Qualitative Research
Methods *in*
Human Geography

Qualitative Research
Methods *in*
Human Geography

Second Edition

Edited by Iain Hay

UNIVERSITY PRESS

2005

OXFORD

UNIVERSITY PRESS

253 Normanby Road, South Melbourne, Victoria 3205, Australia

Oxford University Press is a department of the University of Oxford.
It furthers the University's objective of excellence in research, scholarship,
and education by publishing worldwide in

Oxford New York

Auckland Cape Town Dar es Salaam Hong Kong Karachi
Kuala Lumpur Madrid Melbourne Mexico City Nairobi
New Delhi Shanghai Taipei Toronto

With offices in

Argentina Austria Brazil Chile Czech Republic France Greece
Guatemala Hungary Italy Japan Poland Portugal Singapore
South Korea Switzerland Thailand Turkey Ukraine Vietnam

OXFORD is a trade mark of Oxford University Press
in the UK and in certain other countries

National Library of Australia
Cataloguing-in-Publication data:

Qualitative research methods in human geography.

2nd ed.
Bibliography.
Includes index.
ISBN 0 19 555079 X.

1. Human geography — Methodology. 2. Qualitative research —
Australia. 3. Human geography — Australia. I. Hay, Iain,
1960– .

304.2072

Typeset by OUPANZS
Printed by Sheck Wah Printing Press Ltd, Hong Kong

Contents

7 Oral History and Human Geography   106

Karen George and Elaine Stratford

8 Focusing on the Focus Group   116

Jenny Cameron

12   Knowing Seeing? Undertaking Observational Research   192
Robin A. Kearns

13   Participatory Action Research   207
Sara Kindon

PART 3   'Interpreting and Communicating' the Results of Qualitative Research   221

14   Coding Qualitative Data   223
Meghan Cope

15   Computers, Qualitative Data, and Geographic Research   234
Robin Peace and Bettina van Hoven

16   Writing Qualitative Geographies, Constructing Geographical Knowledges   248

Juliana Mansvelt and Lawrence D. Berg

17   From Personal to Public: Communicating Qualitative Research for Public Consumption   266

Dydia DeLyser and Eric Pawson

List of Boxes

List of Figures

Notes on Contributors

Richard Bedford, BA (Auckland) 1965, MA (Auckland) 1967, PhD (ANU) 1972, is Professor of Geography and Deputy Vice-Chancellor (Research) at the University of Waikato, Hamilton, New Zealand. Prior to taking up the Chair of Geography at the University of Waikato in 1989 he was on the staff of the University of Canterbury. His research interests are mainly in the field of population dynamics, especially migration, in the Asia-Pacific region. He has published widely on population movement and development in the Pacific Islands, including a book co-authored with Harold Brookfield, Tim Bayliss-Smith, and Marc Latham in the Cambridge Human Geography series on the colonial and postcolonial experience of eastern Fiji (1989). His articles have appeared in journals such as *Asia-Pacific Viewpoint; Asian and Pacific Migration Journal; Contemporary Pacific; Espaces Populations Societes; GeoJournal; Journal de la Société des Oceanistes; Journal of Ethnic and Migration Studies; New Zealand Geographer; New Zealand Population Review;* and *Oceania.*

Lawrence D. Berg, BA (Distinction) (Victoria) 1988, MA (Victoria) 1991, DPhil (Waikato) 1996, began his career as a lecturer in the School of Global Studies at Massey University. Lawrence is now Canada Research Chair and Director of the Centre for Human Rights, Diversity & Identity at Okanagan University College, Canada. He has a diverse range of academic interests in radical and critical geography, focusing especially on issues relating to feminist analyses of identity politics and place, and the emplaced cultural politics of knowledge production. Lawrence is editor of *The Canadian Geographer,* co-editor of *ACME: An International E-Journal for Critical Geographies,* and a member of the Steering Committee of the International Critical Geography Group. His current work involves a wide range of activist research projects aimed at contesting and disrupting various taken-for-granted forms of everyday social relations that contribute to oppression in a range of spaces. Lawrence has published extensively in journals such as *Antipode; Geoforum; Gender Place & Culture; Progress in Human Geography; Social and Cultural Geography;* and *Society & Space.*

Matt Bradshaw, BA (Hons) (Tasmania) 1989, MEnvStudies (Tasmania) 1992, PhD (Tasmania) 2000, is an Honorary Associate in the Department of Geography and Environmental Studies, University of Tasmania. He has taught at the University of Tasmania. He is also a social research consultant to the Irish Sea Fisheries Board, the Hobart City Council, and the Tasmanian Aquaculture and Fisheries Institute, among others. His current academic interests include economic geography, the social impact assessment of fisheries, and community involvement in local government planning. He has published in *Antipode; Applied Geography; Area; Australian Geographical Studies; Environment and Planning A; Fisheries Research; Geography, Marine Policy;* and *New Zealand Geographer,* among others.

Jenny Cameron, DipTeach (Brisbane CAE) 1983, BAppSc (QUT) 1990, MA (Sydney) 1992, PhD (Monash) 1998, is Lecturer in the School of Environmental Planning at Griffith University. Prior to taking up this position she was a Research Fellow in the School of Public Policy at Monash University, and has also worked as a researcher in the Queensland Department of Housing, Local Government and Planning, and a primary school teacher in Brisbane and Thursday Island. Most recently she has been using a participatory action research approach to work with economically marginalised groups to develop community economic projects and has also collaborated with the Queensland Department of Local Government and Planning to evaluate, through action research, public participation in regional planning. She has published articles in journals that include *Australian Geographer*; *Geoforum*; *Gender, Place and Culture*; *Rethinking Marxism*; *Socialist Review*; and *Urban Policy and Research*; and chapters in various books including *Class and Its Others* (Minnesota University Press, 2000) and *Community and Local Governance in Australia* (University of New South Wales Press, 2005). She is also committed to communicating research outcomes to a general audience and has produced a documentary and several resource kits.

Meghan Cope, AB (Vassar) 1989, MA (University of Colorado) 1992, PhD (University of Colorado) 1995, is an Associate Professor in the Department of Geography at the State University of New York at Buffalo. Her current research project is on 'Children's Urban Geographies', in which she works directly with low-income children with diverse ethnic and racial backgrounds in Buffalo, New York. From this work and her love of walking and cycling has grown a new activist interest in fostering 'child-friendly cities' through design, outreach, and education. Her other academic interests are post-industrial cities of the USA, race and place, labour and housing markets as experienced by low-income women, and qualitative methods in geographic research. She has published articles in several journals, including *Environment and Planning A*; *Professional Geographer*; and *Urban Geography*; as well as contributing chapters to several books on feminist geography.

Dydia DeLyser, BA (University of California, Los Angeles) 1992, MA (Syracuse University) 1996, PhD (Syracuse University) 1998, is Assistant Professor of Geography at Louisiana State University. Her qualitative research has been both ethnographic—on landscape and social memory in a California ghost town—and archival—on tourism and the shaping of nineteenth and twentieth century southern California. She teaches cultural geography, qualitative methods, and writing at the graduate and undergraduate levels. Dydia has published over a dozen articles and chapters on these topics in such journals as the *Annals of the Association of American Geographers*; *Journal of Geography in Higher Education*; *Journal of Historical Geography*; and *Social and Cultural Geography*; as well as a book, *Ramona Memories: Tourism and the Shaping of Southern California* (University of Minnesota Press, 2005).

Robyn Dowling, BEc (Hons) (Sydney) 1988, MA (British Columbia) 1991, PhD (British Columbia) 1995, is Senior Lecturer in the Department of Human Geography at Macquarie University, NSW, Australia. Her current research explores the material and cultural geographies of home in Australian suburbia; and gendered aspects of transport and mobility. Robyn's publications include a chapter in *Cities of Difference* (Guilford, 1998) and papers in

Antipode; *Australian Geographical Studies*; *Housing Studies*; *Social and Cultural Geography*; and *Urban Geography*; as well as a book with Alison Blunt, *Home* (Routledge, 2005).

Kevin Dunn, BA (Hons) (Wollongong) 1990, PhD (Newcastle) 1999, is Senior Lecturer in the Geography Program at the University of New South Wales. Like other contributors to this volume, Kevin has a broad range of academic interests, including geographies of racism; identity and place; theories of migrant settlement and ethnic concentration; media representations of place and people; and the politics of heritage and memorial landscapes. His PhD focused on opposition to mosques in Sydney. He co-authored *Introducing Human Geography* (Longman-Pearson Education Australia, 2000), which won the *Australian* award for excellence in publishing, and *Landscapes* (Pearson, 2003) and has published more than thirty chapters and articles in various books and in journals including *Australian Geographer*; *Australian Geographical Studies*; *Environment and Planning A* and *D*; *Social and Cultural Geography*; and *Urban Studies*.

Karen George, BA (Hons) (Adelaide) 1984, MA (Australian National University) 1988, PhD (Adelaide) 1994 is a consultant historian and writer. She is sole proprietor of *Historically Speaking*, a business she has operated since 1993. From 1993 to 2001 she was oral historian for the Corporation of the City of Adelaide and is past president of the South Australian branch of the Oral History Association of Australia. She is author of *A Place of Their Own: the men and women of War Service Land Settlement at Loxton after World War II* (Wakefield Press, Adelaide, 1999); *City Memory: A Guide and Index to the City of Adelaide Oral History Collection 1978-1998* (Corporation of the City of Adelaide, 1999); and contributor to Doreen Mellor and Ann Haebich (eds)*, Many Voices: Reflections on experiences of Indigenous child separation* (National Library of Australia, 2002) and the *Wakefield Companion to South Australian History* (Wakefield Press, 2001). As a consultant historian, she specialises in oral history and has worked on numerous projects ranging over many subject areas. She is currently completing a major research project for SA Link-Up, identifying and describing surviving records of homes and institutions into which Aboriginal children were placed.

Iain Hay, BSc (Hons) (Canterbury) 1982, MA (Massey) 1985, PhD (Washington) 1989, GradCertTertEd (Flinders) 1995, MEdMgmt (Flinders) 2004, is Professor of Geography and Head of the School of Geography, Population and Environmental Management at Flinders University, South Australia. He is author of *The Caring Commodity* (OUP, 1989); *Money, Medicine and Malpractice in American Society* (Praeger, 1992); *Communicating in Geography and Environmental Studies* (OUP, 1996, 2002); and *Making the Grade* (OUP 1997, 2002 with D. Bochner and C. Dungey). Iain is also Asia–Pacific editor of *Ethics, Place and Environment*, and Australasian editor of *Journal of Geography in Higher Education*. His research interests include geographies of oppression (exploitation, marginalisation, powerlessness, cultural imperialism, violence); media; and professional development (including research ethics and professional communication).

Richie Howitt, BA (Hons) Dip Ed (Newcastle) 1978, PhD (UNSW) 1986, is Associate Professor in the Department of Human Geography, Macquarie University, NSW, Australia. He is author of *Rethinking Resource Management* (Routledge, 2001) and co-editor of *Resources Nations and Indigenous Peoples* (OUP, 1996, with J. Connell and P. Hirsch). Richie is also

Director of Macquarie's Bachelor of Environmental Management program, and teaches and researches in areas of resource management, social impact assessment, social justice, and geographical education. He received the Australian Award for University Teaching (Social Science) in 1999 and became Fellow of the Institute of Australian Geographers in 2004.

Robin A. Kearns, BA (Auckland) 1981, MA (Hons) (Auckland) 1983, PhD (McMaster) 1988, is Associate Professor in the School of Geography and Environmental Science at the University of Auckland. He has published *Putting Health into Place: Landscape, Identity and Well-being* (Syracuse University Press) and *Culture/Place/Health* (Routledge) with Wilbert Gesler, as well as over 100 refereed articles and book chapters. His research interests include the relationships between health and place, the cultural politics of place; and the social relations of research. Robin is an editor of the *New Zealand Geographer* and maintains a range of involvements within the research community including the Board of the Centre for Housing Research Aotearoa New Zealand and the Public Health Research Committee of the Health Research Council.

Sara Kindon, BA (Hons) (Durham) 1989, MA (Waterloo) 1993, DPhil (Waikato) in progress, is Senior Lecturer in Human Geography and Development Studies at Victoria University of Wellington, New Zealand. She was also a Visiting Lecturer in the Geography Department at the University of Edinburgh in 1997. Sara's interests lie at the intersection of feminist praxis, participatory research, and community development as they are applied to understanding place–identity relationships, particularly within indigenous communities. Her current thesis work focuses on the politics and practices of participatory video within geographic research with a North Island *iwi*. She has published in *Area*; *Asia Pacific Viewpoint; New Zealand Geographer; Progress in Development Studies; Singapore Journal of Tropical Geography*; and *The Contemporary Pacific*, and has contributed a number of chapters on gender and development and participatory research to various edited collections and text books.

Juliana Mansvelt, BA (Hons) (Massey) 1989, PhD (Sheffield) 1994, is currently employed as a Lecturer in Geography in the School of People, Environment and Planning, Massey University, New Zealand. Her teaching and research interests include geographies of leisure and ageing, and consumption. Her recent research on retirement villages as lifestyle choices has involved focus groups and qualitative interviews to explore relationships between ageing, place, and leisure. Juliana has published papers in various journals, and has contributed chapters to a number of books including: *Leisure Recreation and Tourism in New Zealand and Australia* (Longman, 1998); *Explorations in Human Geography* (Oxford University Press, 1999); and *Developing Scenario-based Learning. Practical Insights for Tertiary Educators* (Dunmore, 2003). She has recently completed a textbook for Sage Publications entitled *Geographies of Consumption* due to be published in February 2005.

Pauline M. McGuirk, BA (Hons) (Dublin) 1986, Dip Ed (Dublin) 1987, PhD (Dublin) 1992, is an urban geographer who lectures in the School of Environmental and Life Sciences at the University of Newcastle, NSW, Australia, where she is Deputy Director of the Centre for Urban and Regional Studies. Pauline's research focuses on the study of urban governance and policy and the politics of planning in the context of global neo-liberalism.

She has published widely in leading international journals and is joint-author of *Introducing Human Geography: Globalisation, Difference, Inequality* (Pearson, 2000). She is also President of the Geographical Society of NSW, and Associate Editor of *Australian Geographical Studies*.

Janice Monk, BA (Hons) (Sydney) 1958, MA (Illinois at Urbana-Champaign) 1963, PhD (Illinois at Urbana-Champaign) 1972, is Research Professor in the Southwest Institute for Research on Women (SIROW) and Professor of Geography and Regional Development at the University of Arizona. For over two decades she served as Executive Director of SIROW where she was responsible for funded research and educational projects supported by an array of governmental agencies and private foundations. She was President of the Association of American Geographers (2001–2) and has been honoured by the Association of American Geographers, the Institute of Australian Geographers, the National Council for Geographical Education, and the Royal Geographical Society (with the Institute of British Geographers). Janice's interests include gender studies, the history of women in American geography, and geography in higher education. Among her numerous publications are *The Desert Is No Lady* (Yale UP, 1987; 1989; University of Arizona Press, 1997, with V. Norwood), *Full Circles* (Routledge, 1993, with C. Katz), *Women of the European Union* (Routledge, 1996, with M.D. Garcia-Ramon); and *Encompassing Gender* (Feminist Press, 2002, with M.M. Lay and D.S. Rosenfelt). Her articles appear in such journals as *Annals of the Association of American Geographers; Journal of Geography in Higher Education; Journal of Geography;* and *Professional Geographer*.

Phillip O'Neill, BA (Hons) Dip Ed (Macquarie) 1975, MA (Hons) (Macquarie) 1986, PhD (Macquarie) 1995, is Head of Geography in the School of Environmental and Life Sciences at the University of Newcastle, and the Director of the University's Centre for Urban and Regional Studies (CURS). Phillip is a member of the Council of the Institute of Australian Geographers, and the international editorial boards of the *Journal of Economic Geography* and *Progress in Human Geography*. He is also a regular newspaper columnist and a frequent national media commentator and public speaker on economic change and regional development issues. Phillip is widely published in the fields of industrial, urban, and regional economic change and has a keen interest in the geographical behaviours of large corporations.

Eric Pawson, MA, DPhil (Oxon) 1975, is Professor of Geography at the University of Canterbury, New Zealand. He teaches at most levels in the curriculum from large first-year classes to PhD students, while his research interests include environmental history, and landscape and memory. He was Contributing Editor and Chair of the Advisory Committee of the *New Zealand Historical Atlas* from 1990 to 1997, is Chair of the Editorial Board of the New Zealand Geographical Society, and in 2004 completed a six year term as Head of Canterbury's Geography Department.

Robin Peace, DipTchg (Christchurch College of Education) 1978, BA (Canterbury) 1993, BSocSci (Hons) (Waikato) 1993, DPhil (Waikato) 1999, is a Principal Analyst in the Centre for Social Research and Evaluation in New Zealand's Ministry of Social Development in Wellington. She lectured in the Department of Geography at the University of Waikato from 1994 to 2000. She has a broad range of research and teaching experience, having been Head of Geography at Wellington East Girls' College, Lecturer in Professional Studies at the

Hutt Valley Outpost of the Christchurch College of Education, and visiting research worker at the University of Edinburgh. Her research interests include contemporary geographical thought, geography and social policy, geographical education at the tertiary and secondary levels, and qualitative methods and computer assisted qualitative data analysis.

Michael Roche, MA, PhD (Canterbury), is Professor of Geography and currently Head of the School of People, Environment and Planning at Massey University at Palmerston North in New Zealand. He has written on historical and contemporary aspects of forestry and agriculture in New Zealand. His publications based on archival research have appeared in *Historical Geography; Journal of Historical Geography; New Zealand Forestry; New Zealand Geographer; South Australian Geographical Journal;* and the *Historical Atlas of New Zealand*. He is a Life Member of the New Zealand Geographical Society.

Stan Stevens, BA (University of California, Berkeley) 1983, MA (University of California, Berkeley) 1986, PhD (University of California, Berkeley) 1989, is Associate Professor of Geography in the Department of Geosciences at the University of Massachusetts, Amherst. His research in political ecology, cultural ecology, environmental history, protected areas, and tourism has been based on postcolonially informed ethnographic, collaborative fieldwork with more than thirty Sharwa (Sherpa) co-researchers. He is particularly concerned with issues of indigenous peoples' land use, community-based resource management, conservation values and practices, and struggles for sovereignty and self-determination. These projects have involved fieldwork in the Chomolungma (Mt Everest) region during 17 of the past 23 years and in more than sixty villages. Stan is author of *Claiming the High Ground: Sherpas, Subsistence, and Environmental Change in the Highest Himalaya* (University of California Press, 1993); and editor and contributor to *Conservation Through Cultural Survival: Indigenous Peoples and Protected Areas* (Island Press, 1997). He has also contributed chapters to edited books and articles including *Journal of Cultural Geography; The Geographical Journal;* and *The Geographical Review.*

Elaine Stratford, BA (Flinders) 1984, BA (Hons) (Flinders) 1986, PhD (Adelaide) 1996, is Senior Lecturer in the School of Geography and Environmental Studies, University of Tasmania. Her current academic interests include issues of identity, peripherality, and globalization in island places; the governance of oceans, coasts, and their resources; and the political ecologies of the urban. Elaine has published widely in journals such as *Environment and Planning B; Health and Place; Local Environment; Social and Cultural Geography;* and *Transactions of the Institute of British Geographers;* as well as in various edited collections. Among her other duties, Elaine is Treasurer of the Institute of Australian Geographers, Inc., a member of the board of the Global Islands Network, and serves on the Tasmanian Resource Management and Planning Appeals Tribunal.

Bettina van Hoven, BA (Plymouth, UK) 1996, PhD (Plymouth, UK) 1999 is Lecturer and Researcher at the Department of Cultural Geography at the University of Groningen in the Netherlands. Her interest has long been concerned with Eastern Europe, gender issues, and identity. Recently, a four-year research grant shifted her main interest to the geographies of prison. She has published in *Area* and *Antipode* and edited the books *Europe: Lives in transition* (Pearson, 2003) and *Spaces of Masculinities* (Routledge, 2004).

Gordon Waitt, MA (Hons Soc Sci) (Edinburgh) 1985, PhD (Edinburgh) 1988, is Associate Professor in the School of Earth and Environmental Sciences at the University of Wollongong, NSW, Australia. His research interests include social and cultural geographies, particularly tourism geographies and the geographies of sexuality. He co-authored *Introducing Human Geography* (Longman-Pearson Education Australia, 2000), which won the *Australian* award for excellence in educational publishing. He co-edited a special edition with Kathy Mee on 'Culture Matters' for *Social and Cultural Geography*. He has written over forty articles in various journals including the *Australian Geographer; Environment and Planning D;* and *Urban Studies*. Gordon is actively involved in the professional activities of the Cultural Study Group of the Institute of Australian Geographers and the Geographical Society of New South Wales.

Hilary P. M. Winchester, BA (Hons) (Oxford) 1974, MA (Oxford) 1977, DPhil (Oxford) 1980, is Pro Vice Chancellor and Vice President: Organisational Strategy and Change at the University of South Australia. She joined UniSA in 2003 from Flinders University where she was Pro Vice Chancellor (Academic) for two years, after a decade at the University of Newcastle, NSW, during which time she held various positions including Head of the Department of Geography and Environmental Science, and President of the Academic Senate. Hilary has a wide range of interests in population, social, and cultural geography, specifically including marginal social groups (especially one-parent families), the social construction of place, the geography of gender, and urban social and landscape planning. She is co-author of *Landscapes: Ways of Imagining the World* (Pearson, 2003), and numerous articles and book chapters.

Preface

Qualitative Research Methods in Human Geography has been revised and expanded substantially. This second edition provides an extended yet concise and accessible selection of introductory materials on qualitative research methods. Although the book still gives particular emphasis to examples drawn from 'social/cultural geography', one of the most vibrant areas of inquiry in geography over the past fifteen years, its content is relevant across human geography and related disciplines. The book is aimed primarily at an audience of upper-level undergraduate students, but feedback on ways in which the first edition was used indicates that the volume is of considerable interest to people commencing Honours theses and postgraduate study and, indeed, some professional geographers with many decades of research experience have let me know—quietly in some instances—that they have learned a great deal from the first edition. Chapters have been written with the dual intent of providing novice researchers with clear ideas on how they might go about conducting their own qualitative research thoroughly and successfully, and offering university academics a teaching-and-learning framework around which additional materials and exercises on research methods can be developed. The text remains unique in its dedication to the provision of practical, 'how to' guidance on methods of qualitative research in geography.

Without knowing it at the time, I started work on this book in 1992 when I was asked to teach a topic called 'Research Methods in Geography' at Flinders University. I developed lectures and extensive sets of notes for my classes. I also referred students to helpful texts of the time such as Bernard (1988), Kellehear (1993), Patton (1990), Sarantakos (1993), and Sayer (1992). All of these books came from disciplines other than geography or referred to the social sciences in general. It disturbed me that despite the renewed emphasis on qualitative research and the teaching of qualitative methods in the discipline, no geographer had produced an accessible text on the day-to-day practice of qualitative research.

In the meantime, during their regular visits to my office, publishers' representatives asked what sorts of books might be useful in my teaching. I repeatedly mentioned the need for a good text that dealt with qualitative research methods in geography. That message came back to haunt me when I was asked if I would like to write a book on qualitative methods for Oxford University Press. I declined, but offered instead to try to draw together the expertise and energies of a group of active and exciting geographers from Australia and Aotearoa/New Zealand to produce an edited collection.

Of course, in the period during which I planned the first edition of this book and fulfilled the terms of the publishing contract, a new group of research methods texts emerged! This group included Flowerdew and Martin (1997), Kitchin and Tate (2000), Lindsay (1997), and Robinson (1998). Despite their various merits, none of these books deals exclusively, or as comprehensively, with qualitative methods as the first edition of this volume. While other volumes on research methods in geography have now emerged (e.g., Clifford and Valentine 2003; Moss 2002), *Qualitative Research Methods in Human Geography* continues to be received very well and has sold much better than anticipated in North America and more recently in the United Kingdom.

This second edition is revised and expanded to respond to constructive comments made about its predecessor. In overview, *Qualitative Research Methods in Human Geography* is sub-divided loosely into three main sections: 'introducing' qualitative research in human geography, 'doing' qualitative research, and 'interpreting and communicating' the results of qualitative research. Issues considered within these broad sections are also raised, where appropriate, within chapters: matters of ethical practice, data reduction, and communicating research results are amongst the more prominent of these. The second edition has nine new chapters on topics that include: cross-cultural research, archival research, oral history, participatory action research, and coding. Authorship has been expanded to take in more contributors from the USA in particular where the first edition of this book has been especially successful. Nevertheless we give emphasis in our examples to the Asia–Pacific region. Despite that regional focus, the examples should still inform the learning, teaching, and research work of 'northern' readers. Indeed, it seems from the success of the first edition that just as teachers in Australia, Aotearoa/New Zealand, South-East Asia, and the Pacific elaborate on British and North American texts by referring to local examples, colleagues in 'our' antipodes have been willing to supplement this volume's examples with local illustrations of their own.

As I note above, I have subdivided the book into three sections: 'introducing', 'doing', and 'interpreting and communicating'. To some extent it is imprudent to make such separations. I acknowledge, for instance, the ways in which writing—which might be seen superficially as a part of communication—is embedded in the process of 'doing' qualitative research in human geography. Similarly, 'doing' qualitative research typically implies ongoing interpretation and reinterpretation. The ordering of the book's contents is the product of the medium in which the contents are communicated (a book of linear structure). It is a device to help make more quickly comprehensible a book of seventeen chapters. And it follows the organising sequence followed in many research methods classes—such as the one that gave rise to this book—for which this might serve as a textbook.

The first section of the book deals with 'introducing' qualitative research methods in human geography. In chapter 1, Hilary Winchester situates qualitative research methods within the context of geographic inquiry. She outlines the range of qualitative techniques used commonly in human geography and explores the relationship between those methods and the recent history of geographic thought. On this foundation, Robyn Dowling builds a review in chapter 2 of some critical issues associated with qualitative research. These include power relationships between researchers and their co-researchers, questions of subjectivity and intersubjectivity, and points of ethical concern. Similar issues are taken up in further detail in a long new chapter by Richie Howitt and Stan Stevens who—drawing from their considerable experience working with indigenous communities in Australia and in Nepal respectively—present an illuminating and engaging conversation on ethics, methods, and relationships in cross-cultural qualitative research. This is followed by another chapter new to this volume by Jan Monk and Dick Bedford whose range of research and research management experience makes them extraordinarily well qualified to discuss compelling ways to propose qualitative research projects to others. Chapter 5 by Matt Bradshaw and Elaine Stratford examines the difficult but vitally important matters of design and rigour in qualitative research.

The second section of the book focuses on the 'conduct' of qualitative research methods in human geography. Each of the eight chapters offers concise, yet comprehensive, similarly structured outlines of good practice in some of the main forms of qualitative research practice employed in geography. I have grouped together three chapters on research that focus on spoken testimony; three that emphasise 'texts', or inscription; and two that emphasise worlds of observation and participation.

First, Kevin Dunn draws on his extensive experience of interviewing in cross-cultural settings to provide a complete and valuable outline of interviewing practice. Karen George and Elaine Stratford then offer a chapter new to this edition that sets out the basic scope of oral history, discussing the ways in which its practice differs from interviewing, and describing how oral history can enhance our understandings of space, place, region, landscape, and environment. In chapter 8 Jenny Cameron discusses the research potential of focus groups in geography, outlines key issues to consider when planning and conducting successful focus groups, and provides an overview of strategies for analysing and presenting the results.

All three chapters in the section on 'texts' are new to the second edition. They deal, in turn, with archival research, the use of questionnaires in qualitative human geography, and discourse analysis. Mike Roche provides a short, new chapter on the use of archival resources, a sometimes neglected, yet enormously productive and rewarding activity for human geographers. In chapter 10 Pauline McGuirk and Phil O'Neill explore the ways in which questionnaire surveys can be used in qualitative research in human geography. I suggest you read this chapter in conjunction with that on research design and rigour by Bradshaw and Stratford. In the final chapter of this section Gordon Waitt has prepared a rich review of the theory and conduct of discourse analysis. He draws from work by Gillian Rose and Norman Fairclough to suggest how a Foucauldian approach to understanding 'texts' might be applied. This chapter is longer and certainly more complex than many of the others but I encourage you strongly to persist with it. The rewards will justify your efforts.

Two chapters deal directly with issues of observation and participation. In chapter 12 Robin Kearns reviews the purposes and practice of observational techniques in human geography. Then, taking up some of the issues about participant status for researchers that Robin introduces, Sara Kindon offers another new chapter on participatory action research. There is strong complementarity between Sara's chapter and that of Richie Howitt and Stan Stevens on cross-cultural research and it is helpful to consider them in conjunction with one another.

Four chapters in a section on 'interpreting and communicating' follow. In the first, Meghan Cope offers a succinct and very helpful chapter discussing several ways of undertaking coding in a qualitative project. It is worth reading this chapter with that by Gordon Waitt on discourse analysis. The following chapter, published originally in the first edition by Robin Peace, is now updated with contributions from both Robin and Dutch geographer, Bettina van Hoven. The chapter explores some of the ways in which computers may be used to make sense of qualitative data. Juliana Mansvelt and Lawrence Berg provide the penultimate chapter discussing some of the practical and conceptual issues surrounding representation of qualitative research findings. Finally, Dydia DeLyser and Eric Pawson consider issues associated with the vital task of communicating the results of qualitative research for public consumption.

Like the first edition, this book has chapters of different lengths, 'densities', and complexity. Whilst some of the chapters are challenging to read I would like to think that the challenges lie in comprehending the ideas presented and not in wading through obfuscatory text. In every case authors in this volume have strived to present material that is as clear and well illustrated as possible. As an editor with a career interest in matters of effective communication, the matter of clarity is one to which I have devoted considerable attention.

As I have already observed, the chapters of this volume offer a comprehensive overview of qualitative research methods in human geography. However, the book is not intended to be a 'one-stop' resource or prescriptive outline (indeed, how could it be?) for qualitative researchers and students. It is instead a starting point and framework. Accordingly, each chapter includes direction to a number of additional key readings and relevant sources that may be consulted to follow up material introduced here. There is, of course, a consolidated list of all references cited for those readers who might wish to enquire even further. Chapters also include review questions intended for classroom discussion or as individual exercises. These questions might also serve as prompts for quite different exercises. Indeed, if you have discovered or created any useful exercises to illustrate some of the matters covered within these chapters, I would be delighted to hear about them.

The book features an extensive glossary. While the individual authors have made efforts to ensure that their chapters are written in a language that is accessible to undergraduate readers, there are—without doubt—terms that will be somewhat alien to many readers in the first instance. The glossary should help resolve that sort of difficulty. Terms included in the glossary are drawn primarily from the lists of key words associated with each chapter.

I owe thanks to many people who have been involved with the production of this book. Students in research methods classes at Flinders University encouraged me to put the book together and offered honest and helpful comments on many of its chapters. Every chapter in this collection was reviewed by at least two experts in the field who provided timely, critical, and comprehensive opinion. Those reviewers listed here alphabetically, and their place of affiliation at the time of review were: Stuart Aitken (San Diego State), Kay Anderson (Durham), Nicola Ansell (Brunel), Andrew Beer (Flinders), Alison Blunt (Queen Mary, London), Mark Brayshay (Plymouth), Michael Brown (Washington), Jacquie Burgess (University College, London), Jenny Cameron (Griffith), Garth Cant (Canterbury), Bev Clarke (Flinders), Mike Crang (Durham), Jon Goss (Hawai'i), Ellen Hansen (Emporia State), Andy Herod (Georgia), Richie Howitt (Macquarie), Mark Israel (Flinders), Jane Jacobs (Melbourne), Lucy Jarosz (Washington), Ron Johnston (Bristol), Minelle Mahtani (New School), Murray McCaskill (Flinders), Pauline McGuirk (Newcastle), Eric Pawson (Canterbury), Meryl Pearce (Flinders), Chris Philo (Glasgow), Joe Powell (Monash), Lydia Mihelic Pulsipher (Tennessee), Lyn Richards (La Trobe), Mark Riley (Exeter), Mark Rosenberg (Queen's, Ontario), Pamela Shurmer-Smith (Portsmouth), Robert Summerby-Murray (Mount Allison), Lynn Staeheli (Colorado), and Eileen Willis (Flinders).

I must also express a special note of thanks to the contributors to this volume. As with the first edition, contributors put up with repeated emailed requests and comments from me that were often as long as the chapters themselves! I remember sending out those messages uttering, as I clicked the 'send' button, a quiet prayer to the effect: 'please, please don't let them spit the dummy and pull out of this project!' I admire the authors' tolerance, persistence, and fortitude in the face of both my editing style and the various other forms of personal and professional adversity they encountered during the course of this project.

Finally, I would like to comment on some of the partnerships forged through this book. Most of the new or most heavily revised chapters of this volume have been co-authored, in many instances by geographers who have yet to meet one another face-to-face! From my conversations with all of the authors, I know these virtual relationships have proved intellectually rewarding and I conclude this Preface by thanking contributors for their faith in the partnerships I proposed and for all of their efforts to make them work.

Iain Hay
Adelaide

PART 1

'Introducing' Qualitative Research in Human Geography

Qualitative Research and its Place in Human Geography

Hilary P. M. Winchester

CHAPTER OVERVIEW

This chapter aims first to provide an overview of contemporary qualitative research methods in human geography. The range of methods commonly used in human geography is considered and categorised, together with some of the ways in which those methods are used to provide explanation. Second, the chapter aims to review briefly the context from which qualitative research has developed in human geography. This is achieved by examining changing schools of thought within the discipline, recognising changes are messy, overlapping, and coexisting. Third, the chapter aims to link methodological debates to wider theoretical perspectives in geography.

INTRODUCTION

Contemporary human geographers study places, people, bodies, **discourses,** silenced voices, and fragmented **landscapes**. The research questions of today's human geographers require a multiplicity of conceptual approaches and methods of enquiry. Increasingly, the research methods used are qualitative ones intended to elucidate human environments, individual experiences, and social processes. This introductory chapter aims to set the scene of qualitative research in human geography and to highlight issues and techniques that are examined in more detail in later chapters. The chapter has three main and interlinked objectives.

First, it provides an overview of qualitative methods, their context, and the links between methodology and theory. The categories used and established here are relatively fluid; they are designed merely as a way of organising this growing field, and are not meant to be fixed or constraining. Indeed, some recent research, such as that on the body and embodied experiences in place, essentially defies categorisation. A number of issues raised in this introduction are more fully developed later in the volume, particularly those that relate to ethical practices (chapters 2 and 3), the positioning of the author relative to the audience (chapters 2 and 16), as well as the broad issues of **credibility**, **dependability**, and **confirmability** (chapter 5).

Second, the chapter outlines the arguments about, and differences (and some of the similarities) between, qualitative and **quantitative methods.** Furthermore, the current debate on combining methods through **triangulation** and mixed-method approaches is reviewed. The resurgence of qualitative techniques and the current qualitative/quantitative debate in human geography are set in the context of the discipline's development and evolution. Inevitably a thumb-nail sketch of the evolution of geographical thought in part of just one chapter will necessitate some broad generalisations. However, in this context it is important to recognise that controversy about the nature and validity of research methods has existed for decades. Methodological debates may entrench polarised positions, for example between quantitative and qualitative, **objective** and **subjective.** The apparent polarity between those positions may in fact prove to be largely a false dichotomy. In the past, such debates in geography have raged around other extremes (Wrigley 1970). Geographers in the early decades of the twentieth century have argued, for example, over the merits of determinism versus possibilism (the extent to which humans have control over or are controlled by their environment) (Wrigley 1970). The current airing of the qualitative versus quantitative debate may in one sense be likened to the resurrection of a dinosaur in the shape of a false dichotomy, while in another sense it is a sign of healthy debate and intellectual vigour within the discipline.

Finally, the chapter focuses particularly on links between theory and methodology and raises issues of ethics, authorship, and power. The contemporary use of qualitative methods in human geography is positioned within the theoretical debates and intellectual evolution of the discipline, while raising issues for consideration by reflexive and committed researchers. Intense arguments about methodology are often as much to do with researchers' beliefs and feelings about the structure of the world as about their regard for a particular research method, such as **participant observation** or in-depth **interviews**. While creationists and catastrophists clearly subscribe to a particular world-view (giving credence to the biblical account of earth's creation and catastrophic geomorphological events such as the Great Flood), other geographers may hold equally strong, but perhaps less obvious, views about the order, structure, measurement, and knowability of phenomena. In complex ways, **ontology** (beliefs about the world) and **epistemology** (ways of knowing the world) are linked to the methods we choose to use for research (Sayer and Morgan 1985).

WHAT IS QUALITATIVE RESEARCH?

What questions does qualitative research answer?

Qualitative research is used in many areas of human geography. In a broad sense, qualitative research is concerned with elucidating human environments and human experiences within a variety of conceptual frameworks. The term 'research' is used here to mean the whole process from defining a question to analysis and interpretation. 'Method' is used as a much more specific term for the investigative technique employed. A huge range of methods is used in many different situations. Some of the variety of methods that spring to mind range from interviews about disability rights in the Australian state of Victoria (Smith 2003); through participant observation with homeless children (Winchester and Costello 1995); to **deconstruction** of media events and textual material involved in the place-making of the former industrial city of Newcastle (McGuirk and Rowe 2001). Inevitably, it is difficult to summarise the questions addressed by such a variety of research. However, it is instructive to recall the answer to a similar question posed two decades ago in relation to statistical analysis in geography. In that text, Ron Johnston (1978, pp. 1–5) argued that the gamut of statistical techniques answered two fundamental questions. Those questions were either about the relationships between phenomena and places, or the differences between them. The elegant simplicity of Johnston's questions can be paralleled by a different, but similarly broad, pair of questions that qualitative research is trying to answer.

The two fundamental questions tackled by qualitative researchers are concerned either with **social structures** or with individual experiences. This dualism is one that in practice may be hard to disentangle, but is of fundamental importance in explanation. The behaviour and experiences of an individual may be determined not so much by their personal characteristics but by their position in the social structure, 'together with their associated resources, constraints or rules' (Sayer 1992, p. 93).

The first question may be phrased as:

Question One: *What is the shape of societal structures and by what processes are they constructed, maintained, legitimised, and resisted?*

The structures that geographers are analysing may be social, cultural, economic, political, or environmental. Structures may be defined as internally related objects or practices. Andrew Sayer (1992, pp. 92–5) gives the example of the landlord–tenant relationship, where structures exist in relation to private property and ownership, where rent is paid between the two parties, and where the structure may survive a continual turnover of individuals. Furthermore, he emphasises that tenants almost certainly exist within other structures; for example they may be students affected by educational structures, or migrants constrained by racist structures. The coexistence of rented housing, students, and minority groups produces a complex linkage and mutual reinforcement of structures, within which individuals live out their lives. Qualitative geographers balance a fine line between the examination of structures and processes on the one hand and of individuals and their experiences on the other. Structures constrain individuals and enable certain behaviours, but in some circumstances individuals also have the capacity to break rather than reproduce the mould. An overemphasis on structures and processes rather than individuals could lead to a dehumanised human geography. On the other hand, individuals do not have all-powerful free will and ability, which would enable them to overcome the powerful structures embedded in society, such as capitalism, patriarchy, or racism.

Sayer (1992, p. 95) considers that the key question for qualitative researchers about structures may be phrased as: 'What is it about the structures which produce the effects at issue?' Geographers have studied structures qualitatively in a number of ways. A significant focus has been on the ways in which they are built, reproduced, and reified: for example Kay Anderson (1993) has analysed the documentary history that has led to stigmatisation of the suburb of Redfern in Sydney, while more recently Wendy Shaw (2000) has examined the physical and ideological context of this stigmatisation. In this example the structures are essentially indistinguishable from the processes that build, reinforce, and contest them. Other authors have considered either the material or symbolic **representations** of structures: in their 1994 analysis of British merchant banking, McDowell and Court emphasise media representations of banking patriarchs and the importance of dress and body image for younger female and male bankers. A further aspect of the investigation of structures may be concerned with their oppressive or exclusionary nature: Gill Valentine's (1993) interviews with lesbian workers considered the ways in which workplace structures naturalise hetero-sexual norms, and thereby contribute to the oppression and marginalisation of workers who do not conform to these norms. More recently, her work on young people 'coming out' is placed within the structures of the family (Valentine et al. 2003). Most of the qualitative geographical work on structures in fact emphasises the processes and relations that sustain, modify, or oppose those structures, rather than focusing specifically on their form and nature.

The second question is concerned with individual experiences of structures and places:

Question Two: *What are individuals' experiences of places and events?*

Individuals experience the same events and places differently. Giving voice to individuals allows viewpoints to be heard that otherwise might be silenced or excluded: Jane Jacobs' (1993) account of the conflicts over mining at Coronation Hill in Australia's Northern Territory gives voice to Aboriginal perspectives on naturalised notions of land and country. Dissident or marginalised stories may be 'given voice' through the use of diaries, oral histories, recordings of interviews and conversations, or through the use of 'alternative' rather than 'mainstream' media. Participant observation by immersion in particular settings allows multiple viewpoints to be heard and acknowledged. A study of the post-school celebrations of Schoolies' Week on the Gold Coast of Australia (Winchester et al. 1999) gives voice not only to the partying Schoolies (i.e., high school students celebrating the end of the academic year), but also to agents of control (for example, police). Women's activist groups in urban and rural areas of Australia used public and private spaces differently and strategically, to give voice and space for their concerns (Fincher and Panelli 2001). The experiences of individuals and the meanings of events and places cannot necessarily be generalised, but they do constitute part of a multifaceted and fluid reality. Qualitative geographical research tends to emphasise multiple meanings and interpretations rather than seeking to impose any one 'dominant' or 'correct' interpretation.

The experiences of a single individual have been used in a generalisable sense to illuminate structures and structural change; Rimmer and Davenport (1998) use the travel diaries of Australian geographer Peter Scott as an example of the huge changes in mobility and technology that have characterised air transport since the 1950s. An autobiographical example by Reginald Golledge (1997) tells his personal story to outline the difficulties experienced by geographers and other academics faced with major physical disabilities. In some cases, the boundary between structure and individual experience is blurred: in a study of the daily geographies of caregivers Wiles (2003, p.1307) found that 'the social and physical aspects of the many interconnected scales and places which caregivers negotiate on an everyday basis both shape and are shaped by caregiving'. In other words, the experience itself could not be analytically separated from the structures that form the context for that experience.

Types of qualitative research

It is clear, even from the brief preceding section, that qualitative research in geography is currently used to address a huge range of issues, events, and places, and that these studies utilise a variety of methods. Nonetheless, some methods are much more commonly employed than others. This section identifies three main types of qualitative research: the oral (primarily interview-based), the textual (creative, documentary, and landscape), and the observational.

Clearly the most popular and widely used methods are oral. Talking with people as research subjects encompasses a wide range of activities. The spoken testimony of people is used in ways that range from the highly individualistic (oral histories and autobiographies) to the highly generalised (the individual as one of a **random sample**). The latter type of survey technique borders on the quantitative, where responses can be counted, cross-tabulated, and analysed statistically (for example, Oakley 1981). The former approach, often achieved through **oral history** methods, lies at the more qualitative, individualistic end of the spectrum. Such methods are considered in more detail in chapters 6 and 7. A middle ground is occupied here by the increasingly popular technique of using **focus groups** (see chapter 8). Jackson and Holbrook (1995) effectively used focus groups differentiated by age, gender, and social group to analyse the complex meanings of the 'everyday' activity of shopping. The range of ways in which **oral methods** are utilised in geography—whereby subjects are allowed to speak with their own voice—is outlined in Box 1.1. It should be noted that the research questions will to some extent shape the methods that will be used. In particular, the methods range from answering the research question about individual meanings and experiences at the biographical end of the spectrum, to answering the research question about societal structures at the survey end. Surveys are undertaken to obtain information from and about individuals that is not available from other sources. While an interview is undertaken with an individual, a survey involves a more standardised interaction with a number of people. Oral surveys of personal information, attitudes, and behaviour usually (but not inevitably) utilise questionnaires. Questionnaires are more closely structured and ordered than interviews, and every **respondent** answers the same question in a standard format. These are discussed fully in chapter 10.

BOX 1.1 ORAL QUALITATIVE METHODS IN HUMAN GEOGRAPHY

General method	*Specific method*	*Research questions*
	Autobiography	Individual
Biography	Biography	
	Oral history	
	Unstructured	
Interviews	Semi-structured	
	Structured	
	Focus groups—open-ended	
Surveys	Surveys—structured	
	Questionnaires—structured	General / Structural

The second major type of qualitative research is textual analysis. Such texts are wide ranging but more diffuse in the human geography literature than the oral testimonies described above. Important groups of textual methods utilise creative, documentary, and landscape sources. Creative texts are likely to include poems, fiction, films, art, and music. Documentary sources may include maps, newspapers, planning documents, and even postage stamps! Rose (2003) uses family photographs in a study of domestic space, while Waitt and Head (2002) examine the role of postcards in Australian frontier myths. Landscape sources may be very specific, such as the micro landscapes of the retailing street (Bridge and Dowling 2001) or the 'cemeteries and columbaria, memorials and mausoleums' that Lily Kong (1999) uses in her analysis of deathscapes. Frequently, landscape sources are more general, such as the landscapes of suburbia as indicators of social status (Duncan 1992). The analysis of creative sources, including fictional literature, film, art, and music, has shown increasing complexity in recent years. (For a survey of this field see Winchester and Dunn (1999) and for a brief Australian introduction, see Carroll and Connell (2000). See also chapter 11 of this volume.) Geographers have searched such sources for underlying structures, looking at paintings, for example, to understand changing perceptions of landscape (Heathcote 1975, pp. 214–17; Lowenthal and Prince 1965) or using film to examine both the impact of city restructuring and the ways in which it is represented (Winchester and Dunn 1999).

Written texts have also been used as the source of underlying discourses that underpin and legitimate social structures. Analysis of media representations demonstrate their myth-making power, whether this relates to myths of the inner city (Burgess and Wood 1988) or to the imagery of national identity (Pickles 2002) and urban place-making (Dunn et al. 1995; Schollmann et al. 2000). Herman (1999) has argued that changing place names in Hawai'i reveal a transformation from Hawai'ian political and cultural economy into Western capitalist forms, while Sparke (1998) shows convincingly some of the ways in which *The Historical Atlas of Canada* is enmeshed in the postcolonial politics of that country.

A significant and controversial source of textual analysis is the landscape itself. The argument that landscape may be read as text is epitomised in the work of Duncan and Duncan (1988) where the residential landscape is decoded of its social nuances. A study of roadside memorials in the Australian state of New South Wales concluded that the roadside crosses and flowers were indicative not only of individuals' behaviour but also of a 'problematic masculinity' characterised by aggression, fast driving, and reckless behaviour (Hartig and Dunn 1998). Textual analyses of particular landscapes such as model housing estates use techniques derived from **semiotics** (the language of signs) to demonstrate literally the in-built naturalisation of social roles according to gender and family status (Mee 1994). Schein (1997) interprets landscape architecture, insurance mapping, and other elements of a 'discourse materialised' to explore the ways they symbolise and constitute particular cultural ideals. Waitt and McGuirk (1996) examine both documentary and landscape texts to explore the selective representation of the heritage site of Millers Point in Sydney; the choice of particular buildings as 'heritage' both reflects and reproduces a white, male, coloniser's view of Sydney's history while silencing other views and voices. Bishop (2002) uses the Alice Springs to Darwin railway as a corridor of 'difference, struggle and reconciliation' in the redefinition of national identity and its relationship with the land.

The third significant type of qualitative research in human geography consists of forms of participation within the event or environment that is being researched (see chapters 12 and 13). The most common form of qualitative geographical research involving participation is participant observation. Within participant observation, there may be a wide variation in the role of the observer from passive to pro-active (Hammersley and Atkinson 1983, p. 93). All forms of observation involve problems of positioning of the author in relation to the subject of the research (for example, Smith 1988). In particular, very active participation may clearly influence the event that is being researched, while researchers who are personally involved, for example by researching the community in which they grew up, may find it hard to wear their 'community' and 'researcher' hats at the same time. Participant observation allows the researcher to be, at least in part, simultaneously 'outsider' and 'insider', although differences in social status and background are hard to overcome (Moss 1995). The positioning of the researcher in relation to the 'researched' raises some significant ethical issues, especially if the research is covert (Evans 1988, pp. 207–8). It can, however, have some important advantages, for example for the student whose research work also provided him/her with paid work at a fast-food outlet (see Cook 1997 for an excellent account of this and other student projects). In-depth participant observation is essentially indistinguishable from ethnographic approaches, which often involve lengthy fieldwork. That fieldwork can enable meaningful relationships to develop with the research subjects and may facilitate deep understanding of the research context (Cooper 1994; 1995; Eyles 1988, p. 3). It is useful to follow Cook's (1997, p. 127) terminology where he states that participant observation is the means or method by which ethnographic research is undertaken.

The contribution of qualitative techniques to explanation in geography

In this chapter I have discussed two fundamental questions of geographic enquiry, those concerned with individuals and those concerned with social structures. I have also indicated three main groups of methods: the oral, the textual, and the participatory. There is no simple relationship between the method used and the research questions posed. It is tempting to say that oral methods may be directed predominantly towards elucidating the experiences of individuals and their meanings; however, this is overly simplistic. People's own words do tell us a great deal about their experiences and attitudes, but they may also reveal key underlying social structures. In my own work on lone fathers, I found that the in-depth interviews illuminated underlying structures of patriarchy and masculinity in ways that were much more profound than anticipated (Winchester 1999). Depths of individual anger and despair reflected mismatches between those individuals' romanticised expectations of marriage and gendered behaviour and their actual experience of married life. In this sense, the oral method chosen elucidated both individual experiences and social structures in the holistic sense that would most frequently be associated with participant observation.

Similarly, it might appear that textual methods would most commonly be employed to throw light upon the social processes that underpin, legitimate, and resist social structures. This generalisation would probably be more widely accepted than any equation of oral methods with research questions that focus on the individual. Textual methods have indeed been used to analyse some of the many social processes studied by contemporary human geographers. Examples that spring to mind include the discursive construction of place (Dunn et al. 1995; Mee 1994), processes of social exclusion (Duncan and Duncan 1988), marginalisation (Hay et al. 2004) and expressions of 'problematic' masculinity (Hartig and Dunn 1998).

A recent area of study in human geography focuses on the body and on our embodied experiences. Longhurst's (1995) study of the experiences of pregnant women in shopping malls showed how the embodied experiences of individuals (of feeling marginalised, of needing more toilets, of being uncomfortable in particular places such as bars and lingerie shops) are indicative of the way the pregnant body is socially constructed as **'other'** (i.e., oppositional to or outside the mainstream) to be confined to particular places and roles, medicalised, and marginalised. Resistance to such marginalisation is manifest in a number of ways, notably documented in her study of 'bikini babes', pregnant women who participated in and thereby destabilised a bikini-clad beauty contest (Longhurst 2000). The study of the body may also be as a text or as a landscape that may be marked or shaped in particular ways either as a form of identity (McDowell and Court 1994 identify bodily performances of male and female merchant bankers) or as a form of resistance (Bell et al. 1994 commented on lipstick lesbians as practising resistance to heterosexual norms). The study of the body as text, as performance, or as social construction illuminates some of the richness of methods that cannot be easily pigeon-holed into the types of qualitative method and types of geographical explanation identified for convenience earlier in the chapter.

THE RELATIONSHIP BETWEEN QUALITATIVE AND QUANTITATIVE GEOGRAPHY

In the last twenty-five years the pendulum of geographical methods within human geography has swung firmly from quantitative to qualitative methods. The two are generally characterised as in opposition or as conflicting methodologies. Qualitative methods have been in the ascendant since the 1980s. The trend towards the resurgence of qualitative sources and methods in geography has been chronicled in, and stimulated by, recent books and collections on qualitative methods and mixed methods (Brannen 1992b; Eyles and Smith 1988; Flowerdew and Martin 1997; Holland et al. 1991; Limb and Dwyer 2001; Lindsay 1997).

Typically the gulf between qualitative and quantitative methods has been presented as a series of dualisms. Hammersley (1992) listed seven 'polar opposites' between qualitative and quantitative methods (Box 1.2). Similarly, Brannen (1992a) characterised qualitative approaches as viewing the world through a wide lens and quantitative approaches as viewing through a narrow lens. A dualistic view of methods is highly problematic, as Hammersley (1992, p. 51) recognised: it represents quantitative methods as focused, objective, generalisable and, by implication, value-free. On the other hand qualitative methods are often presented as soft and subjective, an anecdotal supplement, somehow inferior to 'real' science.

Such a view misleadingly represents quantitative methods as objective and value-free; increasingly this assumption about the nature of science has been questioned (see chapter 16). Our choices of what we study and how we study it reflect our values and beliefs. For

BOX 1.2 DUALISMS IDENTIFIED BETWEEN QUALITATIVE AND QUANTITATIVE METHODS

Qualitative methods	*Quantitative methods*
Qualitative data	Quantitative data
Natural settings	Experimental settings
Search for meaning	Identification of behaviour
Rejection of natural science	Adoption of natural science
Inductive approaches	Deductive approaches
Identification of cultural patterns	Pursuance of scientific laws
Idealist perspective	Realist perspective

Source: after Mostyn (1985) and Hammersley (1992).

example much early feminist geography uncovered sexist assumptions in how geographers had typically studied and measured human behaviour (Monk and Hanson 1982). Measurements of migrants and shoppers that ignored 'half of the human population' were clearly demonstrated to be unobjective and value-laden, and in many cases strongly coloured by naturalised assumptions about gendered roles and behaviour. If the subjectivity and value-laden nature of all research methods is admitted, then the apparent gap between the two groups of methods is dramatically reduced. Geographers using qualitative methods often outline their personal subjectivity and possible sources of **bias** by summarising their own background as researchers and their relationship to the research and to its intended audience. Furthermore, the increasingly cultural 'turn' within human geography has made such openness more widespread across the discipline to include not only social and cultural geographers but those with more economic and political interests (for example, Thrift 1996). It is arguable that researchers who define their own position in relation to their research could be more objective than their colleagues who hide behind the supposed objectivity of quantitative methods without revealing the many subjective influences that shape both the research question and the explanations that they find to be true. In short, the equation of 'objectivity' with the quantitative and of subjectivity with the qualitative is highly contested (Philip 1998). This contest is discussed further in chapters 5 and 16.

As qualitative methods have again become prominent within the discipline, they have increasingly had to be justified in a scholarly environment that had come to value measurement and scientific observation more highly than individual experience or social process. Within a largely unfriendly hegemonic scientific framework, advocates of qualitative studies have generally drawn from three arguments. First, some studies of individual experiences, places, and events have been represented as essentially non-generalisable case studies that have meaning in their own right but are not necessarily either representative or replicable (for example, Donovan 1988). The second argument, appropriate to some large-scale studies, has been to suggest that they have generated sufficient data to allow general, and sometimes quantified, conclusions to be drawn from their research (for example, Oakley 1981;

Wearing 1984). More usually, however, qualitative methods have been justified as a complementary technique, as an adjunct or precursor to quantitative studies from which generalisations can be drawn, and as explorations in greater depth as part of multiple methods or triangulation (Burgess 1982a). In making these arguments, qualitative geographers have often been on the defensive, aiming to present their studies as legitimate in their own right and as research that produces not just case studies or anecdotal evidence, but that has added immensely to the geographical literature through powerful forms of geographical explanation, including analysis, theory building, and geographic histories. Mixed methods are increasingly being used in an effective and powerful way without the self-consciousness evident in some of the studies from the 1990s (Longhurst 2000; Nolan 2003).

Classically, qualitative and quantitative methods, such as interviews combined with questionnaires, are seen as providing both the individual and the general perspective on an issue (for example, England 1993) while similar arguments have been raised for mixed methods more broadly (McKendrick 1996; Philip 1998). This triangulation of methods and use of multiple methods are sometimes deemed to offer cross-checking of results by approaching a problem from different angles and using different techniques. Brannen (1992a, p. 13), however, has argued that data generated by different methods cannot simply be aggregated, as they can only be understood in relation to the purposes for which they were created. This question of purpose is intimately related to the theoretical perspectives from which the techniques derive and is considered further in chapter 5.

THE HISTORY OF QUALITATIVE RESEARCH IN GEOGRAPHY

Geography has existed as an academic discipline in Australia since the early years of the twentieth century (Gale 1996). Essentially, for the bulk of the time, geographical work has been dominated by qualitative research of a scholarly and informed, but unquantified nature, drawing assessments of evidence from both physical and human environments (for example, Powell 1988). It should be recognised that qualitative methods of many sorts have been used widely throughout the twentieth century, particularly in the development and writing of sensitive and nuanced regional geography, such as that of Oskar Spate on the Indian subcontinent (Spate and Learmonth 1967), in the landscape school of both human and physical geographers with 'an eye for country', but also in interviewing and field observation (Davis 1954; Wooldridge 1955). The postwar era of the 'quantitative revolution' may, in hindsight, be seen as an aberration rather than the revolutionary **paradigm** (mode of thought) that it was claimed to be at the time (Wrigley 1970).

The early history of geographical thought has been represented classically as a series of paradigm shifts, each triggered by dissatisfaction with the previous prevailing paradigm. A schematic representation of paradigm shifts in academic geography is presented in Box 1.3 (Holt-Jensen 1988; Johnston 1983; Wrigley 1970). For example, dissatisfaction with the crude environmental determinism of the early twentieth century prompted the study of unique places around the world. When this regional approach degenerated into stale layers of facts, and geographers had totally marginalised themselves from the academy by their commitment to 'the region'—both as object of study and research method—then an alternative,

BOX 1.3 PARADIGM SHIFTS AND RESEARCH METHODS IN GEOGRAPHY DURING THE TWENTIETH CENTURY*

Time	Paradigm	Research questions	Research methods	Characteristics	Trends
Early 20th century	Exploration/Discovery	Discovery	Exploration	Colonial	Decrease in spatial and time scale
	Classical Geography	General/Theoretical/ Contextual	Qualitative/Quantitative	Environmental determinism	
	Regional Geography	Unique/Empirical	Qualitative/Regional delineation and description	Region both method and object of study	Increasing separation of physical from human geography
	Spatial Science	General/Theoretical and Empirical	The 'Quantitative Revolution'	Scientific method	Increasing diversity in approaches
1980s +	Critical Social Science	Theoretical/Structural/ Individual	Qualitative	Pluralist	Rise of environmental studies
	Radical Feminist	Theoretical/Structural Structural/Individual			
	Phenomenological Postmodern	Unique/Individual Theoretical	Qualitative	Local	
	Postcolonial/Subaltern	Theoretical/Empirical	Qualitative	Global and local	

*The shifts identified post 1980 are most relevant to human geography, rather than to geography in general.

more credible to the academic community, was sought. The strategic alliances of the discipline shifted away from history and geology to newer and more innovative disciplines such
as psychology and economics. By the 1960s, the quest for academic credibility, combined
with a technological and data revolution, propelled more scientific ways of thinking into the
discipline. This scientific approach combined the use of quantitative method, model making,
and hypothesis testing. The regional idiosyncrasies were condemned as 'old hat' and geographers turned themselves into spatial scientists. This very compressed 'history' has some validity for the earlier years of this century, although the notion of paradigm shifts has been
challenged (for a concise review, see Gregory 1994).

The notion of paradigm shifts essentially becomes inapplicable in the confusing and
exciting world of post-quantitative human geography (Billinge et al. 1984). It is recognised
that in recent human geography there are coexistent, contradictory, and competing communities of scholars adhering to different views of the world, different schools of thought,
and different approaches to research questions. Box 1.3 shows that the recent period is occupied by a number of competing viewpoints jostling for space and credibility. The reactions
against normalising spatial science have spawned a huge diversity of approaches; by the early
1980s radical, feminist, and environmental geographers were reasserting the importance of
the social, the agency of the individual, and the particularity of place. Qualitative research
requiring qualitative methods reasserted its respectability.

From the schema outlined in Box 1.3, a few major points can be drawn:

1   The period of spatial science is unique and aberrant in focusing on quantitative methods.
2   The paradigm shifts within geography have involved an increasing separation in the
    methods and philosophies of human geography from those of physical geography. The
    reactions against 'scientific' geography established since the 1970s have drawn human
    geography more and more into the realms of critical social science, while physical geog-
    raphy has remained essentially within the scientific paradigm.
3   The questions that geographers have asked have oscillated between elucidating general
    trends and patterns in one period to examination of the individual and unique in sub-
    sequent phases of geographic enquiry. The multitude of post-quantitative approaches
    allows both individual and structural research questions to be tackled.
4   In general, the scale of geographic enquiry has shifted from the global, to the regional, to
    the local. However, recent writings are concerned not only with the specifics of individ-
    ual experiences and places, but have re-engaged with both the theoretical and the global.

Qualitative methods are currently used by all the major groups within the critical social science approaches utilised in human geography and identified in the lower half of Box 1.3.
Much of the drive for qualitative research has come initially from humanistic geography of
the late 1970s, which focused geographers sharply on values, emotions, and intentions in
the search to understand the meaning of human experience and human environments (for
example, Ley 1974). Another significant influence in the reassertion of qualitative methods
has been the work of feminist geographers establishing links between the personal and the
political. A clear example of this might be Cupples and Harrison's (2001) work on media
representations of sexual assault by establishment figures or Mackenzie's earlier (1989) work

on women and environments in a postwar British city. This approach also predominates in studies of gay communities and environments (for example, Seebohm 1994). More recently, many studies that might be grouped as postcolonial give voice to people defined as 'other', enabling multiple interpretations of events to be heard. Much qualitative work within contemporary human geography cannot be clearly categorised within any of the schools of thought listed in the final section of Box 1.3 (critical social science), but is concerned with the broad questions of elucidating human environments and human experiences within a variety of conceptual frameworks.

CONTEMPORARY QUALITATIVE GEOGRAPHY— THEORY/METHOD LINKS

Contemporary human geography adopts a broad range of research methods. Although not tied specifically to particular theoretical and philosophical viewpoints, the methods discussed in the preceding sections of this chapter are often more frequently associated with one standpoint than another. For example, feminist geography is often associated with qualitative methods through a naturalised association of the feminine with the 'softer' qualitative approaches. However, feminist questions can be stated within a variety of theoretical frameworks, and may use a variety of methods (Lawson 1995).

Qualitative methods have been used more widely in human geography throughout the past century than is commonly believed. They have been used in conjunction with quantitative methods in a search for generality, and have also been used to explain difficult cases or to add depth to statistical generalisations; above all they have traditionally been used as part of triangulation or multiple methods in a search for validity and corroborative evidence. However, qualitative methods have also been used in different conceptual frameworks to reveal that which has previously been considered unknowable—feelings, emotions, attitudes, perceptions, and cognition. Overwhelmingly, qualitative methods have been used to verify, analyse, interpret, and understand human behaviour of all types.

Studies that utilise qualitative methods in their own right to express individual meanings are much more limited in number. Although humanistic geographers of the 1980s laid claim to this territory, the output of the humanistic school per se was both limited and short-lived; even by 1981, Susan Smith was calling for 'rigour' in humanistic method in a way akin to the current calls for validity and **replicability** and (by implication) respectability (Baxter and Eyles 1997; Philip 1998).

Similarly the aims of critical realism expressed by Sayer and Morgan (1985) have given pre-eminence to individuals' actions and their meanings, yet contributions in this mould to geography literature have been slim. The schools of thought that may have made the greatest contribution to answering qualitative research questions have been the feminist and the poststructural (including the postmodern and the postcolonial). These frameworks both recognise that multiple and conflicting realities coexist. They deliberately give voice to those silenced or ignored by hegemonic (modern, colonial) views of histories and geographies. They embody and acknowledge previously anonymous individuals. Paradoxically, however, the voice of the oppressed not only speaks for itself: it is part of a wider whole. Reality is like an orchestra: poststructural approaches differentiate the instruments and their sounds and bring the oboe occasionally to centre-stage; usually dominated by the strings, the minor instruments too have a tune to play and a thread that forms a distinct but usually unheard part of the whole. It is the voices of the women and children, the colonised, the indigenous, the minorities, that, when released from their silencing, enable a more holistic understanding of society to be articulated (for example, Jane Jacobs' (1993) interpretation of the Aboriginal and mining representations of the conflict over Coronation Hill).

Sayer and Morgan (1985) make the point that exactly the same research technique can be used in different ways for different purposes, according to the theoretical stance of the researcher. Interviews, for example, may be used to gain access to information from gatekeepers about structures or to give voice to silenced minorities. John McKendrick (1996, table 1) considers the relationship between methods and their applications in different research traditions. He contrasts the use of interviews in the humanistic tradition, to 'explore the meaning of the migration of each individual migrant', with their use in a postmodernist framework, whereby in-depth interviews with women may be used 'to "unpack" their rationalisations of their migrations'.

Qualitative methods raise an immense number of difficult issues that are considered in more detail in several of the chapters of this volume. Among those issues are concerns over authorship, audience, language, and power (discussed in chapters 2, 3, 16, and 17). Ethnographic research is often highly complex, within which the individual subject and the audience for the research are often intermingled and mutually dependent. The position of the author as observer in relation to the object of research raises issues of power relations and control. The engagement of the researcher does not necessarily allow the voices of the researched to speak as they are mediated through the researcher's experience and values. The language of research reporting may also exclude those researched, although language varies according to the audience towards which the research is directed. The key issue of the outsider gazing, perhaps voyeuristically, at those defined as 'other' is an intractable problem that needs to be recognised even if it cannot be solved. Even participant observation cannot surmount inbred and naturalised class differences, as demonstrated by Moss (1995) in her immersion in manual labour in hotels. Moss never managed to bridge the cultural, linguistic, and social gap between herself as middle-class researcher and the housemaids who spent their lives in manual labour. The engagement with human research subjects raises significant questions about ethical research practice, which are only now being addressed seriously within the discipline.

SUMMARY

This chapter has outlined three major groups of qualitative methods currently used in human geography. These are oral, textual, and participatory methods. The range of methods is used to answer two broad research questions, relating either to the experiences of individuals or to the social structures within which they operate. Qualitative methods have often been categorised as oppositional to quantitative methods, yet in many respects this is a false dichotomy. The differences between qualitative and quantitative methods are related to the conceptual frameworks from which they have been derived. In elucidating human experiences, environments, and processes, qualitative methods attempt to gather, verify, interpret, and understand the general principles and structures that quantitative methods measure and record. Furthermore, qualitative methods have very frequently been used in conjunction with other methods. The use of qualitative methods alone to explore human values, meanings, and experiences has been more limited. Currently some of the most rewarding qualitative research in human geography is being carried out in feminist and postcolonial frameworks to enable silenced voices to be heard and to foster better comprehension of those naturalised discourses that exclude and marginalise certain groups.

KEY TERMS

deduction

discourse

epistemology

induction

interviews/interviewing

landscape

mixed methods

objective

ontology

oral methods

'other'

paradigm

participation/participant observation

postcolonial

quantitative methods

replicability

semiotics

structures/social structures

subjective

text/textual

triangulation

validity

REVIEW QUESTIONS

1   What research questions may be answered by qualitative methods? Give examples.
2   What are the main types of qualitative research methods used in human geography?
3   How may different types of qualitative methods be linked to theoretical approaches within the discipline?
4   Outline what is meant by the quantitative/qualitative debate.

SUGGESTED READING

Anderson, K. J. 1995, 'Culture and nature at the Adelaide Zoo: at the frontiers of "human" geography', *Transactions of the Institute of British Geographers*, vol. 20, no. 3, pp. 275–94. This article examines discourses surrounding the 'natural' world.

Cook, I. 1997, 'Participant observation', in R. Flowerdew and D. Martin (eds), *Methods in Human Geography*, Addison Wesley Longman, Harlow. This chapter contains many useful hints and stories that make it very useful for students thinking about starting projects. It focuses on the third type of method discussed in this chapter (i.e., participatory).

Jackson, P. and Holbrook, B. 1995, 'Multiple meanings: shopping and the cultural politics of identity', *Environment and Planning A*, vol. 27, pp. 1913–30. This article employs focus groups and provides an example of the 'deconstruction' of an everyday activity.

Kong, L. 1999, 'Cemeteries and columbaria, memorials and mausoleums: narrative and interpretation in the study of deathscapes in geography', *Australian Geographical Studies*, vol. 37, no. 1, pp. 1–10. This article analyses landscape, described in this chapter as the second main type of qualitative method.

Longhurst, R. 1995, 'The geography closest in—the body...the politics of pregnability', *Australian Geographical Studies*, vol. 33, pp. 214–23. A highly readable article that focuses on embodied experience and the discourses surrounding embodiment, but which is grounded in the reality of women's shopping experiences.

Winchester, H. P. M., McGuirk, P. M., and Everett, K. 1999, 'Celebration and control: Schoolies Week on the Gold Coast Queensland', in E. Teather (ed.), *Embodied Geographies: Spaces, Bodies and Rites of Passage*, Routledge, London. This chapter uses oral qualitative evidence to examine a cultural phenomenon of a rite of passage. It provides an example of oral methods.

Power, Subjectivity, and Ethics in Qualitative Research

Robyn Dowling

CHAPTER OVERVIEW

This chapter aims to introduce issues that arise because qualitative research typically involves interpersonal relationships, interpretations, and experiences. I discuss three issues of which qualitative researchers need to be aware: (1) the more formal ethical issues raised by qualitative research projects; (2) the power relations of qualitative research; and (3) objectivity, subjectivity, and intersubjectivity. Rather than advocating simple prescriptions for dealing with these issues, the chapter proposes that researchers be 'critically reflexive'.

INTRODUCTION: ON THE SOCIAL RELATIONS OF RESEARCH

Chapter 1 outlined the types of research questions asked by qualitative researchers, namely our concerns with the shape of societal structures and people's experiences of places and events. This chapter takes you one step closer to conducting qualitative research. It discusses some of the implications of research as a social process. Collecting and interpreting social information involves personal interactions. Interviewing, for example, is essentially a conversation, albeit one contrived for research purposes. Interactions between two or more individuals always occur in a societal context. Societal norms, expectations of individuals, and structures of power influence the nature of those interactions. For instance, when you are conducting a focus group, you may find men talking more than women, and people telling you what they think you want to hear. Societal structures and behaviours are not separate from research interactions. This places all social researchers in an interesting position. We may use a variety of different methods to understand society, but those methods cannot be separated from the structures of society. The converse is also true. The conduct of social research necessarily has an influence on society and the people in it. By asking questions or participating in an activity we alter people's day-to-day lives. And communicating the results of research can potentially change social situations.

Both qualitative and quantitative researchers recognise this lack of separation between research, researcher, and society. What distinguishes qualitative researchers' approach to this issue is the emphasis they give to it. For those who use the qualitative methods discussed in this volume, the interrelations between society, the researcher, and the research project are of critical and abiding significance. They permeate all methods and phases of research. These relationships cannot be ignored, and raise key issues that must be considered when designing and conducting research. This chapter outlines three issues that arise because of the social nature of research and suggests an approach to dealing with them.

The chapter begins with a discussion of ethical guidelines commonly applied to research projects. It moves beyond these guidelines to introduce the concept of critical reflexivity. The chapter then focuses on the ways power traverses the conduct of qualitative methods. Finally, the chapter considers the significance that a researcher's subjectivity and intersubjective relations have for the collection of qualitative data.

A word of caution to begin. In general, most of the chapters that follow offer practical guides to different qualitative methods. They explain how to be a participant observer, how to conduct a focus group, and so forth. This chapter is different in two important respects. First, it is not about any specific method. It is about issues common to each of the methods discussed in this volume. This chapter should be used in combination with those on particular methods to help you think about the specific challenges you are likely to encounter in your research. Second, this chapter does not—and cannot—offer hard and fast rules on conducting ethical research that is responsive to matters of power and **intersubjectivity**. The conduct of good, sensitive, and ethical research depends, in large part, on the ways you deal with your unique relationships with research participants at particular times in particular places.

UNIVERSITY ETHICAL GUIDELINES

Ethics, broadly defined as being about 'the conduct of researchers and their responsibilities and obligations to those involved in the research, including sponsors, the general public and most importantly, the subjects of the research' (O'Connell-Davidson and Layder 1994 p. 55), constitute an issue that must be dealt with in your research. University ethics committees focus on the researcher's responsibilities to research subjects, and formulate guidelines about what researchers should and should not do. It is useful to consider such formal guidelines as a first step in thinking through the social context of your research. In most universities graduate students or those in charge of courses are required to gain the formal approval of a university ethics committee before beginning research that involves people. The committee will not evaluate your research design, but will want to know the aims of the research and the methods you will use. It will be concerned primarily with your responsibilities to research participants with regard to matters of privacy, informed consent, and harm.

Privacy and confidentiality

Qualitative methods often involve invading of someone's privacy. You may be asking very personal questions or observing interactions in people's homes that are customarily considered private. Ethics committees are concerned that these private details about individuals are not released into the public domain. Accordingly, you may have to show that your original field-notes, tapes, and transcripts will be stored in a safe place where access to them will be restricted. You may also need to ensure that your research does not enable others to identify your informants. There are various ways of ensuring the anonymity of informants, including using pseudonyms and masking other identifying characteristics (for example, occupation, location) in the written version of your research. You should note, however, that when dealing with significant public figures it is sometimes not possible or desirable to ensure anonymity. For example, in O'Neill's (2001) research on the Australian-based transnational BHP (Broken Hill Proprietary Company Limited) he identified both the firm and the executives with whom he spoke.

Informed consent

For most geographical research, participants must consent to being part of your research. In other words, they have to give you permission to involve them. However, this criterion is somewhat stricter than a simple 'yes, you can interview me'. It must be *informed* **consent** (see the helpful discussion of this in chapter 3). Informants need to know exactly what it is that they are consenting to. You need to provide participants with a broad outline of what the research is about, the sorts of issues you will be exploring, and what you expect of them (for example, the amount of time required to complete an interview). Most ethics committees recognise that there are exceptions to informed consent. Simple observation of people in a place like a public shopping mall, for example, may not need the explicit consent of those individuals. Indeed, it may be physically impossible to secure the consent of everyone involved. Sometimes informed consent may be waived, although an ethics committee will typically ask you to justify that decision. There are some relatively rare instances when research may involve deception. Deception is where research participants either do not know that you are a researcher (for example, Routledge 2002) or do not know the true nature of your research. Set against the principle of informed consent, deception is clearly an ethically difficult issue and you should think carefully and seek advice before contemplating a research project that involves deception. Moss' (1995) discussion of why and how she used deception in her study of domestic workers may be useful.

Harm

Your research should not expose yourself or your informants to harm—physical or social. As social scientists it is highly unlikely that you will be subjecting people to physical harm. You may, however, be bringing them into contact with 'psycho-social' harm. You may raise issues that may be upsetting or potentially psychologically damaging. This does not mean that your research cannot proceed. Rather, it means your research should cater for this possibility. For example, in work with gay men in western Sydney, Stephen Hodge (reported in Costello and Hodge 1998) had ready the contact details of a counselling service in case participants became upset during interviews. You should also avoid putting yourself at risk during the research. For example, a young woman planning a participant observation project on single women's safety at night on public transport could meet a very cautious response from an ethics committee or research supervisor because of the potential dangers to herself while conducting that work.

MOVING BEYOND ETHICAL GUIDELINES: CRITICAL REFLEXIVITY

Although important, ethical rules and ethics committees are not unproblematic. Iain Hay (1998), for instance, argues that rigid codes cannot always deal with 'the variability and unpredictability of geographic research' (p. 65). What is appropriate in one situation will be inappropriate in another. The blanket application of rules for informed consent, for example, does not take account of the specificity of individual circumstances and character of some research projects (for example, observing people in a public park or plaza). In relation to harm, it is not always possible to predict the impact of research on participants, especially over a longer term (Bailey 2001). More relevant to this chapter is the suggestion that as geographers engaged in research, we must constantly consider the ethical implications of our activities. Because research is a dynamic and ongoing social process that constantly throws up new relations and issues that require constant attention, self-critical awareness of ethical research conduct must pervade our research. Our engagement with ethical behaviour does not end when we submit our research proposal to an ethics committee.

As the foregoing discussion of ethical research conduct might imply to you, human geographers have come to appreciate more fully than ever before the social nature and constitution of our research. Indeed, we now recognise and acknowledge this location through the concept of **critical reflexivity**. Reflexivity, as defined by Kim England (1994), is a process of constant, self-conscious, scrutiny of the self as researcher and of the research process. In other words, being reflexive means analysing your own situation as if it were something you were studying. What is happening? What social relations are being enacted? Are they influencing the data?

Critical reflexivity is difficult but rewarding. It is rewarding in that, as some of the examples used in this chapter indicate, it can initiate new research directions. Critical reflexivity is however difficult in two respects. First, many geographers do not write about the research

BOX 2.1 THE RESEARCH DIARY AS A TOOL FOR THE REFLEXIVE RESEARCHER

Your task in being reflexive will be helped by keeping a research diary. The contents of a research diary are slightly different from those of a fieldwork diary. While a **fieldwork diary**, or fieldnotes, contains your qualitative data—including observations, conversation, and maps—a research diary is a place for recording your reflexive observations. It contains your thoughts and ideas about the research process, its social context, and your role in it. You could start your research diary by including answers to the questions posed in the checklist set out in Box 2.3 at the end of the chapter.

process in their published work. Linda McDowell (1998) comments, for example, that many of the details of how her merchant banking research proceeded and, as a result, her reflections on the process, do not appear in the book based on that research. However, discussions of reflexivity are becoming more common and a guide to some of these is provided in the 'Suggested Reading' section at the end of the chapter. Second, reflexivity is difficult because we are not accustomed to examining our engagement with our work with the same intensity as we regard our research subjects. You may be helped in this matter by keeping a **research diary**, which is outlined in Box 2.1.

The rest of the chapter focuses on two of the important issues about which you need to be reflexive: power and subjectivity. For those readers who are especially interested, the discussion of reflexivity is extended in chapter 16.

POWER RELATIONS AND QUALITATIVE RESEARCH[1]

One important outcome of the social character of qualitative research is that research is also interleaved with relations of power. Power intersects research in a number of ways. It can enter your research through the stories, or interpretations, you create from the information you gather. Power is involved here because knowledge is both directly and indirectly powerful. Knowledge is directly powerful through its input into policy. Some studies are specific analyses of policy issues and their results have a direct impact on people's lives. Knowledge is also indirectly powerful. The stories you tell about your participants' actions, words, and understandings of the world have the potential to change the way those people are thought about. Power is also involved in earlier parts of the research process. In undertaking qualitative research you are attempting to understand—participating in, and sometimes creating situations whereby people (yourself included) are differently situated in relation to social structures. Both you and your informants occupy different 'speaking positions'. Not only do you and your informants have different intentions and social roles, but you also have different capacities to change situations and other people.

England (1994) identifies the different sorts of power relations typically entered into by social researchers. She divides these relationships into three types. ***Reciprocal* relationships** are those whereby the researcher and the researched are in comparable social positions and have relatively equal benefits and costs from participating in the research. You may, for example, be conducting focus groups with your fellow students on how they are adjusting to university life. Although not absent, power differences in this relationship are minimal compared with two other sorts of relationships. In ***asymmetrical* relationships** those being studied are in positions of influence in comparison to the researcher. Interviews with corporate executives may fall into this category because of such executives' relative access to cultural and financial resources (see McDowell 1992). In ***potentially exploitative* relationships** the researcher is in a position of greater power than the research participant. Tracy Skelton's research with young people is an example of a potentially exploitative relationship (Skelton 2001).

Power cannot be eliminated from your research since it exists in all social relations. Human geographers typically have one of two responses to issues of power. The first, responding directly to potentially exploitative relationships, is to involve participants in the design and conduct of the research. In their research on young people's experience of crime and victimisation, Pain and Francis (2003) explicitly sought young people's perceptions of what required investigation and then gave participants a number of opportunities to verify or refute the researchers' interpretations. Pain and Francis also conducted a number of meetings and workshops to disseminate their findings. Through these two strategies they hoped to effect some social change and alter potentially exploitative relationships.

Such participatory forms of research are not always the most appropriate for every research project or for student researchers. A second response that recognises and negotiates relations of power is critical reflexivity. For example, when collecting data, our responsibility to the research participants is such that we should not take advantage of someone's less powerful position to gather information. In the case of homeless youth, for example, you would

---

BOX 2.2   SEXISM IN RESEARCH

Sexism can present problems in many different sorts of research projects. Eichler (1988) identifies four primary problems of sexism in research:

- *androcentricity/gynocentricity*—a view of the world from male/female perspectives respectively. For instance, concepts of 'group warfare' developed through reference to men's experiences only.
- *overgeneralisation*—a study is only about one sex but presents itself as applicable to both sexes. By way of example a study that is exclusively concerned with men's location decisions might be misleadingly entitled 'Residential location decisions in Auckland'.
- *gender insensitivity*—ignores gender as an influential factor in either the research process or interpretation. For instance, a study of the geographical effects of a free-trade agreement that fails to consider any gender-specific effects.
- *double standards*—identical behaviours or situations are evaluated, treated, or measured by different means or criteria (for example, drawing different conclusions about men and women on the basis of identical answers to a survey or aptitude test).

Eichler also identifies three 'derived' forms of sexism:

- *sex appropriateness*—the notion that some characteristics and behaviours are accepted as being more appropriate for one sex than the other (for example, designing a research project on parental perceptions of children's play space, and interviewing women only because you assume they will know more about the issue).
- *familism*—using family as the unit of analysis when the individual might be more appropriate or vice versa (for example, working at the family scale in evaluating the social costs and rewards of in-home care for the elderly, rather than exploring the different implications this might have for males and females within the family).
- *sexual dichotomism*—postulating absolute differences between women and men (for example, women are sometimes claimed to be 'naturally' more timid than men).

not make the possibility of gaining access to shelter dependent on that person's participation in the study. But you cannot eliminate the power dimension from your research, since it exists in all situations. The best strategy is to be aware of, understand, and respond to it in a critically reflexive manner. Critical reflexivity does not necessarily mean altering your research design but it does imply that you reflect constantly on the research process and modify it where appropriate. When you are formulating your topic think about the various ethical and power relations that may be enacted during your research (see, for example, Box 2.2). Are you happy with the situation? Would you like to do anything differently? Could you justify your actions to others? You should also think about how you communicate the results. Have you reflected as faithfully as possible what you have been told and/or observed without reproducing stereotypical representations? Are you presenting what you heard and saw, or what you expected to hear and see? Remember, the stories you tell may change the worlds in which you and your research participants live (for more detail on this matter, see chapter 16).

OBJECTIVITY, SUBJECTIVITY, AND INTERSUBJECTIVITY IN QUALITATIVE DATA COLLECTION

Objectivity has traditionally been emphasised in geographic discussions of quantitative research methods. Objectivity has two components. The first relates to the personal involvement between the researcher and other participants in the study. The introduction to this chapter suggested that it is impossible to achieve this sort of objectivity because of the social nature of all research. Objectivity's second component refers to the researcher's independence from the object of research. This implies that there can be no interactive relationship between the researcher and the process of data collection and interpretation. Clearly, however, dispassionate interpretation is difficult if not impossible because we all bring personal histories and perspectives to research. *Subjectivity* involves the insertion of personal opinions and characteristics into research practice. Qualitative research gives emphasis to subjectivity because the methods involve social interactions. As will become evident in later chapters, you need to draw on your personal resources to establish rapport and communicate with informants. Discourse analysis also involves your subjectivity in that your everyday understanding of the world helps you decipher texts. If subjectivity is important then so too is *intersubjectivity*. This refers to the meanings and interpretations of the world created, confirmed, or disconfirmed as a result of interactions (language and action) with other people within specific contexts. Collecting and interpreting qualitative information relies upon a dialogue between you and your informants. In these dialogues your personal characteristics and social position—elements of your subjectivity—cannot be fully controlled or changed because such dialogues do not occur in a social vacuum. The ways you are perceived by your informants, the ways you perceive them, and the ways you interact are at least partially determined by societal norms.

Critical reflexivity is the most appropriate strategy for dealing with issues of subjectivity and intersubjectivity. Although you cannot be entirely independent from the object of research, trying to become aware of the nature of your involvement, and the influence of social relations, is a useful beginning that can help you identify the implications of subjectivity and intersubjectivity in your research.

Geographers' work on gender provides some good examples of the role of intersubjectivity in research. Gender is important because we often ascribe characteristics to people on the basis of gender. Furthermore, personal interactions vary with the gender of participants; we tend to react differently to men and women. Therefore gender is a factor that can influence data collection. For instance, Andy Herod (1993) found that male union officials restricted the sort of information he was given during interviews because he was a man. Specifically, his informants downplayed the role of women in the union's struggles. Herod attributes this not only to the perspectives of the union officials, but also to the social (masculine) context of the interviews. The union officials assumed, Herod thinks, that either he was not interested in gender or that it was inappropriate to raise this issue in the context of a male-to-male conversation. By contrast, Hilary Winchester (1996) suggests that being a woman interviewing men aided her research on lone fathers. She found herself adopting a typically feminine role of facilitating conversation with men, which helped considerably in gathering the men's stories.

Your ability to interpret certain situations also depends on your own characteristics. Important here is a debate about the relative merits of being an '**insider**' or '**outsider**'. An insider is someone who is similar to their informants in many respects, while an outsider differs substantially from their informants. As an 'out' lesbian, interviewing other lesbians, Valentine's research on sexuality could be considered insider research, whereas she was an 'outsider' in her interviews with parents and children about childhood (see Valentine 2002). One position in the debate is that as an insider both the information you collect and your interpretations of it are more valid than those of an 'outsider'. People are more likely to talk to you freely, and you are more likely to understand what they are saying because you share their outlook on the world. If you are not a member of the same social group as your informants, then establishing rapport may be more difficult (see chapters 3 and 6). And, since you do not share their perspective on the world and their experiences, then your interpretations may be less reliable. But being an outsider can also bring benefits to the research. It may mean that people make more of an effort to clearly articulate events, circumstances, and feelings to the researcher. Interviewing trade union officials in Eastern Europe, Herod (1999) found it helpful to be from a different country because it guaranteed a warm reception and insightful two-way exchanges of information.

A final perspective to consider is that you are never simply either an insider or an outsider. We have overlapping racial, socio-economic, gender, ethnic, and other characteristics. If we have multiple social qualities and roles, as do our informants, then there are many points of similarity and dissimilarity between ourselves and research participants. Indeed, becoming aware of some of these commonalities and discrepancies can be one of the pleasures and surprises of qualitative research. As a British researcher, Mullings (1999) was far removed from the social worlds of the Jamaican factory workers and employers she interviewed. To her surprise, however, her position as a person of African descent led to shared experiences with local interviews and subsequently rich interviews.

Intersubjectivity also means that neither yourself, your participants, nor the nature of your interactions will remain unchanged during the research project. Your general outlook and opinions may indeed change as result of your research. If you are a participant observer, for example, you will be immersing yourself in a situation that will invariably affect you. Robin Kearns (1997) discusses how both he and his research project changed in response to his inter-actions as an observer. Kearns began his project on Maori health in rural New Zealand in the waiting room of a medical clinic. He did not intend to interact with patients in the waiting room. His attempts to be unobtrusive failed due to the inquisitiveness of patients who talked to him incessantly. These interactions had two immediate effects. First, they forced him to adopt a different stance in his research: he had to be more open about his presence and his research. Second, he modified his method by actively involving the local community in the research design and the findings (Kearns discusses this more fully in chapter 12).

Critical reflexivity can give rise to new and exciting directions in one's research. In a very different context, Gilbert (1994) began a research project believing that the women she was speaking with were not feminists. But responses such as 'she had devoted her life to God because she was not going to let any man stop her from surviving' (p. 92) helped challenge her own preconceived ideas about feminism, and shed new light on the empirical material.

SUMMARY AND PROMPTS FOR CRITICAL REFLEXIVITY

Using the qualitative methods described in subsequent chapters will involve you in various social relations and responsibilities. I have advocated critical reflexivity—self-conscious scrutiny of yourself and the social nature of the research. Critical reflexivity means acknowl-edging rather than denying your own social position and asking how your research interac-tions and the information you collect are socially conditioned. How, in other words, are your social role and the nature of your research interactions inhibiting or enhancing the information you are gathering? This is not an easy task since it is not always possible to anticipate or assess accurately the ways in which our personal characteristics affect the infor-mation we accumulate.

I shall not end this chapter with answers. Instead, I offer a preliminary set of prompts that might help you reflect critically on issues of ethics, power, and intersubjectivity in dif-ferent types and phases of research (see Box 2.3).

BOX 2.3   HOW TO BE CRITICALLY REFLEXIVE IN RESEARCH

Before beginning:

- What are some of the power dynamics of the general social situation I am exploring and what sort of power dynamics do I expect between myself and my informants?
- In what ways am I an insider and/or outsider in respect to this research topic? What prob-lems might my position cause? Will any of them be insurmountable?
- What ethical issues might impinge upon my research (for example, privacy, informed con-sent, harm, coercion, deception)?

After data collection:

- Did my perspective and opinions change during the research?
- How, if at all, were my interactions with participants informed/constrained by gender or any other social relations?
- How was I perceived by my informants?

Remember to take notes throughout data collection and keep them in a research diary. During writing and interpretation:

- Am I reproducing racist and/or sexist stereotypes? Why and how?
- What social and conceptual assumptions underlie my interpretations?

KEY TERMS

asymmetrical power relation
critical reflexivity
ethics
fieldwork diary
informed consent
insider
intersubjectivity

objectivity
outsider
potentially exploitative power relation
reciprocal power relation
research diary
subjectivity

REVIEW QUESTIONS

1   What is critical reflexivity? Read a study in human geography in your field of interest that uses qualitative methods. Is the researcher reflexive about the research process? If so, how? If not, what sort of questions would you like to ask the researcher about the research process?
2   What forms of power relations may be part of a qualitative research project?
3   Read a piece of qualitative research in human geography. Can you identify any or all of Eichler's (1988) forms of sexism in the way the research has been carried out or in the interpretation?
4   How are qualitative methods intersubjective? How might social relations like gender influence the collection of data?
5   Outline and explain the issues of concern to university ethics committees. Find out how your university's committee deals with these issues.

SUGGESTED READING

The journal *Ethics, Place and Environment* often has special issues of relevance to this chapter. See, for example, volume 3, number 1 on disability and volume 4, number 2 on research with children.

Iain Hay discusses the limitations of ethical codes and suggests alternatives in a 1998 article entitled 'Making moral imaginations: research ethics, pedagogy, and professional human geography' in *Ethics, Place and Environment*, vol. 1, no. 1, pp. 55–75.

Paul Cloke and others provide a detailed account of the practice of critical reflexivity in their research into homelessness in 'Ethics, reflexivity and research: encounters with homeless people', *Ethics, Place and Environment*, vol. 3, no. 2. pp. 133–54.

Gillian Rose provides a sophisticated discussion of critical reflexivity and some of its problems in her 1997 article 'Situating knowledges: positionality, reflexivities and other tactics', *Progress in Human Geography*, vol. 21, pp. 305–20.

Note

1   See chapter 3 for further discussion of power-related issues.

3

Cross-Cultural Research: Ethics, Methods, and Relationships

Richie Howitt and Stan Stevens

CHAPTER OVERVIEW: AN EXPLANATION OF OUR WRITING METHOD

Working across the differences that constitute 'cultures' is a common challenge for geographical researchers. Ideas about research are profoundly shaped by cultural contexts. As geographers, we are aware of and engaged by the complex and dynamic relationships between culture and geography—our thinking is shaped by where we conduct research and the people we work with. In discussing how we might write about cross-cultural research as part of a wider discussion of qualitative methods, we initially thought each of us might write sections of the chapter, with a jointly developed introduction and concluding discussion. This approach, we thought, would enable us each to have our own voice (and responsibility for positions that not all might fully share!). But the wonders of email allowed us to explore some alternatives. We decided that it might be better to think of our writing in terms of a conversation across cultures and geographies, with each of us framing key questions arising from our readings of each other's work and the wider literature on cross-cultural research and our frustrations with existing practices and their impacts on people we work with. In the end, we have written the chapter as a conversational text. In many ways, the text parallels what we seek to emphasise about cross-cultural field-based research—it involves respectful listening, difficult and challenging engagements, careful attention to nuances in the lives of 'others', and a critical, long-term consideration of the implications of methods in the construction of meaning.

MODES OF CROSS-CULTURAL ENGAGEMENT: COLONIAL, POSTCOLONIAL, DECOLONISING, AND INCLUSIONARY RESEARCH

Richie: Can we start our conversation by talking about the intercultural spaces in which we might think about 'cross-cultural' research? Conventionally, fieldwork is seen as 'the heart of geography' (Stevens 2001, p. 66), but there has been a lot of discussion about just what we mean by 'the field' in 'fieldwork' (see, for example, special issues of *Professional Geographer* (1994) and *The Geographical Review* (2001), including Blake 2001; DeLyser and Starr 2001; Gade 2001; Katz 1994; Kobayashi 1994; Nast 1994; Zelinsky 2001) and about the multiple versions of 'out-there-ness' and 'in-here-ness' that are constructed around ideas of what constitutes the 'cross-cultural' in 'cross-cultural research'.

As I see it, most human geographic research is 'cross-cultural' because we are drawn into thinking about other people's constructions of place; other people's ways for reading their cultural landscapes—even when they are the landscapes that we live in ourselves in our everyday lives! I remember as an undergraduate being struck by the idea of a 'geographical expedition' into Detroit (for example, Horvath 1971; Pawson and Teather 2002). That was juxtaposed, for me at least, with the whole 'Boy's Own Adventure' representation of fieldwork, and the ethical issues of interpreting someone else's culture for one's own reasons.[1] The critique of that androcentric-style in geography was simultaneously about its sexism *and* its ethnocentricism.

Stan: I agree with you, Richie. A lot of cultural geographical research is cross-cultural. Geographers often face similar ethical and methodological issues whether working close to home or on the other side of the planet. I've chosen to spend nearly a quarter of my time, more than twenty years, living and working in the Himalaya with the Khumbu, Pharak, and Katuthanga Sharwa peoples of the Chomolungma region (better known to the rest of the world in British colonial nomenclature as the Sherpas of the Mt Everest region) (Stevens 1993; 1997; 2001; 2004; forthcoming; Stevens and Sherpa 1993). But one need not go to the other side of the planet to engage with 'others' given the often complex dimensions of diversity created by societal and group constructions of regional, ethnic, linguistic, class, racial, gender, sexual, religious, ideological, and other difference. I suspect that the challenges and moral considerations of cross-cultural communication, learning, and activism might not be much different if I were to undertake research with my neighbours in the rural Massachusetts community I've lived in for the past few years or in the neighbourhoods of nearby cities.[2] Accordingly I think that there may well be broader applicability and utility to some of the lessons I've learned from Sharwas, my Berkeley advisor Bernard Nietschmann (1973; 1979; 1997; 2001; Maya People of Southern Belise, Toledo Maya Cultural Council, and Toledo Alcades Association 1997) and his work with the Miskito and the Maya, and postcolonial studies that challenge 'conventional'—in the sense of common, long-established, and unexamined—views of fieldwork.[3] These lessons revolve around the importance of rejecting the attitudes, assumptions, purposes, and methodologies of what postcolonial theorists refer to as **'colonial' research** in favour of those of 'decolonising', 'postcolonial' research.

Richie: Stan, these are issues that fieldworkers have grappled with for a long time. Even in 'colonial' modes, people such as Clifford Geertz, Charles Rowley, and Nugget Coombs made valuable and very critical contributions.[4] Amongst geographers we might think of the work of people such as Fay Gale, Janice Monk, Elspeth Young, Keith Buchanan, Oskar Spate, Jim Blaut, and others, You also identify 'inclusionary' research as relevant to your work. How do you differentiate these different approaches to research? Do you see them as adopting different positionalities vis-à-vis difference, or do they adopt different methods, conceptual emphases, or perhaps purposes for the research that leads to your particular wording?

Stan: You've written insightfully about these distinctions yourself, Richie (Howitt 2002a; 2002b), which are critical to rethinking research ethics, methods, and relationships. I see colonial and **postcolonial research** as differing fundamentally from all of the standpoints you've just identified. Colonial research reflects and reinforces domination and exploitation through the attitudes and differential power embodied in its research relationships with 'others', its dismissal of their rights and knowledge, its intrusive and non-participatory methodologies, and often also in its goals and in its use of research findings. Postcolonial research, to me, is a reaction to and rejection of colonial research and is intended to contribute to 'others' self-determination and welfare through methodologies and the use of research findings that value their rights, knowledge, perspectives, concerns, and desires and are based on open and more egalitarian relationships. **Decolonising research** goes further still in attempting to use the research process and research findings to break down the cross-cultural discourses, asymmetrical power relationships, representations, and political, economic, and social structures through which colonialism and neo-colonialism are constructed and maintained. I owe the term **'inclusionary research'** to your use of it for a particularly revolutionary kind of decolonising research aimed at helping empower subordinated, marginalised, and oppressed others and to provide training and tools they can use to 'overturn their world' (Howitt 2002a).

Colonial research has unfortunately long been the dominant mode of cross-cultural research in geography and anthropology and continues to be widespread today despite feminist and postcolonialist critiques. Much research continues to be imposed by outsiders for their own purposes and benefits on indigenous peoples, many of the non-indigenous peoples of Asia, Africa, and Latin America, and on women and ethnic and cultural minorities in many societies throughout the world.[5] So much research has been conducted from such ethnocentric perspectives for morally suspect purposes and through ethically dubious ways that, as Linda Tuhiwai Smith (1999, p. 1) notes from Maori and other indigenous peoples' perspectives in her important book, *Decolonising Methodologies: Research and Indigenous Peoples*, 'the word itself, "research" is probably one of the dirtiest words in the indigenous world's vocabulary'. Vine Deloria Jr. made the same observation and indictment, declaring that 'Indians have been cursed above all other people in history. Indians have anthropologists' (1988 [1969] p. 78).

Richie: The Australian (Wadi Wadi) poet Barbara Nicholson makes a similar point in her 2001 poem 'Something there is…' (see Box 3.1).

Stan: Exactly! I hadn't come across Barbara Nicholson's poem, but it should be required reading for prospective cross-cultural researchers. These kinds of **subaltern** critiques of colonial research condemn not only the ways in which research has objectified 'others', violated their privacy and their humanity, and promoted colonising agendas but also the ways in which Western science and scholarship have (mis)represented non-Western, indigenous, and subaltern peoples and groups. Linda Tuhiwai Smith accordingly identifies research as 'a significant site of struggle between the interests and ways of knowing of the West and the interests and ways of resisting of the Other' (Smith 1999, p. 2). [7]

Although colonial research has typically claimed positivistic objectivity, validity, and **reliability**, from the perspectives of the colonised and researched it has instead been seen as

BOX 3.1 SOMETHING THERE IS...
by Barbara Nicholson

...that doesn't like an anthropologist.
You go to a university
and get a bit of paper
that says you are qualified.
Does it also say that you
have unlimited rights
to invade my space?
It seems that you believe your bit of paper
is both passport and visa to my place,
that henceforth you have the right
to scrutinise the bits and pieces
of me.
You have measured my head,
indeed, you preserved it in brine
so that future clones of your kind
can also measure and calculate my
    cognition.
You've counted my teeth and compared
    them with
the beasts of the forest,
you've delved into my uterus,
had a morbid fascination with my sacred
    practices of incision and concision,
with the secret expressions of my rites of
    passage.
On your bit of paper you record how I dress,
earn my money,
what I eat and drink,
with whom I mix and with whom I don't,
where I go and don't go,
what I spend my money on,
the physical, mental and moral state of
    my being,
my marriage habits,
my birthing rituals,
my funerary rites,
the position I hold
in my society.
You analyse to a fine point

my art and music,
dance and composition,
horticulture and agriculture,
pharmacology and technology.
Nothing escapes your keen eye
and your pen records it
so that other aspirants to your
    elevated state
may draw on your findings and
    further explore
the intricacies
of me...
and perpetuate the invasion.

Oh yes...something there is.
If I were to go to university
and get a bit of paper that says,
'Wadi Wadi woman, you are an
    anthropologist',
will that give me the right to invade
    your space,
to visit you
in your three-bedroom brick veneer,
note how many rice bubbles
go into your breakfast bowl,
what colour is on the roll
in your bathroom,
and see if the bathroom is clean?
Will I have the right to sit
on the end of your bed
and count every thrust
as you make love?
You will not complain
when I calculate your expenditure
on alcohol and yarndi,[6]
or count the cost when you visit
    McDonalds?
Remember, because I am an
    anthropologist,

my bit of paper gives me the right!
From now on I have carte blanche
to all the above
in your society,
and I can invade your space,
and I can record my findings
so that for generations to come
my kin can pursue
a relentless investigation
into the fabric of your existence,
into the bits and pieces
of you.

And resulting from my research
into the common cold and its effects
on you, a representative sample
of a cross-section of the population
of Double Bay, Sydney, 1994,
an avalanche of vultures from the media,

the government,
and the tourism industry
will descend on you
in ever increasing hordes
to see for themselves
if what I said
could really be true.
They will take over your lounge-room
and lay down laws for you to live by
—all for your own good of course;
they will point out to you
the necessity of changing your way of life
so that you will be better able to fit into
the prescriptive patterns of social behaviour
devised by them on your behalf.
I will be to you,
in the guise of humane academic inquiry,
as you have been to me, invader!
something there is...

From *Urban Songlines*

Used with kind permission of the poet
from Reed-Gilbert, K. (ed.) 2000, *The Strength Of Us As Women: Black Women Speak*, Ginninderra Press, Canberra
(pp. 27–30). For other work by Barbara Nicholson see the journals *XText* (1996), and *Law, Text & Culture* (2003).

subjective, superficial, and misinformed. Smith (1999) argues that this reflects subjectivity, positionality, situated and partial knowledges, and ethnocentrism. She draws on Said's (1978) seminal postcolonial critique of the West's construction of the Orient, Foucault's (1972) concept of Western knowledge as a cultural archive in which many different cultures' knowledges, histories, and artefacts have been collected, categorised, and represented, and feminist critiques of positivism that highlight the partial and situated character of knowledge (Haraway 1991; Reinharz 1992; Stanley and Wise 1993). Colonial research also reflects and embodies unequal power relationships (and associated discourses and methodologies), and the ramifications these have for cross-cultural relationships and interaction. Imposed, exploitative research denies respect for alternative ways of knowing. It undermines trust, and sabotages communication and collaborative exploration. By thus shaping the interactions and relationships on which cross-cultural fieldwork relies, this colonial model of unreflective fieldwork produces distorted and ethnocentric findings and analysis, fostering **'Orientalism'** in its depictions of 'others'. When it ventures into the realm of activism in the name of development or conservation, such research tends to support paternalism and imposed, external intervention, often with equally regrettable results. Postcolonial research rejects the assumptions and methods of colonial research. Research is instead envisioned as a means of contesting colonialism and neo-colonialism through fostering self-determination and cultural affirmation (Smith 1999). In my view, postcolonial research aims at being emancipatory not simply through being more culturally sensitive or seeking local research approval, but through respect for the legitimacy of 'others' knowledge, ways of knowing and being, and through activism in support of their pursuit and exercise of self-determination. This requires acknowledging and repudiating the dynamics of power that shape colonial research interactions with subordinated and marginalised peoples and groups, attempting to overcome whatever ethnocentrism and paternalism we bring to the research and whatever suspicion we are greeted with, persuading people that we are worthy of being taught and capable of learning, and being willing to put aside preconceptions (and academic and activist preoccupations), to listen and to be of service to local concerns and projects.

Having drawn such strong contrasts between colonial and postcolonial research, I would like to be clear that I am not suggesting that there has been a simple historical progression from colonial to postcolonial research nor even that there is always a clear dichotomy between the two. Nor would I advocate that postcolonial researchers casually dismiss and ignore research findings from less critically informed research or assume that all work prior to the development of postcolonial research methodologies was uniformly exploitative, mis-informed, and paternalistic. We should recognise that much work today, even work cast within postcolonial frameworks, may remain colonial to some degree. And certainly there is much to learn from the research findings and experience of colonial research (as well as to react to and to revise), despite the ethical issues that it raises and the difficulties of evaluating the degree to which its research findings have been distorted by the goals, attitudes, relationships, and methodologies that shape such fieldwork. There is also much to respect and learn from in the work of earlier researchers whose fieldwork in some ways broke with the prevalent colonial research climate of their time.[8]

Richie: Deborah Rose refers to the need to develop critical perspectives on our own work, and to guard against 'deep colonising' (1999, p. 177). She suggests that even the educated and sensitive 'Western' self risks enclosing itself within a 'hall of mirrors', in which it mistakes the endless reflections of its own common sense for a universal truth—and truthfulness. And we often see a romantic idealising of the 'indigenous Other' as a source of some alternative universal truth. How do you see the task of doing research whose methods and approach fosters decolonising peoples' lives and domains—and even of ourselves and our discipline?

Stan: That raises important issues of attitudes, intentions, and relationships. I'd like to first suggest a few practical strategies for such a decolonising approach, and then discuss the post-colonial perspectives and attitudes towards difference that they reflect and embody. I think we need to work to avoid 'deep colonising' and foster decolonising in multiple, interactive ways. One vital part of this is 'critical self-reflexivity', (England 1994; Rose 1997; see also chapter 2 of this volume). Another is fostering relationships with the people we work with that make it possible for them to voice their concerns and other feedback about us and the research project in an open and honest way. This is important on an everyday level, but it can also include seeking formal or informal local authorisation for research as you've written about, Richie (Howitt 2002a), or placing the project under community supervision (Smith 1999). Local research authorisation or community supervision both involve reaching an understanding on appropriate research goals, methodologies (including the **cultural protocols** within which it will be conducted), and how knowledge will be shared and used. If there is no formal process for this, as has been the case in the Sharwa regions I've worked in, one can try to achieve something similar through working with a set of local residents or—still better—with local mentors and co-researchers. As I see it the greatest potential for fieldwork to be decolonising for all involved is to give up 'control' of the research and develop either truly collaborative research or to contribute to local or indigenous research in which we offer our skills as colleagues, consultants, or allies (see chapter 13 for further discussion; also Herlihy 2003; Herlihy and Knapp 2003; Maya People of Southern Belize, Toledo Maya Cultural Council, and Toledo Alcades Association 1997; Park 1993; Nietschmann 1995; Smith 2003).

Decolonising research thus requires a fundamental shift in research approach and conduct that begins with a perception and response to difference and 'others' that is the antithesis of the perspective and practice of colonial research. Colonial research is grounded in the binary, polarising perception of other peoples as the 'Other', a position of distance in opposition to the 'Self', 'Us', (and often also to the 'West') that is fraught with ethnocentrism and hierarchy and undergirds cross-cultural and interpersonal dynamics of dominance and exploitation.[9] To me postcolonial research is instead grounded in the perception of other peoples as 'others' who are different but not intrinsically different or alien, who differ culturally but not in essential humanity and value. It is attracted to difference rather than wary of it, it seeks to interact rather than to remain distant, it coexists with, respects, and honours difference rather than dominating or exploiting it. This difference of attitude and intention makes for very different conceptions of the purposes of research. Colonial research promotes, deliberately or inadvertently, a colonising (and now globalising) agenda that includes political, economic, and cultural imperialism and neo-colonialism; national, transnational, and global exploitation and commodification of 'resources' (natural and human); Western or other colonial discourses about 'civilisation', 'development', or 'conservation'; Western conceptions of 'science'; and promotion of a Western over-preoccupation with 'self' and self-gratification (not excluding such selfish motivations as the pursuit of academic status or the satisfying of intellectual curiosity). With postcolonial approaches, the purposes of research instead become cross-cultural understanding, the celebration of diversity, and especially empowerment or emancipation—a decolonising project based on rejecting the ethnocentrism and exploitation of colonialism through cross-cultural respect and through support for self-determination.

These differences in attitudes and intentions in turn tend to be manifest in research topics and conceptual frameworks. I would like to think that postcolonial researchers approach research with a high level of idealism, that they may tend to be less concerned with research topics for their self-serving value in enhancing their career or bringing financial gain or with scholarly/scientific intellectual pursuits as ends in themselves.[10] Postcolonial researchers are often strongly drawn to research topics that enable them to engage in advocacy and activism and to theory and concepts that enable them to study and affect exploitative/oppressive political, social, and economic relationships, processes, and contexts. This has attracted postcolonial researchers particularly to **postmodernism** (including poststructuralism as well as postcolonialism itself), feminist theory, neo-Marxism, and the perspectives and language of independence struggles, 'subaltern' social justice movements, and indigenous rights campaigns.

From these perspectives, values, and conceptual frameworks, postcolonial research has developed methodologies that differ in significant ways from those of colonial research—a topic that will be the focus of much of our remaining discussion in this chapter.

Richie: That makes me think of David Harvey's call as President of the American Association of Geographers for an **'applied peoples' geography'** (1984, p. 9), where the skills of geographical analysis might be harnessed to the service of marginalised 'others'. That idea always sat comfortably in my mind with the educational philosophies of Paulo Freiere (for example, 1972b; 1976) and more recent discussion of using Goulet's ideas of 'border pedagogy' in geographical education and research settings (for example, Cook 2000; Howitt 2001). But universities are themselves a major element in the construction of power and privilege. Academic institutions harness well-intentioned efforts to their own purposes—not all of which are consistent with the liberal values of education and research for the common good. In some cases, much narrower institutional concerns and specific ideological concerns become dominant. Yet universities also continue to provide opportunities for discursive, and even practical, dissent. Indeed, allowing a small space for difference while reinforcing the status quo of privilege is a defining characteristic of the liberal academy. The task of harnessing these opportunities in pursuing the core values of social justice, economic equity, ecological sustainability and the acceptance of cultural diversity has been a central element in my projects for inclusionary geographies—they straddle intercultural spaces both discursively and practically (Howitt 2001).

Stan: I would certainly agree with that. I'd add one more point here relative to the discussion of 'deep colonising', though, that is that prospective researchers should be aware that despite good intentions even what might be intended as postcolonial, applied peoples' geography can still be exploitative, paternalistic, and ethnocentric in practice. This is one reason that some indigenous advocates of postcolonial research have strong reservations about research by outsiders, particularly outsiders who are not under indigenous guidance (Smith 1999). It is not enough, for example, to *intend* to carry out advocacy and activism-directed research if the means we use reflect our own ethnocentric baggage or if our preconceived notions of what needs to be studied and what needs to be done are considered patronising, irrelevant, or threatening to the people we wish to work with and for. I am reminded here, Richie, of your call (Howitt 2002a) for 'inclusionary research', your accounts of your early experience in Australia, and my own early experiences with the Sharwas of the Chomolungma region. I arrived in Khumbu in 1982 with the idea that I could best 'help out' by documenting and exposing the adverse impacts of international tourism. That project was welcomed by local Sharwa leaders, and from the outset of the fieldwork in 1982–83 Sharwas actively participated in and assisted the research. Yet when I returned in 1984 and was taken under the guidance of two Sharwa mentors I was gently taught that Sharwas had their own perspectives about what kinds of research they needed, their own critique of previous research (much of which had been 'colonial' in character), and their own ideas about the kinds of contributions that I could make. I came as a result to work closely with them and with other Sharwa co-researchers on a series of projects that Sharwas thought important, including documenting oral traditions and oral histories at the request of elders who were concerned about their possible loss, reporting the perspectives of Sharwas who wanted to correct outsiders' mis-impressions and 'orientalism' of their culture and homeland, and working with Sharwas to document 'counter-knowledge' and 'counter-history' that they can use in their efforts to redress the Nepal government's seizure of their territory and authority over their land use and management (Stevens 1993; 1997; 2004; forthcoming).

GETTING STARTED: RESEARCH LEGITIMACY AND LOCAL AUTHORISATION

Richie: Yes, I remember heading off to western Cape York in late 1978 as an enthusiastic young student researcher intent on 'studying land rights around the Weipa bauxite mine'. I called in on a regional Aboriginal organisation in Cairns on my way to Weipa, expecting to be welcomed with open arms. But I was taken aside and told in no uncertain terms that the last thing local Aboriginal people wanted or needed was a study that told the mining companies about their land rights. 'If you want to help, why don't you do something useful?' I was asked. 'Why don't you do a study of the companies that we can use?'

This question reoriented not just my first foray into geographical research, but my relationship with the discipline. I read Laura Nader on 'studying up' (1972), and enthused about 'applied peoples' geography' (Harvey 1984). I shifted my audience from a scholarly focus to a community focus, and began to ask questions that other social scientists hadn't really asked before. When I started working on research projects with Aboriginal people, there was no formal process of ethics review required—although Mary Hall, my honours supervisor, required detailed research protocols and critical engagement with participating or affected community groups about ethical concerns. In many ways she anticipated the shift away from an assumption that academic researchers have a 'right to research', and the increased accountability for formal ethical oversight of research. The legal and institutional requirements for ethical oversight and the support for ethical engagement from formal institutional quarters has been quite an important shift in the last ten years. In that time most institutions have increasingly put procedures in place that require researchers to establish strong ethical foundations for cross-cultural work, particularly with vulnerable groups, rather than allowing them to assume a right to research non-Western 'others'. For example, recent guidelines for researchers working with Aboriginal and Torres Strait Islander groups in Australia advocate 'building of robust relationships' as the basis for ethical engagement, with no implicit checklist to ensure conformity (NHMRC 2003, p. 3). [11]

Stan: I've found university human subjects protocols a useful starting point for pursuing decolonising research. For cross-cultural work generally, and not only with indigenous peoples, however, I think formal or informal community-based research agreements are critical to creating a space in which non-local researchers are held accountable to local, cultural research protocols. In breadth and specificity these may go far beyond the usual university research protocols with 'informed consent', confidentiality, and avoiding harm to those with whom we work, identifying appropriate research goals and questions, appropriate ways to seek knowledge (culturally specific, appropriate methodologies), and appropriate ways for research findings and knowledge to be shared. There is usually no place for this in the other kinds of 'research permission' that may be required for foreign fieldwork. The process of obtaining research permission from the government of Nepal and from the Department of National Parks and Wildlife Conservation, for example, in part involves crafting research proposals and logistical arrangements to meet the self-interest of various government agencies and institutions, and requires no consultation with the communities where research would be carried out, no consideration of culturally appropriate research methods, nor any concern with the research being co-ordinated with local residents or with knowledge or other research products being shared with them. Regardless, however, of whether or not university, governmental, or local research agreements specify cultural protocols, I would suggest that as researchers we have an ethical responsibility to learn about and respect them. How well we work within them, moreover, will often greatly shape the reception we receive, the kinds and quality of information and insight we obtain, and indeed whether we can carry out research at all.

Richie: Yes. That ethical responsibility can be focused in the process of complying with formal institutional ethics requirements very constructively, I've found. For example, in supervising graduate students, it's helpful to take the student through my university's application form for ethics clearance, and ensure that they have considered the ethical and cultural dimensions of various methodological choices, and that they have considered the implications of philosophical pluralism and multiple viewpoints in the real-world context of their research interests (for example, Howitt 2001; Howitt and Suchet-Pearson 2003).[12]

DOING THE WORK

The scale politics of cross-cultural research projects

Richie: One of the things that I've been drawn to over the years is the ways in which a politics of scale is implicated in the construction of cross-cultural research (for example, Howitt 1992; 1997; 2001; 2002c; 2003). In the indigenous studies' domain, there is an assumption—often rooted in the ways that power relations are constructed between indigenous and non-indigenous domains in Australia—that the 'correct' entry point for cross-cultural research of any sort is through a 'local' or 'regional' Aboriginal organisation, or through a 'community'. Indeed, many ethical review procedures are predicated on the need for researchers working with indigenous Australians to demonstrate their accountability to 'local' or 'community' interests. This implies, however, a relatively naive conceptualisation of scale. In contrast, people working in overseas locations often depend on national agency approval as an entry point to their research topic and are forced to conceptualise their study to conform to the window of opportunity offered by such links.

Working on the social impacts of transnational mining company strategies or major development projects in mining, tourism, conservation, and transport over recent years, however, made it impossible to restrict my vision to the naively 'local'. Multi-locational fieldwork in locations linked by various aspects of the mining production cycle (e.g., common ownership; downstream process integration; competition; government policies) meant that the local quickly emerged as a set of particular kinds of relationships that linked to a much wider set of scale relationships rather than as a singularity focused on a bounded location. And any local was always and inescapably contextualised for me by a range of critically important power relations that were constructed at several scales: in a nation that denied its indigenous populations a right to self-government (or self-determination); in industries characterised by corporate strategies of integration, cartelisation, and financial innovation.

This raises a number of methodological questions, both in relation to how we might conceptualise the places in which we situate ourselves as cross-cultural researchers, and to how we conceptualise the range of topics suitable for research in cross-cultural settings. Indeed, in my work, it has even raised serious questions about just what we might mean by 'research' and how we might be held ethically responsible for our work as 'researchers'. How does one engage research participants in 'informed consent' for their involvement in, for example, a PhD study, when not a single person from the language group has completed high school and no-one has been to a university? What sort of sense might they make of the question of informed consent? And even if one concedes that some sort of consent can be constructed in such circumstances, how is one really held accountable for one's immediate or subsequent actions in relation to the people involved, their representations of their lives and cultures, and one's interpretation of them for other audiences?

Stan, you've raised some important questions that also seem to have implications in terms of scale and the scale politics of research in 'foreign' settings, whether they are an unfamiliar part of one's home town, or a location on the other side of the world. Your identification of 'research affiliations' as an issue is, to my mind, immediately drawing in some critically important scale issues, and I've just had a discussion with some young colleagues about the ways in which development studies and indigenous studies enter the field via quite different (scaled) windows of 'government' (or NGO—Non-Government Organisation) and 'community' respectively. You also identify many of the key issues of collaboration and accountability.

Stan: The scale issues you've raised, Richie, are quite familiar. They are likely to face researchers carrying out political ecological work with indigenous peoples anywhere. This often involves research with—and about—multiple actors and processes in order to analyse patterns of regional land use and environmental change. Typically this requires not only fieldwork with indigenous communities but also with government agencies and often with regional, national, and transnational NGOs, and national entrepreneurs or transnational corporations (Blaikie and Brookfield 1987; Bryant and Bailey 1997; Zimmerer and Bassett 2003). When my Sharwa mentors, co-researchers, and I began to examine forest issues in Khumbu in 1984 and in the Pharak and Katuthanga regions in 1994, for example, they made it clear from the outset that it would be necessary to look at forest use and management by a range of people (Sharwa villagers, non-local Sharwa timber merchants, Nepali foresters and national park staff, and international tourists) and to assess this within the complex politics of contestation over control of territory and the management of forest commons that was being waged within and between villages and between villages and the central government's district forest office and departments of national parks. In such situations the research 'site' becomes not only indigenous settlements but also offices and archives in regional centres, national capitals, and abroad. This also often required conducting more than one kind of cross-cultural research, because in Nepal, as in many countries where indigenous peoples live in states controlled by other peoples, trying to understand local economic and environmental change involved work with non-indigenous government officials, NGO staff, and entrepreneurs (Stevens 1993; 1997; 2004; forthcoming; Stevens and Sherpa 1993). .

Cross-cultural research often not only requires work at multiple scales but also requires negotiating relationships at those scales. This takes place at the national level (and with central government officials stationed at the local level), moreover, within a highly charged context because in many domestic and foreign fieldwork situations research authorisation processes are often controlled by state agencies that seek to influence the direction of research, benefit from it, and prescribe procedures to hold researchers accountable to its dictates. Often research funding agencies and universities expect researchers to adhere to these research authorisation requirements. In practice, however, there is often a great range of variation in the degree to which researchers are controlled, how much cooperation and coordination is expected, and how well potentially awkward expectations can be defused. Researchers who aim to carry out decolonising work may be inclined to focus on the ethics of the relationships they develop with indigenous communities and may well find government requirements inimical. Negotiating these ethical and practical dilemmas may be critical to our work and can derail it before we can begin. Such situations can be particularly intimidating when one lacks familiarity with the internal politics, institutional culture, and bureaucrats involved. It can help to seek advice from other researchers with recent experience.

Richie: In these settings, it is important to contextualise one's work—to recognise that the state and its agencies have ambiguous relationships with many indigenous and tribal minorities and their territories—that there is a scale politics in the development discourse itself, and that research is easily drawn into that scale politics in ways that are not obvious to new researchers in a region. There is a substantial literature on the ways in which nation states, even mature democratic nation states, respond to developmentalist imperatives to develop remote corners of 'their' territories and the people whose homelands they have been since time immemorial (see, for example, Berger 1991; Clarke 2001; Howitt 2001; Wolf 1982; also more generally Tully 1995). Yet there are also elements of accountability, ethics, and responsibility to grapple with in working with state agencies, transnational corporations, and environmental NGOs. In many ways there is a very different sort of responsibility and accountability in being an informed critic in such complex situations rather than an ignorant critic!

Social/cultural transmission and creation of knowledge

Richie: We face a tension in how we conceptualise and bring the creation of knowledge to life and negotiate its various purposes. In some situations, research orientation is towards demonstration of a theory or salvaging a 'lost' or fragile way of life (for example, Singer and Woodhead 1988). But in many situations, the sorts of research local people themselves prioritise is concerned with exploration of the possibilities of the intercultural domain, or explanation of 'the other side' of the cross-cultural relationships they experience. For many of my research students, it is their capacity to explain how the institutions, values, and practices of non-Aboriginal society work that is their greatest value for Aboriginal people—not their expertise in cross-cultural matters. Indeed, it is often our lack of facility in listening to and learning from local research participants and collaborators that limits our capacity to frame knowledge and understanding of our own culture and its operations in ways that are accessible and meaningful to local people. It is in listening to and engaging with interpreters about the concepts underpinning the knowledge we create that we make some of the most important realisations about our work. For example, in work on Aboriginal contributions to the central Australian economy in the late 1980s (Howitt et al. 1990), we found that Warlpiri interpreters were translating the concept 'wealth' with the Warlpiri term for 'money'. Our analysis was seeking to explore the contributions of non-monetary wealth to Aboriginal futures—including culture, children, health, and so on—and we needed to tackle the terms in which these ideas were being conveyed in workshop discussions with Warlpiri speakers. More recently, in South Australian work (Agius et al. 2003; 2004), Antikarinja interpreters and speakers spent half a day discussing the conceptual differences between ideas of 'agreement' and 'negotiation' after they realised we were using different words that were being translated with the same Antikarinja term. This discussion of the different implications of a term that sought to signify a process and another that addressed an outcome was a careful exploration of how meaning is constructed, and the implications for meaning-making in cross-cultural settings. It is through such conversations with the most direct users of our research that I often find my most inspirational collaborators and peers.

Although producing materials for these groups is important, there are other times when producing more conventionally academic publications is important. Ensuring the credibility of our work through peer review procedures, for example, can ensure that work that local or indigenous collaborators are relying on in their own efforts to change their circumstances has credibility with governments and others. And we have a responsibility to contribute ideas into those academic discourses that reflect the learning made possible by the work we do in our intercultural engagements. Those more academic papers can provide transformational opportunities well beyond the confines we might have previously imagined for our modest endeavours.

Collaborative and participatory research[13]

Stan: Yes, we've been talking all along about methodology in the sense of approaches to knowing rather than as only a set of research techniques. As a reaction against colonial research there has been increased interest in research that is more culturally sensitive and emancipatory in its orientation and often focused on **collaborative research**, locally guided research, and indigenous research. In some indigenous societies, as Smith (1999) describes for the Maori, histories of colonial research have led some people to demand that outsiders cease research on indigenous peoples and issues, and in such cases some have called instead (as she so powerfully does) for indigenous research and research methodologies. I feel that both research by 'insiders' and cross-cultural research by 'outsiders' are important, and on the basis of my own experience I have come to believe that 'others' can value decolonising relationships and friendships with outside researchers, consider outsiders' cross-cultural perspectives and insights into their societies and situations useful, seek to mentor and work with outside researchers out of interest in the research and belief in its significance, and view outside researchers as useful advocates and allies. While Smith (1999) is sceptical of research by non-indigenous researchers, she and other Maori researchers and critics of colonial research indicate some avenues to cross-cultural research that are both ethical and concerned with outcomes that benefit indigenous peoples, and which would be equally as valuable in other cross-cultural research. In her view such efforts begin with critical awareness of how research is shaped by relationships, power, and ethics. Researchers also can make an effort to work in more culturally sensitive ways, prepare for research by learning the local language, interact with 'others' on their terms in their own social/political community venues, and become informed about local concerns, seek local support and consent for research, and honour local cultural research protocols and negotiated research agreements. And they can change the nature of their research by making local participation integral to it. This can be done in several ways, as Graham Smith (in Linda Tuhiwai Smith 1999) has suggested for research with indigenous peoples. Researchers can work under the guidance of local mentors. They can become adopted as members of the community, with all the life-long obligations and responsibilities this entails. They can establish a 'power-sharing' approach in which they seek community support for research. And they can adopt an 'empowering outcomes' approach, in which research becomes a vehicle through which 'others' can obtain information they seek and which they can use to their benefit. To these Linda Tuhiwai Smith adds a more deliberately 'bicultural or partnership' approach in which local and outside researchers design and carry out a project together, a process that requires negotiation and agreement on many important aspects of research methodology, design, and use.

In exploring the idea of 'bicultural or partnership research' I feel that it is worth drawing a distinction between the attitudes and relationships embodied by participatory research in general and what I would call truly collaborative research. In participatory research an effort is made to create a space for more involvement by 'others' as an integral part of the research approach. Participation itself does not, of course, necessarily represent a break from colonial research since it can amount to nothing more than enlisting local cooperation in a research project that continues to be driven by outside researchers' definitions of its purposes, methods, and use. Participatory research can also be carried out with an agenda of activism and empowerment by addressing locally relevant issues, supporting self-determination, human rights, and indigenous rights, providing new knowledge that is of use to subordinated peoples, groups, and individuals, and transferring research skills that they can employ in the future on their own behalf.[14] Even in this case, however, there may still be attitudes of intellectual arrogance, paternalism, and evangelism (Bishop 1994; Smith 1999). Who, it might be asked, is being given the opportunity to participate in whose project?[15]

Richie: Stan, this is important in so many settings, where young, well-intentioned researchers feel their university credentials give them an expertise in situations they know relatively little about. The risk is in allowing this to frame the collaboration. In native title research in Australia, for example, we often find Aboriginal groups having to tell an expert who they are, how their society works and what their historical and geographical setting is, because only an accredited 'expert' can give evidence on these topics to a court. The claimants themselves are not trusted to represent their societies adequately (or perhaps truthfully), and the intervention of (well-paid) experts is mandatory—an extraordinarily arrogant mis-reading of the nature and source of such knowledge. Although it is the evidentiary system that drives this, many of the researchers accept the mis-reading without challenging it.

Stan: Collaborative research—truly collaborative research—reflects a sharper break from imposed, colonial research based on different attitudes towards 'others', and different relationships among researchers. Collaborators work as equals on a mutual project. This decolonisation of the relationships within the research team can generate an interactive, cross-cultural synthesis of knowledge and skills through which research conducted with community and other local authorisation and within local cultural protocols can be used to address community concerns. Local and non-local researchers conceive and design the research together, including making the key decisions on defining research goals and questions, where and how to seek funding, affiliation, and authorisation, who should be on the research team, what methodology should be used, how cultural research protocols should be honoured, how the day-to-day conduct of fieldwork should be handled, what kinds of analyses should be attempted, and how research findings should be shared and used. This requires non-indigenous researchers to give up 'control' over a project, and for all involved to contribute their time and efforts in order to work together towards shared goals. This is not easy to do, and can only really take place if all researchers can move beyond often quite strong assumptions and behaviours conditioned by their statuses in their own societies and by asymmetrical cross-cultural power relationships. On the basis of my own experience of working within collaborative research relationships with several different Sharwa co-researchers, I would advise not to underestimate the time, care, emotional commitment, self-reflection, learning, and stress this can entail on everyone's part.[16]

Collaborative research approaches and locally guided ones are based on conducting research that works within what are considered to be culturally appropriate ways of seeking and transmitting knowledge. There are several important dimensions to this. One of the most basic of these, and often also the most difficult for researchers to accept, is that in many societies knowledge and information are not necessarily shared openly within communities, much less with outsiders. There may thus be particular types and levels of knowledge that are considered appropriate to share with or withhold from outside researchers (Stevens 2001).[17] Knowledge may also be considered to be ethnic, gender, age, class, religion, or subculture specific. Researchers should also be aware that there may be types of knowledge that may be shared with outside researchers with the understanding that they are not to be otherwise shared with outsiders. Outside researchers should accept that honouring these concerns may greatly affect the design and conduct of research and the publishing of research findings.

Cultural protocols about acquiring knowledge also may include an understanding that knowledge must be earned by working within culturally sanctioned methodologies. This may apply only to certain kinds of knowledge, and may not preclude the use of other culturally sensitive and authorised research methods to learn about local conditions and practices, methods that may produce new knowledge, insight, and community empowerment. But the importance of working within existing local systems of the transmission of knowledge should not be ignored. This may mean, for example, that one must be found worthy of being mentored and then undertake a possibly long period of instruction. Researchers whose projects do not have the documentation/translation of a particular type of specialist's knowledge as a goal may be inclined to decline involvement in such a relationship (and knowledge specialists may have their own reasons for declining to take one on as a student). But it may often be the case that a great deal of information that is important to the project can only be obtained through such culturally sanctioned means. Researchers must then weigh whether to make the commitment to the relationship, the process, and the project. Those who persevere may find great personal and research rewards from a kind of cross-cultural communication and learning that ordinary interviewing (much less group-meeting-based rapid research) cannot approach.

Cultural protocols also may have considerable ramifications for the use of particular research techniques. The use of questionnaires or formal, structured interviews, for example, may be considered by some peoples to be intrusive, rigid, and exploitative. Informal, semi-structured interviews, on the other hand, may not conflict with local etiquette about social interaction and communication because they can be interactive discussions or conversations in which there can be reciprocal exchanges of information. Interviewees may indeed value such interviews as social occasions that provide an opportunity to get to know the researchers, inquire about research findings, and learn about the outside world. Researchers may find that elders and knowledge specialists do not wish to be interviewed, or may think requests for assistance are appropriate only after a process of acquaintance and relationship, or may initially speak only in generalities. Yet in other cases, if properly approached, they may be willing to act as mentors. People may be uncomfortable with group discussions or consider them essential. Mapping may be highly suspect if one is not well known and respected, while in other contexts it may be invited and welcomed. Cultural protocols and negotiated local research agreements may also influence research design in terms of whom it is appropriate to interview, what topics are considered suitable, and when interviews are and are not appropriate (such as not being appropriate during festivals or times when people are busy with subsistence activities). Local etiquette may also influence conversation in very specific ways, such as when there are taboos against using the names of the dead.

Another aspect of honouring local cultural protocols that can significantly affect research arises in cases in which societal discourses and practices promote relationships and interactions of inequality and domination between women and men or between people of different ethnicity, race, class, religion, age, or other socially defined categories and groups. Such cultural protocols can pose a formidable dilemma for outside researchers who wish to respect local concerns but object to the character of the interactions and relationships created by societal discourses and asymmetries of power and do not wish to engage in or to tacitly accept them. Local societal attitudes towards difference may also complicate the interactions and relationships of team members and affect the degree to which their research is fully collaborative. And cultural protocols that discourage or constrain interaction between women and men or between people of different ethnicities, classes, castes, or other social groups can make research across socially defined boundaries of difference difficult or impossible for both local and outsider researchers.[18]

Constructing legitimacy

Stan: The reception that we and our research projects receive depends in part on local perception of the projects' legitimacy in terms of whether or not they address local concerns, needs, and interests, partly on how the projects are conducted and whether they meet cultural protocols, and partly on local perception of our character and that of our co-researchers. The importance of the perception of our character should not be underestimated. Often this will be based primarily on our personal qualities, the evaluation of which can vary considerably among cultures, but may well include whether we are considered to have a good heart or spirit, whether we can be trusted, how we treat and interact with people, how well we listen, and what skills and resources we bring to the community (see Smith 1999). While our academic achievements and status may matter little, we should be aware that how we are perceived can be very much affected by the company we keep, or are perceived to keep. Research teams will often be judged also by the character, reputation, and actions of all of their members, including local ones (see, for example, Berreman 1972). And we may need to work hard to counter suspicions that we are agents of the central government, a transnational corporation, or a locally unpopular NGO, and to reassure people that research findings will not find their way into such hands. Affiliation with local, regional, national, or transnational NGOs or with particular government programs can also, however, enhance one's legitimacy when they are well regarded locally, and this can sometimes both smooth the issue of negotiating for research authorisation from government agencies and serve as an easy entré into communities. The problem is that it can be difficult to know how agencies, organisations, and programs are locally perceived until one has spent time in an area and people trust one well enough to be candid. This is one of many reasons why it is often ideal to carry out an extended reconnaissance of a potential research site before establishing affiliations and research authorisations. In any event we need to be clear with community members on our relationships (if any) with government agencies and NGOs, and to be prepared to rethink those relationships based on community concerns.

Richie: Of course this means that many students have to rely on the credibility and experience of a supervisor. That can open doors, but in my experience it is ultimately the student's own credibility and qualities that carry them through into worthwhile working relationships with people. Because those relationships are so dependent on personal integrity rather than status, it becomes important for students and new researchers to think about what this integrity might mean in the setting they hope to work in. But this also means that the timeframes involved in negotiating these matters can be inconsistent with the bureaucratic expectations around a students' candidature.

Stan: Legitimacy is also created through social relationships. Working in places and within communities fosters the development of relationships, and these bring with them expectations of reciprocity and diverse responsibilities. Meeting these obligations over time can greatly enhance our acceptance in a community and attitudes towards our work. And over time we also establish networks of friends and allies who will vouch for our character and intentions.

MAKING SENSE, REACHING CONCLUSIONS

Richie: One of the really important issues that we've hardly touched so far is the question of audiences in cross-cultural research. Working in an academic environment, we are inevitably influenced by the publication culture of our institutions. Our own legitimacy as intellectuals is constructed in our 'public' work. But in many cross-cultural settings, the primary audience for our work is neither academic nor reached by academic publications. 'Publishing' to community-based audiences is often the most important element of cross-cultural research. It is the point at which we become accountable to our participants and collaborators for the ideas and knowledge our work produces. And it often involves exceptionally rigorous scrutiny, with multilingual discussion, careful (re)contextualisation of ideas and information, checking of facts and interpretations, challenges and debate. While this is some of the most demanding peer reviewing one experiences as an academic, it is not acknowledged as such by the institutional academic community. Many of the publication formats it involves (for example, community newsletters, comic books, radio broadcasts, long debates in community settings, joint submissions to inquiry processes, manifestos, and community statements) will not count for credit when it comes to thesis examinations, academic tenure, and promotion. Yet, if we are in the business of producing ideas that change the world, this can be our most effective and influential work, and it is powerfully tested in communities' efforts to actually change their own circumstances!

Of course we cannot escape the requirement to publish in more academic and professional settings, but that also raises important questions about how one represents the intercultural domain for other audiences. It is easy to be cast in a role as an 'expert' on another culture—however limited our grasp of or engagement with that culture in all its complexity. In some cases, a range of outputs or different types and formats for publications can reframe quite sophisticated academic outputs for multiple audiences (Coombs et al. 1989; and Rose 1996b offer impressive examples).

Stan: Yes. There is a responsibility for researchers to share findings with the people they work with. This is more than the courtesy of ensuring that copies of our subsequent academic publications are widely available in the research area. We need to seek out culturally appropriate and effective ways of sharing knowledge. Academic publication is often not a very effective way of doing this in any cross-cultural situation, and non-academic writing specifically produced for local audiences may have a limited impact in societies where literacy is rare. In societies where knowledge is shared face-to-face and orally it may be effective to discuss the research findings in group meetings, community meetings, or workshops. It can also be very effective and rewarding to discuss findings directly with individuals, although this takes considerable time to do widely. These methods also have the major benefit that they are interactive and provide opportunities for feedback that may correct mis-impressions and over-generalisations, provide alternative information and analyses, clarify concerns with the communication of some information or particular portrayals to the outside world, and provide opportunities to discuss how findings from the research can be used by individuals and communities in their lives and actions. Co-researchers also play a major role in disseminating research findings since they become in-place, living repositories of that knowledge and the skills and experiences through which it was created, and they can use these directly in their own lives and to inform community discussions and action. This can be much more powerful than anything an outside researcher can contribute.

Finally, for me, another important aspect of making sense of the research is coming to terms with how that experience reshapes our lives and the lives of those with whom we work. Cross-cultural research can lead to long-term relationships between researchers and 'others', and with them come obligations and responsibilities that can far transcend the sphere of the research itself and the relatively brief time that most researchers devote to living in places and carrying out fieldwork. The closeness that we develop with co-researchers, mentors, and friends can lead to continuing, life-long affection and interaction, and in these relationships there can be strong cultural expectations of generosity and mutual aid that extend also to each other's relatives, children, and associates. For some researchers (as Barney Nietschmann and I both found) field experiences and relationships can create strong sense of commitment to a people, particular communities, and a region that leads us to return repeatedly to the place, the people, and further rounds of research and activism.

Richie: Yes, what might be conceptualised academically as 'cross-cultural' is simultaneously interpersonal, and it has profound implications for just what sort of human beings we imagine ourselves to be, or capable of becoming! To some extent one is drawn into more activist and advocate roles than many of one's colleagues, and even framing our academic roles as 'teacher' and 'researcher' somewhat differently. I have long considered the links between my own intellectual nourishment from research and teaching and the construction of critical engagements with students and the wider society/ies of which I am part to be a central element of my responsibility as a public intellectual. That sort of engagement is not limited to the classroom. It happens in a great range of places where one tries to make new sorts of sense that might disrupt the certainties of colonial (and deep colonising) practices. For many researchers finding the balance between scholarship and activism is far from easy.

KEY TERMS

applied people's geography
collaborative research
colonial research
cultural protocols
decolonising research
inclusionary research

Orientalism
Other
postcolonial research
postmodernism
subaltern

REVIEW QUESTIONS

1   What are some key differences between colonial and postcolonial research in assumptions, attitudes, relationships, and methodologies?
2   How can researchers go about attempting to carry out decolonising research and inclusionary research?
3   How can research be made more truly collaborative in all aspects of a project, and how might this affect the time, energy, and outputs involved and affect a student's progress towards her or his degree?
4   Why might university research protocols often need to be supplemented by local cultural protocols?
5   How might issues about research with indigenous peoples raised in this chapter be relevant to cross-cultural research in your own situation?

SUGGESTED READING

Ivanitz, M., 1999, 'Culture, ethics and participatory methodology in cross-cultural research', *Australian Aboriginal Studies*, vol. 2, pp. 46–58.
Maya People of Southern Belize, Toledo Maya Cultural Council, and Toledo Alcades Association, 1997, *Maya Atlas: the Struggle to Preserve Maya Land in Southern Belize*, North Atlantic Books, Berkeley.

Mullings, B., 1999, 'Insider or outsider, both or neither: some dilemmas of interviewing in a cross-cultural setting', *Geoforum*, vol. 30, pp. 337–50.

Smith, L.T. 1999, *Decolonising Methodologies: Research and Indigenous Peoples*, University of Otago Press and Zed Books, Dunedin and London.

Notes

1   For me (Richie Howitt) it was my awareness of the US Government sponsorship of 'research' on social movements in Latin America and hill tribes in Indo-China in the 1960s and the disputes that produced within anthropology (e.g., Horowitz 1967; also Gough 1968; Jorgensen 1971). This helped push me into engaging with intercultural research ethics early in my strange career! It also drew me into a critical consideration of our own discipline's implication in colonising efforts (e.g., Howitt and Jackson 1998).

2   One example of a similar approach close to home is Herman and Mattingly's (1999) effort to negotiate 'reciprocal research relations', cultivate 'the authority of self-representation', and implement 'ethical responsibility', through community action as well as research methodology in their work in the most culturally diverse neighbourhood in San Diego, California. Also see chapter 13 and Katz 1994; Kobayashi 1994; Nast 1994.

3   Postcolonial or post-colonial can signify both 'after' colonialism and 'rejecting', 'against', or 'anti' colonialism. I use the term in the sense of 'rejecting' colonialism. Even in cross-cultural settings that are not appropriately characterised in these terms, rethinking research relationships in terms of participant action frameworks (see chapter 13) can redefine research outcomes towards mutual recognition and benefit.

4   In Australian public policy the work of Charles Rowley (e.g., 1970; 1971a; 1971b) and Nugget Coombs (e.g., 1978; but see also Rowse 2000) reflected a deeply reflective and non-paternalistic approach within a predominantly 'colonial' period. Reynolds (1998) refers to such dissent as a 'whispering in our hearts' and notes that 'In each generation people have expressed their concern about the ethics of colonisation, the incidence of racial violence, the taking of the land and the suffering, deprivation and poverty of Aboriginal society in the wake of settlement' (1998, p. xiv). Geertz (e.g., 1973; 1980; 1984) similarly throws a different light on 'colonial' efforts to understand cultural difference.

5   Many of the criticisms of colonial research can also be applied to much cross-cultural research with subordinated and marginalised peoples and groups in non-colonial contexts (although some postcolonial scholars would prefer to define the term more narrowly), as in Nietschmann's (2001, p. 183) remark that 'Who studies and who gets studied reflects power, economics, status, class, color, and identity'.

6   Yarndi: marijuana.

7   **Stan**: I prefer to use 'others' in preference to 'the Other' to acknowledge cultural diversity, although I remain uncomfortable with the distance and attitudes implied in any form of the word and prefer less polarised language.

   Richie: Yes, I find that too, but there is something important in acknowledging that the language of power reflects something significant about the relationships it represents. As the philosopher Levinas suggests, that awkward singularity of a generalised 'Other' annihilates something very significant in a relationship 'whose terms do not form a totality' (Levinas 1969, p. 39). In the case of the 'self–other relation', there is no larger concept higher in some implied hierarchy that encompasses these two terms. So, for Levinas, aggregation of the self and the other does not produce a new, larger singularity because to do so would be to deny the ethical (or unethical) power relations that create differences. While the more generalised singularity 'human' might encompass such differences, the risk is that in seeking to challenge the realities of the relationships of power, we use language that obscures it. It's a good reminder of the need to problematise language and to reflect on and challenge many aspects of the hidden constructs of injustice in the work we do.

8   In the case of Sharwa studies this has included research by pioneering anthropologists Christoph von Furer-Haimendorf (1964; 1975; 1984), Sherry Ortner (1978; 1989; 1999), and James Fisher (1990).

9   Said (1978) notes that such views of 'others' go back to the ancient Greek delineation of themselves and 'barbarian' others, although the ancient Chinese developed a similar perception early on and it might be argued that such ethnocentrism is very old, very widespread, and common outside of imperial and colonising situations as well as in them.

10   In practice many of us find we must negotiate multiple personal motives in our work, and I would suggest that while our ideals and commitments may often call for a measure of self-sacrifice in our work that it is also legitimate to be concerned with such matters as completing one's degree or attaining tenure.

11   These new guidelines seek to establish grounds for developing ethical relationships between indigenous communities and research groups, rather than offering a checklist of how to make a project application look like it conforms to institutional ethics requirements. This approach shifts the orientation of ethics oversight away from formal legal concerns about risks to the institution and constructs a framework for higher levels of accountability to those participating in or affected by the research and will require some degree of rethinking in institutional compliance structures—as does the recognition of native title.

12   There is material related to project-based agreements for research ethics available on Richie Howitt's website <http://www.es.mq.edu.au/~rhowitt/>.

13   Readers are encouraged to consult chapter 13 for a complementary discussion of participatory approaches to research.

14   The term 'participatory research' is often used to refer to exactly this kind of collaborative, empowering research (see Park 1993).

15   This also brings up the issue of local 'research assistants', as it has long been conventional in geography and anthropology to refer to local members of a research team. In recent years I have come to feel that this practice needs to be examined critically because of the way it can narrow local project members' participation in research by fostering hierarchical relationships among team members and restricting—and in some cases not properly acknowledging—local project members' contributions and roles.

16   On collaborative research see Park 1993, Herlihy and Knapp 2003, and the approach that Barney Nietschmann and Berkeley geography students working for GeoMap developed with the Maya of Belize (Maya People of Southern Belize, Toledo Maya Cultural Council, and Toledo Alcades Association 1997). This 'community-based cartography' is both more collaborative and more empowering than most participatory mapping.

17   This is a somewhat different thing from the issue of local perceptions of what levels of knowledge that outside researchers are capable of understanding. Local residents may often over-generalise and simplify in response to what they perceive to be an outside researcher's rather basic level of understanding of their homeland and ways of life. This is a major problem for short-term research and for researchers who do not realise that there are multiple levels of explanation and understanding.

18   For reflections on the issues raised by these situations see the 2001 special issue of the *Geographical Review* on 'Doing Fieldwork', the 1994 special issue of the *Professional Geographer* on 'Women in the Field', several other collections of essays by feminist geographers working within and outside of their own societies and communities (Berreman 1972; Jones III, Nast, and Roberts 1997; Moss 2002; Wolf 1996).

4

Writing a Compelling Research Proposal

Janice Monk and Richard Bedford

CHAPTER OVERVIEW

This chapter aims to help you with the challenging task of initiating research by writing a proposal that will focus your thoughts, plan your approach, and convince others that your project is important. We address how ideas for research originate, how to specify research questions, how to demonstrate your ideas' significance, and how to define your research methods. We discuss the process of writing research proposals and comment briefly on how reviewers evaluate these. Our concluding comment sums up why we think writing compelling research proposals is so challenging while at the same time being one of the most enjoyable parts of a geographer's tertiary training.

THE RESEARCH CHALLENGE

Writing a compelling research proposal is a real challenge. In our view, it is probably the most demanding task that any undergraduate or graduate experiences. It is also one of the most exciting because it is a chance for you to define your research questions, frame them in the context of existing knowledge, identify appropriate methods of inquiry to address the question, negotiate ethical issues, and establish data collection and analysis procedures.

Writing a research proposal requires you to bring into focus all of the essential elements of your university education. It demonstrates your ability to synthesise and question existing knowledge on a topic and your understanding of how ideas are used to formulate theoretical frameworks. It draws on your knowledge of, and experience with, different ways of approaching problems and asking questions, as well as your ability to construct a coherent design for new research. It indicates the extent to which you are stimulated by the 'cutting edges' of knowledge and inquiry in those geographical questions that really interest you.

As we show in this chapter, a proposal offers a road map for the research journey but, as on many journeys, you are likely to encounter crossroads, road blocks, and many twists and turns that you need to negotiate. You need to be flexible enough to accommodate those changes. Your proposal is not a static, definitive statement; it is a vibrant, living component of your research. It is subject to revision, extension, and amendment as the research unfolds.

Writing research proposals is stimulating and challenging. Carrying out the research to address the questions in the proposal is even more of an adventure. Research is to be enjoyed, not endured, even if at times it is difficult to see how you will ever address all the research questions you started with. No worthwhile journey is easy; research is not easy; but research makes university-based study really rewarding.

WHERE DO RESEARCH IDEAS COME FROM?

The first thing one has to establish when developing a research proposal is a topic. In our experience, ideas for research come from at least three sources: personal experience, reading, or conversations with other geographers and scholars. In most cases some combination of these is involved. It is important to appreciate that you need to have a strong personal interest in the research you are planning to do. The work has to be something you care about and have the skills to carry out (or know where you can get these skills).

If you are writing a thesis you will be spending a lot of time on the research, so you want to be sure you have a topic that really interests you. Do not be surprised if it takes time to refine the topic; the initial idea may come from some experiences you have had a long time before you actually get involved in research. In the course of writing a proposal the ideas will be clarified and you may find by the time the proposal is written the original idea you started with is substantially altered and refined.

To illustrate how research ideas can evolve, we draw on our own experiences as graduate and postgraduate students embarking on our first major research exercises (see Boxes 4.1 and 4.2).

BOX 4.1	THE ORIGINS OF A DISSERTATION IN SOCIAL GEOGRAPHY

Jan Monk grew up in a fairly low-income family in Australia at a time when non-English speaking immigrants were arriving in substantial numbers. She was conscious of social inequalities, ethnic differences, and stereotyping of those we would now label 'Other'. Shortly after graduating with her BA, she participated in a work camp that built a house for an Aboriginal family so that they could move from a reserve into a small town in New South Wales. The project reflected the state's policy of aiming to assimilate Aboriginal people into the white community. The government paid for the building materials and a church group brought together young professional men and women who donated the labour.

The project raised geographic questions about who lives where and who has the power to shape those residential patterns. The experience, and some of the project's ethical and political implications, made a strong impression on Jan. At that time, Australian geographers had not been writing about Aboriginal affairs[1] and anthropologists were mainly interested in 'traditional' cultural patterns or in psychological questions about life on reserves. There was really no geographic precedent for Jan to link her personal interests and potential research at this time. The ideas for possible research were stimulated by personal experience; further reading in the social sciences while undertaking postgraduate studies was needed before the research proposal could be developed.

Jan moved on to doctoral study in geography in the United States. Attention to relations between groups was rare in geography, but she took courses in sociology and anthropology that spoke to her interests. The anthropology professor's ecological framework took into account demography, economy, and politics. With this new perspective, Jan saw a way to address what had been on her mind in Australia. It so happened that Australian policies towards Aboriginal people were also coming under scrutiny at the time she embarked on doctoral research, so her ideas happened to coincide with an emerging area of policy concern. This was a bonus—government officials were also interested in the research, and this made the whole project seem more useful and relevant.

She now had context that identified her question as one of policy importance, she was more familiar with a relevant interdisciplinary literature, and had a set of research tools to apply to questions grounded in personal experience. Imbued with the geographical perspective that place matters, Jan designed a comparative analysis of the social and economic lives of Aboriginal communities in six small towns in New South Wales and went on to explore how the lives of these Aboriginal people were influenced by white social, political, and economic history.

BOX 4.2 BEGINNING A CAREER IN RESEARCH ON MIGRATION

Serendipity can play a major role in the selection of research topics. Richard Bedford's undergraduate training in geography, history, geology, and Pacific studies at the University of Auckland led him to consider two quite different directions for a graduate research degree: fluvial geomorphology and population geography. In the end it was an invitation to visit a central Pacific atoll country (Kiribati) for a holiday that swung the balance towards research about people rather than rivers. There are no rivers on atolls, but there are some very interesting people–environment relationship issues, especially apparent to someone from a much larger, mountainous country, who visits coral atolls for the first time.

A combination of reading for a graduate paper on the geography of the Pacific Islands, discussions with senior government officials in Kiribati, and several months of field work in the islands provided the ideas that were to become the basis for a Masters thesis on migration in an atoll environment. As was the case with Jan Monk's research on Aboriginal social geography,

Richard Bedford's research on migration as a response to population pressure on coral atolls was of interest to the colonial government of the day. The concerns the government had about population change thus fed into informing the ideas that underpinned the research proposal that was developed to guide the research over the subsequent twelve months. This interest in the migration of Pacific peoples then took Richard to the Australian National University's Research School of Pacific Studies (now the Research School of Pacific and Asian Studies) where he completed his doctorate.

Doctoral research in Vanuatu, and post-doctoral research in Papua New Guinea and Fiji during the 1970s and 1980s, as these countries moved from colonial rule to independence, was exciting and very challenging for a 'white' male New Zealander. A mix of research methods and sources of information was always required: **archival research**, analysis of census data, questionnaire surveys, in-depth interviews, group discussions. It was not a question of 'either quantitative or qualitative research methods and approaches'; it was always necessary to use a mix of both, especially if the analysis of population movement, as described in the reports of government officials and the statistics collected in surveys and censuses, was ever to be informed by the personal experiences of those who moved.

Something we both found highly motivating about our research was that the ideas that contributed to the development of our research proposals were of interest to participants, local government officials, and to other academics studying contemporary social, cultural, and economic transformation. Personal as well as broader interest in what you are researching can be critically important, both for sustaining your own engagement with the project as well as for stimulating new research ideas and opportunities.

One of the great benefits of much research done by geographers is that it seems 'relevant' to others: that is often very important for researchers when they are trying to define a topic on which they will work for a substantial period. However, it should be noted that research does not have to be 'relevant' to particular interest groups to be worthwhile; much theoretical inquiry is driven by curiosity and not a concern to address a question that is of interest to a particular group. As we have already said, the key thing about doing research is to be genuinely interested in the topic you chose to work on.

GETTING STARTED

When and how you start work on a research proposal will depend on the stage of your tertiary education, what your department and supervisor expect, the nature of your project, and whether or not you need funding for the research. If you are an undergraduate, your department may offer a course that includes some training in writing a research proposal. At this level it is likely you will be expected to develop a full research proposal, but you may not be required to actually carry out the proposed research or to seek outside funding to support your research. If you are an Honours, Masters, or Doctoral student, however, you will usually be expected to write a proposal and present it in a colloquium prior to having it approved. Once it is approved, you will then undertake the proposed research. You may also need to prepare a proposal to a granting body to gain financial support for the research.

Even if you are not required to write a formal proposal, along the lines of what is suggested in Box 4.3, we suggest that you do so—it will clarify your ideas, taking them from a broad theme to specific questions. The proposal will provide you with a road map for the research journey. It will help you to say why your project is important, how you will carry out the work, what resources (financial and other) you will need, and what timetable you will follow for collecting data, analysing the materials, and writing up your results.

In Box 4.3 we summarize some of the key components of a research proposal. Several of the items that are bulleted in this summary are discussed in greater detail in subsequent sections.

In the next three sections we use examples from a research proposal prepared by Ranjana Chakrabarti, a doctoral student in the United States, who has given us approval to quote from her work, to illustrate the major parts of the proposal. These are: specifying the research questions, framing the research in terms of its theoretical and empirical contexts, and developing the methodology for the project. We then provide some suggestions about the way successful research proposals are written, and return briefly to the issue of funding.

BOX 4.3 COMPONENTS OF A RESEARCH PROPOSAL

A good proposal will enable the reader to appreciate immediately:

- the *question/problem* that is being addressed in the research
- the current state of *knowledge* on the topic that is the subject of inquiry
- the *methods* that will be used to collect the information required
- the *ethical issues* that have to be addressed before undertaking any field work
- the *resources* that will be required to collect the required information and complete the research report
- the *intended outcomes* of the research.

The proposal will have several sections in which the points raised above will be covered. The key sections are:

- introduction and background to the proposed research, including a statement as to why the topic is worth studying
- the key research questions/problems (these might be specified in the form of hypotheses but this is not always appropriate)
- the wider theoretical and empirical context for the research
- research methods and associated ethical issues
- research plan (timetable outlining the various stages of the research)
- budget and sources of funding for the research
- references cited.

SPECIFYING YOUR RESEARCH QUESTION

One of the most challenging aspects of writing a proposal is articulating your major research question, and the sub-questions that flow from it. Everything else follows. You have to keep the 'big picture' in mind, but think through how to identify its component parts so that you have a manageable project. Suppose you are interested in policy aspects of housing and homelessness in Australia. You know, stereotypically, that homelessness is associated with urban areas and 'vagrant' men; remedies are couched in terms of providing shelters, mostly in inner city neighbourhoods. Then you see a report that young people make up almost one-third of the homeless.[2] You grew up in a rural area and know of students who dropped out of your high school and ended up homeless within the local community. This knowledge prompts your first decision: you will conduct research on aspects of youth homelessness in country towns.

Now you have more decisions to make. Will you emphasise the causes of the problem, the experiences of homeless youth themselves, focus on the types of services provided or needed, or on some combination of these? Will you undertake a **case study** of a single community or of several? What criteria will you use to select the study area(s)? Will you focus on homeless young men, young women, or both? How will you connect your research back to policy concerns? There is no 'right' answer to these questions. Which questions you address will depend partly on the time and resources you have and also on what you learn about existing related research so that you can show yours will make a new contribution.

Your choice of research question will also be heavily influenced by your knowledge of, and skills with, different research methods. Some geography students have a strong interest in statistical analysis, especially if they work with Geographic Information Systems, or have subjects like psychology and economics in their degrees. Other students have a strong preference for qualitative modes of inquiry, especially if they have studied cultural geography, critical perspectives, gender and ethnicity, and so on. There is no 'right' set of skills that everyone doing research must have, aside from an ability to think and write clearly. The particular research and analytical skills needed will depend very much on the nature of the research questions being addressed.

Research offers the best opportunity there is to use the skills you have already developed in the course of getting your degree, while at the same time enabling you to gain new skills. You should not feel constrained to work just with methods you are familiar with; research for a thesis will often encourage you to extend your understanding of research methods. But be realistic when developing your research questions; make sure when you are specifying questions that you have or can develop the skills to address them. Over-ambitious research proposals can make for very frustrating research experiences.

The sorts of questions raised above in the example of homelessness amongst rural youth lend themselves to analysis using qualitative research methods, and students with a good understanding of such methods may be both more interested in and better placed than others to undertake research on this topic. We discuss the development of the methodology section of a research proposal later in this chapter, but it is important to appreciate that the definition of research questions is very much influenced by your preferences for and understanding of different research methods and modes of analysis.

BOX 4.4   RESEARCH QUESTIONS FOR A HEALTH GEOGRAPHY STUDY

Much of public health research on prenatal care has focused on the role of individual-level maternal risk factors in explaining low levels of utilization of prenatal care. A large number of sociodemographic, structural as well as attitudinal and psychological factors have been identified in previous studies. However, the ways these barriers are experienced and expressed differ among women from different ethnic backgrounds. This difference can be understood through an appreciation of the complex interactions between place, culture, and health. (Chakrabarti 2004)

Ranjana's primary research question is: what causes the low rates of utilisation of prenatal care facilities by South Asian immigrant women in New York?

The sub-questions she identified to assist her frame the study and develop the research proposal are:

- How and why does prenatal care use by South Asian immigrant women vary within New York City?
- How do South Asian women gain access to prenatal services?
- How does the experience of place mediate the prenatal care practices of these women?
- How do these women relate to and gain knowledge from the formal and informal prenatal care resources in their local environment? What geographical, economic and cultural barriers do they face?
- How does culture affect the prenatal care knowledge and practices of these women? Are such practices place-based and at what scale?
- How do South Asian women create and utilize place-based social networks at the local, national or transnational scales to gain access to formal and informal prenatal care services and advice? (Chakrabarti 2004)

It is useful to cite a further example to illustrate how research questions are formulated and incorporated into a research proposal. Ranjana Chakrabarti (2004), a doctoral student at the University of Illinois at Urbana-Champaign, went to the United States for study after completing a Master's degree in India with a focus in medical/health geography. She is interested in how place shapes women's health care practices. Given her background and current location she has chosen to study South Asian immigrant women in the United States, specifically in New York where she has personal connections. Her research addresses their low rates of prenatal care utilisation since this has consequences for their health and that of their babies. In the rest of this chapter we use sections of her dissertation proposal to illustrate some of the key points we seek to make. Box 4.4 summarises how Ranjana defined the research question and the sub-questions for her dissertation research on the roles of place, context, and culture in shaping South Asian immigrant women's prenatal health care practices in New York.

Once the research questions have been defined in draft (they will be refined as the proposal is developed) the **literature review** and the identification of an appropriate theoretical framework and methodology for conducting the research can be completed. We now turn to the critically important component of all research proposals that addresses the theoretical and empirical contexts within which the research questions are situated.

FRAMING YOUR RESEARCH

As you develop your research questions it is important to think about how you will convey their significance to others and what theoretical and **conceptual frameworks** you will employ. If your audience and study are primarily academic, you will mostly rely on the research literature to justify your project's approach and significance. If your work has a strong applied component, you should also study the perspectives and needs of the group(s) with which you will work. Among the various questions that need to be addressed while framing your research, the following four are especially important:

- Does the project deal with a significant and meaningful problem that lends itself to a substantial research effort?
- Why is the problem of interest to other scholars or practitioners in the field?
- Has a persuasive case been made as to why the problem is worth solving?
- Is it clear who or what will be aided by the research findings?

Source: *Dissertation Proposal Writing Tutorial* Undated (online)

Writing a review of the literature is essential for preparing the proposal. To situate the research in an appropriate theoretical framework will require careful study of some of the key journals in the discipline (see Box 4.5 below). This literature review should not be confused with an annotated bibliography or a summary of all you have read. It should be both constructive and critical in tone, identifying the strengths of the pieces you select in order to show how they support your own work and reveal weaknesses or gaps that demonstrate why your work is fresh and significant. The final report or thesis that you write will always include reference to earlier research on the topic and, if it is a thesis, a substantive assessment of previous findings and how your proposed research furthers our understanding of the topic.

Using a literature review to help establish the context for your research is a demanding and time-consuming task. It is not something that is done overnight! There are some suggestions in Box 4.5 about how you can approach this very important component of a research proposal.

A useful source of examples of research contexts, and the literature reviews associated with these, is the introductory sections of published articles. A recent paper by Marianna Pavlovskaya (2004), on her doctoral research on household economies in post-Communist Moscow, is one such example. She begins by noting that the existing literature on the transition from Communism tends to emphasise macroeconomic themes. Next she draws attention to the theoretical writing by geographers on the importance of scale and connections over space in shaping the social and spatial relations of people and the environments within which they conduct their lives. This geographical literature is used to justify her approach to the topic through an analysis of households and the ways in which they link formal and informal economies in the city. This theoretical perspective leads her to a research design that will enable her to integrate in-depth interviews with households in selected neighbourhoods of

BOX 4.5 THE RESEARCH CONTEXT

The key questions that are addressed when describing the *context* for your research are:

1   What does your work offer to the available field of knowledge that helps us understand better the issue/topic you have chosen to address in your research?
2   How do existing studies inform your work?

In answering these questions, keep in mind that there are two important dimensions to the context of any research proposal:

1   The theoretical ideas that inform research on the topic (these will tend to come mainly from the existing literature)
2   The empirical or 'real world' situation that relates to your research topic (there will usually be examples of research on your topic or a closely related one that you can find in the literature).

Make sure you address both of these dimensions when framing your research.
   Heath (1997) suggests that when describing the context for your research you should:

*   Use specific language to name and describe the conceptual foundation for your research—that is, the research perspective that informs your approach to the topic. Show clearly *why* this perspective is appropriate and relevant for your study. For example, you may be using insights from a poststructuralist perspective to provide a theoretical context for your research. Make sure you explain clearly, and simply, what the approach means for the way you will do your research and how you will interpret your results. Useful definitions of most of the main theoretical approaches used in human geography can be found in the recent editions of *The Dictionary of Human Geography* (Johnston et al. 2000).
*   Cite authors who have already used this approach to address questions/problems similar to the ones you are researching. An excellent starting point for recent reviews of the theoretical and the empirical literature in most of the main areas of research currently being addressed by human geographers is the journal *Progress in Human Geography*. This journal, and its companion, *Progress in Physical Geography*, contain regular updates on new ideas, methods, and findings in contemporary geography.

inner Moscow (taking into account their gender and class dimensions), with a GIS-based reporting of spatial patterns of neighbourhood characteristics and interactions.

The research context thus establishes the rationale for the particular research methods that will be used to undertake the study. We now turn to this very important component of all research proposals.

DEVELOPING YOUR METHODOLOGY

Identifying how you plan to carry out your research is one of the most demanding aspects of writing a proposal. Reviewers of proposals repeatedly find that the discussion of the

BOX 4.6 THINKING ABOUT A RESEARCH METHODOLOGY

- Be realistic. You will have limited time and resources to conduct the project. If your work involves individual interviews, how many, for example, will you be able to complete while still getting sufficient information to explore the range of views people may hold? Consider that you will have to recruit people, schedule the interviews, deal with some refusals, or cancelled meetings. How do you know people will talk to you? What strategies will you use to recruit them? Be careful not to over-commit yourself.

- Will your work be served best by combining methods? Researchers frequently use a combination of quantitative and qualitative approaches (see, for example, Tashakkori and Teddlie (1998)). How can you do this and be realistic in relation to your resources and context?

- Assess the strengths of the approach you propose over alternatives. Would focus groups serve your needs better than individual interviews? Why or why not? What are the strengths and limits of the methods you are proposing?

- Show that you know what data you may need to draw from (e.g., public records) and that you will be able to gain access to them and in time to complete the project.

- Consider what you will do if you run into data collection problems. Strong proposals identify potential obstacles and show that you have thought of alternatives. The best laid plans are not always feasible at the time and place you want to implement them.

- Prepare and include a timeline showing when you will undertake specific tasks. One (but not the only format) for a timeline is a matrix that lists tasks on one axis and time periods (for example, months) on the other. This allows you to show that some components of your work will overlap in time (for example, you may be arranging for interviews at the same time that you are researching background information from other sources on the context). Box 4.7 provides an example of a timeline based on Ranjana Chakrabarti's PhD dissertation.

- If possible, undertake pilot research to demonstrate the feasibility of your study and refer to this in your proposal.

- Finally, do not forget to allow time to gain approval from the departmental or the university committee responsible for overseeing ethical issues in research.

methodology is the least satisfactory part of the document. This seems to be a particular problem with research that plans to use qualitative methods. The researcher may not go much beyond indicating that data will be collected through focus groups or in-depth interviews, perhaps naming software that will be used for analysis but failing to *show why and how these methods will allow the specific research questions to be answered fully and ethically.*[3] In Box 4.6 we summarise some of the most important considerations that need to be borne in mind when developing a research methodology. We do not discuss specific methods in this chapter in any detail; these are the subjects of other chapters in this volume.

In Box 4.8 we draw again on Ranjana Chakrabarti's doctoral research proposal to provide a specific example of a statement of research methodology. These ideas about research methods should be read in the context of her key research question and sub-questions outlined in Box 4.4.

BOX 4.7 EXAMPLE OF A PHD TIMETABLE

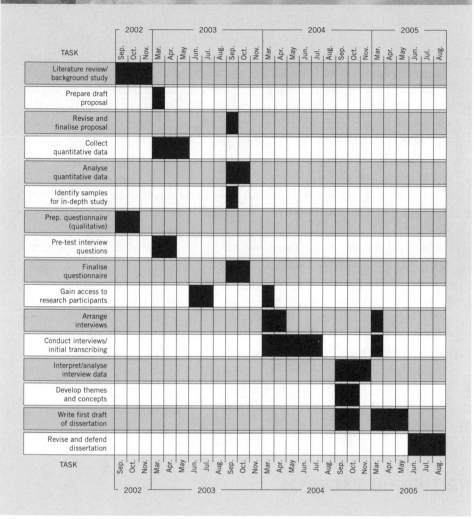

BOX 4.8 RESEARCH METHODOLOGY FOR A HEALTH GEOGRAPHY STUDY

In this study a mix of qualitative and quantitative methods will be used, and these relate to two distinctive, but related, parts of the proposed research into the use of prenatal care services by South Asian mothers...The first phase involves a quantitative analysis of spatial variation in the use of formal prenatal care services by South Asian mothers in New York City (NYC). This work uses data from the births master file of the NYC Department of Health. A Geographical Information System (GIS) will be used for mapping and analyzing the geographic distribution of South Asian mothers and for exploring geographic variation in prenatal care use for the major South Asian groups. Logistic regression techniques will be used to shed light on the influence of factors such as education and insurance coverage on the use of prenatal care.

The second phase of the research involves an extensive field-based qualitative study to understand how the everyday lives of immigrant South Asian women shape their prenatal care practices. Interviews will be carried out with approximately 60 immigrant South Asian women in New York City. The main goal is to understand the type of barriers women face in using formal prenatal care and how women utilize social networks, both national and transnational, to gain knowledge, social support, and prenatal services during pregnancy. The types of questions that will be used to obtain this information are discussed in the proposal.

The sample women for the in-depth interviews will be chosen to reflect the geographic, economic and cultural diversity amongst South Asian immigrant population in New York City...Based on the quantitative GIS analysis, place-based stratification is proposed to identify neighborhoods for intensive study. The initial research participants in each neighborhood are to be contacted through South Asian organizations, nongovernmental organizations working for immigrant South Asian women, and through informal networks and social gatherings...and through '**snowball-sampling**' procedures.

The qualitative phase of the project began in February, 2004 and is expected to last for 6–8 months. Interviews are being tape-recorded and transcribed, and the interview data will be analyzed using interpretive methods. The qualitative analysis software, NUD*IST, will be used to assist in identifying major themes from the interviews and in aiding the data interpretation. The proposal makes reference to the fact that Ranjana conducted pilot interviews with a small sample of South Asian women in Champaign, Illinois, to pretest the format and questions for the in-depth interviews. Based on that experience, a detailed set of interview questions were formulated.

The Institutional Review Board [i.e., ethics committee] at the University of Illinois granted final approval for the project in December 2003. (Chakrabarti 2004)

WRITING THE PROPOSAL

Exactly how you organise the final proposal will depend on who will read it. If you are writing it for your supervisor or a class in research methods, you may be given guidelines to follow. If you are applying to a funding agency, it will usually have guidelines that should be followed very carefully. A cover sheet or letter and an abstract, for example, may be required. You will probably write these last to make sure they are accurate and compelling statements about your project.

In whatever form the proposal is written, it should address the key questions of *what, why, how, and when*, as this chapter has discussed, and if you are applying for funding, it will need to identify *who* you are and what are your qualifications, and *how much* (a justified budget) the research will cost. Ancillary information may well include items such as a list of the references cited in your text, the ethics/institutional review clearance, letters of recommendation, and your credentials in the form of a biographical statement or curriculum vitae.[4]

As we have noted earlier, when outlining the key components of a research proposal, we think that the opening one or two paragraphs of the research proposal should capture the reader's attention by succinctly answering the *what, why, how* questions. Anthony Heath (1997) provides a useful outline of the content of the introduction to a proposal advocating that you address what it is you want to know or understand, how you became interested in the topic, why the research is needed, and referring briefly, for example, to the lack of existing knowledge or limits of other work, and to whom the work will be of value. We also suggest that you indicate briefly what conceptual or methodological approach the research will adopt. In Box 4.9 we offer the opening paragraphs from Ranjana Chakrabarti's research proposal for illustrative purposes.

This kind of approach is more effective than beginning with a lengthy 'background' statement and failing to define your project until several pages into the proposal. It is especially important to have a strong opening if you are applying for funds in a national competition. Reviewers have many proposals to evaluate in a short time. The easier you make their task the better chance you have of being successful. In this regard it is a good idea to specify in the opening paragraphs what is innovative about your research.

We observed at the outset of this chapter that you should allow plenty of time to write your proposal. Just how much time depends on your career stage and the context in which you are

---

BOX 4.9   INTRODUCING THE PROPOSAL

Ranjana Chakrabarti's (2004) proposal began with the following two paragraphs:

The main objective of this PhD dissertation is to understand the roles of place, context and culture in shaping prenatal health care practices of South Asian immigrant women in New York City. These women have very low levels of prenatal care utilization compared to US-born women and women from other immigrant backgrounds (NYC Department of Health and Mental Hygiene, 1999; South Asian Public Health Association, 2002; Coalition for Asian American Children and Families, 2001). This puts at risk the maternal and infant health of one of the most vibrant immigrant populations in the country, because low and inadequate prenatal care use can result in low birth weight babies and other adverse pregnancy outcomes (Kieffer et al., 1992; McDonald et al., 1998).

Little is known about the complexity of circumstances that leads to inadequate utilization of formal prenatal care by South Asian women in New York City. This research is intended to fill this gap by exploring how the geographical contexts of everyday life influence their prenatal care practices. The primary focus is to understand how the experiences of place, culture and context mediate prenatal health care practices. Using quantitative methods and qualitative in-depth interviews I seek to understand how women's situatedness in local and transnational social and geographical networks constrains access to prenatal care and how women draw on such networks in creating new spaces of prenatal care access.

writing. Six months preparation is not unusual for a doctoral proposal. Six weeks might be typical for an Honours proposal. You should expect to write multiple drafts, to seek critiques from peers, your supervisor(s), and other relevant academic staff members. You should seek out models of other successful proposals. Web sites that provide helpful examples exist and we list some of these at the end of the chapter in 'Suggested reading'. Some, such as that of the United States' National Science Foundation, also include reviewers' critiques. If program officers in a relevant funding agency are willing to discuss your proposal with you, or if they offer workshops at professional meetings, by all means take advantage of such opportunities.

While your ideas are clearly extremely important, your writing style and the format of the argument are critical features of a successful proposal. Use clear language rather than excessive technical jargon. Make sure the typeface is easily legible. Make judicious use of underlining, bold, or italic type where appropriate. Proofread carefully and check/double-check all details. If you have written a proposal for external funding, be especially careful about the funding agency's requirements. Does the proposal have to be mailed by or received by a specific date? How many copies must you send? Is the proposal to be submitted electronically or as paper copy? Do you require approval by your institution before you submit your proposal to an external agency? What does that process involve? How much time does it take? Failure to follow the required guidelines for research proposals can lead to significant delays in getting the project approved or funded or, more likely, to rejection of the proposal.

SEEKING FUNDING FOR RESEARCH

Obtaining funding for research operates very differently in different settings, and for this reason we will deal with this topic only briefly. We suggest that you talk with your supervisor and other students who may have had grants, check the Web and libraries for information sources, and consult offices in your university that assist in identifying funding sources. You may also wish to check if funding is available for a **pilot study** that will enable you to demonstrate your main project is feasible.

If you need funding, start the application process well before you expect to begin the research. You may wait as much as six months to learn if you have been successful in a national competition. It is sometimes argued that research involving qualitative methods—for instance collecting detailed information from small numbers of interviewees—has less chance of getting financial support from external sources than, say, large quantitative surveys. This was much more of an issue a decade ago than it is now. Well-argued research proposals, which rely heavily on qualitative rather than quantitative data, are likely to be funded. A critical issue with regard to funding research is the nature of the research question that is being addressed, and the relevance this has for the priorities of the funding agency.

Before applying for funding, check the agency's guidelines *very carefully*: are you eligible for an award, what is required in the proposal (for example, format, page length, type style, budget, bibliography, letters of reference, your credentials), and what is the deadline for receipt of proposals. Writing your research proposal and associated funding proposals is time consuming. Experienced supervisors often suggest beginning your draft up to six months before submission. So, begin early!

A CONCLUDING COMMENT

We pointed out in the introduction to this chapter that writing a research proposal is probably the most demanding task any undergraduate or graduate student will experience. We have found that students invariably tell us that the requirement to design and carry out their own research project was the highlight of their geography training at university. One of the hardest things to do is to decide on what you think is a good research topic. As we noted when drawing on our own experiences of graduate and postgraduate research, there is no single source of inspiration for topics. One useful piece of advice, with the wisdom of hindsight, is to choose a topic that can be specified and explained simply and clearly. A real trap when choosing topics for research is to try and be very clever in order to convince the reader that this really is an original idea. In reality, very few research ideas are completely novel or 'original'; most research builds on existing ideas and extends these in interesting ways.

The key to success in writing a compelling research proposal is your own excitement about doing the research. If you are interested in the topic, you will think more clearly about all of the issues we have raised in this chapter. Strong commitment on your part to the topic will tend to ensure that the research questions will be well specified, the research will be framed effectively, the methodology will be appropriate, and the proposal will be well written. Undertaking research does not appeal to everyone, and a lack of interest in this aspect of university training usually shows up very quickly in the content of a research proposal. We hope you will want to carry out research into a topic that is of interest to you; in both our cases it was a transformative experience that led us on to careers where research is at the heart of the job. We can think of no better challenge in a university program than the challenge of writing a compelling research proposal.

KEY TERMS

conceptual framework
literature review

REVIEW QUESTIONS

1   Identify two or three possible topics you will consider for your research project, thesis, or dissertation. Describe how these ideas originated. Why do you think they will sustain your interest? What preparation will you need in order to address them?
2   Select a published research article in your area of interest. What does the author identify as the main research questions? Write an opening paragraph that you think would be a strong introduction for a research proposal that will address these research questions.
3   List the information you will include in a proposal for research you will undertake to demonstrate that you have considered how your methodology will be implemented (for example, how you will select people to interview).

4 Outline the 'big picture' question and up to four related sub-questions for a research topic of your choice. Identify the main elements of the methodology you would need to employ to address these questions.

SUGGESTED READING

Bouma, G.D. 1996, *The Research Process*, 3rd edn, Oxford University Press, New York.

Hay, I. 2002, *Communicating in Geography and the Environmental Sciences*, 2nd edn, Oxford University Press, Melbourne.

Heath, A.W. 1997, 'The proposal in qualitative research', *The Qualitative Report* (online), vol. 3, no. 1, Available: <http://www.nova.edu/ssss/QR/QR3-1/heath.html> (Accessed: 9 September 2004).

Institute of International Studies, University of California, Berkeley 2001, *Dissertation Proposal Workshop* (online), Available: <http://globetrotter.berkeley.edu/DissPropWorkshop/> (Accessed: 9 September 2004). In addition to sections on conceptualising, writing, and revising proposals, this site includes sample proposals and comments by the authors reflecting on how they regarded the proposal after they had completed the research.

McIntyre, J. 2001, *Guide to Writing a Research Proposal* (online), Available: <http://www.education.uts.edu.au/research/degrees/guide.html> (Accessed: 9 September 2004).

National Research Foundation (South Africa) undated, *Proposal Writing Resources* (online), Available: <http://www.nrf.ac.za/methods/proposals.htm> (Accessed: 9 September 2004).

Punch, K. F. 2000, *Developing Effective Research Proposals*, Sage, London.

Przeworski, A. and Salmon, F. 1995, *The Art of Writing Proposals: Some Candid Suggestions for Applicants to Social Science Research Council Competitions* (online), Available: <http://www.ssrc.org/publications/for-fellows/art_of_writing_proposals.page> (Accessed: 9 September 2004).

Sarantakos, S. 2005, *Social Research*, 3rd edn, Palgrave, Melbourne.

Sides, C.H. 1992, *How to Write and Present Technical Information*, 2nd edn, Cambridge University Press, Oakleigh, Victoria.

Notes

1   Though Fay Gale was shortly to complete her doctoral research in South Australia on regional patterns of Aboriginal communities in South Australia (Gale 1964).

2   Andrew Beer drew our attention to this research idea.

3   Keep in mind that any research involving collection of information from human subjects will necessitate a process of ethical approval for the project. Writing the ethics approval application can be a time-consuming task that should be factored into your timetable. See chapter 2 for a fuller discussion of ethical issues.

4   For an example of agency guidelines for proposal preparation (and just how specific they can be) see the U.S. National Science Foundation's Web site section on doctoral dissertation programs. This is available online at: <http://www.nsf.gov/pubsys/ods/getpub.cfm?nsf01113>.

5

Qualitative Research Design and Rigour

Matt Bradshaw and Elaine Stratford

CHAPTER OVERVIEW

Careful design and **rigour** are crucial to the dependability of any research. Research that is poorly conceived results in research that is poorly executed, and in findings that do not stand up to scrutiny. Thoughtful planning of research and the use of procedures to ensure that research is rigorous should therefore be central concerns for qualitative researchers. The research questions we ask, the cases and participants we involve in our studies, and the ways we ensure the rigour of our work all need to be considered in any dependable research.

INTRODUCTION

In this chapter, we focus on some matters of design and rigour that qualitative researchers need to consider throughout a project to ensure that the work satisfies its aims and its critical audiences. We outline various principles of qualitative research design as well as some specific means by which rigour can be achieved in our work.

The chapter is organised into three main sections. First, we discuss influences on us as researchers, as well as the influence we have over the conduct of research. This discussion makes a link between the interpretive communities in which we work and the sorts of issues that are raised when we begin a research project. Second, we elaborate on how to select suitable cases and participants for study. In qualitative research, the number of people we interview, communities we observe, or texts we read is less important than the quality of who or what we involve in our research, and how we conduct that research. Third, we outline some ways of ensuring rigour in qualitative research to produce work that is dependable.

Careful research design is an important part of ensuring rigour in qualitative research, and while texts and topics on research methods and design often imply that studies should be conducted in a particular way (Gould 1988), no single correct approach to research design can be prescribed. For certain kinds of work, the order and arrangement of stages may be different, stages can overlap, other stages might well be included, and the combination of qualitative and quantitative research is also possible. Nevertheless, by the end of the chapter we will have moved through a number of stages of qualitative research design, and summarised this passage in three diagrams. We consider that you will find this movement helpful in approaching your own qualitative research work.

ASKING RESEARCH QUESTIONS

Each of us needs to acknowledge that our fellow geographers and other colleagues are *already* involved in our studies (Box 5.1). None of us ever formulates research questions or undertakes research in a vacuum. We are all members of **interpretive communities** that involve established disciplines with relatively defined and stable areas of interest, theory, and research methods and techniques (Butler 1997; Fish 1980). Our interpretive communities influence our choice of topic, and our approach to and conduct of study. We also fold our own values and beliefs into research, and these can influence both what we study and how we interpret our research (see Jacobs 1999 and chapter 16 of this volume for more detail).

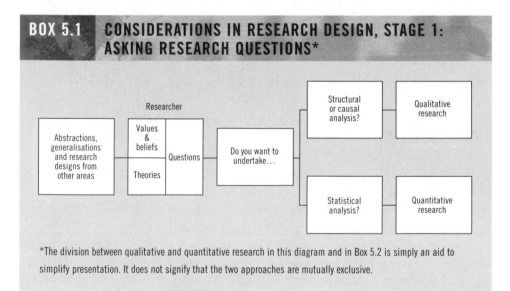

BOX 5.1 **CONSIDERATIONS IN RESEARCH DESIGN, STAGE 1: ASKING RESEARCH QUESTIONS***

*The division between qualitative and quantitative research in this diagram and in Box 5.2 is simply an aid to simplify presentation. It does not signify that the two approaches are mutually exclusive.

From asking research questions to conducting research

Research aims affect research design. For example, asking 'how many skaters frequent a particular public place compared with other types of users?' will involve a research design different from one that aims to answer the question 'why do skaters use this place and how do they interact with other types of users?' The first question focuses on quantification and statistical analysis, and the second is more concerned with the qualitative investigation of underlying causes of skaters' behaviour and how this partly expresses various structural relations.

In considering how we conduct research, we need also to ask what we want to do with the information we collect. Answering this question will also help us to decide what kind of research to do. Before making this decision, we need to be aware of some of the differences between qualitative (intensive) and quantitative (extensive) research. As Sayer (1992) suggests, each method helps us to answer different research questions, employs different research methods, has different limitations, and ensures rigour differently. Extensive research is characterised by identifying regularities, patterns, and distinguishing features of a population, often through a sample that has been selected using a random procedure to maximise the possibility of generalising to a larger population from which it is drawn. Extensive methods are designed to establish statistical relations of similarity and difference among members of a population, but they can lack explanatory power. For instance, we may be able to determine that N number of respondents in a sample think P, but we may not readily be able to determine why they hold this opinion. Intensive methods require that we ask how processes work in a particular case (Platt 1988). We need to establish what actors do in a case, why they behave as they do, and what produces change both in actors and in the contexts in which they are located.

For example, the issue of multiple-use conflict in a public place can be investigated using quantitative methods. Wood and Williamson (1996) decided to distribute a standardised questionnaire to a random sample of the users of Franklin Square, an inner-city square in Hobart, Tasmania, that had been partly claimed through day-to-day use by skaters. The data from their study were aggregated and statements were made about the degree to which these data were likely to reflect the opinions of all the square's users about the presence of skaters. This extensive approach produced useful information suggesting the existence of common characteristics and patterns; for instance, skaters used certain parts of the square, while other users avoided these. But such findings did not account for the shifting quality of various people's different experiences of Franklin Square and of each other, or the reasons behind their opinions. Also selecting Franklin Square as a case by which to examine multiple-use conflict in public places, Stratford (1998; 2002) and Stratford and Harwood (2001) have used intensive methods such as in-depth interviews and observation to understand various responses to skating in the square and around Tasmania more generally. If we are interested in working through the elements of structure and process that arise from analysing responses rather than in data that make statistical analysis possible, then we are pointed in the direction of intensive research.

In summary, in moving towards a qualitative research design, we are influenced by the theories we are concerned to use, by studies undertaken by other researchers in our interpretive communities that we have found interesting, and by the research questions we wish to ask—all of which are interrelated.

SELECTING CASES AND PARTICIPANTS

Definitions of the terms '**case**' and '**participant**' will differ between interpretive communities. However, it is our view that cases are examples of more general processes or structures that can be theorised. Researchers should be able to ask 'that categorical question of any study: "What is this case a case of?"' (Flyvbjerg 1998, p. 8). Franklin Square is a *case* of multiple-use conflict in a public place, with this more general process involving, for example, theories of consumption, citizenship, and government (Stratford 2002). *Participants* make up some of the elements of the case in question, for example, skaters, the elderly, the business community, and Council.

Selecting cases

Sometimes we find a case, and sometimes a case finds us. In both instances, selection combines purpose and serendipity (Box 5.2). On the one hand, we may read about multiple-use conflict in public places in other cities, and want to see if causal explanations advanced there have merit in—or inform our understanding of—situations with which we are familiar. In this instance, the general or theoretical interest 'drives' the research and we must narrow the field, selecting cases and participants for research. On the other hand, perhaps a local government Parks Manager draws our attention to conflict among various groups in one site in the city, and wishes us to investigate options to manage this conflict. In this situation, the case has 'found' the researcher—and theories about multiple-use conflict in public spaces are subsequently woven into it. It is worth noting that if, for example, a Community Development Officer rather than a Parks Manager had contacted us about the same issue, we may well have been presented with a different brief which would in some ways make for a 'different' case.

Irrespective of how a case is selected, it is usually advisable to work in sites or on cases that are both practical and appropriate. In our example of skaters' use of public places, ambiguous sites—such as shopping malls, which are generally private places behind public façades—may need to be eliminated. In practical terms, we must be able and be permitted to work in the site or sites we select.

One final issue needs to be considered in case selection. On the one hand, we might choose to work with cases that are deemed typical on the grounds that these will provide useful insights into causal processes in other contexts. Alternatively, we might deliberately seek out **disconfirming cases**. Such cases might include individuals or observations that challenge a researcher's interpretations or do not confirm ways in which others portray an issue. It might be, for example, that we have studied media reports in which it is suggested that there is unmitigated conflict between youths and the elderly in a public square. However, interviews with elderly pensioners lead us to understand that certain aged people regularly frequent the square at the same times as youths because they seek to be among the young, whose company they find enjoyable. Such disconfirming cases can be important in the research process, requiring us to think through how different institutions and the practices used by them (such as the media and their tendency to sensationalise events) create stereotypes. Such cases also require us to ask how various actors are represented (and for what reasons) and how they represent themselves.

Selecting participants

Generally speaking, the more focused our research interest becomes, and the better our background information and understanding, the more certain we are about who we wish to involve in our research and why. Exploratory work (for example, reading, observation, viewing television documentaries, conducting preliminary interviews) will often give us the

BOX 5.2 CONSIDERATIONS IN RESEARCH DESIGN, STAGE 2: SELECTING CASES AND PARTICIPANTS

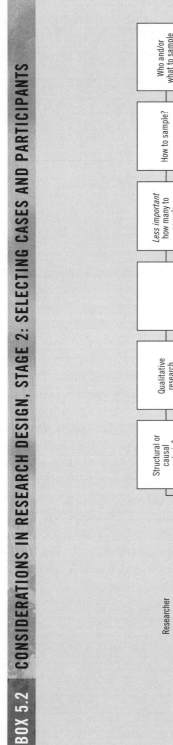
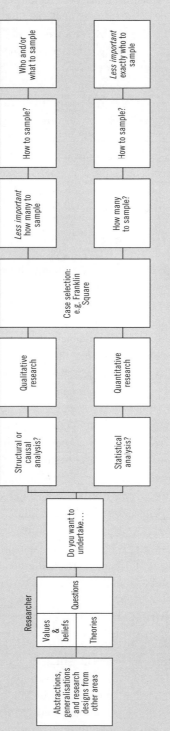

capacity to begin to comprehend the perspectives of key informants. Understanding key informants in complex cultural situations usually requires semi-structured, in-depth interviewing (see chapter 6 for details) or observational methods (see chapter 12 for details) that, though time-consuming, often result in a deeper or more detailed appreciation of the complicated issues involved (Geertz 1973; Herod 1993).

Talking with, or observing people as long as necessary (or at least as long as possible), to understand their different experiences and perspectives is a good way to develop an in-depth understanding of the positions and issues surrounding any particular research interest. In point of fact, it is feasible that conducting in-depth interviews with a small number of the 'right' people will provide significant insights into a research issue. In selecting the right people, however, we rely heavily on early and ongoing secondary research to allow us to approach appropriate key informants to unlock a topic with us. The next matter to be resolved is how to select participants for possible involvement in our research.

How to select participants

Michael Patton's (1990, pp. 182–3) work on **purposeful sampling** is among the more useful summaries on the topic available to researchers. Patton refers to fifteen forms of purposeful sampling, including the following commonly employed strategies. *Extreme* or *deviant case* **sampling** is designed to help researchers learn from highly unusual cases of the issue of interest, such as outstanding successes/notable failures, top-of-the-class students/dropouts, exotic events, or crises. *Typical case sampling* illustrates or highlights what is considered 'typical', 'normal', or 'average' (such as the early 1990s television documentary *Sylvania Waters*, which depicted life in a 'typical' Australian family). *Maximum variation* **sampling** documents unique or diverse variations that have emerged in adapting to different conditions and identifies important common patterns that cut across variations. *Snowball* or *chain* **sampling** identifies cases of interest from people who know other people with relevant cases (such as Kirby and Hay's (1997) work involving homosexual men in Adelaide). *Criterion* **sampling** involves picking all cases that meet some criterion, such as all children held back a grade at some time in their schooling. *Opportunistic* **sampling** requires that the researcher flexibly follows new leads during fieldwork and takes advantage of the unexpected. *Convenience* sampling involves selecting cases or participants on the basis of access (for example, interviewing passers-by in the street). While this final strategy saves time, money and effort, it often provides the lowest level of dependability, and can yield information-poor cases. Much purposeful sampling combines a number of these strategies.

How many participants to select

In both qualitative and quantitative research it is usual that only a sub-group of people or phenomena associated with a case is actually studied. The size of this group is more relevant in quantitative research where representativeness is important. In qualitative research, however, the sample is not intended to be representative since the 'emphasis is usually upon an analysis of meanings in specific contexts' (Robinson 1998, p. 409).

Some of the ways in which the issue of how many respondents to select is different in qualitative as opposed to quantitative research are introduced in the following analogy between a case and an island. Suppose you are looking at a special kind of aerial photograph of an island, so detailed that you can see all of its inhabitants.

> Clearly, if the population of the island were ten thousand instead of ten, enumeration would count for a great deal...But this is because of the investigator's limitations: [s/he] cannot really get to know ten thousand people and the various ways in which each interacts with others. The use of formalist techniques is a second-best approach to this problem because the ideal technique is no longer feasible. Even on this big island, the old technique will count for a great deal, but that is not the main point. The point is that counting and model building and statistical estimation are not the primary methods of scientific research in dealing with human interaction: they are rather crude second-best substitutes for the primary technique, story-telling (Ward 1972, p. 185).

Numbers *do* tell us things about the island, and if what we are interested in is the frequency and geographic distribution of the island's population then we need no more than the photograph. If we are interested in a particular 'story', such as might revolve around an aspect of the cultural geography of the island, for example multiple-use conflict in public places, then we will need more than the photograph to go on.

One way to conduct our investigation is to talk with the island's inhabitants. We could also engage in participant observation or we could consult relevant texts such as submissions to government, letters to the editor of the island's newspaper, or television news stories that might give us an insight into multiple-use conflict in the island's public places. As researchers, however, we are usually resource-limited, both in terms of funding and time, and we must make decisions about what/who to include and what/who to exclude from our study. It is clear, however, that we remain faced with the issue of how many people to talk with or how many texts to read and so forth. While it may seem disconcertingly imprecise, Patton's (1990, pp. 184 and 185) brutally simple advice remains accurate:

> *There are no rules for sample size in qualitative inquiry.* Sample size depends on what you want to know, the purpose of the inquiry, what's at stake, what will be useful, what will have credibility, and what can be done with available time and resources...
>
> The validity, meaningfulness, and insights generated from qualitative inquiry have more to do with...information-richness...and the observational/analytical capacities of the researcher than with sample size. (Emphasis in original.)

In the final analysis, then, it is you as the researcher who must be able to justify matters of case and participant selection to yourself, your supervisor, your interpretive community, and reader–users of your work.

ENSURING RIGOUR

It is no frivolous thing to share, interpret, and represent others' experiences. We need to take seriously 'the privilege and responsibility of interpretation' (Stake 1995, p. 12). This responsibility to informants and colleagues means that it must be possible for our research to be evaluated. It is important that others using our research have reason to believe that it has been conducted dependably. (An extensive literature on these matters includes works by Anfara et al. 2002; Baxter and Eyles 1997; Bogdan and Biklen 1992; Ceglowski 1997; Denzin 1978; Dey 1993; Flick 1992; Geertz 1973; Jick 1979; Johnson 1997; Keen and Packwood 1995; Kirk and Miller 1986; Lincoln and Guba 2000; Manning 1997; Mays and Pope 1997.)

Ensuring rigour in qualitative research (Box 5.3) means establishing the *trustworthiness* of our work (Bailey et al. 1999a; 1999b; Baxter and Eyles 1999a; 1999b). Research can be construed as a kind of 'hermeneutic circle' starting from our interpretive community, and involving our research participant community and ourselves, before returning to our interpretive community for assessment (Burawoy et al. 1991; Jacobs 1999; Reason and Rowan 1981). This circle is a key part of ensuring rigour in qualitative research; our participant and interpretive communities check our work for credibility and good practice. In other words, trust in our work is not assumed but has to be earned.

There are two particular steps that need to be followed to ensure and argue the rigour of our research for our interpretive communities. First, strategies for ensuring trustworthiness need to be formulated in the early stages of research design and applied at various stages in the research process (Baxter and Eyles 1999a; 1997; Lincoln and Guba 1985). These should include appropriate checking procedures in which our work is opened up to the scrutiny of interpretive and participant communities. Second, we need to document each stage of our research carefully so that we might report our work to our interpretive community for checking; 'we should focus on producing analyses that are as open to scrutiny as possible' (Fielding 1999, p. 526).

Rigour is a matter that needs to be considered from the outset of our research, underpinning the early stages of research design. It is important to incorporate appropriate *checking* procedures into our research process. These procedures are outlined in Denzin (1978) and Baxter and Eyles (1997) as the four major types of triangulation: multiple sources, methods, investigators, and theories. For example, as we move through various research stages, we might check: (a) our sources against others (re-search); (b) our process and interpretations with our supervisors and/or colleagues; and (c) our text with our research participant community to enhance the credibility of our research (although this last check can be problematic if that community has considerable power, such as might be the case with a multinational corporation whose managers refuse us permission to publish work related to findings derived from the corporation). Reason and Rowan (1981) elaborate on some of these matters.

Examining the research stages in Box 5.3—which often overlap as they become a whole research composition—we also need to document our work fully: how we came to be interested in the research, why we chose to do it, and for what purpose. We may declare our own philosophical, theoretical, and political dispositions, and we will almost certainly review literatures dealing with both the general area of our research and the research methods we intend to use. This elaboration of context permits us to establish the plausibility of our research by demonstrating that we embarked on our work adequately informed by relevant literatures and for intellectually and ethically justifiable reasons. We will most likely have checked the plausibility of our research with supervisors and/or colleagues before embarking on detailed research design. At the final stage of reporting research we can also attempt

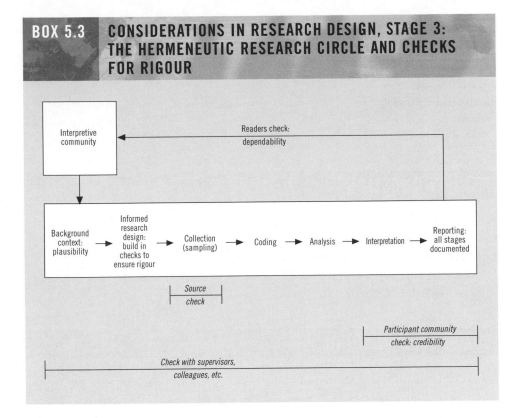

| BOX 5.3 | CONSIDERATIONS IN RESEARCH DESIGN, STAGE 3: THE HERMENEUTIC RESEARCH CIRCLE AND CHECKS FOR RIGOUR |

to acknowledge limits to the **transferability** of our research due to particularities of the research topic, the research methods used, and the researcher. In this way, we confirm that the methods we use and the interpretations we invoke influence our research outcome. Thus, it is vital that we document all stages of our research process. Such documentation allows members of our interpretive and participant communities to check all of these stages so our work might be considered dependable.

FINAL COMMENTS

We began this chapter by suggesting that consideration of research design and rigour is essential to the conduct of dependable qualitative inquiry. We have addressed issues of case selection and participant selection, and outlined some reasons to be concerned with rigour, as well as some means by which rigour might be achieved.

Most research is undertaken to be shared with others. We therefore need to ensure that our research can stand up to the critical scrutiny of our interpretive and participant communities. The work presented in this chapter provides some of the conceptual and practical tools by which this outcome of sharing plausible, credible, and dependable work can be achieved.

KEY TERMS

case

disconfirming case

interpretive community

participant

purposeful sampling

rigour

triangulation

REVIEW QUESTIONS

1   Why is rigour important in qualitative research?
2   What is an 'interpretive community'?
3   What is meant by the phrase 'participant community'?
4   What are some ways we might check our research to establish its dependability to members of
     our interpretive community?

SUGGESTED READING

Anfara, V.A., Brown, K.M. and Mangione, T.L. 2002, 'Qualitative analysis on stage: making the
    research process more public', *Educational Researcher*, vol. 31, no. 7 (October), pp. 28–38.

Baxter, J. and Eyles, J. 1997, 'Evaluating qualitative research in social geography: establishing "rigour"
    in interview analysis', *Transactions of the Institute of British Geographers*, vol. 22, no. 4, pp.
    505–25.

Jacobs, J. M. 1999, 'The labour of cultural geography', in E. Stratford (ed.), *Australian Cultural
    Geographies*, Oxford University Press, Melbourne.

Patton, M. Q. 2002, *Qualitative Evaluation and Research Methods*, 3rd edn, Sage, Beverly Hills.

Platt, J. 1988, 'What can case studies do?', *Studies in Qualitative Methodology*, vol. 1, pp. 1–23.

Sayer, A. 1992, *Method in Social Science: A Realist Approach*, 2nd edn, Routledge, London.

PART 2

'Doing' Qualitative Research in Human Geography

6

Interviewing

Kevin Dunn

CHAPTER OVERVIEW

This chapter provides advice on interview design, practice, transcription, data analysis, and presentation. I describe the characteristics of each of the three major forms of interviewing and critically assess what I see as the relative strengths and weaknesses of each. Applications of interviewing are outlined by referring to examples from economic, social, and environmental geography.

INTERVIEWING IN GEOGRAPHY

Interviewing in geography is so much more than 'having a chat'. Successful interviewing requires careful planning and detailed preparation. A taped hour-long interview will have involved days of preliminary background work and question formulation. It would have required the diplomacy of contacting **informants** and negotiating 'research deals'. A sixty-minute interview will require at least four hours of transcription if you are a fast typist and verification of the record of interview could stretch out over a couple of weeks. After all that, you have still to analyse the interview material. These are involved and time-consuming activities. Is it all worth it? In this chapter I outline some of the benefits of interviewing, and provide a range of tips for good interviewing practice.

An interview can be defined as 'a face-to-face verbal interchange in which one person, the interviewer, attempts to elicit information or expressions of opinion or belief from another person or persons' (Maccoby and Maccoby 1954, p. 499). An interview is a data-gathering method in which there is a spoken exchange of information. It is a method that requires some form of direct access to the person being interviewed.

Types of interviewing

There are three major forms of interviewing: structured, unstructured, and semi-structured. These three forms can be placed along a continuum with the **structured interview** at one end and the **unstructured interview** at the other (see also chapter 1, Box 1.1). Structured interviews follow a predetermined and standardised list of questions. The questions are asked in almost the same way and in the same order. At the other end of the interviewing continuum are unstructured forms of interviewing such as oral histories (discussed fully in chapter 7). The conversation in these interviews is actually directed by the informant rather than by set questions. In the middle of this continuum are **semi-structured interviews**. This form of interviewing has some degree of predetermined order but still ensures flexibility in the way issues are addressed by the informant. Different forms of interview have varying strengths and weaknesses that should be clear to you by the end of this chapter.

Strengths of interviewing

Research interviews are used for four main reasons (see also Krueger 1994; Minichiello et al. 1995, pp. 70–4; Valentine 1997, pp. 110–12):

1 to fill a gap in knowledge that other methods, such as observation or the use of census data, are unable to bridge efficaciously
2 to investigate complex behaviours and motivations
3 to collect a diversity of meaning, opinion, and experiences. Interviews provide insights into the differing opinions or debates within a group, but they can also reveal consensus on some issues
4 when a method is required that shows respect for and empowers those people who provide the data. In an interview the informant's view of the world should be valued and treated with respect. The interview may also give the informant cause to reflect on their experiences and the opportunity to find out more about the research project than if they were simply being observed or if they were completing a questionnaire.

Interviews are an excellent method of gaining access to information about events, opinions, and experiences. Opinions and experiences vary enormously between people of different class, ethnicity, age, and sexuality. Interviews have allowed me to understand how meanings differ among people. Geographers who use interviewing should be careful to resist claims that they have discovered the *truth* about a series of events, or that they have distilled *the* public opinion (Goss and Leinbach 1996, p. 116; Kong 1998, p. 80). Interviews can also be used to counter the claims of those who presume to have discovered *the* public opinion. This can be done by seeking out the opinions of different groups, often marginalised or subaltern groups, whose opinions are rarely heard.

Most of the questions posed in an interview allow for an open response, as opposed to a closed set of response options such as Yes or No. In this way, each informant can advise you as researcher about events or opinions in their own words. One of the major strengths of interviewing is that it allows you to discover what is relevant to the informant.

Due to the face-to-face verbal interchange used in interviewing the informant can tell you if a question is misplaced (Box 6.1). Furthermore, your own opinions and tentative conclusions can be checked, verified, and scrutinised. This may disclose significant misunderstandings on your part or issues that you had not previously identified (Schoenberger 1991, p. 187).

BOX 6.1   **ASKING THE WRONG QUESTION: A TALE FROM CABRAMATTA**

On 23 June 1990, I began my first formal research interview. The informant was a senior office-bearer from one of the Indo-Chinese cultural associations in New South Wales. My research interest was in the social origins of the concentration of Indo-Chinese–Australians around Cabramatta and the experiences of these migrants and their families. The political context of the time was still heavy with the racialised and anti-Asian overtones of the 1988 'immigration debate' in which mainstream politicians and academics such as John Howard (later Prime Minister 1996 to the present) and Geoffrey Blainey (Professor of History) had expressed concern about 'Asian' immigration and settlement patterns in Australian cities. Specifically, Vietnamese migrants were accused of congregating in places like Cabramatta (Sydney), and Richmond and Springvale (both in Melbourne), and of purposefully doing so in order to avoid participating with the rest of Australia. I had hypothesised that Vietnamese–Australians did not congregate voluntarily, but that they were forcibly segregated by the economic and social constraints of discrimination in housing and labour markets. Indeed, the geographic literature supported my assertion at the time. I was a somewhat naive and colonialist investigator, who saw his role as 'valiant protector' of an ethnic minority.

But back to my first interview. One of my first questions was: 'Please explain the ways in which discrimination has forced you, and members of the community you represent, to reside in this area?' The answer: 'I wouldn't live anywhere else'. This informant, and most subsequent informants, described the great benefits and pleasures of living in Cabramatta. They also explained how residing in Cabramatta had eased and assisted their expanding participation in Australian life (Dunn 1993). I had asked the wrong questions and had been told so by my informants. I decided to focus the project on the advantages and pleasures that residence in 'Cab' brought to Indo-Chinese–Australians. The face-to-face nature of the exchange, and the informed subject, makes interviews a remarkable method. The participants can tell the researcher: 'you're wrong'!

INTERVIEW DESIGN

It is not possible to formulate a strict guide to good practice for every interview context. Every interview and every research issue demands its own preparation and practice. However, researchers should heed certain procedures. Much of the rest of this chapter focuses on strategies for enhancing the credibility of data collected using rigorous interview practice. In the next section we look at the organisation of **interview schedules** and the formulation of questions.

The interview schedule or guide

Even the most competent researcher needs to be reminded during the interview of the issues or events they had intended to discuss. You cannot be expected to recall all of the specific questions or issues you wish to address and you will benefit from some written reminder of the intended scope of the interview. These reminders can take the form of interview schedules or **interview guides.**

An interview guide or **aide-mémoire** (Burgess 1982c), is a list of general issues you want to cover in an interview. Guides are usually associated with semi-structured forms of interviewing. The guide may be a simple list of key words or concepts intended to remind you of discussion topics. The topics initially listed in a guide are often drawn from existing literature on an issue. The identification of key concepts and the isolation of themes is a preliminary part of any research project (see Babbie 1992, pp. 88–164).

One of the advantages of the interview guide is its flexibility. As the interviewer, you may allow the conversation to follow as 'natural' a direction as possible, but you will have to redirect the discussion to cover issues that may still be outstanding. Questions can be crafted in situ, drawing on themes already broached and from the tone of the discussion. The major disadvantage of using an interview guide is that you must formulate coherent questions 'on the spot'. This requires good communication skills and a great deal of confidence. Any loss of confidence or concentration may lead to an inarticulate and ambiguous wording of questions. Accordingly, a guide is inadvisable for first-time interviewers. It is more appropriate for very skilled interviewers and for particular forms of interview, such as oral history.

An interview schedule is used in structured, and sometimes semi-structured, forms of interviewing. They are also called question schedules or 'question routes' (Krueger 1994). An interview schedule is a list of carefully worded questions (see Box 6.2).

BOX 6.2 FORMULATING GOOD INTERVIEW QUESTIONS

- Use easily understood language that is appropriate to your informant.
- Use non-offensive language.
- Use words with commonly and uniformly accepted meanings.
- Avoid ambiguity.
- Phrase each question carefully.
- Avoid leading questions as far as possible (i.e., questions that encourage a particular response).

I have found that a half-hour interview will usually cover between six and eight primary questions. Under each of these central questions I nest at least two detailed questions or prompts. In some research it may be necessary to ask each question in the same way and in the same order to each informant. In others, you might ask questions at whatever stage of the interview seems appropriate. The benefits of using interview schedules mirror the disadvantages of interview guides. They provide greater confidence to the researcher in the enunciation of their questions and allow better comparisons between informant answers. However, questions that are prepared before the interview and then read out formally may sound insincere, stilted, and out of place.

A mix of carefully worded questions and topic areas capitalises on the strengths of both guides and schedules. Indeed, a fully worded question can be placed in a guide and yet be used as a topic area. The predetermined wording can be kept as a 'fall-back' in case you find yourself unable to articulate a question 'on the spot'. I find it useful to begin an interview with a prepared question. There is little that is more damaging to one's confidence than the informant saying 'what do you mean by that?' or 'I don't know what you mean' in response to your first question.

Interview design should be dynamic throughout the research (Tremblay 1982, pp. 99, 104). As a research project progresses you can make changes to the order and wording of questions/topics as new information and experiences are fed back into the research design. Some issues may be revealed as unimportant, offensive, or silly after the initial interview. These can be dropped from subsequent interviews. The interview schedule or guide should also seek information in a way that is appropriate to each informant.

While the primary purpose of interview schedules and guides is to jog your memory and to ensure that all issues are covered as appropriately as possible, it is also useful to provide informants with a copy of the questions or issues before the interview to prompt thought on the matters to be discussed. Interview guides and schedules are also useful note-taking sheets (Webb 1982, p. 195).

TYPES OF QUESTIONS

Interviews utilise **primary** (or original) **questions** and **secondary questions**. Primary questions are opening questions used to initiate discussion on a new theme or topic. Secondary questions are prompts that encourage the informant to follow up or expand on an issue already discussed. An interview schedule, and even an interview guide, can have a mix of types of original questions, including descriptive questions, storytelling prompts, structural questions, contrast and opinion questions, and devil's advocate propositions (see Box 6.3). Since different types of primary questions produce very different sorts of responses, a good interview schedule will generally comprise a mix of question types.

On an interview guide or schedule you might have a list of secondary questions or prompts (Box 6.5). There are a number of different types of prompts, ranging from formal secondary questions to nudging-type comments that encourage the informant to continue speaking (Whyte 1982, p. 112). Sometimes prompts are listed in the interview guide or schedule, but often they are deployed, when appropriate, without prior planning.

Ordering questions and topics

It is important to consider carefully the order of questions or topics in an interview guide or schedule. Minichiello et al. (1995, p. 84) advise that the most important consideration in the ordering of questions is preserving **rapport** between you and your informant. This requires

BOX 6.3 PRIMARY QUESTION TYPES

Type of question	Example	Type of data and benefits
Descriptive (knowledge)	*What is the full name of your organisation?* *What is your role within the organisation?* *How many brothers or sisters do you have?*	Details on events, places, people, and experiences. Easy-to-answer opening questions.
Storytelling	*Can you tell me about the formation and history of this organisation and your involvement in it?*	Identifies a series of players, an ordering of events, or causative links. Encourages sustained input from the informant.
Opinion	*Is Canadian society sexist?* *What do you consider to be the appropriate size for a functional family?*	Impressions, feelings, assertions, and guesses.
Structural	*How do you think you came to hold that opinion?* *What do you think the average family size is for people like yourself?*	Taps into people's ideology and assumptions. Encourages reflection on how events and experiences may have influenced opinions and perspectives.
Contrast (hypothetical)	*Would your career opportunities have been different if you were a man? Or if you grew up in a poorer suburb?*	Comparison of experience by place, time, gender, and so forth. Encourages reflection on (dis)advantage.
Devil's advocate	*Many of your own colleagues are privately voicing concern about your policy. Are you about to…?*	Controversial/sensitive issues broached (opinions of political opponents) without associating the researcher with that opinion.

See also Box 6.4.

BOX 6.4	ASKING THE TOUGH QUESTIONS WITHOUT SOUNDING TOUGH

My work with Indo-Chinese communities in Cabramatta occurred within a political context in which Vietnamese–Australians were being publicly harangued by academics and politicians (Dunn 1993). I felt it was important to get the informants to respond to the views of their critics. My interview schedule had the following two devil's advocate propositions. I also used a preamble to dissociate myself from the statements.

> In my research so far, I have come across two general explanations for Vietnamese residential concentration. I would like you to comment on two separate statements, that to me, represent these two explanations:
>
> First: that Vietnamese people have concentrated here because they don't want to participate with the wider society.
> Second: that the Vietnamese are segregated into particular residential areas through social, economic, and political forces imposed upon them by the wider society.

The aim was to gather peoples' responses to both statements. In most cases, informants were critical of both views. Some informants took my question as a request for them to select the explanation which they thought was the most appropriate. Those people selected the second statement. Others were in no doubt that I disagreed with both views. Either way, devil's advocate propositions are often leading. My political views were noticeable in the question preamble and wording, as well as in the preliminary discussions held to arrange the interviews. It is fairer that the researcher's motives and political orientation are obvious to the informant rather than hidden until after the research is published (see chapters 2, 5, and 16 of this volume).

that discomfort for the informant be minimised. There are two broad sorts of advice regarding the order in which issues should be addressed: the 'funnel' and the 'pyramid structure' approaches.

Funnelling involves an initial focus on general issues, followed by a gradual movement towards personal matters and issues specific to the informant. This strategy allows for conversational development towards more sensitive issues: 'The assumption made in using this strategy is that informants and interviewers would find it uncomfortable to start talking directly about an issue which may be personally threatening or uncomfortable to think about' (Minichiello et al. 1995, p. 84).

As an ordering strategy, funnelling draws on long-held advice in interviewing to keep sensitive questions until the end (Sudman and Bradburn 1982, pp. 73, 78). The advantage of this strategy is that the interview begins in a relaxed and non-threatening manner. Rapport between informant and interviewer can develop and the chance that the informant will discontinue the interview is reduced. Even if an informant ends an interview at a sensitive point, you will nonetheless have gathered some data. Funnelling might usefully be employed, for example, when investigating an informant's experiences of oppression. The

BOX 6.5 TYPES OF PROMPT

Prompt type	Example	Type of data and benefits
Formal secondary question	Primary Q: *What social benefits do you derive from residing in an area of ethnic concentration?* Secondary Q: *What about informal child-care?*	Extends the scope or depth of treatment on an issue. Can also help explain/ rephrase a misunderstood primary question.
Clarification	*What do you mean by that?*	Used when an answer is vague or incomplete.
Nudging	*And how did that make you feel?* Repeat an informant's last statement.	Used to continue a line of conversation.
Summary (categorising)	*So let me get this straight: your view, as just outlined to me, is that people should not watch shows like* Survivor?	Outline in-progress findings for verification. Elicit succinct statements (for example, 'quotable quotes').
Receptive cues	Audible: *Yes, I see. Uh-huh.* Non-audible: nodding and smiling.	Provides receptive cues, encourages an informant to continue speaking.

interview might begin with a discussion of the general problem of homophobia or racism: how widespread it is; how it varies from place to place; and how legal and institutional responses to those forms of oppression have emerged. Having broached these general or macro-level aspects of oppression the interview might then turn to the particular experiences of the informant.

In an interview with a **pyramid structure** the more abstract and general questions are asked at the end. The interview starts with easy-to-answer questions about an informant's duties or responsibilities, or their involvement in an issue. This allows the informant to become accustomed to the interview, interviewer, and topics before they are asked questions that require deeper reflection. For example, to gather views on changes to urban governance you might find it necessary to first ask an informant from an urban planning agency to out-line their roles and duties. Following that, you might ask your informant to outline the actions of their own agency and how those actions may have changed in recent times. Once the 'doings and goings-on' have been outlined it may then make sense to ask the informant why agency actions and roles have changed, whether that change has been resisted, and how they view the transformation of urban governance.

A final question-ordering option is to use a hybrid of funnel and pyramid structures. The interview might start with simple-to-answer, non-threatening questions, then move to more abstract and reflective aspects, before gradually progressing towards sensitive issues. This sort of structure may offer the benefits of both funnel and pyramid ordering.

When thinking about question and topic ordering, it can be helpful to have key informants comment on the interview guide or schedule (Kearns 1991, p. 2). Key informants are often initial or primary contacts in a project. They are usually the first informants and they often possess the expertise to liaise between the researcher and the communities being researched. Key informant review can be a useful litmus test of interview design, since these representatives are 'culturally qualified'. They have empathy with the study population, and can be comprehensively briefed on the goals and background of the research (Tremblay 1982, pp. 98–100).

STRUCTURED INTERVIEWING

A structured interview uses an interview schedule that typically comprises a list of carefully worded and ordered questions (see Boxes 6.3 and 6.5 and the earlier discussion on ordering questions and topics). Each respondent or informant is asked exactly the same questions in exactly the same order. The interview process is question focused.

It is a wise idea to pre-test a structured interview schedule on a subset (say three to ten) of the group of people you plan to interview for your study to ensure that your questions are not ambiguous, offensive, or difficult to understand. Though helpful, 'pre-testing' is of less importance in semi-structured and unstructured interviews, where ambiguities (but not offensive questions!) can be clarified by the interviewer.

Structured interviews have been used with great effect throughout sub-disciplines of geography, including economic geography (Box 6.6).

BOX 6.6   INTERVIEWING—AN ECONOMIC GEOGRAPHY APPLICATION

In 1991 Schoenberger argued that most industrial geography research had been on the outside looking in, deducing strategic behaviour from its locational effects rather than investigating it directly (1991, p. 182). One of the assumptions challenged by the use of structured interviews was that the location of firms was strongly associated with the location preferences of the industries in question. Using structured interviews with managers, Schoenberger was able to show that the location of foreign chemical firms in the USA was as much, if not more, related to historical and strategic contingencies than to contemporary location preferences.

For example, one of Schoenberger's case studies was a German-owned chemical firm. Her interviews revealed that the firm's Board of Directors had decided on a major expansion in the US market. But the Board had been split between establishing a 'greenfields' site, which would be purpose-built to company needs, and acquiring an already established chemical plant, which would hasten their expanded presence in the market. Plans to establish a greenfield facility were foiled by organised community opposition. The directors who argued for an acquisition then gained the upper hand, and at about the same time a US chemical firm came up for sale. For many decades German chemical firms had agreed among themselves to specialise in certain parts of the chemical sector. These agreements were about to end, and Schoenberger's case-study firm was keen to expand horizontally into another speciality. The US firm that came up for sale happened to specialise in that area. A host of historical and strategic events had combined to produce a particular location result.

The historical and strategic contingencies that accounted for the location of the German chemical company were revealed through structured interviews. Their location was in fact quite at odds with the apparent preferences of the firm and reveals nothing about the firm's location preferences (Schoenberger 1991, p. 185). The US chemical sector has a high level of foreign ownership, and most of it was established through acquisition. Replicated interviews with managers and directors across the chemical sector revealed the prevalence of location choices being determined by historical and strategic contingency. Interviewing was therefore an essential method for unravelling the location determinants of chemical plants in the USA.

SEMI-STRUCTURED INTERVIEWING

Semi-structured interviews employ an interview guide. The questions asked in the interview are content focused and deal with the issues or areas judged by the researcher to be relevant to the research question. Alternatively, an interview schedule might be prepared with fully worded questions for a semi-structured interview, but the interviewer would not be restricted to deploying those questions. The semi-structured interview is organised around ordered but flexible questioning. In semi-structured forms of interview the role of the researcher (interviewer or facilitator) is recognised as being more interventionist than in unstructured interviews. This requires that the researcher redirect the conversation if it has moved too far from the research topics (see also chapter 16).

UNSTRUCTURED INTERVIEWING

Various forms of unstructured interviewing exist. These include oral history, **life history,** and some types of group interviewing and in-depth interviewing. Unstructured interviewing focuses on personal perceptions and personal histories. Rather than being question focused like a structured interview, or content focused as in a semi-structured format, the unstructured interview is informant focused. Life history and oral history interviews seek personal accounts of significant events and perceptions, as determined by the informants, and in their own words (see chapter 7 and also McKay 2002). Each unstructured interview is unique. The questions you ask are almost entirely determined by the informant's responses. These interviews approximate normal conversational interaction and give the informant some scope to direct the interview. Nonetheless, an unstructured interview requires as much, if not more, preparation than its structured counterpart. You must spend time sitting in musty archive rooms or perched in front of dimly lit microfiche machines gaining a solid understanding of past events, people, and places related to the interview. But through these interviews we can 'find out about' events and places that had been kept out of the news, or that had been deemed of no consequence to the rich and powerful (Box 6.7).

BOX 6.7   ORAL ENVIRONMENTAL HISTORIES

Oral history interviews can collect data about environmental history. This type of interviewing helps produce a more comprehensive picture of the cause and process of environmental change than is available through physical methods of enquiry. Data collected might include peoples' memories of changes in local land use, biodiversity, hydrology, and climate.

Lane (1997) used oral history interviews to reveal changes in watercourses, weeds, and climate in the Tumut Region high country of the Australian Alps. Interviews were conducted with five main informants, firstly in their homes, and then while driving and walking through the countryside where they had resided. The informants told of the waterholes and deep parts of creeks where they would fish and swim, and where they and their children had learnt to swim. One informant commented that one of the creeks used to be almost a river…and now you could step over it (Lane 1997, p. 197). The same informant noted the change in colour and quality of the water. Lane's informants described how the water level and quality had steadily degraded since pine plantations had been planted in the 1960s. This description was consistent with 'scientific' understandings of the impact of pine plantations in which there is an ever decreasing level of run-off as the pines grow.

Such specific observations from local residents may often be the only detailed evidence on environmental change that is available. Oral history can fill gaps in the 'scientific record' or it can be used to complement data gathered using physical or quantitative methods. More importantly, with the use of oral history environmental change can be set in a human context and related to the history of people who lived in the region (Lane 1997, p. 204).

INTERVIEWING PRACTICE

Rapport with another person is basically a matter of understanding their model of the world and communicating your understanding symmetrically. This can be done effectively by matching the perceptual language, the images of the world, the speech patterns, pitch, tone, speed, the overall posture, and the breathing patterns of the informant (Minichiello et al. 1995, p. 80).

Achieving and maintaining rapport, or a productive interpersonal climate, can be critical to the success of an interview. Rapport is particularly important if you need to have repeat sessions with an informant. Even the first steps of arranging an interview are significant, including the initial contact by telephone and other preliminaries that might occur before the first interview. Interviews in which both the interviewer and informant feel at ease usually generate more insightful and more valid data than might otherwise be the case. In the following paragraphs, I outline a set of tips that can help you enhance rapport before, during, and while closing an interview.

Contact

Informants are usually chosen purposefully on the basis of the issues and themes that have emerged from a review of previous literature or from other background work (see chapters 4 and 5). This involves choosing people who can communicate aspects of their experiences and ideas relevant to the phenomena under investigation (Minichiello et al. 1995, p. 168). Decisions about the selection of informants also depend on your ability to gain access to people. Once you have identified a potential informant you must then negotiate permission for the interview. This means getting the consent of the informants themselves and, in some circumstances, it will also involve gaining the sanction of 'gatekeepers' like employers, parents, or teachers. This might occur for example if you wanted to interview school children, prisoners, or employees in some workplaces.

Your first contact with an informant will often be by telephone, or by some form of correspondence. In this preliminary phase you should do at least four things (Robertson 1994, p. 9):

1 Introduce yourself and establish your bona fides. For example: 'My name is Juan Folger and I am an honours student from Java State University'.
2 Make it clear how you came to get the informant's name and telephone number or address. If you do not explain this people may be suspicious and are likely to ask how you got their name. If you are asked this question, rapport between you and your informant has already been compromised.
3 Outline why you would like to conduct the interview with this informant in particular. Indicate the significance of the research and explain why the informant's views and experiences are valued. For instance, you may believe they have important things to say, that they have been key players in an issue, or that they have experienced something specific that others have not. On the whole, I have found that most people are flattered to be asked for an interview, although they are often nervous or hesitant about the procedure itself.
4 Indicate how long the interview and any follow-up is likely to take.

Making an informant feel relaxed involves dealing with all of the issues mentioned above, and in addition spelling out the mechanics of the interview and negotiating elements of the interview process. All of these can be outlined in a 'Letter of Introduction' which may be sent to an informant once they have agreed to an interview, or while agreement is still being negotiated. This formal communication should be under the letterhead of your organisation (for example, your university), and should spell out your bona fides, the topic of the research, the manner in which the interview will be conducted, and any rules or boundaries regarding confidentiality. You must, of course, seek permission from your supervisor to use the letterhead of an organisation such as a university, although 'ethics' procedures within your institution (see chapter 2) are likely to have made this mandatory. In the absence of a letter of introduction informants should be made aware of their rights during the interview. This is sometimes referred to as brokering a 'research deal' or a 'research bargain'. The research deal may be agreed to over the telephone, or just before an interview begins. The deal can be set out in written form. (See Box 6.8 for some of the rights of informants that can be established. Chapter 2 of this volume includes material relevant to the ethics of interviewing.) These preliminary discussions are important to the success of an interview. Indeed they set the tone of the relationship between interviewer and informant.

BOX 6.8   CODIFYING THE RIGHTS OF INFORMANTS

In their research on the Carrington community in Newcastle, New South Wales, Winchester, Dunn and McGuirk (1997) decided to codify informants' rights in the oral histories and semi-structured interviews that were to be conducted. They included the following list of informants' rights on university letterhead, and gave a copy to each of the informants:

- Permission to tape the interview must be given in advance.
- All transcribed material will be anonymous.
- Tapes and transcripts will be made available to those informants who request them.
- Informants have the right to change an answer.
- Informants can contact us at any time in the future to alter or delete any statements made.
- Informants can discontinue the interview at any stage.
- Informants can request that the tape-recorder be paused at any stage during the interview.

To this list, one might make additional statements (for example, that informants could expect information about the ways in which their contributions to the research would be used). A codification of rights was deemed necessary for two reasons. First, it was done to empower the informants and assure them that they could pause or terminate the interview process whenever they deemed it necessary to do so. Second, the researchers had employed an articulate local resident to conduct the interviews and so it was important that the interviewer was also constantly reminded of the informants' rights.

The interview relation

The relationship established between interviewer and informant is often critical to the collection of opinions and insights. If you and your informant are at ease with each other then the informant is likely to be communicative. However, there are competing views on the nature of the interviewer–informant relationship. On the one hand there is an insistence on 'professional interviewing' and on the other there is 'creative' or empathetic interviewing. Goode and Hatt (in Oakley 1981, pp. 309–10) warn that interviewers should remain detached and aloof from their informants: 'the interviewer cannot merely lose himself [sic] in being friendly. He must introduce himself as though beginning a conversation, but from the beginning the additional element of respect, of professional competence, should be maintained…He is a professional in this situation, and he must demand and obtain respect for the task he is trying to perform' (Goode and Hatt, in Oakley 1981, p. 191).

A very different, indeed opposite, sort of relationship was proposed by Oakley (1981) and Douglas (1985). In their view, a researcher who remains aloof would undermine the development of an intimate and non-threatening relationship (Oakley 1981, p. 310). Rather than demanding respect from the informant, Douglas' model of 'creative interviewing' insists that each informant must be treated as a 'Goddess' of information and insight. Douglas recommends that researchers humble themselves before the Goddess. The creative or empathetic model of interviewing thus advocates a very different sort of relationship between the informant and interviewer than that recommended for 'professional' interview relations. Overall, there is a range of interview practice that lies between the poles of 'professional' or 'creative' interview relationships.

Decisions about the interview relationship will vary according to the characteristics of both the informant and the interviewer. The cultural nuances of a study group will at times necessitate variations in the intended interaction. However, it is wise to remember that despite any empathy or relationships that are established, the interview is still a formal process of data gathering for research. Furthermore, there is usually a complex and uneven power relationship involved in which information, and the power to deploy that information, flows mostly one way: from the informant to the interviewer (see chapter 2, and also McKay 2002; Stacey 1988).

Rapport may increase the level of understanding you have about the informant and what they are saying. There are a number of strategies for enhancing rapport. The first is through the use of respectful preliminary work. The second involves the use of a warm-up period just before an interview commences. Douglas (1985, p. 79) advises that rather than getting 'right down to business' it is better to engage in some 'small talk and chit-chat (which) are vital first steps'. This warm-up discussion with an informant could be a chat about the weather, matters of shared personal interest, or 'catching-up' talk. In their surveys and interviews of Vietnamese–Australians in Melbourne, Gardner, Neville and Snell (1983, p. 131) found that 'The success of an interview (when measured by the degree of relaxation of all those present and the ease of conversation) generally depended on the amount of "warm-up" (chit-chat, introductions, etc.)'.

My own warm-up techniques have included giving the informant an overview of the questions I plan to ask, presenting relevant diagrams or maps, as well as discussing historical documents (see also Tremblay 1982, pp. 99, 103). Maps, diagrams, tables of statistics, and other documents can also be used as references or stimuli throughout an interview. If an informant offers you food or drink before an interview it would be courteous to accept them.

You should also have acquainted yourself with the cultural context of the informants before the interview. As Robin Kearns pointed out, 'If we are to engage someone in conversation and sustain the interaction, we need to use the right words. Without the right words our speech is empty. Language matters' (Kearns 1991a, p. 2). For instance, you must be able to recognise the jargon or slang, and frequently used acronyms of institutions or corporations, as well as the language of particular professions or cultural groups.

Listening strategies can improve rapport and the productivity of the interview. Your role as interviewer is not passive, but requires constant focus on the information being divulged by informants, and the use of cues and responses to encourage them. Your role as an active participant in the interview extends well beyond simply asking predetermined questions or broaching predetermined topics. You must maintain an active focus on the conversation. This will help prevent lapses of concentration. You must also avoid 'mental wandering', otherwise you may miss unexpected leads. Moreover, it is irritating to the informant, and a threat to rapport, if you ask a question they have already answered (Robertson 1994, p. 44).

Adelman (1981) advises researchers to maintain a **critical inner dialogue** during an interview. This requires that you constantly analyse what is being said and simultaneously formulate the next question or prompt. You should be asking yourself whether you understand what the informant is saying. Do not let something slide by that you do not understand with the expectation that you will be able to make sense of it afterwards. Minichiello et al. (1995, p. 103) provide a demonstration of how critical inner dialogue might occur: 'What is the informant saying that I can use? Have I fully understood what this person is saying? Maybe, maybe not. I had better use a probe. Oh, yes I did understand. Now I can go on with a follow-up question'.

Strategies to enhance rapport should continue throughout the interview. Support the informant through verbal and non-verbal techniques that indicate that their responses are valued. Informants may sometimes recount experiences that upset them or stir other emotions. When an informant is becoming distressed, try pausing the interview or changing the topic and possibly returning to the sensitive issue at a later point. If the informant is clearly becoming very distressed you should probably terminate the interview.

There may be a stage in an interview when your informant does not answer a question. If there is a silence or if they shake their head, the informant may be indicating that they have not understood your question, or simply do not know the answer. They might be confused as to the format of the answer expected: is it a 'Yes / No' or something else (Minichiello et al. 1995, p. 93)? In these cases try restating the question, perhaps using an alternative wording or providing an example. You should always be prepared to elaborate on a question. It is important to remember, however, that choosing not to respond is the informant's right. If the informant refuses to answer, and says so, you should not usually press them. They may have chosen not to answer because the question was asked clumsily or insensitively (or for some other reason—if the question dealt with sensitive commercial matters, for instance). If you prepare your questions carefully you should avoid this sort of problem and the consequent loss of empathy and data.

BOX 6.9 FINISHING SENTENCES, INTERRUPTING, AND 'RUSHING-ON'

During February 2001, Minelle Mahtani (then of the University of British Columbia) joined me in Sydney to undertake joint, and comparative, research on the media and representations of ethnic minorities. This involved interviews with managers and employees within newsrooms. These were powerful and confident informants. Dr Mahtani had a wealth of expertise in such environments, having been a producer with the flagship Canadian Broadcasting Corporation's *The National*, a news television program. Our first field interview was with a Network News Editor for one of the commercial networks in Australia. Our questions included themes such as media representations of ethnic minorities, attempts by the organisation to improve the portrayal of ethnic minorities, the presence of 'minority' journalists, and circumstances where they or their staff had challenged stereotypical storylines. The questions had been developed and agreed in advance, but what very different styles we had! The informants would sometimes provide very short and dismissive responses to some questions. When it was clear they had answered I would probe, or move to another question. Dr Mahtani would wait however. The silence would hang heavy over the interview. I felt uncomfortable, but these powerful informants got the idea that we wanted a fuller response, and would attempt to justify the view they had briefly dismissed, or they would admit that there were alternative viewpoints to that they had expressed. Rushing-on or interrogating prompts were vastly inferior to the 'sounds of silence' for uncovering richer insight into ethnic minority representations and the dynamics of the newsroom (Dunn and Mahtani 2001).

As an interviewer, you should also learn to distinguish between reflective silence and non-answering. Robertson cautions, 'Do not be afraid of silences. Interviewers who consciously delay interrupting a pause often find that a few seconds of reflection leads interviewees to provide the most rewarding parts of an interview…There is no surer way of inhibiting interviewees than to interrupt, talk too much, argue, or show off your knowledge' (Robertson 1994, p. 44).

It is important to allow time for the informant to think, meditate, and reflect before they answer a question (see Box 6.9). It is also important to be patient with slow speakers or people who are not entirely host-language fluent. Resist any temptation to finish peoples' sentences for them. Supplying the word that an informant is struggling to find may seem helpful at the time, but it interrupts them and inserts a term they might not have ordinarily used. In some instances, such as in 'corporate interviews', non-answering may relate to commercial confidentiality or the protection of information that is being kept secret for other reasons. In such instances, a non-answer also becomes data.

Closing the interview

Do not allow rapport to dissipate at the close of an interview. It is critical to maintain rapport—especially if you intend to re-interview the informant. You must prepare for the closure of an interview otherwise the ending can be clumsy. Because an interview establishes a relationship within which certain expectations are created, it is better to indicate

---

BOX 6.10 TECHNIQUES FOR CLOSING INTERVIEWS

Four types of verbal cue:

- direct announcement
  'Well, I have no more questions just now.'
- clearing-house questions
  'Is there anything else you would like to add?'
- summarising the interview
  'So, would you agree that the main issues according to you are…?'
- making personal inquiries and comments
  'How are the kids?' or *'If you want any advice on how to oppose…just ring me.'*

Six types of non-verbal cue:

- looking at your watch
- putting the cap on your pen
- stopping or unplugging the tape recorder
- straightening your chair
- closing your notebook
- standing up and offering to shake hands.

Source: adapted from Minichiello et al. (1995, pp. 94–8).

a sense of continuation and of feedback and clarification than to end the interview with an air of finality.

Try not to rush the end of an interview. At the same time do not let an interview 'drag on'. There is an array of verbal and non-verbal techniques for closing interviews (Box 6.10). Of course, non-verbal versions should be accompanied by appropriate verbal cues otherwise you could appear quite rude. The most critical issue in closing an interview is to express not only thanks but also satisfaction with the material which was collected. For example you might say: 'Thanks for your time. I've got some really useful/insightful information from this interview'. Not only is gratitude expressed this way, but the informant is made aware that the process has been useful, and that their opinions and experiences have been valued.

RECORDING AND TRANSCRIBING INTERVIEWS

Interview recording, transcription, and fieldnote assembly are referred to as the mechanical phases of the interview method. These are the steps through which the data are collected, transformed, and organised for the final stages of analysis.

Recording

Audio recording and note-taking are the two main techniques for recording an interview. Other less commonly used techniques in geography include video recording, compiling records of the interview after the session has ended, and using cognitive maps. Both audio recording and note-taking have associated advantages and disadvantages, as will become clear in the discussion to follow. Therefore, a useful strategy of record keeping is to combine note-taking and audio recording.

The records of an interview should be as close to complete as possible. An audio recorder will help compile the fullest recording (Whyte 1982, pp. 117–18). Interviewers who use note-taking would need excellent short-hand writing skills to produce verbatim records. However, the primary aim in note-taking is to capture the gist of what was said.

Audio or video recording can allow for a natural conversational interview style because the interviewer is not preoccupied with taking notes. Instead, you can be a more attentive and critical listener. Audio recording is also preferable to note-taking because it allows you more time to organise the next prompt or question, and to maintain the conversational nature of the interview. The note-taking researcher can be so engrossed in note-taking that they can find themselves unprepared to ask the next question. Note-takers can also miss important movements, expressions, and gestures of the informant while they are hunched over and scribbling at a furious pace (Whyte 1982, p. 118). This all undermines rapport and detracts from attentive listening.

On the other hand, an audio recorder may sometimes inhibit an informant's responses because the recorder serves as a reminder of the formal situation of the interview (Douglas 1985, p. 83). Informants may feel particularly vulnerable because someone might recognise their voice if the recording was to be aired publicly. Opinions given by the informant on the 'spur of the moment' become fixed indelibly on tape (or disc or memory stick) and have the potential to become a permanent public record of the informant's views. This may lead to the informant being less forthcoming than they would have been if note-taking had been used. Some informants become comfortable with an audio recorder as the interview progresses, but others do not. If you find the latter situation to be the case, consider stopping the recorder and reverting to note-taking.

If you use an audio recorder, place it somewhere that is not too obvious without compromising the recording quality. The use of long-playing tapes will diminish your concern about whether a tape has stopped and minimise the interruption associated with changing tapes but, as George and Stratford point out in chapter 7, long tapes bring their own problems. Digital audio recorders pose less of a problem in this regard, with vastly longer recording capacities. However, this equipment can be quite expensive, especially when we add the cost of transcription pedals and software for your computer.

Take care when using an audio recorder not to be lulled into a loss of concentration by the feeling that everything is being recorded safely. There may be a technical failure. You can maintain concentration and avoid the problem associated with recorder failure by taking some written notes. If you are taking notes, there is little likelihood of mental wandering. Everything is being listened to, interpreted, and parts of it written down, demanding that you maintain concentration. I find this particularly important if I am conducting the second or third interview of a long day's fieldwork.

Because an audio recorder does not keep a record of non-verbal data, non-audible occurrences such as gestures and body language will be lost unless you are also using a video recorder or taking notes. If an informant points to a wall map and says: 'I used to live there', or if they say: 'The river was the colour of that cushion', then the audio recording will be largely meaningless without some written record. These written notes can be woven into the verbal record during the transcription phase (described later in this chapter). Written notes also serve as a back-up record in case of technical failures. Overall, then, a strategic combination of both audio recording and note-taking can provide the most complete record of an interview with the least threat to the interview relationship.

Transcribing the data

Whether using a tape (memory stick or disc) or notes, the record of an interview is usually written up to facilitate analysis. Interviews produce vast data sets that are next to impossible to analyse if they have not been converted to text. A transcript is a written 'reproduction of the formal interview which took place between researcher and informant' (Minichiello et al. 1995, p. 220). The transcript should be the best possible record of the interview, including descriptions of gestures and tone as well as the words spoken (although see Box 6.13 below). The name or initials of each speaker should precede all text in order to identify the interviewer(s) and informant(s). Counter numbers at the top and bottom of each page of the transcript enable quick cross-referencing between the **transcript** file and tapes or digital records of the interview. Converting interview to text is done either through a reconstruction from hand-written notes, a transcription of an audio or video recording, or through the use of voice recognition computer software (See Box 6.11). Issues particularly pertinent to the reconstruction of note-taking-based interviews are outlined below.

BOX 6.11 VOICE RECOGNITION COMPUTER PACKAGES AND INTERVIEWS

Computing packages have been developed that convert the spoken word into computer text. Packages such as NaturallySpeaking by Dragon Systems that convert text at the rate of 150 or 160 words per minute do not require that each word be enunciated separately. However, these systems will only convert the speech of a single speaker. Each system has to be 'trained' to understand a single 'master's voice', and multiple voice systems are still many years away. The success of these packages for converting interview data has been mixed. The researcher has to simultaneously listen to a recording and verbally repeat the informant's contributions to enable the system to convert the data. Gestures and indications of intonation have to be typed into the **word processing** document manually. Nonetheless, typists can train the software and then re-speak the interview, typing corrections (using the 'correct that' command) and inserting notations as they go (using hot-keys for speaker initials etc). Tiredness, flu, and alcohol have all been reported to reduce recognition accuracy.

Limitations of voice recognition software include the cost of the packages and the need for very powerful personal computers and a host of computer add-ons such as sound cards. Nonetheless, listserve reports lodged by researchers have claimed accuracy rates as high as 95% once the program has been 'trained'. I have read a claim that the new age of software requires only fifteen minutes of training, although my experience was that even after four hours of coaching the software was still getting every third word 'wrong', and some of the conversions were hilarious. It is critical that you save your speech files (the training) after each use, and it is advised that you use a very good quality microphone. It should also be noted that serious investigation of methodological issues that may surround voice recognition software has barely begun.

Interview notes should be converted into a typed format preferably on the same day as the interview. If there were two or more interviewers it is a good idea to compile a combined reconstruction of what was said using each researcher's notebook. This will improve the breadth and depth of coverage. The final typed record will normally comprise some material recalled verbatim as well as summaries or approximations of what was said.

Recorded interviews should also be transcribed as soon as possible after the interview. Transcription is a very time-consuming and therefore resource-intensive task (Whyte 1982, p. 118). On average, most interviews take four hours of typing per hour of interview. Transcription rates vary according to a host of variables such as typist skill, the type of interview, the informant, and the subject matter. You can facilitate transcription by using a purpose-built transcribing recorder. You should transcribe your own interviews for two main reasons. First, since you were present at the interview, you are best placed to reconstruct the interchange. You are aware of non-audible occurrences and therefore know where such events should be inserted into the speech record. You are also better able to understand the meaning of what was said and less likely to misinterpret the spoken words. Second, transcription, although time consuming, does enable you to engage with the data again. Immersion in the data provides a preliminary form of analysis.

BOX 6.12 SYMBOLS COMMONLY USED IN INTERVIEW TRANSCRIPTS

Symbol	Meaning
//	Speaker interrupted by another speaker or event: //phone rings//
:	Also used to indicate an interruption
KMD	The initials of the speaker, usually in CAPS and bold
—	When used at the left margin refers to an unidentified speaker
Ss	Several informants who said the same thing
E	All informants made the same comment simultaneously
…	A self-initiated pause by a speaker
…. or ……	Longer self-initiated pauses by a speaker
-	Speech which ended abruptly but without interruption
( )	Sections of speech, or a word, that can not be deciphered
(jaunty)	A best guess at what was said
(jaunty/journey)	Two alternative best guesses at what was said
*	Precedes a reconstruction of speech that was not taped
(…)	Material that has been edited out
But I didn't want to	Underlined text indicates stressed discourse
I got nothing	Italicised text indicates louder discourse
[sustained laughter]	Non-verbal actions, gestures, facial expressions
[hesitantly]	Background information on the intonation of discourse

While there is no accepted standard for symbols used in transcripts, some of the symbols commonly used are set out in Box 6.12.

Once completed, the transcript should be given a title page stating the informant's name (or a code if there are concerns of confidentiality), the number of the interview (for example, first or third session), the researcher(s) name(s) (i.e., who carried out the interview), the date of the session, the location, duration of interview, and any important background information on the informant or special circumstances of the interview. Quotations that demonstrate a particular point, and that could be presented as evidence in a final report on the research, might be circled or underlined.

The transcript can be given to the informant for vetting or authorising. This will normally improve the quality of your record (see Box 6.13). This process of **participant checking** continues the involvement of the informants in the research process and provides them with their own record of the interview.

BOX 6.13 DEBATES ABOUT CHANGING THE WORDS: VETTING AND CORRECTING

In general it has been thought a transcription should be a verbatim record of the interview. This would include poor grammar, false starts, 'ers' and 'umms'. There are a number of good reasons advanced for this position. A verbatim record will include the nuances of accent and **vernacular**, it will maintain a sense of hesitancy, and could demonstrate an embarrassment that was present. For example, Sarah Nelson (2003, p. 16) reflected on how the 'humming and hawing' of Ulster politicians when asked about sectarian killings was reflective of their hesitancy and hypocritical stances on sectarianism. Transcripts that are not exact textual replications of an interview will lose the ethnographic moment of the interview itself. Also, it may be difficult to search for key terms if they are 'mis-spelt' in a transcript (mis-spelt as a means to indicate accent or mis-pronunication).

However, a range of researchers working in different disciplines and countries have expressed some concern at the political effects of exact transcription. Many have reflected on the embarrassment that many informants articulate when they receive the transcript of their interview. They angst about the grammar, the false starts to their sentences, repetition, and the 'ers' and 'umms', and 'you knows'. This is even more strongly felt by informants who are living in societies where the dominant language is not their first language. Informants might be so concerned as to withdraw their interview, and avoid any future ones. Moreover, research reports on the less powerful in society (the poor, single mothers, youth groups) that use the real language of informants, and which are largely sympathetic to those people, can often portray them in a way that reproduces negative images and stereotypes. Nelson (2003) reflected on the way such quoted material reconstructs images of illiteracy, powerlessness, and inferiority. As stated earlier, transcription is a transformation of verbal encounter into text, it is a constructed document that is of the researcher's making (Green et al. 1997). As bell hooks (1990, p. 152) famously stated: 'I want to know your story. And then I will tell it back to you in a new way...Rewriting you, I write myself anew. I am still author, authority'. This seems to undermine some of the central claims for verbatim transcripts. It is also clear that informants are much more interested in the interpretation of their words and the outcomes. Many researchers recommend sending informants summaries or interpretations of the interview rather than transcripts. It is certainly a good idea to send informants the eventual publications and reports.

Assembling fieldnote files

Assembling interview records marks the beginning of the analysis proper. This begins with a critical assessment of the interview content and practice and is followed by formal preparation of interview logs. To my mind the best and most recent explanation of assembling fieldnote files is that by Minichiello et al. (1995, pp. 214–46). In the wide margins of the transcript file you can make written annotations. Comments that relate to the practice of the interview, such as the wording of questions and missed opportunities to prompt, should be placed in the left margin. These annotations and other issues concerned with contact, access, ethics, and overall method should be elaborated upon in a **personal log** (Box 6.14). The right margin of the transcript file can be used for annotations on the substantive issues of the research project. These comments, which generally use the language and jargon of social science, are then elaborated upon in the **analytical log**. The analytical log is an exploration and speculation about what the interview has found in relation to the research question (Box 6.14). It should refer to links between the data gathered in each interview and the established literature or theory.

BOX 6.14   FIELDNOTE FILES

Transcript file	*Personal log*	*Analytical log*
Includes the record of speech, and the interviewer's observations of non-audible data and intonation. Also includes written annotations in the margins on the practice and content of the interview.	Reflection on the practice of the interview. Includes comments on the questions asked and their wording, the appropriateness of the informant, recruitment and access, ethical concerns, and the method generally.	Exploration of the content of the interview. A critical outline of the substantive matters that have arisen. Identification of themes. Reference to the literature and theory. In-progress commentary on the research aims and findings.

Source: adapted from Minichiello et al. (1995, pp. 214–46).

ANALYSING INTERVIEW DATA

Researchers analyse interview data to seek meaning from the data. We construct themes, relations between variables, and patterns in the data through content analysis (see chapter 14). Content analysis can be based on a search of either manifest or latent content (Babbie 1992, pp. 318–19). **Manifest content analysis** assesses the visible, surface content of documents such as interview transcripts. An example would be a tally of the number of times the words 'cute' and 'cuddly' are used to describe koalas in interviews with members of the public. This might contribute to a broader assessment of the political significance of culling in areas of koala overpopulation (for example, Muller 1999). Searching interview data for manifest content often involves tallying the appearance of a word or phrase. Computer programs such as **NVivo** or N6 are particularly effective at undertaking these sorts of manifest searches (see chapter 15).

Latent content analysis involves searching the document for themes. For example you might keep a tally of each instance in which a female has been portrayed in a passive or active role. Latent content analysis of interview texts requires a determination of the underlying meanings of what was said. This determination of meanings within the text is a form of coding.

A coding system is used to sort and then retrieve data. For example, the text in transcripts of interviews with urban development authorities could be coded based on the following categories: structures of governance (for example, legislation, party political shifts), cultures of governance (with sub-codes like 'managerialist perspective' and 'entrepreneurial perspective'), coalitions and networks (of various type and agenda), the mechanisms through which coalitions operate, and the various scales at which power and influence emanate and are deployed (see McGuirk 2002). Once the sections of all the interviews have been coded, it is then possible to retrieve all similarly coded sections. These sections of text can be amalgamated and re-read as a single file (Box 6.15). This might allow a researcher to grasp the varying opinions on a certain issue and to begin to unravel the general feeling about an issue.

BOX 6.15   CODING INTERVIEW DATA: FIVE SUGGESTED STEPS

Coding step	*Specific operations:* computing */ manual versions*
Develop preliminary coding system	Prepare a list of emergent themes in the research. Draw on the literature, your past findings, as well as your memos and log comments. Amend throughout.
Prepare the transcript for analysis	Meet the formatting requirements for the computing package being used. / *Print out a fresh copy of the transcript for manual coding.*
Ascribe codes to text	Allocate coding annotations using the 'Code Text' function of computing packages. / *Place hand-written annotations on transcript.*
Retrieve similarly coded text	Use the 'Retrieve Text' function of computing packages to produce reports on themes. / *Extract and amalgamate sections of text that are similarly coded.*
Review the data by themes	Assess the diversity of opinion under each theme. Cross-referencing themes allows you to review instances where two themes are discussed together. Begin to speculate on relations between themes.

Not every section of text needs to be coded. An interview will include material that is not relevant to the research question, particularly warm-up and closing sections, and other speech focused on improving rapport rather than gathering data. Sections of text can also be multiple-coded. For example in one sentence an informant may list a number of causes of fish kills including open-cut mine run-off, super phosphates, acid sulphate soils, and town sewage. This may require that the sentence is attributed four different coding values. Coding is discussed more fully in chapter 14.

PRESENTING INTERVIEW DATA

Material collected from interviews is rarely presented in its entirety. Most interview data must be edited and (re)presented selectively in research publications. While it is difficult to locate a 'genuinely representative' statement (see Connell 1991, pp. 144–5; Minichiello et al. 1995, pp. 114–15), it is usually possible to indicate the general sense and range of opinion and experience expressed in interviews. One way to indicate this is to present summary statistics of what was said. Computing packages such as NVivo can help you calculate the frequency with which a particular term or phrase appeared in a document or section of text (see chapter 15). However, the more common method is through a literal description of the themes that emerged in the interviews (see for example, Boxes 6.6, 16.1 and 16.2, and the discussion in chapters 16 and 17 on presenting results).

When describing interview data you must cite transcript files appropriately. For example, in her interview-based honours research on the changing identity of the industrial city of Wollongong, Pearson (1996, p. 62) noted that 'Several respondents asserted that elements excluded by the new identity were of little significance to the overall vernacular identity of Wollongong' (Int.#1, Int.#6, and Int.#7). The transcript citations provided here indicate which of the informants expressed a particular type of opinion. In research publications the transcript citations can indicate the informant's name, number, code, or recorder count. Whenever a direct quotation from an informant is presented then a transcript page reference or recorder count should be provided.

Transcript material should be treated as data. A quotation, for example, ought to be treated in much the same way as a table of statistics. That is, it should be introduced and then interpreted by the author. The introduction to a quotation should offer, if it has not already been provided, some background on the informant. It is important that readers have some idea of where an informant is 'coming from'; information about their role, occupation, or status is important in this regard. Also important, as Baxter and Eyles (1997, p. 508) point out, is 'some discussion of why particular voices are heard and others are silenced through the selection of quotes'. Quotations should be discussed in relation to, and contrasted with, the experiences or opinions of other informants. Statements of opinion by an informant should also be assessed for internal contradiction. Finally, a quotation cannot replace a researcher's own words and interpretation. As the author you must explain clearly what theme or issue a quotation demonstrates.

Knowledge is a form of power. The accumulation and ownership of knowledge is an accumulation of power: power to effect change, power to support arguments, or to construct proofs. In most interviews, information and knowledge flow from the informant to the researcher. The researcher accumulates this knowledge and ultimately controls it. There is a host of strategies and guidelines to which researchers can adhere to reduce the potential political and ethical inequities of this relationship (see chapters 2, 4, and 16). In terms of data presentation it will sometimes be important that an informant's identity be concealed.

Pseudonyms or interviewee numbers have been used by geographers to disguise the identity of their informants where it has been thought that **disclosure** could be harmful. Informants can be given the opportunity to select their own pseudonym. Robina Mohammed (1999, pp. 238–9) used this technique, with some success, in her interviews with young Pakistani Muslim women in England. The interviews included discussion of patriarchal authority, 'English cultures', and the cultures and dynamics of the Pakistani Muslim community in Britain. Some informants selected Pakistani Muslim pseudonyms for themselves, others chose very English names. These selections were themselves very interesting, and provided further insight into the cultural perspectives and resistances of these women. Gill Valentine (1993) felt it necessary to disguise the name of the town in which her interviews with lesbians had taken place. Similarly, Pulvirenti (1997, p. 37) disguised the street names that were mentioned by female Italian–Australians when discussing their housing and settlement experiences in Melbourne.

Naming an informant (or locating them in any detailed way), and directly associating them to a quotation, could be personally, professionally, or politically harmful. Researchers must be very careful when they deploy data they have collected. Interviewers are privileged with insights into people's lives. Some researchers recommend instituting an alias or pseudonym for informants very early in the mechanical phase, such that there are no electronic records that bear the informant's real identity and to aid cross-referencing between files. However, it can prove difficult to remember who the real people were behind the aliases, and some researchers only impose the pseudonym in the presentation phase of the research. Research deals and promises should be respected. In this way the integrity of the researcher, and of the entire research community, will also be enhanced (Hay 1998).

Finally, the presentation of interview-based research must contain an accessible and transparent account of how the data were collected and analysed (Baxter and Eyles 1997, p. 518). This account should outline the subjectivity of the researcher, including their biases or 'positioned subjectivity' (see chapters 2, 4, and 16). Some indication should also be given on what procedures were used for selecting interview excerpts for presentation and of how instances of shared or divergent opinion were determined by the researcher. As we have already seen from the discussion in chapter 3, it is only through transparent accounts of how interview-based research was undertaken that the trustworthiness and wider applicability of the findings can be assessed by other researchers.

CONCLUSION

The rigour of interview-based research is enhanced through adequate preparation, diverse input, and verification of interpretation. Being well informed and prepared will allow a deeper understanding of the 'culture' and discourse of the group(s) you study. You can then formulate good questions and enhance levels of rapport between you and your informants. You should also purposely seek out diversity of opinion. Interviewing more than one informant from each study group will begin to draw out and invite controversy or tensions. An opinion from one informant should never be accepted as demonstrative of group opinion unless it is shown to be the case. Finally, some means of verifying your interpretations of interview data are necessary (for example, participant checking, peer checking, and cross-reference to documentary material).

Interviews bring people 'into' the research process. They provide data on peoples' behaviour and experiences. They capture informants' views of life. Informants use their own words or vernacular to describe their own experiences and perceptions. Kearns (1991, p. 2) made the point that 'there is no better introduction to a population than the people themselves'. This is what I find to be the most refreshing aspect of interview material. Transcribed interviews are wholly unlike other forms of data. The informant's non-academic text reminds the researcher and the reader of the lived experience that has been divulged. It reminds geographers that there are real people behind the data.

KEY TERMS

aide-mémoire

analytical log

critical inner dialogue

funnelling

informant

interview guide

interview schedule

latent content analysis

life history

manifest content analysis

NVivo

oral history

participant checking

personal log

primary question

prompt

pyramid structure

rapport

semi-structured interview

structured interview

transcript

unstructured interview

REVIEW QUESTIONS

1   Select one of the four questions below and spend about fifteen minutes constructing an interview schedule for a hypothetical five-minute interview with one of your colleagues. Use a mix of primary question types and prompts. Think about the overall structure of your schedule and provide a sense of order to the way the issues are covered. Try to imagine how you will cope if the interviewee is aggressive, very talkative, or non-communicative. Will your schedule still work?

   a   Most of us would agree that a greater use of public transport is an environmentally and economically sound goal. However most of us would personally prefer to use a private car and only pay lip service to such noble goals. Why?

   b   Beach activity is decidedly spatial. Performances are expressive and behaviour is at times territorial.

   c   The re-integration of the differently abled into 'normal society' is a noble ideal. However, this integration will always be confounded by the organisation of public space and the reactions of the able-bodied when the differently abled are in public space.

   d   The Local Environment Plan (LEP) of every local council should allocate a specific area for sex industry uses.

2   Conduct two semi-structured in-depth interviews with someone of an older generation than yourself. It could be an older relative (however, do not interview a sibling or parent). Limit both interviews to approximately thirty minutes. Construct an interview guide that operationalises key concepts in the following research question: 'Ours is a patriarchal society. We are often told, however, that the society of our parents and grandparents was structured by an even more restrictive and oppressive system of sexism and compulsory heterosexuality. Investigate how the opportunities, resources, and experiences differed according to gender for earlier generations. Pay particular attention to gender variations in the use of, and access to, space'.

3   Devise a list of rapport strategies you could use if you were to interview an older relative not well known to you. Consider the preliminary, contact, warm-up, and closing phases of the interview.

SUGGESTED READING

Baxter, J. and Eyles, J. 1997, 'Evaluating qualitative research in social geography: establishing "rigour" in interview analysis', *Transactions of the Institute of British Geographers*, vol. 22, no. 4, pp. 505–25.

Bennett, K. 2002, 'Interviews and focus groups', in P. Shurmer-Smith (ed.), *Doing Cultural Geography*, Sage, London.

Blunt, A. 2003, 'Home and identity', in A. Blunt, P. Gruffudd, J. May, M. Ogborn and D. Pinder (eds), *Cultural Geography in Practice*, Arnold, Euston.

Cloke, P., Cook, I., Crang, P., Goodwin, M., Painter, J. and Philo, C. (eds) 2004, 'Talking to people', in *Practising Human Geography*, Sage, London.

Douglas, J. D. 1985, *Creative Interviewing*, Sage, Beverly Hills.

Edwards, J. A. and Lampert, M. D. (eds) 1993, *Talking Data: Transcription and Coding in Discourse Research*, Lawrence Erlbaum Associates, Hillsdale, New Jersey.

Findlay, A. M. and Li, F. L. N. 1997, 'An auto-biographical approach to understanding migration: the case of Hong Kong emigrants', *Area*, vol. 29, no. 1, pp. 34–44.

Kearns, R. 1991, 'Talking and listening: avenues to geographical understanding', *New Zealand Journal of Geography*, vol. 92, pp. 2–3.

Minichiello, V., Aroni, R., Timewell, E. and Alexander, L. 1995, *In-Depth Interviewing: Principles, Techniques, Analysis*, 2nd edn, Longman Cheshire, Melbourne.

Oakley, A. 1981, *From Here to Maternity: Becoming a Mother*, Penguin, Harmondsworth.

Robertson, B. M. 2000, *Oral History Handbook*, 4th edn, Oral History Association of Australia SA Branch Inc, Adelaide.

Schoenberger, E. 1991, 'The corporate interview as a research method in economic geography', *Professional Geographer*, vol. 43, no. 2, pp. 180–9.

Tremblay, M. A. 1982, 'The key informant technique: a non-ethnographic application', in R. G. Burgess (ed.), *Field Research: A Sourcebook and Field Manual*, Allen & Unwin, London.

Valentine, G, 1997, 'Tell me about…: using interviews as a research methodology', in R. Flowerdew and D. Martin (eds), *Methods in Human Geography: A Guide for Students Doing a Research Project*, Longman, Harlow, pp. 110–26.

Whyte, W. F. 1982, 'Interviewing in field research', in R. G. Burgess (ed.), *Field Research: A Sourcebook and Field Manual*, Allen & Unwin, London.

7

Oral History and Human Geography

Karen George and Elaine Stratford

CHAPTER OVERVIEW

This chapter describes ways in which oral history can be used in geographical research. After defining oral history, we outline the unique aspects of oral history that distinguish it from other forms of interviewing. These include: establishing rapport, dealing with sensitive issues, understanding the ethics of interviewing, ways to ask questions, and the importance of sound quality.

INTRODUCTION

It was a blinking dust storm. Every time you come up to Loxton there was you got off the track oh well that's where you was until you got yourself out again and it was always blowing dust. I thought 'Gawd' I always used to say, 'Fancy living up in this hole' (Ruth Scadden in George 1999a, p. 161).

These are the words of Ruth Scadden, the wife of a soldier settler, who was eyewitness to major environmental change in the horticultural town of Loxton in South Australia's Riverland after World War II. Over the past 50 years this farming area and 'dust bowl' has been gradually transformed into an irrigated oasis producing citrus fruits, grapes, and stone fruits for Australian and overseas markets. Ruth is now witnessing further change as long-term irrigation affects the River Murray. Her perceptions, understanding of rural life, and representations of that life to others are threads of everyday and ordinary existence whose cumulative weavings constitute a rich tapestry of geographical knowledge.

Ultimately what has always struck me as being remarkably interesting about how one is influenced is that there is a local geography involved. For example, when I was working in Bougainville, there was one other academic working on the island, an anthropologist, and simply because we met fairly frequently we managed to produce two or three joint articles together and that situation seems to me to have always continued. So there are these local factors which no one can actually build into an intellectual trajectory or even practical planning, have been incredibly important at how one actually shapes what it is one does (John Connell, Geographer).

These are the recollections of a scholar in the field, recorded at interview for the Institute of Australian Geographers' Millennium Project on Australian Geography and Geographers. His words trace just some of the complex lines that ultimately form the web of an individual's life experiences and locales.

This chapter outlines the basic scope of oral history as a technique in gathering information from participants in social research—people such as Ruth Scadden and John Connell. It describes how oral history can be a powerful source of situated learning and can facilitate enhanced understandings of space, place, region, landscape, and environment—the five central filaments of human geography. Importantly, the chapter also summarises a range of ethical, technical, and communicative guidelines for the effective conduct of oral history.

WHAT IS ORAL HISTORY AND WHY USE IT IN GEOGRAPHICAL RESEARCH?

The practice of oral history involves a prepared interviewer recording a particular kind of interview. The interview is usually conducted in an informal question-and-answer format with a person who has first-hand knowledge of a subject of interest. Background preparation allows the interviewer to follow-up responses and prompt further information. Oral history interviews may concern a very specific subject or cover an entire lifespan.

Historian Alan Nevins first used the term 'oral history' in the 1940s to describe a project at Columbia University in which the memories of a group of eminent Americans were recorded (Robertson 2000, p. 3). While 'oral *tradition*' as a method of passing stories down through generations has existed for centuries, oral *history* was defined differently because its aim was to record the first-hand knowledge and experience of interviewees. During the 1960s and 1970s the value of oral history in discovering and preserving the experiences of ordinary people was recognised. Since then oral history has become an important tool in studying hidden histories and geographies, the place-based lives and memories of disadvantaged people, minority groups, and others whose views have been ignored or whose lives pass quietly, producing few, if any written records. In short, there are insights to be gained from oral histories to better understand space, place, landscape, region, and environment in ways that are sensitive to context and that reflect the cultural turn in geography (Stratford 1997, 1999).

American geographer Isaiah Bowman suggested that 'Geography tells what is where, why and what of it' (Rivera 1997). To borrow Bowman's phraseology, oral history tells what happened, how, why, and what it was like from a personal perspective. For this reason it has become a useful tool in human geography, enabling insights into how recollections and representations are *placed* over extended periods, and allowing researchers and participants to track and understand changes across spatial scales as well as temporal ones. In this respect, oral history has been described as the voice of the past (Thompson 2000) and as 'a picture of the past in people's own words' (Robertson 2000, p. 2). As a research method, it provides a means to step back to the mix of past times and places *as these are mediated* through the words and memories of another person in the present.

Another way of thinking about oral history in relation to human geography is to acknowledge that people are witnesses to and participants in all change, including environmental change—and here we mean 'environment' broadly as 'that which surrounds'. While documents and photographs may tell part of the story, eyewitness accounts can deepen the image and provide unique detail from many different perspectives. Take, for example, how oral history helps to uncover people's experiences of the built environment and to trace the narratives of their geographical engagements there. As oral historian for the Adelaide City Council, Karen George learned from statistical records in Annual Reports that during the 1950s and 1960s the population of the City declined markedly. Many buildings were declared unfit for human habitation and residents were forced out of the city as it was being transformed into a business district. Only when she interviewed such former residents did Karen understand the significance of this phenomenon. The city was not only the home of individual families, but also a community and a support network. Destruction of homes resulted in the breakdown of this network. People described meeting places that no longer exist and reminisced about people they used to see every day. From such stories Karen reconstructed an image of the city before the exodus. Interviews with a health inspector who had declared many of the houses unfit allowed her to see the event from another perspective. Ironically, events have now gone full circle and the Council is vigorously encouraging people to move back to the city to live and to build new community networks and sense of place (City of Adelaide Oral History Collection, Adelaide City Archives).

A second example shows how oral history can uncover how geographers themselves understand their professional contributions to how space, place, region, landscape, and environment are constituted. As coordinator of the Millennium Project since 1996, Elaine Stratford has been encouraging members of the profession to 'gather' oral histories from eminent geographers (Stratford 2001; see also Hay 2003b; Sheridan 2001). Interviewees are asked to give some thought to the contributions that geography has made or may make to Australian society. Two responses begin to hint at the wealth of disciplinary knowledge that can be gained by the extended and in-depth interview style of oral history.

> I think that geography could continue its contribution to the development of Australian society by expanding the public imagination and...values about [the public's]...relationship with the environment and so on. Because it is a very special place here, a very special environment with special needs and so on (Joseph Powell).

> I think geography has made an enormous contribution. It would be difficult to look at that in its totality because different geographers are obviously looking at that component from the perspective of the work that they themselves have done. I think geography has contributed or could contribute again enormously to the understanding of the habitation of this country and what this means for the future (Elspeth Young).

HOW IS ORAL HISTORY DIFFERENT FROM INTERVIEWING?

In chapter 6, Kevin Dunn describes in detail how to conduct research interviews. Most of his guidelines hold true for oral history. However, oral history practice does differ from interview practice in a number of ways, which we set out in the sections below.

Perhaps one of the clearer differences between interviewing for research and conducting oral history interviews is that many elements in the oral history process place particular emphasis on the role of the interviewee. Through preparations and techniques that make an interviewee comfortable with taping an interview, oral historians aim to record as natural, rounded, and complete a story as possible.

Starting ethically

Matt Bradshaw and Elaine Stratford note in chapter 5 that because it is a significant matter to engage with research participants and share, interpret, and represent their experiences, these acts require an ethical approach. Oral history work involving researchers from tertiary institutions must be assessed and approved by those institutions' ethics committees. Similarly, private practitioners must be ethical in their approach, and membership of oral history associations demands this. Thus, in describing below the various stages and techniques of oral history we assume that ethical considerations and/or clearances are in place before research commences—a matter that has parallels with interviewing more generally and on which subject Kevin Dunn elaborates in chapter 6 of this volume.

On matters of ethics in oral history as a specific mode of research practice distinct from interviewing, it is useful to note that the Oral History Association of Australia (<http://cwpp.slq.qld.gov.au/ohaa/>) was established in 1978 to promote the practice and methods of oral history; educate in the ethical use of oral history methods; encourage discussion on all aspects of oral history; and foster the preservation of oral history records. There are branches of the association in each state and similar organisations exist internationally.

As well as providing advice and training in oral history, the Association has drawn up 'Guidelines for ethical practice'. It strongly advises that these guidelines, which protect the rights of both interviewee and interviewer, are followed by anyone involved in oral or life history. These guidelines are available from the association. Similar organisations exist in the UK (<http://www.oralhistory.org.uk/>), the USA (<http://www.dickinson.edu/oha/>), Canada (<http://www.ncf.carleton.ca/oral-history>), and New Zealand (<http://www.oral-history.org.nz/>). Many such associations belong to the International Oral History Association (<http://www.ioha.fgv.br/>).

Getting to know your informant—the preliminary meeting

Establishing rapport with an interview participant is integral to success. Oral historians use a particular approach to help establish rapport and the **preliminary meeting** is a key part of this. After contact by letter or phone, the interviewer arranges a meeting, usually at the home of the participant. No audio recorder is produced at this orientation session. Rather, the time is used to establish a relationship, gather background information, and 'assess' the participant and interview environment. Some practitioners use an information sheet to record information about their informant, such as where and when they were born, aspects of their school, employment and/or personal background, and other data that might be pertinent to the interview. Although much of this material might be covered again in the recorded interview, preliminary notes establish context and ensure accuracy, for instance in spelling and pronunciation.

The preliminary meeting also offers opportunities to ask to see materials that may enhance research. News-clippings, letters, diaries, or photographs may suggest new questions not previously considered. If a new topic is raised in the interview proper, you may be unprepared to ask questions about it. If it emerges in a preliminary session, you have time to conduct further research about it before the interview.

Assessing the participant sounds clinical, but some people remember things and are able to talk about them more readily than others. You may find that someone you thought would provide you with great material remembers very little, is extremely nervous, or overly wary about their responses. Thus at a preliminary meeting you have the opportunity to defer or cancel the interview by saying that your participant has provided what you needed. This strategy can be less embarrassing for participant and interviewer than a stilted recording, filled with clipped responses and phrases like 'I don't remember', 'I don't recall'.

Sensitive issues

If a project deals with sensitive issues (including personal, political, or professional details that may require the researcher to guarantee the confidentiality of parts of the oral history transcript), a preliminary meeting will allow you to discover how your participant feels about answering particular questions or exploring aspects or phases of their life or the subject under investigation. Even when interviewing in a subject area that seems uncontentious, it is good practice to assure the participant of their right to provide no answer or to withdraw from the research altogether without prejudice. Discussing these matters in advance saves embarrassment during an interview and allows participants to think in advance about what they might wish to say about difficult subjects.

Sensitive subjects can arise unexpectedly during interview. If this happens, exercise care and consideration. Ask your interviewee if s/he wishes to continue or would rather stop. If they wish to continue, let them speak. If the subject material becomes very personal and you think that it should be excluded, let the interviewee know this. University ethics committees often make the useful suggestion that if the participant is distressed, you might ask if s/he would like you to call a friend or family member, or provide details of a helpful counsellor.

After the interview is over, allow time for winding down. Winding down can be as simple as accepting another cup of tea, or listening to other stories not related to the research subject.

Multiple interviews

Unless there are unavoidable constraints, oral history recordings with an interviewee may be completed over several sessions. Where longer recordings are feasible, individual sessions may be confined to an hour or so, and second and subsequent occasions used to complete the history.

Multiple interviews can be very valuable. There is time between appointments for you to listen to the initial recording and note responses to enlarge upon later. Participants may also reflect on their answers: remembering triggers further memories to be shared at ensuing meetings. By a third or even fourth meeting a bond between interviewer and participant has usually developed, which can result in an even better interview.

The question of questions

Open questions are integral to effective oral history. These questions begin with words like who, what, where, when, why, and how. They reveal who was involved in an event, what happened, where and when it happened, how it felt, and why that was so. They yield the details that make oral history such an effective source of nuanced (if always partial) recollections.

In chapter 6 Kevin Dunn refers to secondary questions or 'prompts', which oral historians often label '**follow-up questions**'. These often comprise the body of an interview. Most are prompted by a participant's response to an initial question. If a participant says that his or her first day on the job was 'frightening', the logical follow-up question is 'why?' or 'in what way?' If he or she responds by saying that 'fellow-workers were aggressive', a logical follow-up question is, 'can you give me an example?'. Through follow-up questions, great depth may be added to the detail of information being sought.

Interview structure

Oral histories can appear to be 'unstructured', but such is not really the case. Interview guides or *aides-mémoire* are often used. Interviews in the tradition of oral histories can often be divided into a three-part format, comprising orientation, common, and specific questions. As Robertson points out, this:

> three part structure provides an excellent framework for interviews. It helps you to avoid aimless or superficial interviews and it can lead to recordings that are easier to use for research, publication or broadcast because of their well-defined structure and focus (Robertson 2000, p. 22).

Orientation questions establish the participant's background. **Common questions** are those asked of each participant in a project. They build up varying views and information about certain themes. **Specific questions** relate to individual experiences and are developed through follow-up work. The flow of the interview is determined by participant responses, so follow-up questions are always different across interviews.

Questioning the source

As the sections above suggest, oral history is active and shared; you can question the source. For example, as part of Karen George's South Australian research on post War Service Land Settlement after 1945, she consulted written records of applicant interviews with the Land Board. Although these documents included Board members' notes about applicant responses, she could not ask them 'what do you mean by that?' When conducting oral histories with people who had appeared before the Board, she could. Karen then created as complete a picture of those Board interviews as memory allowed. She was able to ask what happened that particular day, what the interviewers were like, how respondents felt about the questions when they were asked, and after the experience (George 1999a).

Sound quality, interview sites, and other technical issues

Oral history is *always* recorded via audio- and sometimes audio-visual technologies, and predominantly on analogue and digital tape recorders: a significant aim is to create **sound documents**. Oral history preserves the participants' voices and content of their interviews. High-quality sound allows the emotion, inflections, and tone of each voice to be heard. It is also important because material may be used for broadcast. Background noises, interruptions, substandard recording equipment, and a too-talkative interviewer diminish sound quality.

Because you are recording a unique sound document, it is important to tape interviews in a location that is as quiet as possible, and to use the best equipment available. Oral History Associations in all countries are the best place to make enquiries about equipment hire. High-quality recorders are often available for loan from libraries and, in Australia, from branches of the Oral History Association of Australia (OHAA). Some of these organisations also run workshops on the conduct of oral history and the correct use of recording equipment.

Even if you are using a basic audio recorder, a high-quality recording is possible if you use an external microphone. Recorders that have internal microphones record so much of their own workings that they never produce a high-quality outcome. If you are using audiotapes, always use 60-minute ones (30 minutes each side) as they are much less likely to break or become damaged than the thinner 90- and 120-minute varieties. Robertson's *Oral History Handbook* is an excellent source of information on all recording equipment, from budget priced, to super high-quality (see Robertson 2000, chapter 4). Recording technology is constantly undergoing change and many types of new digital recording devices are now becoming available. It may be prudent to seek professional advice from organisations such as the OHAA before investing in new equipment. Extra tapes and batteries are a must whether using analogue or digital tape-based technology. If using other forms of digital recording technology, it is important to remember to download sound files after each interview to ensure that you have back-up copies of work completed.

No matter what type of recorder you are using, always try to find somewhere quiet and free from interruptions to conduct an interview—office or work environments are among the worst locations. Private homes usually offer a dining room or lounge, both of which can be quieter. Avoid kitchens where possible. Refrigerators are renowned for droning away in the background or cutting in and out with a thump. Ticking or chiming clocks should be stopped or removed as their regular pulse in the background is distracting. If you cannot avoid background noises completely, such as traffic sounds from a busy road, direct the interviewee's microphone away from the noise. Close doors and windows to minimise background noises. If you talk about these things at your preliminary meeting, participants will usually help out and will not think you are being rude when you ask them to stop great-grandmother's cuckoo clock or to turn off the fridge!

Interpreting non-verbal responses and gestures is common to oral histories and other interviews. The comment 'It was about this big' needs to be translated by the interviewer into, 'about a metre high'. It is best to say this on tape as you might forget later. Recall, too, that an interviewer's verbal responses can be detrimental to a sound recording, particularly one for broadcast purposes. A litany of 'yes, yes', 'mmm', 'oh really', or 'wow' remarks that commonly occur in a conversation interrupts the recorded flow of a story. Respond with a nod or a smile instead. Let participants know you will remain quiet *and* involved. Listen to your own recordings to gauge how silent you actually are. A pause, a moment of quietness, may be the instant before the best story. Oral history also can be a demanding process for participants and they may need time to stop and reflect. Be sure to allow them this time. Silence on tape can also be very emotive. Long seconds of silence recorded in the midst of a painful story reveal a struggle with strong emotions better than words ever could.

WHY AND HOW TO MAKE ORAL HISTORY ACCESSIBLE?

Interviews conducted for research often have very limited circulation. However, in oral history, practitioners are encouraged to deposit their tapes into libraries or archives. This step ensures the preservation of master or original tapes, and, if the participant has agreed, allows recordings to be made available to other researchers. It is always worthwhile to search oral history collections *before* you begin an interview to make sure that your informant has not already been interviewed, and to check whether there are other tapes that might provide data for your project. Even interviews concerning completely different topics may contain useful information. For example, as the majority of the men and women Karen George (1999a) interviewed about soldier settlement in South Australia grew up during the Depression, a researcher interested in that period of history could glean a lot of information from their answers to questions about their background and childhood.

Another advantage of depositing tapes in a library is that some larger repositories offer limited assistance with the transcription of interviews. Whether you produce full transcripts, timed tape logs (which note subjects discussed at different time points in the recording), or broad interview summaries is normally dependent on the project's aim and on funding. Professional transcription is expensive, but worthwhile if material from interviews is to be reproduced in a publication. It is worth noting here that professional transcriptionists are trained to reflect pauses and the unique cadences of the spoken word through punctuation and layout. Transcripts are rarely completely verbatim as it is a common phenomenon for interviewees to become concerned at poor grammar, repetition, and crutch phrases (such as 'you know'), common in speech, when they see them in print (see chapter 6 for additional discussion on this matter).

Making interviews, both tapes and transcripts, accessible to others should only be done with the signed agreement of your participants. It is essential that you draft a **'conditions of use' form** outlining what will happen to the material they share with you— what their rights are, who will own copyright, where the tapes will be stored and for how long, and what they will be used for. Although interviewees should be encouraged to share their stories with a wide audience, they must be allowed to add conditions to this agreement, to restrict portions of the recording, or the entire interview until after their death if they wish to do so.

USES OF ORAL HISTORY—SPREADING THE WORD

As well as depositing oral history tapes into libraries or archives and using information from interviews in published and unpublished writing, there are other ways of sharing the results of your project. If you have made high-quality recordings, the possibilities are extensive. While quotations from interviews can be presented in displays and on the Web in written form, it can be even more effective to use sound excerpts. Sound bytes used on a web page allow users to hear as well as read about your interviews. Listening posts—that is, posts with speakers in them—may be used as part of exhibitions, or portions of interviews can be used in taped audio commentary.

Well-recorded interviews offer much scope for presentations to groups, in radio, film, and video. For example, the voices of long-term employees of Balfours, one of the last city-based factories in Adelaide, were used effectively in conjunction with video recording of the working of the bakery (Starkey and George 2003). By using images and oral history excerpts, this project recorded and preserved images and descriptions of the original factory and of the processes that will no longer be used when the factory relocates to modern suburban premises. Certainly, narration may be made much more engaging when excerpts from oral histories are played in conjunction with visual materials.

LAST WORDS

Geography's central concern is to understand people in place, spatial relations, landscapes, regions, and environments. It also aims to contribute to research-based outcomes that advance well being. For many geographers, these composite tasks involve philosophical and political investments in learning about—rather than appropriating—marginal, informal, and otherwise-undocumented perspectives (see chapter 3), as well as in comprehending those that are central, formal, and documented. Like the interview or focus group, oral history techniques allow both researchers and participants to explore the nuances of social and spatial interactions, events, and processes in ways that can make these goals possible. However, in the pursuit of these goals, never forget that your 'source' is another human being, a person sharing with you a distinctive and valuable gift, their memory.

KEY TERMS

common questions	orientation questions
conditions of use form	preliminary meeting
follow-up question	sound document
open questions	specific questions

REVIEW QUESTIONS

1   What are some of the ethical issues associated with of oral history?
2   What are some of the relationships between oral history and human geography?
3   What are some of the ways in which oral history might help you explore an area of human geography in which you are interested?
4   Develop an idea for an oral history project; prepare a list of potential interviewees; and search existing oral history collections for previously recorded interviews on related topics.
5   Record an interview paying particular attention to sound quality. Develop a multi-media spoken or Web-based presentation using excerpts from the interview combined with other media—such as photographs and documents. You could present this as a talk or on the Web.
6   Develop a conditions of use form to be used in conjunction with one of the two projects above.

SUGGESTED READING

George, K. 1999a, *A Place of Their Own: The Men and Women of War Service Land Settlement at Loxton after the Second World War*, Wakefield Press, Adelaide.

—— 1999b, *City Memory, A Guide and Index to the City of Adelaide Oral History Collection*, Corporation of the City of Adelaide.

Hay, I. 2003, 'From "Millennium" to "Profiles": Geography's Oral Histories across the Tasman', *Proceedings of the 22nd Conference of the New Zealand Geographical Society*, 6–11 July, University of Auckland, New Zealand, pp. 5–6.

Rivera, M. 1997, *Various definitions of geography* (online), Available: <http://www2.westga.edu/~geograph/define.html> (Accessed: 22 August 2004).

Robertson, B. M. 2000, *Oral History Handbook*, 4th edn, Oral History Association of Australia SA Branch Inc, Adelaide.

Sheridan, G. 2001, 'Dennis Norman Jeans: historical geographer and landscape interpreter extraordinaire', *Australian Geographical Studies*, vol. 39, no. 1, pp. 96–106.

Starkey, A. (video recording) and George, K. (interviews) 2003, *Balfour's City Site, 1910–2003*, Corporation of the City of Adelaide.

Stratford, E. 2001, 'The Millennium Project on Australian Geography and Geographers: An Introduction', *Australian Geographical Studies*, vol. 39, no. 1, pp. 91–5.

—— 1997, 'Memory work in geography and environmental studies: some suggestions for teaching and research', *Australian Geographical Studies*, vol. 35, no. 2, pp. 208–21.

Thompson, P. 2000, *The Voice of the Past: Oral History*, 3rd edn, Oxford University Press, New York.

8

Focusing on the Focus Group

Jenny Cameron

CHAPTER OVERVIEW

An investigation of community responses to literature on environmental sustainability (Myers and Macnaghten 1998), a study of rapid social and economic change in non-metropolitan regions (Gibson et al. 1999), an examination of the construction of identity through shopping (Jackson and Holbrook 1995), and an exploration of the experiences of Filipina domestic workers in Canada (Pratt 2002)—all of these are examples of research projects that employ focus groups as a means of disentangling the complex web of relations and processes, meaning and representation, that comprise the social world. With the shift to more nuanced explorations of people–place relationships in geography the focus group method has been recognised increasingly as a valuable research tool.

Focus groups can be exhilarating and exciting, with people responding to the ideas and viewpoints expressed by others, and introducing you, the researcher, and other group members to new ways of thinking about an issue or topic. This chapter discusses the diverse research potential of focus groups in geography, outlines the key issues to consider when planning and conducting successful focus groups, and provides an overview of strategies for analysing and presenting the results.

WHAT ARE FOCUS GROUPS?

The focus group method involves a small group of people discussing a topic or issues defined by a researcher. Briefly, a group of between six and ten people sit facing each other around a table (see Figure 8.1), the researcher introduces the topic for discussion and then invites and moderates discussion from group members. A session usually lasts for between one and two hours (you might see parallels here with university tutorial group meetings!).

Figure 8.1 The synergistic effect that occurs in a focus group discussion as members listen and respond to each other's contributions.

Interaction between members of the group is a key characteristic of this research method, and it is that which helps differentiate focus groups from the interview method, where interaction is between interviewer and interviewee. The group setting is generally characterised by dynamism and energy as people respond to the contributions of others (see Box 8.1). One comment, for example, can trigger a chain of responses. This type of interaction has been described as the 'synergistic' effect of focus groups and some propose that it results in far more information being generated than in other research methods (Berg 1989; Stewart and Shamdasani 1990). In the focus group excerpt in Box 8.1, for example, the discussion shifts from family farming practices, to people's commitment to an area, to ways of working with government, to projects that address environmental degradation. Yet as the farmer points out at the conclusion of this excerpt, the speakers all highlight the effect that taking a long-term approach has on economic, environmental, and community practices.

The interactive aspect of focus groups also provides an opportunity for people to explore different points of view, and formulate and reconsider their own ideas and understandings. Kitzinger (1994, p. 113) describes this form of interaction in the following terms: '[p]articipants do not just agree with each other. They also misunderstand one another, question one another, try to persuade each other of the justice of their own point of view and sometimes they vehemently disagree'. For researchers who are interested in the socially constructed nature of knowledge this aspect of focus groups makes them an ideal research method; the multiple meanings that people attribute to places, relationships, processes, and events are expressed and negotiated, thereby providing important insights into the practice of knowledge production.

BOX 8.1 THE 'SYNERGISTIC' EFFECT OF FOCUS GROUPS

Farmer A: Where we make a mistake in business is in thinking of tomorrow. The family approach is what's happening to the next generation. It's a much longer term approach. I'm more interested in investing my resources for the next generation and therefore you build a solid business.

Farmer B: My attitude is that I'm the tenant in time.

Farmer A: The custodian.

Farmer B: Yeah, the custodian. My father gave it to me and I'll hand it on to the next generation. And people say you could sell it and make lots of money but that just doesn't come into the equation. The thought of selling it and leaving the good life—the kids probably will. And I think there are an awful lot of farmers with that attitude. And I think it has probably in lots of ways been to our detriment. We could use that asset and make more money—as if money is the most important thing.

Consultant: I think that's right. I think one of the important reasons there have been successes and perhaps less problems here is that even though we have all identified lots of problems, we are really committed to this community and making it better. And I think there are an amazing range of people that do choose to live here—they don't have to—but choose to live here and [have] invested huge amounts of time and energy. And I also think this community, just thinking back to my experience, that it's really open to working with whatever government is in at the time and turning the rules or the policies or the dollars that are around for the best here. Like local government saying we don't want yet another regional development board but we will have the money and this is our structure and this is what we'll do. I think there has been some creative use of government money and good partnerships and also just that huge commitment, that energy to make it work.

Manager: You mention our successes and I think one of the unheralded things we've done really well is look towards the sustainability of the whole area from land management which underpins our whole economy. Because we've poured irrigation water onto this country for years and years and we've never really looked at the repercussions: the drainage problems, the salinity problems. And I think in recent years, in the last fifteen, twenty years, that's really been addressed—the work that's gone into it by some very dedicated people and I think that message has gone across to virtually all land holders in the area. With the advent of some major arterial drains, community drains, the cooperation—the cooperatives virtually that have been formed to bring this into being, really will underpin the future of our economy and the management of our natural resource, which is absolutely vital to the future of our farmers and businesses etc.

Consultant: And a lot of that work's been voluntary.

Farmer A: It all comes back to the notion that it's the next generation. It's a different approach.

Source: videotape excerpt from focus group conducted by Katherine Gibson, Jenny Cameron and Arthur Veno, Shepparton, Victoria, 5 June 1997 (see Gibson et al. 1999).

A second characteristic is the pivotal role of the researcher, who promotes group interaction and focuses the discussion on the topic or issue. The researcher draws out the range of views and understandings held within the group, and manages—and sometimes even encourages—disagreement between participants (Myers 1998). By comparison, in an observation situation, the researcher may have a more 'hands off' role (see chapter 12).

Initially focus groups can be extremely challenging for researchers who are new to the process. They are, however, well worth it. In focus groups the diversity of processes and practices that make up the social world and the richness of the relationships between people and places can be addressed and explored explicitly. A not inconsequential consideration is that group members almost invariably enjoy interacting with each other, offering their points of view, and learning from each other. Researchers also find the process refreshing (for example, see the discussion by two skeptical anthropologists in Agar and MacDonald (1995)).

USING FOCUS GROUPS IN GEOGRAPHY

Focus group discussions—or **focused interviews**, as they were originally known (Merton 1987)—were used by sociologists in the USA during World War II to examine the impact of wartime propaganda and the effectiveness of military training materials (Merton 1987; Morgan 1997). Although this work resulted in several sociological publications on the technique, focus groups were neglected by social scientists in the post-World War II period in favour of one-to-one interviews and participant observation (Johnson 1996). It was in the field of market research that the focus group method found a home. Since the 1980s there has been renewed interest in the technique among social scientists and this has led to considerable diversity in the practice of focus group research (Lunt and Livingstone 1996; Morgan 1997). Focus groups can be a highly efficient data gathering tool but they are also appropriate in 'more critical, politicized, and more theoretically driven research contexts' (Lunt and Livingstone 1996, p. 80), exploring, for instance, the discourses that shape practices of everyday life, the ways in which meanings are reworked and subverted, and the creation of new knowledges out of seemingly familiar understandings. The range of uses and purposes of focus groups is evident in geographic research employing the technique.

Geographers have used focus groups to collect information. Zeigler, Brunn, and Johnson (1996) used them to find out about peoples' responses to emergency procedures during a major hurricane. They claim that the focus group technique provided insights that might not have been revealed through methods like questionnaires or individual interviews. As a consequence they were able to recommend important refinements to disaster plans. J. Burgess (1996) has also used focus groups, in combination with participant observation, to obtain information about factors that inhibit visits to, and use of, woodlands. Her findings have contributed to the development of landscape design and management strategies to enhance the use of woodlands.

One concern of some researchers involved in data gathering is that because of the relatively small numbers of participants in focus groups the findings are not applicable to a wider population (for a discussion of this issue, see chapter 5). Combining focus groups with quantitative techniques is an extremely useful way of dealing with this issue. A survey questionnaire, for instance, might be administered to a random sample of the population from which the focus group was drawn to test the **generalisability** of the insights gained from the group discussions. Quantitative methods can supplement focus groups in other ways.

Preliminary surveys are sometimes helpful in identifying focus group members or the topics for detailed focus group discussion.

Conversely, focus groups can supplement quantitative research. They have been used to generate questions and theories to be tested in surveys (Goss and Leinbach 1996; Pratt 2002), to refine the design of survey questionnaires (Jackson and Holbrook 1995), and to follow up the interpretation of survey findings (Goss and Leinbach 1996), particularly where there seem to be contradictory results (Morgan 1996). It is, however, entirely appropriate to use focus groups as the sole research method rather than in combination with other research techniques.

For geographers interested in the process of knowledge production, focus groups are an excellent research tool. Robyn Longhurst (1996) is a geographer from Aotearoa/New Zealand interested in the absence of a language to talk about pregnancy. She has employed focus groups as a forum in which pregnant women could converse and interact. The narratives, accounts, anecdotes, and explanations offered by these women provided Longhurst (1996) with insights into a new discursive landscape of pregnancy. Similarly, Gibson, Cameron, and Veno (1999) have been concerned to not just reproduce a knowledge of the problems and difficulties confronting rural and non-metropolitan communities in Australia, but to reshape understandings so that new responses might be engendered. The seemingly isolated instances of innovation that several focus group members could readily recall provoked other participants to think of additional examples. The beginnings of a body of knowledge on regional initiative began to emerge through these discussions.

In a report of their Indonesian research on individual and household strategies related to the allocation of land, labour, and capital, Goss and Leinbach (1996) also highlight the collective rather than individual nature of knowledge production. By interacting with other focus group members Javanese villagers developed new understandings of their social conditions. Indeed, Goss and Leinbach argue that 'the main advantage of focus group discussions is that both the researcher and the research subjects may simultaneously obtain insights and understanding of particular social situations *during* the process of research' (Goss and Leinbach 1996, pp. 116–17, emphasis in original). For geographers who are committed to the idea that research can be used to effect social change and empower 'the researched', the potential for focus groups to create and transform knowledges and understandings of researchers and participants is compelling (see also Johnson 1996; Swenson, et al. 1992).

The focus group method has an important contribution to make to geographic research. It is a highly effective vehicle for exploring the nuances and complexities associated with people–place relationships. The material generated in focus groups can add important insights to work that seeks to describe and document the social world. But focus groups serve not just to 'mine', 'uncover', and 'extract' existing knowledges (Gibson-Graham 1994); they can also contribute to the development and construction of new knowledges and understandings for both researcher and 'researched'.

PLANNING AND CONDUCTING FOCUS GROUPS

Given that the focus group method can be used for a range of research purposes in geography, there will be some variation in how groups are organised and conducted. There are, however, basic principles and methodological and theoretical issues that need to be considered. To be sure, the success of a focus group depends largely on the care taken in the initial planning stage.

Selecting participants

Selecting participants is critically important. Generally, participants are chosen on the basis of their experience related to the research topic. J. Burgess' (1996) study is a good example of this **purposive sampling** technique (see chapter 5 for a discussion of participant selection). In work intended to ascertain the perceptions among different social and cultural groups of crime and risk in woodlands she selected women and men of varying age, stage in the life cycle, and ethnicity to participate in focus groups. In another study (Casey et al. 1996) of local perspectives on potential strategies to address agricultural pollution in the Minnesota River Basin, people from the area involved in different aspects of farming were invited to participate. Groups were made up of farmers—who varied in age and gender, and size and type of farm— and local staff from agriculturally based government agencies and non-profit groups.

Composition of focus groups

Should people with similar characteristics participate in the same group or should groups comprise members with different characteristics? This decision will be largely determined by the purpose of your research project.

Holbrook and Jackson (1996), for example, sought to address issues of identity, community, and locality by grouping together people with characteristics like age and ethnicity in common. In their research on environmental responsibility, Bedford and Burgess (2002) had people with similar experiences in each focus group but a range of different focus groups—suppliers, retailers, regulators, consumers, and advocates. They describe this as 'ensur[ing] homogeneity within the group and heterogeneity between them' (p. 124). Other researchers have noted that discussion of sensitive or controversial topics can be enhanced when groups comprise participants who share key characteristics (Hoppe et al. 1995; O'Brien 1993). In some projects it may be more appropriate to have groups made up of different types of people. Goss and Leinbach (1996) were interested in the social relations involved in family decision-making and deliberately chose to conduct mixed gender groups. The different knowledges, experiences, and perspectives expressed by women and men became an important point of discussion.

Another consideration is whether people already known to each other should participate in the same group. Generally it is best not to have people who are acquainted in the same group, but in some research, particularly place-based research, it may be unavoidable. Researchers need to be aware of the limitations this can produce. One is peer pressure with participants not wanting to appear 'out of step' with their acquaintances. Similarly some participants may under-disclose or selectively disclose details of their lives, as Pratt (2002) found in her research.

A different problem is when participants over-disclose information about themselves. One strategy for dealing with this is to outline fictional examples and ask group members to speculate on these. In groups they ran in Indonesia, Goss and Leinbach (1996) provided details of three fictional families and asked group members to discuss which of the families would be most likely to accumulate capital. Participants did not have to disclose information about their own situations but could still discuss family strategies. Participants can also be asked to treat discussions as confidential. As this cannot be guaranteed, it is appropriate to remind people to disclose only those things they would feel comfortable about being repeated outside the group.

Of course, you should always weigh up whether a topic is too controversial or sensitive for discussion in a focus group and is better handled through another technique, like individual in-depth interviews. (Most universities now have ethics committees to ensure that researchers carefully manage material from focus groups and other qualitative research methods. For more on this see chapter 2.)

Size and number of groups

The size of each group and the number of groups are other factors to be considered. Too few participants per group—fewer than four—limits the discussion, while too many—more than ten—restricts the time for participants to contribute.

In terms of the number of groups, one rule of thumb is to hold three to five groups, but this will be mediated by factors (Morgan 1997) such as the purpose and scale of the research and the heterogeneity of the participants. A diverse range of participants is likely to necessitate a larger number of groups. J. Burgess (1996), for instance, conducted thirteen focus groups with people of varying age, stage in the life cycle, and ethnicity, while Secor (2003) held four groups with women migrants to Istanbul. Likewise, Le Heron et al. (2001) held four focus groups with dairy and sheep meat farmers in New Zealand.

The structure of the focus group is also a factor to consider. When less **standardised questions** are used and when there is a relatively low level of researcher intervention and moderation more groups are needed, as both these factors tend to produce greater variability between groups (Morgan 1997). Time, cost, and availability of participants may also limit the number of groups that can be held. The overall research plan—especially whether focus groups are the sole research tool or one of a number of tools—will also affect decisions about the number of groups convened. Finally another guide to the number of focus groups is to use the concept of **saturation** (Krueger 1998, p. 72). This means that you continue to conduct focus groups until you gather no new information or insights.

Recruiting participants

The strategy used to recruit participants will depend on the type of participants you require for your study. Gibson, Cameron, and Veno (1999) recruited business and community leaders in two regions by initially contacting local people who featured in local newspapers and targeting managers of key government and non-government agencies. These initial contacts were asked to suggest other people who would make interesting contributions to the study (this snowball **recruitment** technique is also discussed in chapter 5). A preliminary phone conversation quickly established whether nominees were interested and able to attend. This was followed by a letter with more information about the project. A few days before the focus groups were held, participants were telephoned again to re-confirm their participation.

Twelve people were invited to attend each group to allow for cancellations due to illness, last-minute change of plans, and so on (several people from each group did drop out).

After an unsuccessful attempt to recruit participants by advertising in local newspapers and writing letters to local organisations, Holbrook and Jackson (1996) went directly to places where potential participants were likely to meet and socialise, such as community centres, homes for the elderly, play groups, and clubs. Managers or convenors of the centres helped set up the groups, or the researchers visited venues and invited people to participate. Once people had been involved in a focus group, news of the project spread by word of mouth and other people were recruited easily. Like Holbrook and Jackson, researchers need to think strategically about how best to locate potential participants (see also Burgess et al. 1988).

Questions and topics

Before conducting focus groups, give thought to the questions or topics for discussion. This involves not only the general content of questions or selection of issues for discussion, but also the wording of questions and issues, identification of key phrases that might be useful, the sequencing and grouping of questions (see chapter 7 for additional material on question order), strategies for introducing issues, and the links that might be important to make between different questions or issues.

One way to proceed is to devise a list of questions. Swenson, Griswold, and Kleiber (1992) developed a list of twenty questions to act as **probes** for focus groups comprising rural journalists. Another list of twenty questions was used in separate focus groups with community development leaders. Holbrook and Jackson (1996) identified six themes related to the experience of shopping and then used these to develop questions that were raised spontaneously and that fitted with the flow of the discussion. J. Burgess (1996) preceded each focus group with a walk through a woodland and then introduced for discussion five primary themes related to elements of the walk. As part of the recruitment process, Gibson, Cameron, and Veno (1999) asked each participant to prepare a brief two-minute summary of their perception of social and economic changes in the region over the last twenty years. The similarities and differences between these statements provided the basis for discussion.

Take care when letting people know in advance what the questions or topics will be. If attendance or discussion is likely to be enhanced by providing this information then it may be appropriate. Sometimes, however, it might be necessary for you to paint a very broad picture. For example, it might be more judicious to let a group of men know that you are interested in how they manage the interrelation between work, recreation, and home than to tell them you are interested in contemporary negotiations of masculinity (provided of course that you do want to know about masculinity in work, recreation, and home environments). (See chapter 2 for a consideration of the ethical dimensions of this sort of approach.) This example is also a reminder to be sure to use language that participants will understand when you are providing them with advice on the themes of your research.

Generally, questions or topics should allow for discussion of between one and two hours. With very talkative groups it might be necessary to intervene and move the discussion on to new topics. Alternatively, if you have planned a hierarchy of questions or themes then it may be appropriate to allow the group to focus on the more important areas of discussion. With less talkative groups you may need to introduce additional or rephrased questions and prompts to help draw information out and open up the discussion. These should be thought about in the preparation stage.

Another issue to consider is whether questions and topics will be standardised across all focus groups involved in your study or whether new insights from one group will be introduced into the discussions of the next. In many qualitative research situations it may be appropriate to incorporate material from earlier groups, but this should be determined by referring to the project aim. Information that might identify people who attended earlier groups should not be revealed to subsequent groups.

As well as running meetings with several groups, you may find it useful and appropriate to have each group meet more than once. Burgess, Limb, and Harrison (1988) ran in-depth discussion groups that met each week for six weeks to explore individually and collectively held environmental values. Although this group method is slightly different from the focus group method—it draws on the psychotherapeutic tradition and places an emphasis on the exploration of feelings and experiences—it does not preclude focus groups from meeting more than once.

Multiple focus groups may be a particularly useful strategy when participants are being asked to explore new and unfamiliar topics or to think about an apparently familiar topic in a new way (such as Longhurst's (1996) research on a new language of pregnancy). Multiple groups may also be appropriate as a way of developing trust between the researcher and research participants. For instance, when researching the experiences of single mothers I met several times with one group of teenagers who were very wary of talking with people associated with educational, medical, and media institutions (Cameron 1992).

Conducting focus groups

Generally, focus groups are best held in an informal setting that is easily accessible to all participants. The rooms of local community centres, libraries, churches, schools, and so on are usually ideal. The setting should also be relatively neutral: for example, it would not be advisable to convene a focus group about the quality of service provided by an agency in that agency's offices. Food and drink can be offered to participants when they arrive to help them relax, but alcohol should never be provided. It is also helpful to give out name tags as participants arrive.

There has been much written about the ideal focus group **facilitator** or **moderator** (for example, Morgan 1997; Stewart and Shamdasani 1990). In academic research it is often the researcher, who is familiar with the aim of the research and the purpose of the focus groups, who is best positioned to fill this role. To gain some confidence and familiarity with the process, a less experienced researcher might initially take the role of note-taker while a more experienced researcher facilitates the first groups. Focus groups can also be run with more than one facilitator, and a less experienced researcher might invite a more experienced researcher to take the lead.

When a note-taker is present they should sit discreetly to one side. The notes, particularly a list of who speaks in what order and a brief description of what they talk about, can be helpful when transcribing audio-recordings of the discussion. A seating plan is also essential. As the facilitator has to attend to what participants are saying and monitor the mood of the group, they should not take extensive notes, though they may want to jot down a point or two to come back to in discussion.

It is highly advisable to audio-record focus groups. The group will usually cover so much material that it is impossible to recall everything that was discussed. In addition, because presentation of focus group results generally includes direct quotes to illustrate key points, a transcribable audio-recording can be very helpful. The quality of the recorder and microphone is crucial. (See chapters 6 and 7 for a fuller discussion.) Most recorders come with a built-in microphone, but several flat 'desk' microphones placed around the table will ensure much better sound quality and that quieter voices are recorded. The audiovisual departments of universities are sometimes excellent places to get advice. Ensure you test the equipment long before the focus group, and also later in the room before group members arrive. Spare batteries (and tapes if you are using them) are essential equipment for focus group researchers. Take care that the setting for the group meeting is quiet enough for discussion to be recorded clearly.

The facilitator usually initiates discussion by giving an overview of the research and the role of the focus group in the project. The themes or questions for discussion can then be introduced. As group members may be unfamiliar with the focus group technique, a brief summary of how focus groups operate should also be given. Box 8.2 provides an example of a focus group introduction.

BOX 8.2 A SAMPLE INTRODUCTION TO A FOCUS GROUP SESSION

In this focus group, three researchers acted as facilitators. As people arrived they were greeted by one of the research team, introduced to the other researchers and group members, and offered tea or coffee. When all participants had arrived the group was invited to sit around a table. The primary facilitator for this focus group session explained the consent form that was already laid out in front of each person. Participants were asked to read and sign it. The consent forms were passed to one of the researchers, and the session was ready to begin. The researcher acting as the primary facilitator introduced the project:

Well, I'd like to thank you all for making the time and coming along today and contributing and sharing your knowledge. In this particular project that we're working on, we're looking at how communities negotiate change and the reason that we particularly wanted to look at this community was that it seemed there was a lot of change going on and the community, ummm, seemed to be, ummm—we were interested in how you saw your community handling that change and specifically what we're trying to get is to—in the long term is to generate a set of suggestions for other communities on how to manage and negotiate change. So we're hoping to learn from both the mistakes and the right things you've done. So what we're looking for today is a frank and open discussion about how you see change occurring in your community over the last twenty years and how that has been handled. And a little later on in the session we'll get you to—as we go on through the session we'll ask you specific things to help flesh out answers and issues that might be raised. And anything you feel like contributing or adding to just jump in and have that because these focus groups are to get at what the ideas and issues are as you see them. So I think we mentioned in the initial contact with you that we'd like to start out with a two-minute presentation from each of you as to how you see the critical features of change in your community. So we might start around this way. And if you would introduce yourself and your affiliation as you start.

Once all the group members had made their presentations the primary facilitator opened the discussion up:

Great, thanks very much. Well that's been really informative to get all those different perspectives. What we'd like to do now is to explore some of these issues. But from here on in the process should change and you should feel free enough to ask, agree, disagree, jump in, put your opinion forward, and so on. And if things get a bit noisy then we'll just jump in and try and get some semblance of order. One of the common themes that runs through what you've all said is that the community fabric has been affected in a really negative way by all the changes that have occurred. And what I'm trying to get at is what could have been done to improve that. So what do you think?

From this point on different group members responded to questions from the researchers, asked each other questions, agreed, and disagreed with each other. The topics for discussion flowed as people each contributed adding a slightly different perspective and introducing new ideas. The researchers also asked questions and points of clarification and introduced new areas of discussion.

Source: videotape excerpt from focus group conducted by Katherine Gibson, Jenny Cameron, and Arthur Veno, La Trobe Valley, Victoria, 19 June 1997 (see Gibson et al. 1999).

An example of an introduction is also provided by Myers (1998, p. 90).

The facilitator moderates discussion by encouraging exploration of a topic, introducing new topics, keeping the discussion on track, encouraging agreement and disagreement, curbing talkative group members, and encouraging quiet participants. Examples of the sorts of phrases used by facilitators are outlined in Box 8.3.

Some aspects of facilitation require special comment. Expressing and exploring different points of view is important in focus groups, yet research shows that groups have a preference for agreement (Myers 1998). The facilitator plays a central role in creating the context for disagreement. This can be done by stating in the introduction that there is no correct answer and that disagreement is normal and expected, by asking directly for different points of view, and by making explicit implied disagreement and introducing it as a topic for discussion (Myers 1998, p. 97). Watch for non-verbal signs of disagreement such as folded arms, movement away from the table, and a shaking or downcast head. You might ask the whole group or target the disagreeing member to give a different point of view. Of course, as facilitator, never state that someone is wrong, nor display a preference for one position. In the unlikely event that the discussion becomes heated then intervene immediately, suggest that there is no right answer, and move the group on to the next question.

| BOX 8.3 | EXAMPLES OF PHRASES USED IN FOCUS GROUP FACILITATION |

- Encouraging exploration of an idea:
  'Does anyone have anything they'd like to add to that?'
  'How do you think that relates to what was said earlier about...?'
  'Can we talk about this idea a bit further?'
- Moving onto a different topic:
  'This is probably a good point to move on to talk about...'
  'Just following on from that, I'd like to bring up something we've not talked about yet.'
  'This is an important point because it really picks up on another issue.'
- Keeping on track:
  'There was an important point made over here a moment ago, can we just come back to that.'
- Inviting agreement:
  'Has anyone else had a similar experience?'
  'Does anyone else share that view?'
- Inviting disagreement:
  'Does anyone have a different reaction?'
  'We've been hearing about one point of view but I think there might be other ways of looking at this. Would anyone like to comment on other sorts of views that they think other people might have?'
  'There seem to be some differences in what's been said and I think it is really important to get a sense why we have such different views.'
- Clarifying:
  'Can you give me an example of what you mean?'
  'Can you say this again, but use different words?'
  'Earlier you said that you thought...now you're saying...can you tell us more about what you think/feel about this topic/issue?'
- Curbing a talkative person:
  'There's a few people who've got something to add at this point, we'll just move onto them.'
  'We need to move onto the next topic, we'll come back to that idea if we have time.'
- Encouraging a very quiet person:
  'Do you have anything you'd like to add at this point?'

Source: Drawn from discussions in Carey (1994), Krueger (1998), and Myers (1998) and from personal experience.

Very talkative or very quiet participants can be a problem. Talkative people need to be gently curbed, while quiet ones need to be encouraged to participate. Along with the sorts of phrases listed in Box 8.3, your non-verbal signals can be useful. Pointing to someone who is waiting to speak indicates to the talkative person that there are others who need to have a turn. Making frequent eye-contact with the quieter person and offering encouraging signs, like nodding and smiling when they do speak, is important. Remember though that silence gives people time to reflect and gather their thoughts. Don't feel that you have to fill silences; give people time to respond.

At the conclusion of a focus group you might review key points of the discussion, providing a sense of completion and allowing participants to clarify and correct your summary. Group members should always be thanked for taking the time to attend and for their contributions. You can do this again with a personal letter to each participant.

ANALYSING AND PRESENTING RESULTS

Krueger (1998, p. 46) importantly reminds us that 'analysis begins during the first focus group'. Listen carefully to responses and clarify any unclear or contradictory contributions, as this information may be critical later when presenting the results. For example, if young people say that they would watch television news and current affairs if the coverage was more relevant to them, it is probably important to get them to explain or give examples of how news items could be made more relevant if it is your intent to increase the amount of televised current affairs shows they watch (see also Box 8.3).

Since there is always a richness of material, analysing focus group discussions can be as time consuming as it is interesting. The first step involves transcribing the audio-recording. A complete transcript of the entire discussion takes time, as one hour of recording usually takes over four hours to transcribe. When a detailed comparison of groups is to be undertaken full transcripts may be necessary. Generally a partial or abridged transcription (which involves transcribing only key sections of the discussion) will suffice. This is best done as soon as possible after the focus group with the facilitator/s and note-taker working in collaboration to decide which sections should be transcribed. A record of seating plan and running order of speakers and a brief description of what was said are extremely helpful at this point. If you have the time it is also advantageous for the researcher to transcribe the audio-recording as this is a way to become more fully immersed in their content (and for a researcher new to focus group research to reflect on their facilitation style, and identify strengths and weaknesses). (For a full discussion on transcribing interviews, see chapter 6.)

It is advisable to transcribe and undertake a preliminary analysis of the first focus group before conducting any others. This is a way of checking that your questions are understood by participants and are eliciting the type of information you need for your research. It is also a way of checking that you understand and can interpret the responses of participants. For example, in an initial focus group you might not think to ask young people to clarify what they mean by relevant news coverage, but by carefully reading the transcript you are likely to pick up this omission.

Once you have the complete set of focus group transcripts available, read the material over several times to help make yourself very familiar with the discussion. One relatively straightforward strategy for proceeding draws from the questions or themes that focused the discussion. Write each question or theme on the top of a separate sheet of paper and then on each sheet list the relevant points made. Finally take a note of key quotes that might be used in written material (Bertrand et al. 1992). This is an approach that works well when the discussion did not deviate widely from the questions or themes set by the researcher, or when comparisons are to be made between focus groups (Bertrand, Brown, and Ward 1992). For example, in a research project comparing the land management strategies for dealing with salinity preferred by farmers, policy-makers, and researchers, the sheets with the responses of the different groups to each question or theme might be compared easily.

When the purpose of the research project is to identify key themes or processes associated with a particular issue or topic it may be more appropriate to use **margin coding** (Bertrand et al. 1992). To do this, read through the transcripts, identify key themes or categories, and devise a simple colour, number, letter, or symbol-based coding system to represent the themes or categories. The transcripts should then be reread; words, sentences, and paragraphs related to each category or theme are highlighted by writing the appropriate code in the margin. Once transcripts have been coded, a cut and paste technique—completed either on a computer or manually—can be used to group the discussion related to each theme or process (see chapters 6, 14, and 15 for more information on this). Always keep an original of the transcripts for future reference. Sherraden (n.d.) suggests a variation of this thematic analysis. He develops a list of key words and, in a word-processing package, types two or more key words beside each comment. Using the search function, it is then possible to locate related points of discussion. Computer programs specifically designed for qualitative analysis, like NVivo, can also be used, and are particularly helpful when there is a large amount of transcribed material to be analysed (see chapter 15 for a discussion of this).

Being able to find material quickly is an important consideration as analysis and writing rarely proceed in a linear fashion. During the writing process new insights unfold (see chapter 17) and frequently you may find it necessary to return to the original transcripts to refine and reformulate ideas. Sometimes it will be necessary to listen to and make additional transcriptions of sections of the recordings.

When reporting on focus group research, present your results only in terms of the discussion within the groups. As noted earlier, focus groups do not produce findings that can be generalised to a wider population. Focus group results are also expressed in impressionistic rather than numerical terms. In place of precise numbers or percentages, the general trends or strength of feeling about an issue are typically given. As Ward, Bertrand, and Brown (1991, p. 271) have noted, focus group reports are 'replete with statements such as "many participants mentioned…", "two distinct positions were observed among the participants", and "almost no one had ever…"'. Reporting on their study into people's responses to emergency procedures, Zeigler, Brunn, and Johnson (1996), for example, noted that the people in their focus groups generally responded with either compliant behaviour or underreaction. Zeigler, Brunn, and Johnson then used direct quotes to illustrate the different ways that the responses were expressed (see Box 8.4 for an example of a focus group analysis, and see also the ways that Jackson and Holbrook (1995), Jarrett (1994), and Myers and Macnaghten (1998) discuss focus group findings).

In some projects it might not be the general trends but the ambiguous or contradictory remarks that the researcher particularly wants to explore. The development and presentation of an argument may refer not only to what was talked about, but the way it was talked about in the group setting. This became a significant aspect of the focus group research conducted by Gibson, Cameron, and Veno (1999, p. 29):

The stories of success and hope that emerged when the discussion was shifted onto the terrain of community strengths and innovations were numerous. They came stumbling out in a disorganised manner suggesting that these stories were not readily nor often told. In the face of dominant narratives of economic change perhaps such stories are positioned as less important or effective. It is clear that there is a lack of a language to talk about this understanding of community capacity; yet, as we will argue, this understanding has the potential to contribute to the ability of a region to deal effectively and innovatively with the consequences of social and economic change.

BOX 8.4   **EXAMPLE OF HOW FOCUS GROUP RESULTS CAN BE WRITTEN UP**

The following is an extract from a journal article reporting on findings from Australian focus group research on the impact of television news and current affairs on young people's political participation and active citizenship. The analysis of the focus group discussion starts by highlighting how young people find the reporting of news and current affairs too complex, particularly because of the sophisticated language and the absence of background information. The analysis continues:

> Political current affairs television was viewed by respondents as too complex to incorporate into their everyday viewing habits, but young people also feel it is not worth investing time in television current affairs because any political information received from the programs is usually trivialized and played for entertainment value. For example, *A Current Affair* [a news magazine show] was described by Debra, a nineteen year-old university student, as *Hey Hey It's Ray* after the celebrity of its host Ray Martin, and was seen by her focus group as a form of populist emotional exploitation. As the following responses suggest, there was a strong feeling amongst the groups that television current affairs portrays politicians as being 'full of it'.
>
> Bianka: *The whole politics thing. They're all liars; they're all full of it.*
> Craig: *All the media carry on with is stuff like when they asked Hewson [a former politician] if [the] GST [Goods and Services Tax] would be applied to a birthday cake and they just blew that up. Who gave a shit?*
>
> The respondents felt news and current affairs did not help them develop a political identity. They also expressed distrust in politicians who attempt to 'persuade' them to choose a lesser evil. As Bianka points out: *'They all change their minds when they get what they want. I mean what's the point?'* What eventuates is a distrust of not only politicians but also the media that is supposed to decipher the positive and negative elements of each candidate's actions.

Note how the findings are reported only in terms of the focus groups and in tentative terms with the use of phrases such as 'responses suggest', 'respondents felt', and '[w]hat eventuates'. Main themes that emerged from the focus groups are summarised by the authors and quotes from participants are used to illustrate and elaborate these themes.

Source: Evans and Sternberg (1999, p. 105).

One important element in the process of writing up (or 'writing-in' as Mansvelt and Berg call it in chapter 16) is to find a balance between direct quotes and your summary and interpretation of the discussion. When too many quotes are included the material can seem repetitive or chaotic. Too few quotes, on the other hand, can mean that the vitality of the interaction between participants is lost to the reader. Morgan (1997, p. 64) recommends that the researcher should aim to connect the reader and the original participants through 'well-chosen' quotations (see chapter 17).

CONCLUSION

Focus groups demand careful preparation on the part of the researcher. The selection and recruitment of participants; the composition, size, and number of groups; and the questions and topics to be explored are all key points to consider in the planning stage. Even the apparently mundane details of appropriateness of venue, provision of refreshments, and quality of audio equipment are critical to the success of focus groups. A well-prepared researcher also gives thought beforehand to the process of facilitation, including the points to cover in the introduction; the wording of key questions, topics, and phrases; the probes and prompts that might be useful to explore further a theme or topic; and strategies for drawing out different points of view, keeping the discussion on track, and dealing with both the more talkative and quieter members of the group. As soon as possible after the focus group, start the process of analysis, beginning with transcribing the audio-recordings and followed by the reading and rereading of transcripts, summarising main points, and identifying central themes.

Although they require careful planning beforehand and a great deal of reflection afterwards, focus groups are an exciting and invaluable research tool for geographers to use. Participants almost invariably enjoy interacting with each other, and the discussion can generate insights and understandings that are new to both participants and researchers. The interactive element makes focus groups ideally suited to exploring the nuances and complexities of people–place relationships, whether the research has a primarily data gathering function or is more concerned with the collective practice of knowledge production.

KEY TERMS

disclosure
discourse
facilitator
margin-coding
moderator
probe

purposive sampling
recruitment
saturation
transcription

REVIEW QUESTIONS

1   Find a research project from a recent issue of a geographical journal that you think could have been conducted using focus groups. Why do you think focus groups would be appropriate? Discuss the participants you would select, the composition of the focus groups, the size and number of

groups you would use, the questions you would ask or themes you would use, and strategies for recruiting participants.

2   The University of Pacifica is planning to upgrade its indoor sports facilities. Your research company has been commissioned by the university to conduct a focus group study on the sorts of changes that students think are most important. Discuss your research plan, including the composition, size, and number of focus groups; the process of selecting and recruiting participants; and the questions or topics you would use. Make sure you provide a rationale for each of your research decisions.

3   In a few days time you will be facilitating a series of focus groups. Describe the final steps you would take to prepare for the groups. What are some of the issues you anticipate might arise when conducting the groups? Discuss the strategies you would use to manage these. You might want to consider the following issues: too much agreement between participants; over-disclosure of personal information; groups that are overly talkative or overly silent.

SUGGESTED READING

Barbour, R. and Kitzinger, J. 1999, *Developing Focus Group Research: Politics Theory and Practice*, Sage, London.

Dick, B. 1997, *Structured Focus Groups* (online), Available: <http://www.scu.edu.au/schools/gcm/ar/arp/focus.html> (Accessed: 29 September 2004).

Morgan, D. L. 1997, *Focus Groups as Qualitative Research*, 2nd edn, Sage, Thousand Oaks.

Sherraden, M. n.d., *How to do Focus Groups* (online), Available: <http://www.ln.edu.hk/mkt/courses/howtodofocusgroups.doc> (Accessed: 29 September 2004).

Stewart, D. W. and Shamdasani, P. N. 1990, *Focus Groups: Theory and Practice*, Sage, Newbury Park.

9

Historical Research and Archival Sources

Michael Roche

CHAPTER OVERVIEW

Despite heightened levels of interest in qualitative research methods, human geographers have tended to overlook one of the oldest of qualitative techniques: historical approaches based on the study of primary documents. The interrogation of archival sources is an essential technique for most historical geographers and while other human geographers have been willing to incorporate a historical dimension into their work they do not necessarily have any archival research skills (Driver 1988). Human geographers more generally can benefit from having some of these skills, for they can be deployed for contemporary as well as historical research.

INTRODUCTION

After twenty-five years of working as an historical geographer I still relish the opportunity to undertake archival research. There is a continuing sense of delving into the unknown, of engaging in academic detective work trying to make sense of inevitably fragmentary and partial surviving **records**, of striving to make sense of the evidence you are scrutinising. And yet, my own introduction to archival research was orchestrated only at the graduate level. To a large degree I was able to learn by a process of trial and error, following the tendency of historical geographers to regard archival research as part of their craft, something to be acquired on the job. Good archival scholarship was to be inferred from reading journal articles or books by leading geographers working on related topics and from points of interpretation arising from discussions with supervisors. In many ways this was a laudable model, one that allowed me to develop my skills and understanding at my own pace, but geography students of today wishing to explore archival sources can benefit from a more overt discussion of fundamental steps in exploring **archives**. This is also the case because archival research needs to engage with larger disciplinary theory and the research ethics that are also a part of historical inquiry. Even so, like other methods, archival skills can to some extent only be learned by doing archival research. Expertise improves with experience and this is not easily reduced to a checklist of best practice.

WHAT IS ARCHIVAL RESEARCH?

> Archival scholarship at its best, it seems to me, is an ongoing, evolving interaction between the scholar and the voices of the past embedded in the documents (Harris 2001, p. 332).

Archival sources are a subset of what historical geographers and historians refer to as primary sources. These include non-current records of government departments held in public archives but can be extended to include company records and private papers. As well as documents, handwritten and typed, these can embrace personal letters, diaries, logbooks, minutes of meetings, as well as reports, plans, maps, and photographs. This chapter focuses on official papers, including manuscript and typescript files, maps, and photographs.[1] Most of the comments are also applicable to company archives and private papers. With the target readership of this book in mind this chapter concentrates largely on government archives, the more recent past of the last century or so, and on the 'New World'. This simplifies the discussion as much of this documentation is typewritten and the language of the more recent past is relatively easy to comprehend. As a repository of unique, single documents, created contemporaneously with the events they discuss, the materials lodged in archival repositories provide a particular window

BOX 9.1   IDENTIFYING THE ARCHIVES

Archives New Zealand
  <http://www.archives.govt.nz/index.html>

Library and Archives of Canada
  <http://www.collectionscanada.ca/index-e.html>

National Archives of Australia
  <http://www.naa.gov.au/>

National Archives of Ireland
  <http://www.nationalarchives.ie/>

National Archives of Scotland
  <http://www.nas.gov.uk/>

National Archives of South Africa
  <http://www.national.archives.gov.za/>

Public Record Office (England and Wales)
  <http://www.nationalarchives.gov.uk/>

US National Archives and Records Administration
  <http://www.archives.gov/>

on the geography of earlier times. As such they are a major source of valuable information for geographers. Historical approaches applied to archival sources will not enable all of the research questions of human geography to be addressed; however, they do provide a means to answer questions about the recent and more distant past that are not recoverable by the other techniques and sources available to human geographers.

More often than not the researcher will make use of public archives, a government agency charged with the preservation of non-current records. On other occasions small regional collections, such as those associated with some museums, may be targeted. Sometimes access to the records of private organisations may be sought. Michael Williams (1992) provides a concise summary of a range of archives from the national to the local. The Web increasingly provides the initial contact point between research and archival collections. Some major repositories and their 'WWW' addresses are listed in Box 9.1.

For Mayhew (2003), historical geography has a two-fold significance to the discipline as a whole that lies beyond increasing the understanding of the geography of the past: to include re-evaluation of taken-for-granted concepts, and to develop a comparative perspective so that as geographers we might more fully appreciate what is distinctive about today's world and how we understand it in disciplinary terms. Historico-geographical research based on archival research underpins both of these objectives.

ADVICE ON CONDUCTING GOOD HISTORICAL AND ARCHIVAL RESEARCH

The first step in reconstruction of past stages of a cultural area is mastery of its written documents (Sauer 1941, p.13).

It is an oversimplification to believe that the study of change through time by means of either historical documents or field evidence does not require special training and skills (Perry 1969, p. 96).

So where to begin? Good archival research is difficult to reduce to a checklist of points. However, it is useful to explore chronologically the sorts of things you might need to do and that you might encounter in undertaking archival research. To begin, like any other research project your work ought to be informed by some in-depth reading on current scholarship around the topic but accompanied by an openness to discovery. The point is well made by the highly accomplished Canadian historical geographer Cole Harris (Box 9.2).

Archival research begins before you arrive at the archive. You ought to be familiar with the existing literature before beginning any search for archival material. For instance, for a project involving state agencies, it is important to read any previously published institutional histories, the annual reports of that agency, and to look at parliamentary debates (or their equivalent). You should always write to any archives you intend to visit well beforehand and, if possible, get a letter of support from an academic supervisor. This will help you make best use of what is inevitably too little time. Outline your research topic in reasonable detail, indicate if it is for a small project or for a thesis, and signal what you are seeking to do and

BOX 9.2 APPROACHING ARCHIVAL RESEARCH

The first point to make about archival research is that it cannot be contained within a single methodology. Any sizable archive holds a vast array of material, and even if one's research questions are fairly specific, the chances are good that there will be far more potentially relevant documents than there will be time to examine them…

…[A]rchival research tends to gravitate towards one of two polar reactions—neither, I think particularly helpful. It is easy enough to be taken over by the archives, to attempt to read and record all their relevant information. In this way months and perhaps years go by, and eventually the investigator has a vast store of notes and usually, rather weak ideas about what to do with them. A fraction of the archives have been transferred from one location to another, while the challenges of interpretation have been postponed…

In effect the archives have swallowed the researcher. At the other pole are those who come to the archives with the confidence that they know precisely what they want. They have conceptualized their research thoroughly in advance. They pretty much know how they will argue their case and what their theoretical position is. But they do need a few more data, which is why they return to the archives. As long as they cleave to their initial position, either they will find that data they need and leave fairly quickly or they will not find them and also leave. Fair enough for certain purposes. But they are imposing their preconceptions on the archives. They have solved the problem of archival research by, in effect, denying the complexity of the archives and the myriad voices from the past contained in their amorphous record (Harris 2001, p. 330–1).

how much time you have at your disposal. The **archivist**, with an intimate knowledge of the both the ways in which the materials are organised and of their contents, will be able to help you identify relevant material.

Archives are not like libraries though they may have some similarities. They may operate on quite restricted hours. Some will require that you sign up for a reader's ticket (you may be able to do this electronically). You may also need to have someone vouch for you. If you can, you should check out the specific characteristics and requirements of the archives before you visit.

What should you take to the archives? Take related research notes and pencils and paper. Most archives operate on a **'pencil only' rule**, to minimise damage to the original documents should any be accidentally marked, albeit that many researchers now bring their own laptop computers. Although most public archives will have supplies of scrap paper I would also advise you not to depend on the archivists to supply stationery. Do not expect a small regional archive to supply either pencils or to have a convenient power point for your computer.

Sometimes ingenuity is called for in that research questions may only be able to be addressed obliquely. For instance, recently I have become interested in the discharged soldier settlement scheme implemented in New Zealand after 1916 in order to recognise the contribution made by those who served in the armed forces during World War I. This scheme was portrayed in the 1930s as being a failure. In order to look for evidence of failure and success I have had to understand what these terms meant at the time and search for sources of evidence.

Ultimately I appreciated that the registers listing farm land taken up by discharged soldiers contained incidental material about the percentage of the dairy company milk pay-out appropriated directly by the government to repay deferred rents. This provided a clue to levels of indebtedness and the extent to which the ex-soldier dairy farmers were succeeding or struggling. This information was particularly useful where the individual farm files have not survived. The archivists themselves can sometimes provide helpful, expert advice about record sets that you may not have considered useful. Typically, as a new user you will be given the opportunity to explain what you are researching and why. The archivist will tell you how the **finding aids** work and will be able to offer suggestions about where to start looking. Their experience and expertise can often prove invaluable but it is important to remember that they may have limited time available to provide help to individual researchers.

A crucial difference between a library and an archive lies in the way in which each stores material and by the nature of the finding aids. Libraries typically catalogue books and journals by either the 'Dewey Decimal' or 'Library of Congress' classification systems that group together all books with similar subjects. In contrast, public archivists seek to maintain the integrity of the record sets they obtain from government departments or other agencies in terms of preserving specific files place in the broader record set, maintaining the original ordering of documents in the file, providing storage conditions that will ensure the long term survival of the records, and making them available to the public. Archivists place great emphasis on the **provenance** of the **files**; the actual order of the material within the files in itself tells the researcher something about the situation that prevailed when the file was being created. Thus, whereas in a library you can refer to a catalogue to find a book on a particular subject on an open shelf, in an archive basic finding aids take the form of sequential 'series lists' of all the files held by particular agencies.

In many major archives electronic searching of the collections is now possible. This means that specific items can be searched for so that the process, superficially at least, becomes more like using a library catalogue. In large archives this can increasingly be done from distant places, thus reducing the time spent in the archives themselves searching for material and releasing extra time for reading the materials found. Do not forget about provenance. What survives in the file is likely to be only a fragment and it may be quite partial in terms of insights that it provides about the past. In many cases, however, you will have only the list of files to guide you. The files remain organised along the lines that the original creating agency devised. Inevitably you will find that some of the records staff have been more thorough than others. The name of a file may not always be a clear guide to its contents; material may be misfiled; and some files may have been lost or destroyed.

In the case of some national collections, precious and fragile originals may have been electronically scanned or photographed and made available online or as microfilm copies. Again, it is important to check in advance whether you will be reading originals or copies of the documents that you plan to consult. Some sources have been much studied and are available in published form (e.g., Powell 1973). However, remember to use these sources critically for they may have been edited reflecting the conventions and morals of the age. For example, well-known New Zealand historian Bill Oliver provides a light-hearted reflection on this serious matter when observing that the published correspondence of the Richmond and Atkinson families, who were prominent in nineteenth-century New Zealand politics, 'struck me as curious in places; upon inspecting the originals I found that the editor had not only made mistakes in the transcription (a venal sin) but has defaced the manuscript with overwriting and instructions to his typist a (a mortal sin or if it isn't it should be)' (Oliver 2002, p. 107). Just because some primary source material has been published in printed form does not mean that you can relax your critical judgement.

Other files held may have restricted access. Personnel files typically fall within this category. In different national contexts the period during which restricted access applies may vary, but thirty years after the closing of the file is typical. In some instances a lesser degree of restriction applies where permission to look at files may be granted by a senior archivist, government official, or someone associated with the organisation that created the files. A formal written request outlining your research project may result in access being granted; however, this may have some conditions attached, for example being able to read only a particular portion of the material and having the remainder of the file physically sealed. In other cases the researcher can do nothing but wait patiently until the material is released.

Unlike a library, archived files are not kept on open shelves. They are not necessarily kept on the same site as the reading room and may only be delivered from storage hourly upon request, so be prepared to have several tasks to go on with (for example, searching the finding aids for other files to call up while you wait). Photocopying of material is usually possible, but this can be comparatively costly and you may have to pay in advance of delivery. Some material may be deemed to be too fragile or, if bound, too difficult to photocopy. It is therefore advisable to find out what the policy is beforehand. Large plans, maps and charts in excess of A3 size can be copied by means other than photocopying, but this is sometimes quite expensive. However, it may be the only means of obtaining a copy of an essential document.

When the file is produced for you to work on, you will find in most cases that new items are on top of the older material, particularly if the material is secured by paperclip. You will probably need to work from back to front. Will you answer any of your research questions? It may be immediately obvious that the material is relevant to your inquiry or it may appear only tangentially relevant or even irrelevant. Sometimes it is difficult to make a judgement at first glance and you may have to recall material previously examined whose significance was not appreciated at the time. Alan Baker, a British historical geographer, has offered some guiding thoughts on evaluating primary sources including archival materials (Box 9.3).

Baker's words seem to me to be crucial for those using archives as qualitative sources in human geography. It is essential to understand as fully as possible the original purpose of the document, who created it, and how and when it was made.

On the basis of their extended experience working with documents, historians have identified some generic questions to pose when assessing them in order to better understand their significance (Box 9.4).

These questions provide a useful starting point for geographers as well as historians although I would make three qualifying points. First, it is possible to extend 'document' to include maps and plans (see Harley, 1992). Second, this approach tends to privilege the ideas behind actions. That is to say, the past is being understood in idealist terms where the thought behind the action is regarded as providing the understanding necessary to interpret

BOX 9.3   ASSESSING EVIDENCE IN HISTORICAL GEOGRAPHY

No source should be taken at face value: all sources must be evaluated critically and contextually. The history and geography of a source needs to be established before it can legitimately be utilised and incorporated into a study of historical geography. The historical sources we use were not compiled and constructed for our explicitly geographical purposes; they were more likely to have been prepared, for example, for the purposes of taxation and valuation, administration and control. We also have to understand not only the superficial characteristics of a specific source but also its underlying motivation, background and ideology of the person(s) who constructed it. In order to make the most effective and convincing use of a source we must be aware of its original purpose and context and thus from its limitations and potential for our own project (Baker 1997, p. 235).

BOX 9.4   THE HISTORIAN'S STANDARD QUESTIONS OF DOCUMENTS
(after Kitson Clark 1969)

1   What was the writer's bias?
2   What was the writer's situation and intention at the time of writing?
3   What were the writer's opportunities for knowledge?
4   What were the writer's general standards of truthfulness?
5   What powers of critical observation did the writer usually bring to bear (was the writer credulous)?
6   What was the writer's framework of ideas and what did certain words mean when used by the writer?

these events. Historical geography can be written legitimately from a viewpoint other than that of contemporary observers (Baker 2003). Third, the documents themselves cannot be read in isolation but must be understood in their wider context and even then any conclusions will be provisional rather than absolute.

To some extent all archival researchers develop individualised strategies for note-taking from archival materials. However, there are two basic strategies. This first involves collecting material by topic, noting specific details and suitably referenced quotations. Classically, historical researchers have made use of large index cards for this purpose, though many now use computers to organise these notes. New topics can be added on new cards as more files are read and new research questions formulated. The alternative approach is to record chronologically any pertinent information from each file and then subsequently to identify themes that emerge across the files. Both strategies have advantages and disadvantages. The former depends on identifying key topics at the beginning of the project within which to collect information. Such an approach offers the capacity to add new topics or to identify dead ends and to see how themes merge or diverge. My personal view is that, while this approach means that many diverse sources are brought together, it can blur a researcher's capacity to make good inductive judgments. The latter method is more sensitive to the provenance of files and can give a clearer sense of the role of particular officials or departments. It does however involve a degree of double-handling in that evidence that has already been collected by the researcher needs to be reorganised after each visit to the archives and perhaps annotated further. It is important to follow up other research questions that may emerge from this re-sorting process. The latter approach is one that I have used over many years. It suits me and, as a full-time academic, I can incorporate it into my way of working. I would acknowledge that it probably works best when researching in an area where both the secondary literature and the archival sources are familiar, even if the specific contents of the files are unknown. Students with a relatively short period for archival research may prefer to work to the first model outlined above.

Having located and extracted archival evidence, this must be adequately cited in the written products of the research. The first step is carefully recording the specific document description and file reference. For example, the personnel file for Edward Phillips Turner, Director of Forest in New Zealand from 1928 to 1931, is located in the New Zealand Forest Service files at Archives New Zealand in Wellington. The specific reference is 'F Acc W2338 82/113 E. P. Turner'. The 'F' refers to the Forestry files, 'W2338' is the accessions number for that collection of documents, 82 is the series, and 113 the specific file number, while E. P. Turner is the descriptive label (a little confusing in that the individual in question always used the double-barrelled surname). There is considerable variation among filing systems. You need to quickly become familiar with the system used by the agency whose records you are working on, and here the expert assistance of the archivist can be invaluable. The crucial thing is to record the details carefully. This is important for two reasons. First, it enables you as a researcher to keep track of where you found specific information. Second, it enables a subsequent researcher to relocate the material. The idea is simple enough but given the nature of archival material it is somewhat more exacting than, for example, the standard bibliographic requirements of author, date, title, and publisher/place for a book in the reference list of a thesis. Citing archival materials correctly can also pose problems in that human geography has tended to adopt versions of in-text citation systems, such as Harvard (see Hay 2002). Most archival sources sit uncomfortably within this framework and are generally better referenced in footnotes or endnotes, typically used by historians. Students undertaking archival research may need to negotiate a variation from their university's social science oriented formats for referencing.

The archive does not constitute the only source for historical research. For instance, newspapers, private papers, and unpublished memoirs may provide valuable material for cross-referencing with the archival record. Likewise, once archival work is completed, the researcher may need to follow up on unfamiliar key actors by checking old editions of *Who's Who*, or newspaper obituaries. This 'post-archive' work can of course help to shape and inform the purpose of subsequent trips to the archive.

Moreover, files are not the end point of research, as US cultural geographer Carl Sauer reminded historical geographers over 60 years ago:

> Let no one consider that the historical geographer can be content with what is found in archive and library. It calls, in addition, for exacting fieldwork. One of the first steps is the ability to read the documents in the field for instance of an account of an area written long

ago and compare the places and their activities with the present, seeing where the habitations were and the lines of communication ran, where the forests and the field stood, gradually getting a picture of the former cultural landscape behind the present one (Sauer 1941, p. 13).

While Sauer's words may indicate nostalgia for a pioneering rural past and the focus could just as easily be urban and social, his challenge remains pertinent and remains one only partially taken up by subsequent generations of geographers (for example, Raitz 2001).

CHALLENGES OF ARCHIVAL RESEARCH

There are two sorts of challenges facing researchers working with archives. The first of these is intellectual and the second technical. When dealing, for instance, with the file materials contained in an official government archive it is important to bear in mind the sorts of power relations inherent in the surviving materials. This is rather more than just acknowledging that the surviving files are fragmented and partial. The records are those created by politicians and officials. They reflect the outlooks and understandings of the dominant groups in that national context at the time they were created. Duncan (1999) writes of these concerns in terms of complicity stemming from use of the 'colonial archive'. Thus for much of the nineteenth century and well into the twentieth century they are records created largely by men in the upper echelons of society, and in a colonial situation such as in New Zealand are predominantly the records of colonising British settlers. Summarising the contents of files from the archives merely reproduces these uneven power relations rather than interpreting them. The records of nonofficial community or sporting groups may provide a way into understanding the concerns and aspirations of those who had no position in the public political sphere. Likewise oral histories for the recent past may provide insights into gendered and minority concerns. Furthermore an awareness of the power relations within the archival material may allow the researcher to reinterpret surviving materials. For instance, what I once mapped as examples of illegal felling of forest in New Zealand in the 1870s I would now be inclined to understand as a resistance on the part of Maori forest owners to the imposition of authority by the Crown and of flaunting of government regulations by timber cutters who had limited other means of supporting themselves.

The most fundamental technical difficulty relates to the ability to actually read the documents retrieved in the archive. For the first half of the 19th century many official documents were handwritten in copperplate script. This looks elegant but can take some time for novices to learn to read proficiently, a situation that may be exacerbated when officials wrote both across and along a sheet of papers in order to save paper. Perseverance will pay off. Archives for Australia and New Zealand are from the latter nineteenth century and are generally written in a 'modern hand'. They are generally readable with a bit of effort, the main problems being encountered with faint letterbook copies. However, original manuscripts concerned, for example, with the early settlement of North America in the period before 1700 may be written in 'secretary hand'. This was the script of professional scribes of the time and is difficult to read without specialised instruction. Unless the material has been transcribed and printed, its translation requires additional palaeographical skills. In any case, all kinds of handwritten documents made in the past tend to be difficult to decipher especially when the investigator is trying to read only a faint letter book copy of the original. For instance, in the mid-nineteenth century the 'long s' written similar to an 'f' was frequently used in official correspondence. This means that words with a double 'ss', for instance 'lesson' are rendered as what looks to us like 'lesfon'. Not only do spellings change as you move back in time but so does the very construction of the English language.[2] This makes it more of a challenge to understand the world-view of these earlier times. From around the 1880s, typewritten material becomes more common in government files, but important marginal annotations will be handwritten and often cryptic in meaning.

A good example of some of the challenges posed by handwritten documents is provided by the correspondence of Captain Campbell Walker, the first Conservator of Forests in 1876–77 in New Zealand. His letters were an important source for my PhD research into state forestry but were nearly impossible to decipher. I decided to photocopy and later transcribe them but only managed to do so after painstakingly working out on a letter-by-letter basis how he wrote the alphabet. Anyone contemplating the use of archive material as a source for qualitative research in human geography must be prepared to be patient and resourceful; the use of documentary evidence is rarely easy and generally requires a great deal of time.

The units of land area and currency may also be different from those in use today (for example, acres rather than hectares). This raises the issue of whether to convert every measurement to the current system or to give a general conversion factor and use the units of the period (generally, I prefer the latter). Some facility with the original units is useful. Appreciating that there are 640 acres to a square mile makes it possible to recognise, for example, that the apparently precise data on the forest areas in Otago Province in New Zealand in the 1867 are actually only estimates to the nearest quarter mile or 110 acres. More specialised measures may also need to be understood depending on your field of research. For example, throughout the British Empire from the nineteenth century quantities of sawn timber, for instance, are often given in superficial feet (colloquially referred to as a 'superfoot'), that is: twelve inches by twelve inches by twelve inches (thirty cm by thirty cm by thirty cm). However, in North America the term 'board foot'—which is not a surfing term—was more often used for the same unit.

If you are working through a file and time runs short you may find yourself copying whole documents that could be of use—but do not have the time to read them carefully and decide. In the end you find yourself with page after page of material that may subsequently prove to be marginal to the research. This is particularly important in that when returning to your research material it is too easy for the photocopied document to overshadow your handwritten notes so that you end up with the situation Harris refers to as the archive 'swallowing the researcher' (see Box 9.2).

Mistakes in interpretation can and do occur. I once mistook the numbered applications for the position of Director of Forests in New Zealand for the rankings of candidates. The result was an apparently nonsensical list of candidates. On closer subsequent investigation of the date stamps showing the receipt of application it became clear that the numbers related only to the order in which they had been received. Retrospectively, I can draw three points from this episode. First, scrutinise documents carefully. In this case, the answer was there in the documents but I did not see it first time around. Second, if you are uncertain about what the documents indicate acknowledge this and do not make too definite a claim of the surviving evidence. Third, by 'learning the ropes' as an undergraduate or graduate student you can avoid some of the more obvious pitfalls of interpretation before you have anything published.

ETHICS AND ARCHIVES

It is all too easy for archival researchers to dismiss ethical issues as something relevant only to geographers working on present-day topics with other qualitative or quantitative methodologies. Actually, archival researchers also have some ethical obligations, accentuated by the fact that the individuals who created—or are the subjects of—the records in question are, in all likelihood now deceased and unable to defend themselves. Moreover, the deceased may have living descendants, so sensitivity for their sakes is required. Where more recent records are being used the individuals involved may still be living. The issue is one of making an informed and defensible judgement about past events and the actors involved therein. Scrutiny of social science research projects by university human ethics committees is now increasingly the norm. The ethical aspects involved in archival research have less to do with safety, harm, and risk to the researcher or research participants and more to do with retaining the integrity of the material contained in the files and the preservation of the archives themselves. Those using archives should, after all, regard access to the material as a privilege. Historical records are precious and often irreplaceable. All researchers are under an obligation to look after archival material and to ensure that it is preserved in good order for any subsequent scholars.

The US National Council of Public History identifies three guidelines for using archive material.[3] We can reasonably substitute 'geographer' in each of these.

1 Historians work for the preservation, care and accessibility of the historical record. The unity and integrity of historical record collections are the basis of interpreting the past.
2 Historians owe to their sources accurate reportage of all information relevant to the subject at hand.
3 Historians favour free and open access to all archival collections. (National Council on Public History 2003.)

Those who are living can take a libel action against you if they feel you have defamed them. More often in historical research you are dealing with those no longer living. While you cannot libel the dead, what sensitivity do you need show to them and their descendants? Some of these issues can be illustrated by way of example. As part of the research on World War I soldier settlement I referred to earlier, I have viewed the soldiers' personal files for information on age, previous employment details, residential information, and the like. By examining the hospitalisation details it is possible to identify soldiers who were treated for venereal disease. Do I need to mention this? If it is not relevant to my research questions then arguably it can be omitted. Even over eighty years on it may be embarrassing to descendants, but is this sufficient reason to omit the information? If it becomes relevant in that soldier was too ill to successfully farm then you may decide it is necessary to mention this point. You might do this with varying degrees of subtlety. However if your research topic was focused explicitly on the medical geography of World War I soldiers then you might have to confront these sorts of sensitivity issues directly. Ultimately these decisions rest very much with the individual researcher and are not to be resolved by presenting a checklist but can be worked through in terms of thinking about the ethics of research (Hay 2003a, pp. 46–7).

PRESENTING THE RESULTS OF ARCHIVAL RESEARCH

There is no single correct way of presenting the results of archival research. The theoretical foundation of the research project, the sorts of empirical information retrieved, and the writing style of the researcher all shape how the research project or thesis is expressed.[4] Typically however, archival researchers will make use of direct quotations from key documents in order to demonstrate their case (see also chapter 17 for a discussion). They also make use of case study material to illustrate points. On occasions good use may be able to be made of cartographic or pictorial material.

Adept researchers are often able to move easily from specific points of detail to sketch a much larger picture and to relate this to what is known about related topics. I would recommend critical examination of writings by leading historical geographers (for example, Dennis 2001; Harris 2002; Meinig 1986; Powell 1988). However, it is not just a matter of identifying key quotations, but rather of building an argument. This obliges you to select ideas in a logical way from the pre-existing literature and then to use this to provide an informed discussion based on what has been found in the archives. The desirable end point, however, is to be in command of the source material. Rather than merely reproducing a chronicle of part of what is contained in the archive strive, to make your writing a synthesis of specific detail and informed interpretation.

CONCLUSION

Although it has much to offer human geography in general, archival research tends to have been neglected by other than historical geographers. As a research method, historical research using archival sources:

1 calls for creative thinking in identifying source materials relevant to your research problem
2 needs patience, precision, and critical reflection in collecting and evaluating material
3 requires a sense of historico-geographical imagination in interpreting source material whereby theorisation does not outstrip the evidence
4 is partial and requires that you relate archival material to other contemporary sources of a textual and pictorial sort that may be held in other collections
5 asks researchers to continually negotiate between the theoretical and the empirical.

Archival work can be extremely time consuming, and superficially, at least, frustrating in that the information retrieved may offer only partial answers, particularly where you find yourself under time pressure to complete a research project. Archival work done properly takes time and patience. Rarely will the surviving archival material provide 'full' answers to the questions you pose. In the case of public archives the surviving material typically says more about politics, economics, the concerns of elites, and men than it does about social and private spaces, women, and minority groups. Likewise, surrendering to the temptation to merely summarise the content of files, a trap into which inexperienced archival researchers can fall, is another way of being—as Harris terms it—'swallowed by the archive'.

It is all too easy in discussing archival research to create the impression that there is no room for novices when, in fact, more human geographers need to be encouraged to incorporate archival work into their research programs. I would simply describe archival research as somewhat akin to confidently accepting the challenge of working on a jigsaw puzzle where you can be reasonably certain that pieces are missing and that the box cover with the picture of the completed puzzle will never be found. Good archival research can be extremely satisfying, both in learning the skills to conduct it and in the presentation of results.

KEY TERMS

archives

archivist

files

finding aids

'pencil only' rule

provenance

records

REVIEW QUESTIONS

1   What sorts of research questions can be addressed using archival sources?
2   What are the problems of a researcher being, as Harris terms it, 'swallowed by the archive'?
3   What is meant by provenance and why it is important to archival researchers?
4   What steps are required in assessing historical evidence?

SUGGESTED READING

Baker, A. R. H. 2003, *Geography and History, Bridging the Divide*, Cambridge University Press, Cambridge.

—— 1997, 'The dead don't answer questionnaires: researching and writing historical geography', *Journal of Geography in Higher Education*, vol. 21, no. 2, pp. 231–43.

Cameron, L. 2001, 'Oral history and the Freud archives: incidents, ethics and relations', *Historical Geography*, vol. 29, pp. 38–44.

Hall, C. 1982, 'Private archives as sources for historical geography', in A. R. H. Baker and M. Billinge (eds), *Period and Place: Research Methods in Historical Geography*, Cambridge University Pres, Cambridge, pp. 274–81.

Hanlon, J. 2001, 'Spaces of interpretation; archival research and the cultural landscape', *Historical Geography*, vol. 29, pp. 14–25.

Harris, C. 2001, 'Archival fieldwork', *Geographical Review*, vol. 91, nos 1&2, pp. 328–34.

Harris, C. 1978, 'The historical mind and the practice of geography', in D. Ley and M. Samuel (eds), *Humanistic Geography*, Croom Helm, Chicago, pp. 123–37.

Kurtz, M. 2001, 'Situating practices: the archives and the file cabinet', *Historical Geography*, vol. 29, pp. 26–37.

Mayhew, R. 2003, 'Researching historical geography', in A. Rogers and H. Viles, (eds), *The Student's companion to Geography*, 2nd edn, Blackwell, Oxford, pp. 260–5.

Ogborn, M. 2003, 'Knowledge is power: Using archival research to interpret state formation', in A. Blunt, P. Grufford, J. P. May, M. Ogborn and D. Pinder (eds), *Cultural Geography in Practice*, Arnold, London, pp. 9–20.

Powell, J. M. 1988, *An Historical Geography of Modern Australia: The Restive Fringe*, Cambridge University Press, Cambridge.

Sauer, C. 1941, 'Foreword to historical geography', *Annals of the Association of American Geographers*, vol. 31, no. 1, pp.1–24.

Notes

1   For the purposes of this discussion I will leave to one side the whole question of archival material created in electronic form.

2   Indeed you may be dealing with records in another language. For instance there is good deal of correspondence in Maori in Archives New Zealand: much, but not all, of which is accompanied by an English version prepared by official translators.

3   These are expanded on in the American Historical Association's Statement of Standard of Professional Conduct.

4   Given that this volume focuses on qualitative methods I have omitted discussion of how a researcher might extract and present in tabulated form quantitative information derived from archival sources.

Using Questionnaires in Qualitative Human Geography

10

Pauline M. McGuirk and Phillip O'Neill

CHAPTER OVERVIEW

This chapter deals with questionnaires, an information-gathering technique used frequently in mixed method research that draws on quantitative and qualitative data sources and analysis. We begin with a discussion of key issues in the design and conduct of questionnaires. We then explore the strengths and weaknesses for qualitative research of various question formats and questionnaire distribution and collection techniques. Finally, we consider some of the challenges of analysing qualitative responses in questionnaires and we close with a discussion of the limitations of using questionnaires in qualitative research.

INTRODUCTION

Qualitative research seeks to understand the ways people experience the same events, places, and processes differently as part of a fluid reality; a reality constructed through multiple interpretations and filtered through multiple frames of reference and systems of meaning-making. Rather than trying to measure and quantify aspects of a singular social reality, qualitative research draws on methods that reveal and interpret the complexities, context and significance of people's understanding of their lives (Eyles and Smith 1988). Within this epistemological framework, how can questionnaires contribute to the methodological repertoire of qualitative human geography? This chapter explores the possibilities.

Commonly in human geography, questionnaires pose standardised, formally structured questions to a group of individuals, often presumed to be a sample of a broader population (see chapter 5). Questionnaires are useful for gathering original data about people, their behaviour and social interactions, attitudes, and opinions, and awareness of events (McLafferty 2003; Parfitt 1997). They usually involve the collection of quantitative *and* qualitative data. Since such **mixed-method** questionnaires first appeared with the explosion of behavioural geography in the 1970s (Gold 1980), they have been used increasingly to gather more complex data of a qualitative nature in relation to matters as varied as the environment, transport and travel, quality of life and community, work, and social networks.

While there are limitations to the depth and extent of qualitative data that questionnaires are capable of gathering, they have numerous strengths. First, they provide insights into relevant social trends, processes, and interpretations. Second, they are cost-effective, enabling extensive research over a large or geographically dispersed population. Certainly, they are one of the more practical qualitative research tools. Third, they are extremely flexible. They can be combined very effectively with complementary, more intensive forms of qualitative research to provide more in-depth perspectives on social process and context. For instance, Ruming, Mee and McGuirk's (2004) investigation of the impacts of the social mix policies of New South Wales' Department of Housing on understandings of community combined key informant interviews with housing officials, questionnaires with local residents, and follow-up in-depth interviews with volunteers who had participated in the questionnaire. Qualitative data from the questionnaire provided a framework for the in-depth interviews, allowing key themes, concepts, and meanings to be teased out and developed (see Askew and McGuirk 2004; England 1993; and Winchester 1999 for similar examples). In this mixed-method format particularly, questionnaires can be both a powerful and practical research method.

QUESTIONNAIRE DESIGN AND FORMAT

While each questionnaire is unique, there are common principles of good design and implementation. Producing a well-designed questionnaire for qualitative research involves a great deal of thought and preparation, effective organisational strategies, and critical review and reflection, as an array of literature suggests (for example, de Vaus 1995; Dillman 1978; Fink and Kosecoff 1998; Foddy 1993; Fowler 2002; Gillham 2000; and see the relevant chapters in Babbie 2001; Clifford and Valentine 2003; Flowerdew and Martin 1997; and Hoggart et al. 2002). The design stage is where a great deal of researcher skill is vested and it is a critical stage in ensuring the usefulness of the resulting data. Notwithstanding the quality of the questionnaire devised, we are beholden as researchers to ensure that we have sufficient reason to call on the time and energy of the targeted research subjects. The desire to generate our 'own' data on our research topic is insufficient justification (Hoggart et al. 2002). As with any study, the decision to go ahead with a questionnaire needs to be based on careful reflection on detailed research objectives, consideration of existing and alternative information sources, and appropriate ethical contemplation (see chapters 2, 4, and 5).

The content of a questionnaire must relate to the broader research question as well as to your critical examination and understanding of relevant processes, concepts, and relationships. As a researcher, you need to familiarise yourself with existing local and international work on your research topic. This ensures clarity of research objectives, and will help you to select an appropriate target population and relevant key questions. You need to be clear on the purpose of each question, who will answer it, and how you intend to analyse responses. You also need to be mindful of the limits to what people are willing to disclose, being aware that this varies across different social and cultural groups in different contexts. Public housing tenants, for instance, might be wary about offering candid opinions about their housing authority. Every question, then, needs to be carefully considered, and have a clear role and purpose.

Begin by drawing up a list of topics that you seek to investigate. When you have clarified these, develop specific questions. De Vaus (1995) suggests that it is helpful to think about four distinct types of question content:

1 *attributes* Attribute questions aim to establish respondents' characteristics (for example, age or income bracket, owner-occupier or private renter)
2 *behaviour* With behaviour questions, we are interested in discovering what people do (for example, recreation habits, extent of public transport use)
3 *attitudes* Questions about attitudes are designed to discover what people think is desirable or undesirable (for example, judgment on integrating social housing with owner-occupied housing)
4 *beliefs* Questions about beliefs aim to establish what people believe to be true or false (for example, beliefs on the importance of environmental protection).

A basic guiding principle for all these question types, however, is that you need to be sure that your target population will both understand the questions and have the knowledge to answer them. Asking respondents to comment, for instance, on whether they believe government planning policies have contributed to local coastal degradation might be beyond their ability to answer with any certainty.

Apart from the typology of question content, there is a range of questions types on which to draw. We commonly make a distinction between closed and open questions, each of which offers its own strengths and weaknesses. Closed questions may seek quantitative information about respondent attributes (for example, level of educational attainment) or behaviour (for example, how often and where respondents buy groceries). Some examples are set out in Box 10.1. Closed questions can ask respondents to select categories, rank items as an indicative measure of attitudes or opinions, or select a point on a scale as indicative of the intensity with which an attitude or opinion is held. A major benefit of closed questions is that their responses are easily coded and analysed, a bonus when interpreting a large number of questionnaires. Closed questions are demanding to design, however, as they require researchers to have a clear and full understanding of what the range of answers to a question will be. Respondents' answers are limited to the range of categories designed by the researcher as an exhaustive and exclusive list of possible answers, and this can be a limitation. Moreover, closed questions rest on the assumption that words, categories, and concepts carry the same meaning for all respondents and this may not always be the case. For example, how a respondent answers the question 'How often have you been a victim of crime in the past two years?' will depend on what the respondent includes in their definition of a crime (de Vaus 1995). A criticism of closed questions, then, is that 'one may learn more about the behaviour of the sample in responding to a set a categories...than about the behaviour under investigation' (Cox 1981, p. 264). This limitation can be lessened by offering an answer option such as: 'other (please specify)' or by using combination questions that request some elaboration or explanation for the selection made in a closed question (see Box 10.1).

In general, open questions have greater potential to yield in-depth responses in keeping with the thrust of qualitative research: to understand how meaning is attached to process.

BOX 10.1 TYPES OF QUESTIONNAIRE QUESTIONS

Closed questions

Attribute information

How often do you shop at this shopping mall?

Less than once a week	☐
Once a week	☐
Twice a week	☐
More than twice a week	☐

Category list

What was the main reason you chose to live in this neighbourhood?

Proximity to work	☐
Proximity to family and friends	☐
Proximity to schools or educational facilities	☐
Proximity to shopping centre	☐
Proximity to recreational opportunities	☐
Environment	☐
Housing costs	☐
Good place to raise children	☐
Pleasant atmosphere of neighbourhood	☐
Other (please specify) _____	

Rating

Please rank the reasons for buying your current house (Rank all relevant categories from 1 [most important] to 6 [least important]).

Price	☐
Location	☐
Size	☐
Proximity to job/family	☐
Investment	☐
Children's education	☐

Scaling

Please indicate how strongly you agree/disagree with the following statement:

Having a mix of social groups in a neighbourhood is a positive feature.

Strongly disagree	☐
Disagree	☐
Neutral	☐
Agree	☐
Strongly agree	☐

Combination question

Have changes in the neighbourhood made this a better or worse place for you to live? (*please tick the appropriate box*).

Changes have made the neighbourhood better ☐

Changes have not made the neighbourhood better or worse ☐

Changes have made the neighbourhood worse ☐

Please explain your answer below.

_____

_____

Open questions

What have been the biggest changes to the neighbourhood since you moved in?

_____

_____

_____

_____

_____

_____

What, if any, are the advantages for civic action groups of using the Internet, email and mobile phones?

_____

_____

_____

_____

_____

_____

Please describe any problem(s) you encounter using public transport?

_____

_____

_____

_____

_____

_____

Open questions offer less structured response options than closed questions, inviting respondents to recount understandings, experiences, or opinions in their own terms. Rather than offer alternative answers, which restrict responses, they provide space (and time) for free-form responses. Open questions also allow respondents to question the terms and structure of the questionnaire itself, demonstrating an alternative interpretation. For instance, in a questionnaire used by Winchester et al. (1997) in Carrington, New South Wales, concerning urban redevelopment and its impact on the close-knit nature of the stable community being researched, a respondent pointed out that it could not be assumed that a stable community implied a close-knit community, as the questionnaire seemed to suggest. She recounted examples of her own sense of detachment from that community. Open questions, then, are capable of yielding valuable insights, many of them unanticipated. Such scope, though, has led open questions to be characterised as 'easy to ask, difficult to answer, and still more difficult to analyse' (Oppenheim 1992, p. 113). An open format means responses may lack consistency and comparability. Certainly, respondents answer them in terms that suit their own interpretation. So open questions and the responses they yield are certainly more challenging to analyse than are their more easily coded closed counterparts (see chapter 14).

In summary, using open questions makes it possible to pose complex questions that can reveal, to a greater depth than closed questions, people's experiences, understandings, and interpretations of, as well as their reactions to, social processes and circumstances. Beyond capturing these accounts, answers to open questions can tell us a good deal about how wider processes operate in particular settings. Thus they enable research that addresses the two fundamental questions that Sayer (1992) poses for qualitative research: what are individuals' particular experiences of places and events; and how are social structures constructed, maintained, or resisted (see chapter 1).

Beyond choice of question content and type, general principles of questionnaire wording, sequence, and format are fundamental to a questionnaire's success. These are outlined in Box 10.2. Many of these principles revolve around clarity, simplicity, and logic. In question wording, you need to be sure that questions are sufficiently precise and unambiguous to ensure that the intent of your question is clear and well communicated. You should provide simple instructions on how to answer closed questions (e.g., how many responses the respondent can tick). It is worth being aware too that the ways particular questions are posed or how they relate to preceding questions can influence respondents' answers. For instance, Babbie (2001) demonstrates how greater support in questionnaire surveys is indicated habitually for the option worded as 'assistance to the poor' rather than as 'welfare', and for 'halting rising crime rate' rather than 'law enforcement'.

The flow and sequence of the questionnaire will be fundamental to respondents' understanding of the research purpose and to sustaining their willingness to offer careful responses and, indeed, to complete the questionnaire to its conclusion. Grouping questions into sections of related questions connected by introductory statements will help here. In general, open-ended questions are better placed towards the end of a questionnaire, by which time respondents are aware of the questionnaire's thrust and may be more inclined to offer fluid and considered responses. In terms of layout, aim for an uncluttered and spacious design that is easy and clear to follow. Where you use closed questions, aligning or justifying the space in which the answer should be provided will contribute to clarity as well as simplify-

BOX 10.2 GUIDELINES FOR DESIGNING QUESTIONNAIRES

- Ensure questions are relevant, querying the issues, practices, and understandings you are investigating.
- Keep the wording simple and appropriate to the targeted population's vernacular.
- Avoid double-barrelled questions (for example, do you agree that the Department of Housing should cease building public housing estates and pursue a social mix policy?).
- Avoid confusing wording (for example, why would you rather not use public transport?).
- Avoid leading questions (for example, why do you think recycling is crucial to the health of future generations?).
- Avoid questions that raise as many questions as they answer (for example, 'are you in favour of regional sustainability?' raises questions of what sustainability means, how a region is defined, and how different dimensions of sustainability might be prioritised).
- Order questions in a coherent and logical sequence.
- Ensure the questionnaire takes no longer than participants are willing to spend. This will depend on the questionnaire context (for example, whether it is conducted by telephone, face-to-face or by post). Generally, 20–30 minutes will be the maximum, though longer times (45 minutes) can be sustained if the combination of context and research topic is appropriate.
- Ensure a spacious layout with plentiful space for written responses to open questions.
- Use continuity statements to link questionnaire sections (for example, 'The next section deals with community members' response to perceived threats to their neighbourhood.').
- Begin with simple questions and place complex, reflexive questions or those dealing with sensitive or threatening topics later in the questionnaire.

ing coding responses in the analysis stage. You also need to be conscious with open-ended questions of the need to leave enough space for respondents to answer, without leaving so much as to discourage them altogether from offering a response. Finally, you should write a cover letter to be included with the questionnaire. Box 10.3 provides an example. The letter needs to provide general information about the purpose of the questionnaire, provide assurances about confidentiality, how the respondent was selected for inclusion in the research, how long the questionnaire will take to complete and, when relevant, instructions on how and when to return the questionnaire.

SAMPLING

Before administering a questionnaire, you will need to make a decision about the target audience, or **sample**. In quantitative research, questionnaires are used commonly to generate claims about the characteristics, behaviour, or opinions of a group of people ('the **population**') based on data collected from a sample of that population. The sample is selected carefully to be representative of the population (for example, tenants in public housing, the

BOX 10.3 SAMPLE COVER LETTER

School of Geography
Geography Building
East Valley University
Kingsland 9222
Telephone: (04) 89889778
Facsimile: (04) 89889779

Leisure and recreation services in Port Andrew, East Valley

I am Edith Saunders, an Honours student with the School of Geography at the East Valley University. As part of my Honours research on leisure and recreation services in East Valley, I am investigating the use of and satisfaction with these services. The research is being conducted in collaboration with East Valley Council as part of their preparation for planning the extension of these services across the region.

The attached questionnaire asks about the way you use existing services, your satisfaction with them, and other leisure and recreation services you would see as desirable in the area. My research is focused on the Port Andrew area and you have been selected to receive this questionnaire as a local resident.

The questionnaire will take approximately 30 minutes to complete and completion is voluntary. The questions are asking primarily for your opinions—there are no right or wrong answers. All answers will be treated confidentially and anonymously—individuals will not be identifiable in how the research is reported.

Once you have completed the questionnaire, please return it in the reply-paid envelope provided. Return of the questionnaire will be considered as your consent to participate in the survey.

Your participation will be greatly appreciated. Your opinions are important in helping me to establish local service needs and, ultimately, will assist East Valley Council in planning the future provision of services in the locality.

Inquiries about this research can be directed to me at the above address.

Thank you in advance for your participation.

Yours faithfully,
Edith Saunders

The University requires that all participants are informed that if they have any complaints concerning the manner in which a research project is conducted it may be given to the researcher or, if an independent person is preferred, to the University's Human Research Ethics Officer, Research Unit, East Coast University, 9222, Telephone (04) 8988 1234

residents of a given local government area, or people living with HIV/AIDS) such that the mathematical probability of the sample characteristics being reproduced in the broader population can be calculated (May 2001). In such cases, a list of the population in question, the **sampling frame**, is required so that a sample can be constructed (for example, the tenant list of a given public housing authority; a local electoral register; a health register of all people in a given geographical area receiving treatment for HIV/AIDS). The rules surrounding sampling are drawn from the central limit theorem used to sustain statistical claims to representativeness, generalisability, and replicability (see McLafferty 2003; Parfitt 1997; Robinson 1998).

On the other hand, questionnaires used in qualitative research are likely to be used as a part of mixed-method research aimed at establishing trends, patterns, or themes in experiences, behaviours, and understandings as part of analysis of a *specific context*, without seeking to make generalisable claims about whole populations (Robinson 1998, p. 409). Hence, a more appropriate sampling technique for qualitative research is non-**probability sampling**, where generalisation to a broader population is neither possible nor desirable and sampling frames may not, in any case, be available. Specifically, purposive sampling (see chapter 5) is commonly used wherein sample selection for questionnaire respondents is made according to some known common characteristic, be it a social category (for example, male single parents), a particular behaviour (for example, women who use public transport), or an experience (for example, people who have been victims of crime). There are no specific rules for this type of sampling (de Vaus 1995). Rather, the determinants of the appropriate sample and sample size are related to the precise scope, nature, and intent of the research and to the expectations of your research communities.

As in all research these considerations are overlain by the limitations of resource constraints (time and money). Nonetheless, this does not imply the absence of a systematic approach; quite the opposite. Complex decisions need to be made about how to approach sampling. For instance, in research on what motivates 'sea-changers' to abandon city life and relocate to regional, coastal areas, researchers would need to take into account whether they should seek respondents in all age groups, all household types and all income categories. Research on people living with HIV/AIDS would need to take into account whether the researchers should target early-stage individuals only; both biological sexes or only one; people of any sexual orientation or a specific sexual orientation; only individuals infected from a particular source, and so on. Each decision is liable to have ramifications for how sample recruitment proceeds and what mode of questionnaire distribution is suitable. Both these cases illustrate the fundamental importance of research scope, purpose, and intent in shaping sampling approach and in determining appropriate sample size. Patton (1990) provides detailed treatment of various types of purposive sampling, along with a discussion of sample size, and chapter 5 provides an extended treatment of further pertinent questions regarding selecting cases and participants in qualitative research. In the end, claims de Vaus (1995, p. 78), 'decisions about samples will be a compromise between cost, (the need for) accuracy, the nature of the research problem and the art of the possible'.

PRE-TESTING

It is vital to try out a questionnaire before it is distributed. **Pre-testing** is where a questionnaire is piloted or 'road-tested' with a sub-sample of your target population to assess the merits of its design, its appropriateness to the audience, and whether it does in fact achieve your aims. Getting feedback at this stage from those with extensive questionnaire-design experience and from those who might use the data generated (for example, in the example from Box 10.3, a local authority) will allow possible problems to be identified or improvements made. Scheduling a pre-testing stage provides the opportunity for post-test revisions that might dramatically increase the questionnaire's effectiveness.

Both individual question items and the overall performance of the questionnaire need attention at this stage. Are individual questions and question instructions easily understood? Would any of them benefit from the addition of written prompts? Do respondents interpret questions as intended? Do any questions seem to make respondents uncomfortable? Discomfort and sensitivity (perhaps the question is considered too intrusive) might be indicated by respondents' tending to skip or refuse to answer a specific question or section. Alternatively those outcomes could mean that respondents do not understand the question or do not have the knowledge or experience to answer it. On the questionnaire overall, consider how respondents react to the questions' order? Does it seem to them to flow logically and intuitively? Are there parts where the questionnaire seems to drag or become repetitive? Technical aspects can also be tested: is there enough space for respondents' to answer open questions? How long will the questionnaire take to complete? Do the data being generated present particular problems for analysis? If you plan to conduct the questionnaire face-to-face with respondents, the pre-test stage can also be a useful exercise in training and confidence-building.

MODES OF QUESTIONNAIRE DISTRIBUTION

Consideration of the mode of questionnaire distribution should be one of the earliest stages of your questionnaire design. It has significant implications for design, layout, question type, and sample selection. The main distribution modes are mail, face-to-face, and telephone. Each mode has distinctive strengths and weaknesses and the choice between them depends on the research topic, type of questions, and resource constraints. The best choice is the one most appropriate to the research context and target population while the success of any particular mode is dependent on a design appropriate to context and population. So the question is, what should researchers interested in qualitative research be aware of to inform the choice of mode?

Mail questionnaires have clear advantages of cost and coverage. They can be distributed to large samples over large areas (for example, an entire country or province) at relatively low cost. The anonymity they provide may be a significant advantage where sensitive topics are being researched, for example, those dealing with socially disapproved attitudes or behaviours such as racism or transgressive sexual behaviour, or topics involving personal harm such as experience of unemployment or experience of crime. Respondents may also feel more able to take time to consider their responses if unimpeded by the presence of an interviewer. Clearly, too, the absence of an interviewer means responses cannot be shaped by how, precisely, an interviewer poses a question.

Nonetheless, mail questionnaires are the most limited of the three modes in terms of questionnaire length and complexity. The scope for complex open questions particularly is limited too by the need for questions to be self-explanatory and brief, and this may be a significant consideration for qualitatively oriented research. Once sent out, there is little control over who completes the questionnaire or, indeed, how it is completed; respondents may choose to restrict themselves to brief, unreflective, or patterned responses. A response to the question 'what do you value about living in this community?' might yield a response of several paragraphs from one respondent and the comment 'friends and neighbours' from another. There is no opportunity to clarify questions or probe answers. Nor is there control over the pattern and rate of response. Some parts of the target population may respond at a higher rate than others. It is common, for instance, for mail questionnaires to achieve significantly higher response rates in wealthier neighbourhoods than less socially advantaged neighbourhoods. Finally, mail questionnaires can be subject to low response rates unless respondents are highly motivated to participate. Response rates of 40% are not uncommon though effective follow-up steps can increase this somewhat (May 2001; Robinson 1998).

Distributing questionnaires by email is a recent variation on mail distribution. Distribution will be shaped by the age, class, and gender biases that shape computer-use and email patronage (see Gibson 2003). Careful consideration needs to be given to whether the bias in who can be reached by email is problematic for the research in hand. One distinct advantage of electronic distribution is the ability to incorporate colour images and graphics without associated printing costs. This opens up new opportunities for more complex questions to be posed, increasing their potential for generating rich qualitative data. The few geographers who have taken advantage of this distribution mode report strong response rates with respondents characteristically submitting lengthy commentaries on open questions (Hoggart, Lees, and Davies 2002); a plus for qualitative research.

Qualitative research is often well served by using an interviewer to conduct face-to-face questionnaires, although this is a costly option. The major benefits of this mode arise because having an interviewer present allows complex questions to be asked (see chapter 6). It also enables the interviewer to take note of the context of the interview and of respondents' non-verbal gestures, all of which add depth to the qualitative data collected (May 2001). As an interviewer you can motivate respondents to participate and to provide considered, qualitatively informative responses. Moreover, people are more likely to offer long responses verbally than in writing. Perhaps more crucially, face-to-face questionnaires provide the opportunity for questions to be clarified and vague responses probed (see chapters 6 and 7 for related discussions). For example, adding probes like 'why is that exactly?', 'in what ways?', or 'anything else?' can elicit reflection on an opinion or attitude. Long questionnaires can also be sustained because direct contact with an interviewer can enhance respondent engagement. It is a major benefit for qualitative research to be able to pose complex questions and elicit more in-depth and engaged qualitative responses. Moreover, this level of engagement can also secure high response rates—Babbie (2001) estimates 80–85%—with a minimal number of nil response and 'don't know' answers. However, the level of interviewer skill demanded to secure all of these outcomes should not be underestimated.

As Kevin Dunn discusses more fully in chapter 6, the presence of an interviewer can be a powerful means of collecting high quality data, but it introduces limitations too. Interviewer/respondent interaction can produce 'interviewer effects' that shape the responses offered. People filter their answers through a sense of social expectations, especially when interviewed face-to-face (Lee 2000). They may censor their answers according to perceived social desirability. That is, they may avoid revealing socially disapproved behaviours or beliefs (such as racism) or revealing negative experiences (for example, unemployment). One means of dealing with this is to incorporate a self-administered section in the questionnaire or to reassure respondents of a guarantee of anonymity. Moreover, interviewers' presence (as embodied subjects with class, gender, and race characteristics) can also affect the nature of responses given. For instance, Padfield and Procter (1996) suggest that the gender of the interviewer introduces significant variations. So, while distinct benefits arise from using face-to-face distribution, there are drawbacks. Perhaps the most limiting of these is the practical consideration of cost. Interviewer-administered questionnaires are expensive and time consuming and tend to be restrictive spatially and with respect to population coverage. However, as we suggested before, this may not be a significant drawback if a particular, localised population group is targeted.

While the opportunities for personal interchange are more restricted in telephone than in face-to-face questionnaires, the telephone mode still offers the chance for dialogue between researcher and respondent and can secure some of the associated benefits along with a certain anonymity that may limit problematic interviewer effects. Conducting questionnaires over the phone may encourage respondent participation, being potentially less threatening than opening the door to a caller wishing to administer a questionnaire. However, telephone delivery constrains the scope for lengthy questionnaires, with about thirty minutes being the maximum time respondents are willing to participate (de Vaus 1995). Besides, because they rely on a respondent's memory, the question format must be kept simple and the number of response categories in closed questions needs to be limited. However, the advent of **CATI (computer-assisted telephone interviewing)** and 'Voice Capture' technology is significantly enhancing telephone questionnaires (see Babbie 2001, p. 265) and extending their potential in this regard. Moreover, they can be administered with great convenience and at relatively low cost.

Telephone questionnaires may be reliant on a telephone directory as a sampling frame and this can introduce class and gender biases amongst respondents as well as placing ex-directory numbers beyond reach. If telephone numbers are available for a purposefully selected group of people then this may not pose a problem. Historically, telephone surveys have had good response rates (Feitelson 1991) and follow-ups by a simple call-back can be conducted much more conveniently than for face-to-face or mail questionnaires. However, in the present climate of public concern over unsolicited marketing calls, approaches by telephone are increasingly likely to face rejection by recipients or to be screened out by answering machines.

MAXIMISING QUESTIONNAIRE RESPONSE RATES

Questionnaire response rates are shaped by the research topic, the nature of the sample, and the quality and appropriateness of questionnaire design as much as by the mode of distribution. In any case, questionnaire response rates tend to be higher when using a purposive sample, wherein interest in the research topic may be strong. Regardless of the mode of distribution, response rates can be improved by undertaking a series of strategies before questionnaire distribution and as follow-up (Dillman 1978) in order both to maximise

BOX 10.4 STRATEGIES FOR MAXIMISING RESPONSE RATES

Strategy	Face-to-face	Telephone	Mail
• Ensure mode of distribution is appropriate to the targeted population and research topic	√	√	√
• Send notification letter introducing the research and alerting to the questionnaire's arrival		√	√
• Place newspaper advertisement in local/ community newspaper/magazine introducing the research and alerting to the conduct of the questionnaire	√	√	√
• Ensure questionnaire is concise	√	√	√
• Ensure appropriate location of approach	√		
• Ensure appropriate time of approach	√	√	
• Vary time if no contact is made initially	√	√	
• Pre-arrange time/location for conduct of questionnaire, if appropriate	√	√	
• Ensure reply-paid envelope is included in mail-out			√
• Print questionnaire on coloured paper to distinguish it from introductory material or other mail			√
• Send follow-up postcard thanking early respondents and reminding others (about one week after initial receipt)			√
• Send follow-up letter and additional copy of questionnaire (two to three weeks after initial receipt)			√
• Avoid abrasive manner	√	√	
• Dress appropriately to the target population	√		

participation and minimise non-responses. Box 10.4 summarises the key strategies and indicates to which modes of distribution they are appropriate.

ANALYSING QUESTIONNAIRE DATA

Widespread acceptance of mixed-method research ensures that questionnaire analysis will often involve a search for both quantitative and qualitative data. Quantitative data arises primarily from closed questions that provide counts of categorical data (for example, age and income bands, frequency of behaviour) or measures of attitudinal or opinion data (see Box 10.1 for examples). Questions such as these are relatively easy to code numerically and analyse for patterns of response and relationships between the variables that questions have interrogated (May 2001). Indeed response categories can be pre-coded on the questionnaire, simplifying matters even further (see de Vaus 1995 or Robinson 1998 for more detail). The analysis of qualitative responses is more complex. The power of qualitative data lies in its revelation of a respondent's understandings and interpretations of the social world and these data, in turn, are interpreted by the researcher to reveal the understandings of structures and processes that shape respondents' thought and action (for elaboration see Crang 1997a; Robinson 1998, pp. 426–7). Chapters 14 and 15 attend to the techniques and challenges of coding and analysing qualitative data in detail. Nonetheless, it is worth raising some important points specific to analysing qualitative data arising from questionnaires.

In qualitative responses the important data often lie in the detailed explanations and precise wording of respondents' answers. For qualitative research, then, it is best to avoid classifying qualitative responses into simple descriptive categories so as to report on them quantitatively, stating, for example, that '49% of respondents had positive opinions about their neighbourhood'. There are two problems here. First, such reporting gives the misleading impression that findings are quantitative and could be used to draw generalisations. It may well be statistically misleading, too, to report in this form the results of what might be a relatively small purposive sample. Second, this approach involves 'closing' open questions so that much of the richness of how respondents constructed, in this example, their positive understandings and experiences of their locality, is lost. Certainly, classifying qualitative responses into descriptive categories allows us to simplify, summarise, compare, and aggregate data, but this kind of approach forfeits the nuance and complexity of the original text. To report on observations in this way is unlikely to contribute much to our understanding of the meanings and operations of social structures and processes and people's interpretations and behaviour in relation to them. It is more attuned to the thrust of qualitative research to analyse data gained from a questionnaire by sifting and sorting to identify key themes and dimensions as well as the broader concepts that might underlie them (see the discussion of analytical coding in chapter 14). Reporting findings in these terms is much more meaningful than falling back on awkward attempts to quantify the data.

Further, in analysing qualitative responses we need to be aware that qualitative research makes no assumption that respondents share a common definition of the phenomenon under investigation (be that quality of neighbourhood, experience of crime, understanding of health and illness...). Rather it assumes that variable and multiple understandings co-exist in a given social context. We need to incorporate this awareness into how we make sense of respondents' qualitative answers. Indeed, one of the strengths of using questionnaires in qualitative research can be their ability to identify variability in understanding and interpretation across a selected population, providing the groundwork for further investigation through additional complementary methods such as in-depth interviews.

Finally, keep in mind that qualitative data analysis is sometimes referred to as more of an art than a science (Babbie 2001). It is not reducible to a neat set of techniques. Though useful procedures can be followed (see chapter 14), they may need to be customised to the unique concerns and structure of each questionnaire and the particular balance of quantitative and qualitative data it gathers. For this reason, and others, at all stages of the process of analysis we need to be mindful of engaging in critical reflexivity, especially when considering how our own frames of reference and personal positions shape the ways in which we proceed with analysis (see chapters 2 and 16).

CONCLUSION

In seeking qualitative data, questionnaires aim not just to determine qualitative attitudes and opinions but to identify and classify the logic of different sets of responses, to seek patterns or commonality in responses, and to explore how these relate to concepts, structures, and processes that shape social life. This is no easy undertaking and questionnaires struggle with the tensions of seeking explanation while being limited in their form and format to obtaining concise accounts.

Hoggart, Lees, and Davies (2002) argue that the necessarily limited complexity and length of questionnaires prevent them from being able to explain action (as this requires us to understand people's intentions), the significance of action, and the connections between acts. Compared with the depth of information developed through more intensive research methods such as in-depth interviews, focus groups, or participant observation, questionnaires may provide only superficial coverage. Nonetheless, they can help us begin this explanation in that they are useful for identifying regularities and differences and highlighting incidents and trends (see de Vaus 1995 for an extended critique).

Yet, there are ways to construct and deliver effective questionnaires that are largely qualitative in their aspirations, being mindful of the possibility of acquiring deep analytical understandings of social behaviours through careful collection of textual materials. Certainly, the interview, through its record of close dialogue between researcher and respondent, provides the most powerful way of uncovering narratives that reveal the motivations and meanings surrounding human interactions, and questionnaires can only ever move incompletely in this direction. However, by not requiring close and prolonged engagement with the research subject, the questionnaire offers opportunities to reach a wide range and great number of respondents and to collect data on their lived experiences. This extensiveness and diversity makes questionnaires an important, contemporary research tool.

KEY TERMS

CATI (computer-assisted
   telephone interviewing)
closed questions
combination questions
mixed-method research
open questions

population
pre-testing
probability sampling
purposive sampling
sample
sampling frame

REVIEW QUESTIONS

1   Why are open questions more suited to qualitative research than closed questions?
2   Why is the choice of the mode of questionnaire distribution specific to the nature of the sample and the nature of the research topic?
3   Why should we avoid 'closing' open question responses for the purpose of reporting findings?
4   What are the limitations of the use of questionnaires for qualitative research?

SUGGESTED READING

Babbie, E. 2001, *The Practice of Social Research,* 9th edn, Wadsworth, Belmont, CA, chapters 9 and 13.

de Vaus, D. A. 1995, *Surveys in Social Research*, UCL Press, London, chapter 6.

Hoggart, K., Lees, L. and Davies A. 2002, *Researching Human Geography*, Arnold, London, chapter 5.

Parfitt, J. 1997, 'Questionnaire design and sampling', in R. Flowerdew and D. Martin (eds), *Methods in Human Geography. A Guide for Students Doing a Research Project*, Addison Wesley Longman, Harlow, pp. 76–109.

11

Doing Discourse Analysis

Gordon Waitt

CHAPTER OVERVIEW

My hope in writing this chapter is to generate enthusiasm for geographical research employing discourse analysis. My intention is to provide some advice on doing discourse analysis to facilitate the design of research. I first outline why some geographers have been inspired by this approach. I suggest how Foucauldian discourse analysis is a break from other critical methods applied to textual analysis, including content analysis, semiology, and iconography. The theoretical underpinnings of the method provided by Michel Foucault, a French poststructuralist philosopher, is a key source of difference. I therefore condense Michel Foucault's contribution to discourse analysis by sketching out his key theoretical concepts and their methodological implications. To discuss the methodological implications of doing discourse analysis I draw upon the advice of feminist geographer Gillian Rose and linguist Norman Fairclough. I provide a list of questions to help implement a Foucauldian approach to discourse analysis and illustrate their implications for 'doing' geography by drawing upon examples. This chapter should therefore be read only as an appetiser as there are many forms of discourse analysis. The suggested readings provide a much larger selection of the theoretical and methodological possibilities.

INTRODUCTION: GEOGRAPHICAL KNOWLEDGE AS AN EXPRESSION OF HUMAN IDEAS

> We must not imagine that the world turns towards us a legible face which we would have only to decipher. The world is not the accomplice of our knowledge; there is no prediscursive providence which disposes the world in our favour (Foucault 1981, p. 67).

Many geographers are constantly challenged by the writings of the French philosopher Michel Foucault to reflect upon geographical knowledge. Challenges for both what is geographical knowledge and how it is produced are posed by his argument that people only have access to comprehend the world about them through linguistic description. In other words, there is no geographical knowledge other than the ordering that people impose on the world through their linguistic description of the world. In doing so Foucault is not rejecting the materiality of events, nor the existence of a reality that pre-exists humans, as alleged by some of his critics (see Taylor 1984). Yet, he is arguing that it is often not easy for people to understand the world about them (what is a plant, a human, or an animal), who they are (self) and what they *do* with, and their *attitudes* towards, other people and the bio-physical environment outside of the linguistic structures available to them.

This recognition that the social, how people act, think, and perceive, is actually constituted within linguistic description not merely revealing or reflecting it thrills many geographers (Anderson 1995; Boyle and Rogerson 2001; Costello and Hodge 1998; Dunn and Roberts 2003; Jacobs 1993; McManus 2000; McFarlane and Hay 2003; Mee 1994; Shaw 2000; Suchet 2002; Waitt 1997). First, enthusiasm arises from the fact that no longer is geographical inquiry framed within the positivist or Marxist search for truth, generalisations, or **essentialism** of 'the real'. Moreover, the subjects and objects that comprise geographical analysis are no longer uncritically accepted as given, uniform categories, sometimes referred to as stable referents, such as 'wilderness', 'nature', 'class', 'ethnicity', and 'gender'. Instead, the work of language is argued to *constitute* these categories for a particular audience. Second, excitement stems from how Foucault's **constructionist approach** challenges conventional disciplinary boundaries of geography by enabling a demarcation that includes the voices of those people formerly excluded, including the indigenous, disabled, elderly, queer, lesbian, gay, and bisexual. Finally, many geographers turn to the work of poststructuralist writers, such as Foucault, to examine how particular geographical knowledges have social effects on what people perceive, think, and do. Consequently, a constructionist approach has been employed to investigate processes of social marginalisation and the denial of basic human rights (Dunn 2003), to explore the relationship that tourists have with the bio-physical environment and the people they encounter while on holiday (Lane and Waitt 2001), as well as the effectiveness of environmental management.

Influenced largely by the work of Foucault the term discourse is now in wide circulation in human geography (see Lees 2004 for a comparison between a Gramscian and Foucauldian understanding of discourse analysis). Foucault, however, does not use the conventional linguistic meaning of the word 'discourse'; that is, as passages of connected writing or speech. Instead, he conceptualises discourse within a theoretically informed framework that investigates the rules about the production of knowledge through language (meanings) and its influence over what we do (practice). Yet, providing a clear-cut definition of this term is complicated by the multiple and interchangeable ways Foucault (1972) employs the term. At least three overlain explanations of discourse can be identified in his work: (i) all meaningful statements or texts that have effects on the world; (ii) a group of statements that appear to have a common theme that provides them with an unified effect; and (iii) the rules and structures that underpin and govern the unified, coherent, and forceful statements that are produced. Despite this complexity, clarification is provided on what are the aims and objectives of discourse analysis. Clearly, **discourse analysis** becomes: (i) to explore the outcomes of discourse in terms of actions, perceptions, or attitudes rather than the simply the analysis of statements/texts; (ii) to identity the regulatory frameworks within which groups of statements are produced, circulated, and communicated within which people construct their utterances and thoughts; and (iii) to uncover the support or internal mechanisms that maintain certain structures and rules over statements about people, animals, plants, events, and places in existence as unchallengeable, 'normal', or 'common-sense' rather than to discover the 'truth' or the 'origin' of a statement.

In this chapter I use examples primarily from tourism geographies and the geographies of sexuality to illustrate how some human geographers have actioned discourse analysis in their research. This choice is not accidental. These examples clearly illustrate how a particular discursive-grouping (the academic discipline of geography) also operates to determine what can be said, what is worthy of study, and what is regarded as factual. Research addressing tourism and sexuality were often shunned and avoided in the discipline as almost taboo subjects not worthy of geographical analysis until the 1990s (Binnie and Valentine 1999). Their exclusion illustrated how discursive structures operate to limit what geographers can say. There is nothing intrinsic to sexuality or tourism that makes them more difficult for geographers to study than, say, ethnicity or car manufacturing. What made it seem self-evident that these were topics to be avoided by geographers was in part the range of methodologies that the discipline drew upon to think about what constituted geographical knowledge. Sexuality was avoided because positive thinking produced a subject assumed to be sexed at birth. Homosexual people in particular were avoided because in the views of 'rational' science they were thought of as seemingly 'deviant'. Tourists were avoided as they were positioned as seemingly only engaged in leisure pursuits. Analysis of people having fun, regardless of their social impacts, was not as respectable a topic as, say, the kudos that could be achieved from examining the social relationships of those people working in those industries positioned as 'industrial heartlands': the steel, textile, coal, or automobile industries.

FOUCAULDIAN DISCOURSE ANALYSIS AS A BREAK WITH PREVIOUS TEXTUAL ANALYSIS

Perhaps one of the most helpful ways of thinking about how to conduct discourse analysis signalled by poststructuralist theory is to become aware of how the method is a major break with previous views of the use in geography of qualitative data (including films, photographs, brochures, postcards, fiction, travel guides, novels, newspapers, spoken words, and so forth). Before discourse analysis there were a number of 'tools' used by geographers to conduct qualitative research and interpret these sources so as to clarify their importance as a vehicle of communication about the world and form of representation of the geographical imagination. This task of interpreting the meaning in language, texts, and visual representations is known as **hermeneutics**. In the humanities' 'hermeneutic tool bag' geographers had found helpful a number of methodologies, including content analysis, **semiology**, and **iconography**.

In each case these methods conceptualise the stretch of text or representation as transparent and simply as a vehicle of expression. Emphasis in these methods is given to analysis of the qualitative data itself as a mechanism of communication rather than as a practice, a system operating within its own regulations and checks. In contrast, the priority in discourse analysis is upon the *effects* of a particular cultural text on what an individual may do or think by unravelling its production, social context, and intended audience. The methodological strength of discourse analysis lies in its ability to move beyond the text, the subtext, and representation to uncover issues of power relationships that inform what people think and do.

For example, semiology studies representations and written texts for dominant codes or groups of **signs**. For semiologists the basic units of language for analysis are conceptualised as signs rather than a discourse that produced something else. Let us say for example the word 'alien'. In the terminology of semiology the object that the sign refers to is termed the referent. Consequently semiology is sometimes referred to as a referent system. According to theories of semiology language, signs operate through two mutual relationships. The first is between the sign and the **signified** (the concept or object, let's say 'a person born overseas'). The second is between the sign and the **signifier** (the sound or image attached to a sign, in this case the word 'alien'). However, the important theoretical point that semiologists make is that there is no given or stable relationship between the signifier and signified. The same signifier can have many meanings. 'Alien' can also be an extraterrestrial being, or a term to describe unusual behaviour as well as a term to stereotype social differences between people. Instead, whatever stability is fixed between a signifier and signified is reliant upon the difference between the sign 'alien' and other signs such as 'foreigner', 'migrant', 'tourist', 'temporary resident', 'guest worker', and so on (see Barthes 1973; Burgess and Wood 1988; Hall 1980; Hodge and Kress 1988; Williamson 1978).

Iconography is also a method of interpreting symbols and the imagery of visual texts. This method first relies upon a process of familiarisation with the meanings of historically and geographically specific symbols that would have circulated among the text's intended audience. This necessitates the use of relevant historical sources to provide insights into the symbolic meanings of a visual text, its use of colour, and the various objects, postures, and fashions depicted (Daniels and Cosgrove 1988; Panofsky 1957). This method then relies upon a process of peeling away levels of meanings through a process of visual interpretation. According to the art historian, Erwin Panofsky, there are three levels:

1 primary, natural or pre-iconographic
2 secondary, conventional or iconographic
3 intrinsic, symbolic or **iconological**.

To illustrate these levels of interpretation we can consider the postcard in Figure 11.1 'The Essential Australia', Bungle Bungle Range (Purnululu National Park), printed by Fiona Lake and purchased in Kununurra, Western Australia in 2002. This postcard is one example of how the physical environment has been turned into a tourist commodity in Western capitalist societies. At the primary or pre-iconographic level the postcard depicts a bird's eye view of a dry river-bed in a gorge of the Bungle Bungle Range. At the secondary level this physical environment, devoid of any human inhabitants, stands for the possibilities of discovering an alternative or 'real' self through a transformative encounter with the hostile Australian environment. A clue to this interpretation is provided by the text 'The Essential Australia'. The final level of interpretation, the iconological, is an examination of cultural conventions that underpin the symbolic qualities of the image. This requires drawing on other sources that help the target audience decode the symbolic qualities of the Bungle Bungles. For example,

Figure 11.1 A selection of tourism industry texts portraying The Kimberley, Australia, as the frontier

Consider in what ways these different texts operate individually and together to either challenge or reproduce particular geographical knowledge of the Kimberley as a frontier?

Postcard titled 'The Essential Australia', Bungle Bungle Range (Purnululu National Park). (Source: Fiona Lake, Somerville, Richmond, North Queensland 4822, Australia.)

Look Sea Tours Brochure. (Source: Look Sea Tours, lookseatours@bigpond.com.)

Last Frontier sign at Kununurra Airport. (Source: Gordon Waitt 2003.)

Interpretation sign of Aboriginal rock art, Keep River National Park, Northern Territory. (Source: Gordon Waitt 2003.)

Postcard titled 'Kimberley Vision'. (Source: Kimberley Vision.)

the 'true-self' interpretation relies on popular Western myths of the transformative role of travel that were circulating when the first Europeans encountered the extreme and unique physical environment of Australia. Such transformational encounters have played an important role in the Australian nation-making project, differentiating European Australians from other nationalities. Continued circulation of these ideas in popular culture is apparent in the works of novelists such as Mary Durack (see her 1986 book *Kings in Grass Castles*), films such as *Crocodile Dundee,* the Australian Tourism Commission's travel campaigns that brand Australia (Waitt 1999), and the work of historians such as Ward (1958). These authors all draw on the frontier thesis, which suggests that people encountering the harsh environmental conditions of the 'outback' are stripped of their cultural pasts. In the case of national narratives the encounter recasts colonists with the characteristics of European Australians: battlers and larrikins who valued independence and mateship. For the tourism industry the encounter provides tourists with a potential makeover—an opportunity to discover an alternative self through acts of adventure and exploration in the Australian 'outback'.

Finally, content analysis also often examines text as something that exists in itself, which is apparently transparent and therefore can be analysed in isolation. Therefore, content analysis proceeds by coding and then quantifying the priorities of identified and emergent themes within texts (Lutz and Collins 1993). This is also discussed by Meghan Cope in chapter 14.

At a practical level there are some methodological similarities between discourse analysis and both iconography and content analysis. Both iconography and discourse analysis rely upon **intertextuality**, a term often used to refer to the way in which meanings are sustained through mutually related verbal, written, and visual texts. As Jay Ruby (1995) says in the context of analysing visual images, 'the study of images alone, as objects whose meaning is intrinsic to them, is a mistaken method if you are interested in the ways in which people assign meanings to pictures'. Both iconography and discourse analysis rely upon drawing from a number of related qualitative sources to examine how meanings are (re)produced and circulated.

In regards to discourse analysis and content analysis, both methods require the research to perform the operations of familiarisation, coding, and indexing. Indeed, Rose (2001) offers the structured framework of content analysis as a productive way for the novice to begin discourse analysis through the identification of embedded themes. Yet, at a conceptual level, discourse analysis does not emphasise 'peeling away' the meaning of texts. Rather than uncovering processes operating beneath the surface of texts that operate at the level of the sign, discourse analysis examines how discourses are constituted and circulated within texts and representations, which in turn function to produce a particular understanding or knowledge about the world that is accepted as 'truth' (Foucault 1980).

How discourse analysis can be conceptualised as a break from previous qualitative methods is reliant upon its focus, to identify and to understand how particular ideas are privileged as 'truth'. According to Foucault, this requires careful investigation of **discursive structures**. These are the unwritten conventions that operate to produce some kind of authoritative account of the world, be it the physical environment, an economic process, or social difference. A discursive structure can be detected because of how it demarcates the boundaries within which people think or behave. For example, geographers investigating questions pertaining to sexual citizenship have noted how politicians opposed to same-sex political rights often draw upon an evolutionary narrative to constitute as degenerate people who engage in same-sex acts. The evolutionary narrative positions same-sex attracted people as non-citizens who belong to primitive societies, a remnant of an earlier period of primitive human development (see Hoad 2000). Consequently, same-sex attracted people are positioned as a threat to civilised societies. Geographers have demonstrated how these arguments are widely employed to prevent legislation that prevents discrimination for sexual orientation. Waitt et al. (2000) provide another example. They illustrate how the discourse of globalisation voiced by the 'neo-liberalism' of the New Right restricts the way government economic policy can negotiate the global economy. Neo-liberalism asserts the claim that national economies must be highly competitive in order to survive. Economic globalisation, in political narratives of neo-liberalism, is positioned as inevitable, a natural law. In the evolutionary narratives of neo-liberalism, competition is essential for the national economy to survive. In the face of this global force the only government and industry responses are practices of deregulation. In this way governments help to render as 'natural' free trade and industrial policies that have resulted in, for example, higher prices for certain medicines, threats to jobs in the Australian film and television industry, and the introduction of genetically modified crops.

In terms of thinking about discourse as having support structures that maintain certain rules, McFarlane and Hay (2003) illustrate how the discourses of neo-liberalism are assisted through the mass media. From their analysis of a major Australian newspaper, the *Australian*, they demonstrate how this newspaper scripted the subjectivities of those people who protested in Seattle on 30 November 1999 against neo-liberal policies endorsed by the World Trade Organisation as stupid, actors, fringe dwellers, and/or demons. The media positioned protestors as clueless and undermined their political arguments or belittled them as myths or conspiracy theories. Protestors were also portrayed as actors in a carnival of fun, entertainment, and amusement. Through media focus on appearances—hairy chests, buzz cuts, swimsuits, piercing, and bare-breasted women—protestors were portrayed to the *Australian*'s readers as 'abnormal' people. Finally, scripted as demons, protestors were linked to social chaos through a battle script that emphasised violence, lawlessness, and anarchy. In contrast, suited officials from the WTO were reported to communicate commonsense order and norms provided by globalisation.

Rendering neo-liberalism policies as 'commonsense' or shaping any other political narratives as 'true' or 'natural' can be seen to be constructed through the operation of discursive structures. The organisation of discourse is a process instilled and negotiated within a number of intricate, complex, and utterly social processes. Writing geography informed by the ideas of discourse analysis is concerned with troubling, exposing, and unsettling the 'truth' (Bonnet 1996; Jackson and Penrose 1993). In terms of thinking about discourse as having effects by maintaining particular ideas as 'commonsense' it is therefore critical to consider how discourse analysis draws upon its own theoretical framework found in Foucault's discussions of power, knowledge, and truth.

INTRODUCING DISCOURSE

Important methodological implications arise from investigating some of Michel Foucault's theoretical terminology. Although far more comprehensive reviews of Foucault's theoretical arguments are given elsewhere (see Cousins and Houssain 1984; Hall 1997; McNay 1994; Mills 1997), before discussing the methodological implications of doing discourse analysis I briefly summarise some of his conceptual tools including discourse, episteme, discursive structures/formations, genealogy, and regime of truth.

Discourse is central to Foucault's theory and methodology. Foucault's (1972) theories of discourse demonstrate how the mutual relationships between a group of statements within different cultural texts generate the meaning of a specific item that is understood to construct 'truths' about the social and material worlds and to inform practice. For example, for Foucault the meaning of 'homosexual' is not found by looking up this word in a dictionary. Instead, the homosexual is constituted socially in the utterances, representations, and written publications of medical, religious, and political institutions as well as those of same-sex attracted people. This process was envisaged as a 'privileging' one. That is, processes of exclusion operate on discourse to restrict what can be said. Particular meanings are favoured, often being counted as knowledge, while others are excluded and silenced, reduced to hearsay or folk-law.

Returning to the example of the subjectivity of the homosexual: in nineteenth-century Europe, North America, and Russia, privilege was given to the medical institutional narrative that made same-sex attracted women invisible by constituting sex as a penetrative act. Similarly, a lethal mix of fundamental Christian morals and evolutionary narratives of science were applied to explain social difference that positioned homosexual men as primitive, degenerate, diseased, and sinful. Although there were limits placed on what could be said about same-sex attracted women and men and both were alienated from mainstream society, they did not vanish. The official or hegemonic narrative that masked sexual differences through casting the subject of the homosexual as taboo and passing laws to criminalise sodomy only helped to construct a national closet that operated to conceal and confine same-sex desires. Same-sex venues for men were always present in nineteenth-century New York, London, Paris, Berlin, and Moscow. More is known about the lived experience of white men because of privileges accrued by their ethnicity, class, and gender in a patriarchal society. For example Duberman, Vicinus, and Chauncey (1990) provide evidence of how closeted-spaces operated in very homophobic societies to provide a sense of self, pride, and pleasure. Yet, it is important to remember that such important insights would have never been considered knowledge or worthy of academic publication in the nineteenth century. At this time normative methodologies of science had classified the homosexual as a diseased subject, thus self-evidently only worthy of study to find a medicinal cure. Poststructuralist approaches that examine the lived experience of same-sex attracted men would never have been counted as knowledge. This is illustrative of what Foucault (1972) called the **episteme.** This term refers to how thinking is structured about a particular subject and how certain methodologies produce a particular subject. In this way, discourse consequently operates to limit what can be said, what can become objects of our knowledge, and what is accepted as knowledge. That is, although material objects and social practices exist outside language, they are only 'brought into view' by language. Consequently, as Foucault (1972, p. 32) says, 'nothing has any meaning outside of discourse'. In turn, discourse governs how a topic can be meaningfully explained. It controls how ideas are put into practice. In addition to its power to name and temporally 'fix' particular understandings, discourse also refers to the way people respond to that particular way of thinking (Foucault 1972). Thus, discourse can be used to regulate the lives of people (for example, the denial of lesbians in nineteenth-century Britain, the closeting of sexual minorities in twenty-first-century Egypt and Jamaica).

Returning to the example of same-sex desires but within the context of Conservative Party policies of Margaret Thatcher's Britain in the 1980s, let us again reflect on the important point of how processes of exclusion operate through discourse to limit what can be said and establishing imagined social collective boundaries. Although having decriminalised same-sex acts, Britain was still imagined in the 1980s to be a heterosexual nation underpinned by the heterosexual family. Consequently, same-sex acts positioned the homosexual outside the imagined community of the state. The 'queer' was portrayed as the enemy within the state (Cooper and Herman 1995). Only the 'good homosexual' would be tolerated. Smith (1994) has argued that Conservative political narratives constituted the 'good homosexual' as disease free, and who remained closeted, controlled their sexual desires, and knew that their place was on the secret margins of society rather in Pride Parades or in positions of authority. To further limit what can be said about homosexuality the state introduced legislation that prohibited teaching about same-sex desires within the school curriculum through s 28 of the Local Government Act 1988. In doing so, the subject of homosexuality once again became taboo in the state school curriculum. The effect of such an institutional imposed limitation only helped to make it seem self-evident that homosexuality is a difficult subject that should be avoided and also helped to make homosexual people invisible.

Discursive structures/formations

The inclusions/exclusions I have illustrated in the above two examples from the geography of sexuality are reliant upon the operation of structures and rules of discourse, what Foucault (1972) termed 'archaeology'. These discursive structures or formations refer to a relatively rule-bound set of statements that impose limits on how we construct our thoughts and statements (Phillips and Jørgensen 2002). Discursive structures inform our understanding of objects and events. Discursive formations set limits that make, say in my examples of sexual citizenship, the nation appear to be 'real' and heterosexuality appear to be 'normal'.

The meaning of an object, say an animal or plant; an event, say a fun run, an opening ceremony, or Pride Parade; or a place, for example a resort or nation, is fashioned through a pattern of discursive structures repeated across a number of statements, pictures, books, and magazines (texts), including sets of ideas, practices, rules, subject positions, processes, and attitudes. In the context of discourse, meanings cannot only be confined to a single word, sentences, or particular text, but depend on the outcome of relationships between texts, intertextuality. Individually, texts are not meaningful. Texts are made meaningful through their interconnections with other texts, their different discourses, consumption, circulation, and production. Accordingly, discourse analysis must refer to collections of texts. For example, valuable sources to examine in the context of the emergence of counter-hegemonic resort spaces for same-sex attracted people that have emerged in non-metropolitan centres such as the Florida Keys USA), Mykonos (Greece), or Port Douglas (Australia), include statements made by local and national politicians, brochures of the gay tourism industry, interviews with tour operators, local residents, and tourists as well as gay pornography. Therefore, embedded within gay tourism destinations but also gardens, backyards, streets, suburbs, zoos, beach, cities, national parks, rural areas (the outback or the countryside), and the nation are particular interpretations of place, people, the bio-physical environment, and so on that are contingent on other texts as well as the particular culture, time, and place in which they are produced.

Discursive structures set limits to how people can think and act at a specific historical conjuncture. They impose a solidity and normality beyond which is often very hard to reason and behave. However, meanings are temporally 'fixed' only to achieve a particular purpose within a specific historical context. Again this can be clearly illustrated in the transformation in sexual citizenship of same-sex attracted people in Britain following the election of Tony Blair in 1998 and ideologies of the 'Third Way', 'New Labour', or 'New Britain'. In her discourse analysis of the Blair government's ideology Levitas (1997) identified six rule-bounded sets of statements that New Labour employed to differentiate itself from Conservative politics and 'traditional' socialist policies. These were: social inclusion, rights and responsibilities, community, family, multiculturalism, managerialism, and the law. From an analysis of parliamentary discourse Stychin (2003) argues that the political narratives developed around each of these themes is in some ways 'progressive' in widening and deepening an idea of sexual citizenship from the Thatcherite Conservative discourse. Yet, he acknowledges simultaneously how these themes operate to discipline and normalise same-sex identities through a rhetoric of community, nation, family, and morality. As Stychin points out, what gave many lesbian and gay activists concern is the strong Christian underpinning that can be identified in the Blairite ideology (see Bell and Binnie 2000; Durham 2001; Wilkinson 1999). This example illustrates the key point that the meaning of discursive structures are not stable but regulated through practice (Foucault 1972). Discursive structures are forms of discipline over thought, action, and social outcomes that differ radically from period to period. Foucault therefore conceptualised discourse pragmatically rather than metaphysically. Discursive formations are understood as a tool, an 'action' used by specific people to coordinate their social relationships for a specific purpose during a particular period. The discursive structures of (homo)sexuality impose boundaries upon sexual citizenship; that is, which sexual practices are thought of as normally present within the territorial boundaries of the state.

Genealogy

Another key theoretical point illustrated by the examples is what Foucault terms '**genealogy**'. Foucault (1980) uses this term in his writing that challenged conventional ideas about social identities and subject positions, particularly ideas of a homogenous self, underpinned by a stable, cohesive ego. Following Foucault (1982), people 'take up' subject-positions produced through discursive structures rather than subjectivity being a simple expression of an individual self. Foucault chose to ignore approaching subjectivity through notions of a pre-existent subject, such as 'British', 'American', 'Italian', 'mother', 'father', 'adult', 'teenager', 'youth', 'straight', 'homosexual', 'gay', 'queer', 'feminine', or 'masculine', upon which rules for thought and behaviour are imposed. Instead, he chooses to investigate how discursive structures constitute meanings and actions that frame a particular subjectivity. For example, Foucault (1978) interprets the invention of the homosexual as a type of person in the eighteenth century to have been the result of a number of changes within Western knowledge about the nature of sexuality, rather than the expression of the sexual preference of an individual self. Homosexuality does not have a single meaning, but depends on a wide range of features provided by the historical and geographical social context, for its interpretation and effect. Importantly, all subjectivities are conceptualised as actively working out their subject-position and role in the process of negotiating discursive constraints, rather than casting subjectivities as passive victims of discursive structures.

In summary, Foucault understands human subjectivity as constructed through an individual engagement with discursive processes. A person's particular sense of self is obtained through a negotiated rather than imposed process of acculturation into social practices. Subject positions are actively worked out by individuals and associated with reasons of a particular period and location. Foucault argues that through a subject-position a person communicates a particular understanding about the world through their use of language, comportment, dress, attitudes, and actions. In this way Foucault challenged conventional Western notions of the subject as an autonomous and sovereign entity, an individual who is fully endowed with consciousness and independent source of meaning. Instead, following poststructuralist thinking, the subject cannot exist outside discourse. That is, people take up particular social identities through their own particular gendered, classed, sexualised, and ethnic subject-positions produced within discourse. Therefore, for example, homosexuality becomes something that you do, rather than something to which you are you are subject. Furthermore, social identities are also unstable given their discursive quality, which leaves them open to acts of reinterpretation and refashioning. Consequently, homosexuality does not have a single meaning, but depends on a wide range of contextual features. In short, individuals are conceptualised as actively taking up their subject-positions and roles in a process that involves negotiating discursive constraints for themselves. In doing so, people are positioned as actively aware that the adoption of a certain subject-position is a type of action that has effects.

Power

Power was of central concern to Foucault given that the meanings of items, including subject-positions (for example, femininity, sexuality, and ethnicity), were not conceived as stable but negotiated through discourse. Foucault challenged the ways power has been conventionally conceptualised in the humanities, including human geography, through examining the relationship between discourse and power. Conventionally scripted, power belongs to particular agents such as individuals, the state, or groups with particular interests. Power was a means by which groups or individuals were able to achieve their aims against the will of others. Usually, power was conceptualised as confining (power over: the heterosexuals *versus* homosexuals, masculine *versus* feminine, employers *versus* employees) and in the context of binary power blocs of the core and the periphery (the 'have nots' and the 'have lots'). But following Foucault, power is not conceptualised as a repressive, hierarchical, top to bottom force that comes from a specific source. Instead, power is everywhere. It circulates through negotiated social practices in all levels of social existence. Foucault (1980) suggests that both oppressors and oppressed are each, to some degree, caught up in its circulation through a process of negotiation of discursive norms. Furthermore, power need not only be conceived in negative terms (control, repressive, restraining, and so on), but was also crucial in enabling oppressed groups to establish their own identity. Foucault (1977a, p. 95) claims that: 'where there is power...there is resistance...a multiplicity of points of resistance'. As I demonstrated earlier, in many nineteenth-century cities, including Moscow, New York, Paris, and London, closeted spaces opened up the opportunities for secret locations that were the source of great pleasure for many same-sex attracted men. Homosexual men are not positioned as simply dupes of heteronormative discursive structures. Rather, these men are understood as having agency through actively constructing a social position for themselves in relationship to the discursive norms against which they assume other individuals or groups perceive their subject position to be abnormal. These men then express this agency or effect by actively creating secret locations in which to meet. Consequently, power is also productive; power produces discourse, knowledge, bodies, and subjectivities (Phillips and Jørgensen 2002). As Foucault says:

> What makes power hold good, what makes it accepted, is simply the fact that it does not only weigh on us as a force that says no, but that it traverses and produces things, it induces pleasure, forms knowledge, produces discourse. It needs to be considered as a productive network which runs through the whole of social body, much more than as a negative instance whose function is repression (Foucault 1980, p. 119).

In summary, Foucault conceptualised power not as monopolised by one centre and imposed onto individuals. Instead power is conceptualised to operate through discourse in which social relationships between individuals are negotiated. It is these negotiations of how the individual is positioned to the discursive norms that has the potential to be disempowering through compliance, or empowering through resistance. It is to investigate the effects of how individuals weigh up their own position in relationship to these discursive norms displayed through their actions and attitudes, or the conditions of possibility in power, that geographers have turned to discourse analysis.

Regime of truth

Conceptualising the meanings of animals, plants, places, and subjectivities as a negotiated process in relationship to discursive norms raises the important question about the mechanisms that exist to keep certain discourse in circulation as 'normal' or 'true'. In other words, whilst there is not one but many discourses that contend with each other, a particular discourse is always maintained as 'true'. For example, different 'truths' about same-sex desire may often compete for ascendancy. But a particular discourse often becomes dominant in a particular time. Foucault argued that the ascendancy of a certain discourse relies upon two mutually reinforcing social forces: (a) the source of the statement (often the authoritative voices of scientific, medical, religious, or state institutions with coercive powers such as the police, schools, asylums, or prisons); and (b) assertions of what counts as absolute truth, based upon socially agreed methods as to what constitutes knowledge. The historically and spatially contingent grounds within which a discursive formation sustaining truth is asserted comprise what Foucault termed a **'regime of truth'**. Examples include the Thatcherite

Conservative discourse and the Blairite New Labour discourse around 'homosexuality'. The historical rules of a particular regime of truth lies at the heart of processes of exclusion/inclusion that delimits not only what can be said but also what can be done and to whom. In these case studies, the regimes of truth governed the exclusion of same-sex attracted people from the same rights of citizenship as experienced by heterosexual people. Accordingly, to understand discourse and their effects, it is imperative to understand the social contexts in which they arise. Knowledge does not operate within a social void.

Integral to a regime of truth is the mutually interdependent relationship between power and knowledge. Foucault positions this relationship as indistinguishable from regimes of truth. Foucault (1980, p. 131) argues that: 'Truth isn't outside power...Truth is a thing of this world; it is produced only by virtue of multiple forms of constraint. And it induces regular effects of power'. Hence for Foucault (1980) questions about the 'truth' of knowledge were fruitless for truth is unattainable. Instead, he focused on questions addressing the effectiveness of sustaining knowledge (truth effects). In what ways are effects of truth created in discourse? Which discourses give the impression that they represent the truth? For these questions he coined the analytical term '**power/knowledge**'. Thus, 'there is no power relations without the correlative constitution of a field of knowledge, nor any knowledge that does not presuppose and constitute at the same time, power relations' (Foucault 1977a, p. 27). Knowledge is formed within the practices of power. Furthermore, knowledge is constitutive of the establishment and modification of new techniques of power. Consequently, knowledge operates in each academic discipline within a particular regime of truth to assure that a particular interpretation informed by an agreed method has the power to make itself 'true' over another. This point can be illustrated by drawing upon the work of Neville Hoad (2000) who pointed out how in the nineteenth century new 'scientific' beliefs were employed by social scientists to explain the apparent prevalence of homosexuality in non-Western countries, what Richard Burton (1886) called the 'Sotadic Zone'. Drawing on Darwinian evolutionary theory, Victorian anthropologists writing in the 1800s positioned 'homosexuality' as a moral problem spreading from non-Western nations (see Symonds 1896). Generally, at this time, anthropologists explained homosexuality in terms of hierarchical sequence of humanity. Homosexuality was naturalised as belonging to an earlier phase of human development and spatialised as belonging to 'primitive' societies. Constituted as a practice belonging to 'savages', the presence of same-sex desire was portrayed as a spectre on 'civilised' societies. 'Homosexuals' were therefore categorised as degenerate. In this way the power/knowledge of 'science' contained in Darwinian evolutionary theory was employed to naturalise the alleged superiority of 'heterosexuality'—as well as men, masculinity, whiteness, and the middle class.

DOING FOUCAULDIAN DISCOURSE ANALYSIS AND WRITING GEOGRAPHY

A Foucauldian approach to discourse analysis offers human geographers opportunities for investigating how discursive formations articulate regimes of truth that naturalise particular 'ways of seeing' social difference (gender, ethnicity, class, or sexuality), places, or bio-physical environments. One helpful **metaphor** to conceptualising discourse analysis is perhaps to think about it in terms of unravelling how an individual is woven within a social fabric held together by power relationships, where particular discursive formations comprise its threads. Discourse analysis is a process of unravelling how the producer of a particular text is woven into this fabric. Through conducting discourse analysis, concern lies in revealing the effects of language as practice that makes specific accounts appear 'real', or 'natural' through particular regimes of truth. Consequently, discourse analysis is also concerned with issues of power, expressed through cultural politics. In geography, the Foucauldian strand of discourse analysis can tend to problems that require investigating the social effects of discourse through investigating the consequences of how specific sources (institutions, subject-positions) produce particular subjectivities and meanings about the social relationships between objects, people, and places. Such analysis matters not only to illustrate how particular understandings about the world are privileged but also to demonstrate questions of social justice by identifying how processes of inclusion/exclusion operate through discourse.

Expanding Foucault's methodology from his works, however, is not a straightforward task (Hoggart et al. 2002). He was a prolific writer. His ideas altered as his research focus changed. His methodological legacy is thus multifaceted and dispersed. Furthermore, the trust placed in Foucault's work within his interpretative communities did not stem from explicit methodological statements. Barret (1991, p. 127) described his methodological statements as vague. So, whilst the methodology outlined below adheres to the Foucauldian notion of discourse, I draw upon the work of feminist geographer Gillian Rose (1996; 2001) to outline a guide to discourse analysis.

What sources are required for discourse analysis?

Before starting a discourse analysis it is essential to think systematically about what kinds of sources you require. Discourses are expressed through a wide variety of written texts, visual representations, and practices (speech acts, dress, choice of holiday destination). Any or all of these are legitimate resources. Indeed, intertextuality demands the use of a wide range of sources. This may mean adopting a range of research practices to collect your resources including archival sources, semi-structured interviews, and participant observation. The breadth of source materials required is again underscored by recalling that discursive formations emerge from a coherent pattern of statements that can be identified across a range of sources.

Kevin Dunn (2001) used a diversity of written texts and semi-structured interviews to make his case for how local opponents to the construction of mosques in Sydney in the early 1990s drew upon discursive constructions of what constituted a 'local resident' and 'community' and negative Western stereotypes of Islam that have for centuries depicted Muslims as fanatical, intolerant, militant, fundamentalist, misogynist, and alien. He positioned local resistance to mosques in suburban Sydney as an example of how racism and vilification can become accepted as natural. This opposition relied upon an accumulated Western heritage of what he termed 'Islamaphobia'. Drawing on academic texts he illustrated how Islamaphobia has been born of the recurring theme of Orientalism that relies on a West/East opposition. To investigate the conventional 'discourses of opposition' he used national, regional, and local daily newspapers and a data set compiled from the archives of local authorities (including development applications, planner's reports, campaign leaflets, and correspondence to local authorities from resident objectors). Whilst identifying a counter discursive construction within these sources he also analysed Islamic guidebooks and other introductory material for converts for other sources of geographical knowledge. In his conclusion he reflects upon the importance of intertextuality in writing geography. Dunn (2001, p. 292) says, 'The local is not simply a repository for the expression of meanings constructed from above…[Instead,] the local and national discourses [are] knitted together in a symbolic web'. Dunn provides a reminder of how mutual relationships sustain local, national, and international discourses.

Sources can include a variety of genres (for example, home movies, commercial films, travel writing, official reports, science fiction, scientific reports). The producer (journalists, travellers, academics, medics) is addressing a particular audience. Each source will be produced, circulated, and displayed employing a particular technology (such as printing, painting, photography, hand-writing, and email). Your initial problem will most likely be the breadth of potential source materials. Identifying initial sources from which to begin your analysis is an essential research task. The following questions are designed to help you identify your initial sources:

- *Which sources are likely to be particularly helpful?* Remember you are not concerned with selecting sources based on questions of accuracy or validity. Instead, your focus is on selecting sources that enable you to establish rigour in your research through Lincoln's and Guba's (1981) criteria of credibility (see chapter 5). Claims of credibility in your results will necessitate you demonstrating that each source is a meaningful one in the context of your research aim.
- *Which sources are likely to provide counter discourses?* It may be necessary to conduct interviews with a range of informants and draw from council records and media reports to, say, investigate the conflict over a particular urban development proposal.
- *Which sources are going to be particularly interesting?* This may be a case of thinking about whose geographical knowledge has not been previously investigated. For example in a project investigating 1900–45 'beach-making' activities in the Illawarra, Australia, this included use of surf-life saving documents, beach-inspector reports, council by-laws, state-rail, and bank records.
- *Which sources are going to be qualitatively rich?* Given your analysis is reliant on 'unpacking' the meanings that constitute a particular understanding of the social or physical word it is important to avoid, for example, transcripts that have only 'yes'/'no' answers. Sources such as in-depth interviews, oral histories, parliamentary discussion papers, political documents, television programs, propaganda materials, advertisements, tourist souvenirs, and movies will almost always provide qualitatively rich materials.

Once you have identified your initial key sources the research process is best understood as a continuing building process in which new sources to analyse are added as the research proceeds, rather than being collected during a single period of 'data collection'. Gathering new sources typically takes a good deal of time. Important leads are often found by consulting reference lists in texts published by researchers working on the same or similar research questions. Alternatively texts may be discovered in the archives of local community organisations, libraries, banks, or corporations. In turn, the people who work within these places often can suggest other sources that are likely to be particularly productive; for example, private collections of photographs. Equally, you may wish to conduct interviews (see chapter 6) or ask respondents to take photographs. The later method is termed photo-elicitation, where informants take photographs following instructions of the researcher (see Banks 2001). These photographs can then be employed as source for discourse analysis, as prompts during an interview, or both.

Once you have begun to widen your data collection process your next question undoubtedly will be: how many texts are required for discourse analysis? As Bradshaw and Stratford explain (chapter 5), there are no hard and fast rules for sample size in qualitative research design. Drawing from Patton (1990) they point out that the validity of qualitative research depends on information-richness and the analytical skills of the researcher rather than validity brought by numbers. Tonkiss confirms this important point. 'What matters', she argues, 'is the richness of textual detail, rather then the numbers of texts analysed'

BOX 11.1 QUESTIONS TO HELP LOCATE SOURCES FOR DISCOURSE ANALYSIS

Imagine your project was to investigate the ways Sydney has been positioned as the 'gay capital' of the South Pacific. What might your initial starting point be? How might how widen your search? What sources produce visual or written texts that socially construct Sydney as a 'gay and lesbian capital'? Who may you wish to interview? Could photo-elicitation provide a rich textual source? In what ways could the work of Markwell (2002), which investigated the role of the Sydney Gay and Lesbian Mardi Gras in the refashioning of Sydney as a 'gay capital', help you?

This project raises a number of interesting methodological and theoretical questions. The discursive practices of both the (New) Gay and Lesbian Mardi Gras organisations and the gay and lesbian tourism industry are perhaps the most powerful in constructing Sydney as a 'gay and lesbian capital'. In what ways could possibly competing discourses be constructed? How can you get access to these particular discourses? What about the role of the gay and lesbian media? What about international gay guides and the marketing campaigns of New South Wales Tourism or the former Australian Tourist Commission (now Australia Tourism)? Who is portrayed in the marketing campaigns? Do the adverts show both gay men and lesbians? Or is the fact that usually only clean-cut, white same-sex attracted men are visualised in gay tourism marketing also important? In tourist campaigns, is the invisibility of 'lesbians', 'gay men of colour' and sub-culture same-sex attracted groups such as 'bears' or 'leathermen' a relevant issue to examine? Equally, is it important that 'gay events' appear in adverts targeting a straight audience? How might you find out how same-sex attracted residents or tourists construct Sydney?

(Tonkiss 1998, p. 253). As the researcher you must justify the matter of the texts used to sustain your work.

What strategies are helpful to scrutinise the structure of discourse?

Research rigour requires practitioners to discuss their methodologies. However, interpretation activities are often masked by complex, if not impenetrable, language. For example Elizabeth Edwards (2003) discussed her approach to discourse analysis as 'dense context'. That is, she endeavours to explain:

> a dynamic and dialogical shape of broader discourse which constitute the whole cultural theatre of which the photographs are part…'Dense context' is not necessarily linked to the reality effect of the photograph in a direct way, indeed to the extent that it is not necessarily *apparent* what the photograph is 'of'. Often it is what photographs are *not* 'of' in forensic terms which is suggestive of a counterpoint. 'Dense context' has, literally, a density, opacity and three-dimensional volume (Edwards 2003, pp. 262–3, emphasis in original).

Foucauldian concepts of regimes of truth and discursive formations underpin her methodology, yet the actual interpretation of discourse is never made transparent. Furthermore, several handbooks for qualitative methods in the social sciences are hesitant to give formal guidelines (Phillips and Hardy 2002; Potter 1996). Instead, discourse analysis is positioned as a 'craft skill' (Potter 1996, p. 140), the researcher's ability 'to customise' (Phillips and Hardy 2002, p. 78), 'rigorous scholarship' (Gill 1996, p. 144), or 'human intellect' (Duncan 1987, p. 473). The maxim is 'learning by doing'. Through practice, discourse analysis is typically held to become intuitive. Scholarly passion seemingly underpins critical textual analysis. The methodology is often left implicit rather than made explicit. Undermining the very basis of discourse analysis is research that is too systematic, mechanical, and formulaic (Burman and Parker 1993).

In practical terms, such counsel is not especially helpful for those seeking advice on how to do discourse analysis! While mindful that successful interpretation requires careful reading and passionate engagement with texts, Rose (2001) is concerned by the lack of explicit advice given to students. To fill the void she identified in qualitative research method handbooks, she offered seven axioms for interpreting the linguistic structure of discourse (see Box 11.2). These axioms were not suggested with the intention to straightjacket, mute, stifle, or deaden your interpretation. Instead, they are offered to enliven, encourage, and assist students who are particularly hesitant with how to interpret texts critically. Consideration of these axioms in your research design will also help you to justify your interpretation within the context of the hermeneutic research circle. Such a justification is important given that the underpinning premise of qualitative research is precisely the interpretation of cultural texts and not the discovery of their 'truth'. The assessment by your interpretative community will be in part reliant upon the justification of the strategies that underpin your interpretation. I now turn to briefly elaborate on each of the strategies.

BOX 11.2 STRATEGIES TO SCRUTINISE THE STRUCTURE OF DISCOURSE

Seven strategies for the interpretation of the linguistic structure of discourse:
1 Suspend pre-existing categories: examine your texts with fresh eyes and ears.
2 Familiarisation: absorb yourself in your texts.
3 Coding: identify key themes to reveal how the producer is embedded within particular discursive structures.
4 Persuasion: investigate within your texts for effects of 'truth'.
5 Incoherence: take notice of inconsistencies within your texts.
6 Active presence of the invisible: look for mechanisms that silence.
7 Focus on details.

Adapted from Rose (2001, p. 158).

Suspend pre-existing categories: examine your texts with fresh eyes and ears

Reading, listening, or looking at your text with fresh eyes and ears is regarded by Foucault (1972) as an essential starting point given that the objective of discourse analysis is to disclose the 'naturalness' of constructed categories, subjectivities, particularities, accountability, and responsibility. Foucault (1972) pointed out that all preconceptions:

> must be held in suspense. They must not be rejected definitively, of course, but the tranquillity with which they are accepted must be disturbed; we must show that they do not come about by themselves, but are always the result of a construction the rules of which must be known and the justifications of which must be scrutinized.

Foucault's request to attempt to suspend yourself when approaching your analysis from everything you have experienced or learnt is an impossible task. Yet, his call for a highly reflexive researcher is possible to implement in a number of ways. First, this can be achieved by demonstrating that the categories that you allocate arose from the data rather than being taken-for-granted categories from elsewhere that you imposed on your results. Furthermore, the process of categorisation itself must be considered provisional. All categories must be constantly given reflexive attention (Wood and Kroger 2000). Second, as a reflexive researcher you will have to discuss how you are embedded into the research project. You will have to give careful consideration to a reflexive statement that discusses how your position within the project has changed through its design and implementation.

Familiarisation: absorb yourself in your texts

Equally, familiarisation with your texts is essential. Familiarisation enables you to identify the key themes that will enable you to examine the relationships between statements, groups of statements, and different texts. This is a time-consuming and reiterative process of looking, listening, and/or reading. Only through absorbing yourself in your texts will key themes (descriptive labels or categories) become apparent. Make a list of these themes and note where they occur in your texts. You have begun to code your texts (see chapter 14 for a more detailed discussion). Return to coding your texts again and again. Interpretation becomes an on-going process that can proceed through many cycles and reclassifications. During this coding process think about how the theme is given meaning through the relationships between words (word clusters), and connections between word clusters in different texts (genres and authors). Insights to what particular kind of knowledge is produced may be revealed through investigation of these relationships and connections.

Goss' (1993) discussion of how the tourism industry writes a particular geography of the Hawai'ian Islands illustrates the productivity of discourse in the creation of place meanings and subjectivities. To investigate the effects of marketing the islands as a vacation destination his analysis focused on the recurring images and words employed that portray indigenous Hawai'ians, the plants, the volcanoes, the location, and the climate. To explore the 'official' image of the islands Goss collected thirty-four advertisements commissioned by the Hawai'i Visitors Bureau (HVB) and published between 1972 and 1992 in various North American magazines and newspapers. He identified how the social discourse of these advertisements reinvented the Hawaiian tourist through the depiction of the life-styles and vacation activities.

In the early advertisements (1972–84) tourists were portrayed as exclusively white, middle-aged, heterosexual couples. An HVB report stereotyped couples as wearing Hawai'ian outfits, sandals, and black knee-socks. Since the mid-1980s the target group shifted to younger heterosexual couples. The transformative powers of an encounter with the Hawai'ian environment or social traditions were also emphasised. Slogans employed in the 1989–92 campaigns invited readers to 'Come to life in Hawaii', claiming 'A few days in Hawaii and you'll be a new person'. The theme of these campaigns was the discovery of the 'real' self in Hawai'i. To enable this sense of personal emancipation of the Self repressed by civilisation Goss notes five themes of a spatial discourse that located the Hawai'ian Islands outside the 'normal' construction of North American geography. The paradise status was signified by verbal and visual reference to beaches, palms, waterfalls, tropical gardens, and exotic flowers. By virtue of its position on the periphery of United States' territory the islands are constructed as a place on the social, temporal, and geographical frontier. Hawai'i becomes a timeless location, a portal to the past. A trip to Hawai'i is discovering that, 'time and tide are much the same as in the 1800s'. In this timeless place, people are freed from the repressive regulations of contemporary everyday life. Through the process of discovery Hawai'i becomes feminised and through the use of sexual metaphors the physical environment is eroticised. For example, Kauai has 'distractions spread throughout her verdant valleys'.

The final part of the tourism narrative was the erasure of historical and present socio-economic deprivation and oppression of the Hawai'ian people through a tourist encounter framed by *aloha*. A tourist–host relationship informed by *aloha* casts all Hawai'ians as 'friendly natives': innocent, naive, primitive, and naturally sexually promiscuous. Goss thus identifies five persistent themes of the spatial discourse in the advertisements: earthly paradise, marginality, liminality, feminity, and *aloha*. He argues how their persistence in advertisements depends on intertextuality; in other words, the pre-existence and repetition of these selective themes in a wide range of Western movies, books, songs, and holiday narratives. Finally, Goss acknowledges the contradictions within the advertisements through visual and verbal presence of the familiar and the modern. He argues these are present to reassure tourists, reducing the potential fear or threat posed by an unfamiliar place.

Coding: identify key themes to reveal how the producer is embedded within particular discursive structures

One key objective of coding is to identify how the producer of your source material is embedded within particular discursive structures. You may wish to follow a more systematic coding method to help you start with identifying themes and coding your text. The following questions may help you begin:

- What coding categories are suggested by the research question?
- What effects of discursive structures are you coding for: attitudes, experiences, perceptions, or actions?
- Are the outcomes of the discursive structures specific to a particular place?
- What coding categories are suggested by the broader empirical and theoretical literature from which the research question has been derived?

Whether you devise your coding categories through a process of familiarisation with the material or from the relevant literature it is essential to remember that they must have analytical significance to your discourse analysis. Through examining textual detail you allow the research materials to 'speak'. Do not impose categories in a top-down manner. Always be open to the unexpected and unusual. (See also the discussion in chapter 14.)

Persuasion: investigate within your texts for effects of 'truth'

While you are investigating how a particular kind of knowledge is produced you should also assess your texts for effects of 'truth'; that is, how is a discourse considered to have both validity and worth. In other words, what devices are used to make claims that people are 'speaking in the true'? Identifying such mechanisms is important as they act to exclude from consideration other knowledges that might have been possible. A number of strategies of conviction may be used to keep certain discourses in circulation including the notion of calling upon an academic discipline (science), a 'trustworthy' method (statistics, photography, mapping), a commentary by a key spokesperson, or textual (printed word versus spoken word, quotation of voices versus feelings). Their purpose is to present an argument about an item that is accepted by most people as 'common sense', unproblematic, unquestionable, and apparently 'natural'. They maintain in circulation discourses that are repeatedly commented on by others, thus becoming considered to have both worth and validity. Consequently, texts aimed at settling opposition to particularly controversial claims of certainty are those that most clearly employ these strategies of conviction (Tonkiss 1998).

An example of how photography provides a seemingly accurate depiction or copy of external reality of tourist destinations is the picture postcard. Postcards' apparent realism or 'in the true' relies upon photography being regarded in Western societies as a science (Waitt and Head 2002). Light reflected from the photograph object is etched into chemicals. The result possesses the objectivity of technology. Photographs appear to be a true representation of the physical world and to involve no subjective intervention. Decisions about lighting, colouring, cutting, cropping, etching, and cloning are 'forgotten'. The 'effect of truth' of the postcard is further derived from many viewers commenting that photographs themselves are an actual reflection of the physical world, concealing the opportunities for modification by the photographer for commercial purposes (Jackson 1999).

In her work on representations of sex work in the Philippines over three decades from 1970, Lisa Law (2000) provides an example of how maps also act to embed particular knowledge as 'in the true'. She notes not only how different maps of prostitution there legitimise competing claims about prostitution, but how the official health map of the commercial sex industry drawn by the Health Department of Cebu helps to materialise part of the city as a homogenous 'red light district'. The effect of truth maintained by the Health Department's map of registered sex establishments is to help embed ideas that the sex industry is a distinct, bounded, mappable reality that lies outside 'normal' moral/healthy behaviour. Furthermore, Law points out how this cartography attached a particular identity to women. Those women present in the 'red light district', particularly in the evenings, were marked as 'bad girls'. Furthermore, the notion that HIV/AIDS is contracted from foreigners resulted in the tourist 'red light district' becoming the epidemiological centre and the women working in the sex-industry being understood to be 'dirty', diseased', 'polluting', and 'sick'. Consequently, given that the role of the Health Department is to control and manage sexually transmitted disease, HIV prevention strategies were put in place that attempted to discipline the sex workers through compulsory HIV testing and enrolment in HIV/AIDS education activities.

Incoherence: take notice of inconsistencies within your sources

Having coded your data and considered the effect of truth, expect to identify inconsistencies within the discursive structures/formations of your sources. You will recall that discursive structures/formations are the relatively rule-bound sets of statements that impose limits on what gives meaning (Phillips and Jørgensen 2002). Yet, discursive structures/formations are often organised incoherently and inconsistently within texts. Indeed, a discursive formation may rely upon the irregularities provided by many different points of view.

For example, Law's (2000) research on Philippines' sex workers demonstrates how from the 1970s to the early 1990s the Philippine media, human rights activists, and academics were embedded in a rule-bound discursive structure that constituted prostitutes as victims of a 'flesh' industry. Prostitutes' subjectivity was imposed on women, first, by forces of neo-colonialism, including US military bases, and second, during President Marcos' rule through the institutionalisation of international sex trafficking, and sex tourism. Law demonstrates how three non-governmental agencies (NGOs) (End Child Prostitution in Asian Tourism, the Women's Centre of Cebu, and the Visayas Primary Health Care Services) drew upon the prostitute constituted as victim to position prostitution as a social problem borne out of capitalist social relationships. Yet, in 1993, the 'Brunei Beauties' scandal over high-class prostitution disrupted this portrayal that all women are economically deprived and forced into prostitution borne from capitalist social relationships. An inconsistency became evident in the knowledge that all sex workers were victims of an oppressive social system.

Further inconsistencies were introduced in how some Filipinos constituted prostitution during the 1990s when the community-based AIDS education program of a health organisation, called Kabalikat, appealed to the international discourse on HIV/AIDS prevention to unsettle the 'victim' stereotype. Community-based HIV/AIDS intervention projects are designed to require the active involvement of women involved in sex work in designing and implementing HIV/AIDS prevention policies. Yet, in pointing out this shift Law (2000) warns against neatly categorising this NGO articulating the 'agent' paradigm. She noted how Kabalikat representatives seemingly voiced contradictory statements that situated the prostitute as both 'agent' and 'victim'. She suggests that perhaps within the tensions created by the victim/agent debate that new identities are constituted.

Active presence of the invisible: look for mechanisms that silence

Finally, discourse analysis involves exploration of the active presence of absent items (Thiesmeyer 2003). As Rose (2001, p. 157) says, 'absences can be as productive as explicit naming; invisibility can have just as powerful effects as visibility'. The silences of texts are not necessarily meaningless. On the contrary, silences are very important. They often help to underscore the social differences between people through the erasure of ethnicity, gender, sexuality, and physical ability. Silences also operate to help maintain and heighten understandings of the bio-physical environment constituted as 'pristine', 'wild', or 'untouched' nature. Common sense assumptions about who or what should be present in particular places are often sustained through absences in particular texts. Through the active presence of absent items, nations, cities, or streets, for example, may be maintained as 'heterosexual' (Munt 1998) or National Parks imagined as 'pure' nature, a site apparently removed from human interference (Head 2000).

How silence operates in producing geographical knowledge is illustrated clearly in discursive formations of the frontier (see Turner (1920) for North America, and for Australia see McGregor (1994), Schaffer (1988), and Ward (1958)). Colonial projects of nation-making have often employed the concept of the frontier to erase the presence of indigenous people, or at best, cast them as 'primitive' people. The effectiveness of frontier myths in erasing indigenous people relies on representing the frontier as a place suspended in time (Rose 1997). As a timeless land the frontier was understood as not being owned. In Australia this understanding became law (*terra nullius*). History, brought by European occupation, was yet to begin. Suspended in time, indigenous people are portrayed as an earlier phase of human evolution, people still to evolve from their bio-physical environment. The frontier is depicted not as the home of indigenous people, but as a wild, untouched, and unknown place. The regime of frontier truths that silences the presence of indigenous people draws upon linear interpretations of history that employ evolutionary narratives to demarcate the colonisers as bringing civilisation, domestication, and productivity. In doing so excluded from consideration are indigenous peoples, their knowledges, and issues pertaining to land rights.

Waitt and Head (2002) note how within the contemporary Australian tourism industry the selective discursive formations of the frontier that cast indigenous people as stone-age people still enjoy widespread currency. For example, the Kimberley, a north-west region of Australia, is sold as the 'last frontier'. One brochure for a local airline pitches the Kimberley as 'a mysterious, ancient land. So remote, so immense, so rugged—it challenges you to discover it…the Last Frontier' (Slingair tourist brochure (nd)). Waitt and Head (2002) are not surprised at the selectiveness of the advertising strategies. Potential tourists are offered a portal to a timeless land to fulfil specific market demands, including: to discover the 'real' Australia, imagined as the outback, to experience the bio-physical environment constituted as wilderness; to gaze upon the bio-physical environment portrayed as sublime 'natural' beauty; and/or to explore an extreme bio-physical environment for an adventure setting. The key point is that the commercial value of the imagined frontier geographies to marketing the Kimberley to a primarily urban and Australian audience is one mechanism that has kept this evolutionary discourse in existence. The tourist industry has helped to maintain 'the true' evolutionary narratives about indigenous Australians. Furthermore, the tourism industry and the commentaries it produces may also help exclude, particularly from some tourists, consideration of other knowledges about the Kimberley that challenge and are inconsistent with the frontier discourse, simply because they provide fewer meaningful categories upon which to establish a regional marketing campaign. For example, challenging the absence of humans as a central tenet of frontier discursive structure is the Miriuwung-Gajerrong's (the local indigenous people's) knowledge that this place is their 'home'; named, known, and cared for over tens of thousands of years. Equally, on a Kimberley's cattle station the locality is constructed by Anglo-Celtic Australian pastoralists as a 'workplace' inscribed through personal labour. These alternative geographical knowledges are excluded from consideration in the pitching of Kimberley as the 'last frontier'.

Identifying how discursive structures operate to privilege particular knowledge over other knowledge often has important political implications. For example, discourse analyses of the Native Title policies by geographers and anthropologists assisting Aboriginal land claims suggest that rights to land are also based on the construction of indigenous Australians as an unchanging, timeless people through their continuing 'traditional' associations with land, community structures, and maintenance of 'traditional' religion (Edmonds 1995; Merlan 1996; D. Rose 1996a). In the process of Native Title itself, discourse analysis offers an insight into how 'traditional' cultural forms are given priority over hybrid forms. Indigenous Australians constituted as a 'traditional land-owning group' works to eliminate people whose life paths have distanced them from 'country' and culture (D. Rose 1996a).

What strategies are helpful for investigating the social circumstances in which discourse is produced?

BOX 11.3 TWO STRATEGIES FOR INVESTIGATING THE SOCIAL CIRCUMSTANCES IN WHICH DISCOURSE IS PRODUCED

1 Identification of the subject position of the author.
2 Identification of the intended audience of the text.

It is important to investigate authorship of cultural texts (Box 11.3) as part of discourse analysis because authorship is often used to invest texts with authority (Wood and Kroger 2000). For example, for most academics writing geography in the 1920s, the written publications of historians such as Fredrick Jackson Turner would have been invested with greater authority than say the oral histories of the Miriuwung-Gajerrong people discussed in the previous section. Authorship is linked directly to the production what is considered true within a particular social context. To help examine the social context of authorship you may begin by asking a number of rather obvious questions that include *when, where, how,* and *why* a text was produced. These questions will help you establish the originating context of your document, anchoring it within a particular time and place. Next, you may wish to consider exploring the subject positions of the author. What are the author's gender, class, sexuality, and ethnic subject positions? These questions will help you think about the ways in which the author and their subject position is linked to establishing and maintaining realisms (effects of truth) through the production and circulation of texts. The visual and verbal texts produced by authors endowed with authority—through, for example, membership of socially and institutionally powerful organisations—rather, may be more effective in the process of constructing 'truths' and privileging particular knowledge than those produced by socially marginalised groups.

It is important to investigate the assumed audiences of cultural texts as part of the social context of how discourse is produced. How an item is portrayed will, in part, depend on its audience (television, film, art gallery, video, DVD, Internet, greetings card, and so on). In other words, the interpretative context of each audience produced by different media is likely to affect the meanings of texts. In this way audiences can be conceptualised as co-authors of a text. Foucault did not conceptualise audiences as passive recipients of texts. Instead, if we accept that power is everywhere, it is evident that an audience can produce alternative interpretations to those that might have been intended by the 'author'.

Kathleen Mee and Robyn Dowling (2003) illustrate how one audience, film-reviewers, as cultural intermediators, actively reworked the intended meanings of an Australian film called *Idiot Box.* Filmed in the western suburbs of Sydney, this is a fictional film about a bank robbery. The planning and implementation of the unsuccessful bank robbery by the key characters, Mick and Kev, was—according to the writer-director David Caesar—intended to challenge common-sense assumptions about young, unemployed, suburban, working-class men. Yet, Mee and Dowling (2003) argue that film-reviewers interpreted the representations of social difference depicted in *Idiot Box* through the familiar, stereotyping lens rather than as confronting them as intended by the director. In this way film-reviewers sustained a particular fictional geographical knowledge about western Sydney as 'truth'. The events and characters of the film became rendered as 'natural' through an interpretation that understood young working-class men as 'yobs' and suburbia as 'boring'. Clearly, audiences play an important role in discourse analysis. Important insights can be gained into how particular geographical regimes of truth remain privileged through examining questions pertaining to the audience. As Mee and Dowling (2003) illustrate, pre-existing categories and subjectivities circulating in Sydney at the start of the twenty-first century about young working-class men living in its western suburbs operated to curtail challenges to what is considered true.

Reflecting on the method

My aims in this concluding section are twofold. The first is to draw together and summarise in a checklist the various key aspects of doing Foucauldian discourse analysis introduced in this chapter. The second is to reflect on the effects of writing geography that employs these criteria as a checklist.

Interpretation through discourse analysis is a complex process. Partly this complexity arises from the different aspects of our checklist (Box 11.4). The number of judgements that have to be made further compounds the complexity. For example, do the ways in which authors are writing, speaking, or drawing accord with a particular social or institutional context? Were the authors sincere about their claims? Why did the authors circulate ideas in a particular way? What did the authors intend? In short, discourse analysis involves a large amount of thinking about what is meant.

While not objecting to a checklist, Rose (2001, p.161) encouraged researchers to 'ask a Foucauldian question of them [the items in the checklist]: what are the effects of these criteria?' The effect of writing geography that employs these criteria is inevitably selective. My

---

BOX 11.4 A CHECKLIST FOR DOING DISCOURSE ANALYSIS

1 Assumptions
   a What pre-existing categories or value assumptions are made?
2 Coding
   a What discourses are drawn upon in the text?
   b How are discourses textured together?
   c Is there a mixing of discourses?
3 Coherence: are there any incoherencies within the discourse of your texts?
   a Are there any incoherencies in relationship to previous research?
   b Are there any incoherencies in the analysis itself?
4 Persuasion
   a What types of statement are there (fact, predictions, hypothetical, evaluations)?
   b How are the statements communicated (orally, encyclopaedia, maps, photographs, statistics)?
5 Inclusions/Silences
   a What elements of represented social events are included or excluded?
   b Which people are represented and how?
6 Focus on details
   a What is/are the genre(s) of the text?
   b Is the text part of a series of texts?
   c Which other texts are included/excluded?
   d Whose voices are included/excluded?
   e Are voices directly reported (quoted), or indirectly reported?
7 Focus on social contexts
   a What social event or chain of events is the text a part of?
   b Within what social network are the events framed?
   c Who is the audience of the text?

Based on Fairclough (2003, pp. 191–4), Rose (2001, p. 161) and Tonkiss (1998, pp. 258–60)

checklist offers a partial analysis. Geographers who have chosen to ask these types of questions while conducting their discourse analyses have done so because they are most likely motivated by the belief that texts have political, material, social, and moral effects and outcomes (Dunn 1997). My checklist is integral to writing a critical geography that may help address moral and political questions about contemporary societies. In particular when geographers have conducted discourse analysis they have often given voice to how texts operate in processes of social and spatial marginalisation. The outcomes are expected to enhance the quality of lives of people denied access to possibilities and resources. Equally, the outcome of particular research may not have the outcomes that were either intended or expected, particularly if (re)interpreted by the media (see Hay and Israel 2001). In doing so, these geographers are not attempting to prioritise and privilege their claims as truth. They make no claims of offering an 'objective' analysis of cultural texts. Rather, they recognise that their analysis is inevitably partial and limited by expressing, rather than erasing, the motivational and institutional context of the research. Doing discourse analysis always requires critical reflexivity (see chapter 2).

KEY TERMS

constructionist approach
critical reflexivity
discourse
discourse analysis
discursive structures or formations
genealogy
episteme
essentialism
hermeneutics
iconography
iconology

intertextuality
metaphor
power
power/knowledge
regime of truth
rigour
semiology
sign
signified
signifier
texts

REVIEW QUESTIONS

Consider the photographs in Figure 11.2 that were taken whilst I was backpacking around Aotearoa/New Zealand in 1991. These are just three of many millions of photographs taken by backpackers each year on a circuit around that country. The touristic photographs were taken with the intention of displaying them in an album to help reopen the happy, memorable experiences of this vacation to friends and family back home.

These photographs, or the ones taken on your own vacations, could become a source for a project that aims to examine how tourism helps constitute a particular geographical knowledge about a destination at a particular time, in this case Aotearoa/New Zealand in the late twentieth century. Use the following questions to help review the material in this chapter as if you were to begin a discourse analysis of these photographs, those from your own collection, or indeed other written or visual sources about travel. These questions are designed to assist you focus on what you are required to do to conduct a discourse analysis, rather than seeking specific answers. The aim of these questions is to open out research issues that you may have to address while doing discourse analysis.

Figure 11.2   Backpacking snapshots from Aotearoa/New Zealand, 1991.

Summit of Ben Lomond, Queenstown. (Source: Gordon Waitt 1991.)

Road to Arthur's Pass. (Source: Gordon Waitt 1991.)

Aoraki/Mount Cook. (Source: Gordon Waitt 1991.)

Questions about the social setting in which the discourse of the source material is located

Questions about the maker

1   What are the social identities of the maker of the source material?
2   What is the social relationship between the maker, owner, and the subject of the source material?

Questions about the audience

3   Who comprises the original audience of the source material?
4   How is the source material displayed, stored, and circulated?
5   What are the social conventions of the audience's engagement with your source material?
6   Has the source material been used for an audience other than the one for which it was originally intended? Have the social conventions of engagement changed for this new audience?

Questions about the general ideological context

7   What is the general ideological context within which your source material is located? For example, in the case of my touristic photographs they are embedded in wider ideological contexts of the transformation of the bio-physical environment into an aesthetic landscape, and the transformation of the bio-physical environment into wilderness.

Questions about textual analysis

Questions to help you scrutinise the source material in terms of its effects

8   What are your positions within the research? How has your position changed in respect to the source materials? (See Moss 2001.)
9   How is your source material embedded within the social relationships of its production and reflect the social identities of its makers? In the case of my snapshots, the source material clearly is a reflection of my own social identities, given they were taken on vacation to show friends and family back home. Careful consideration of this question is required in the context of conducting semi-structured interviews where a mixed-up set of social relations and positions is generated (see Herod 1999; and Hughes 1999).
10 What technologies did its maker depend upon for the sources' production, circulation, and display? Say, for example, in conducting semi-structured interviews you will rely upon recording technologies.
11 How did these technologies of production, circulation, and display operate upon audiences' interpretation of the source material? In my example, photography is one way that the source material becomes considered true for its intended audience. Garlick (2002), Markwell (1997), and Nicholson (2002) provide helpful discussions on how the science underpinning film and snapshot production maintains them in what is considered as true representation of the world.
12 What discursive structures can you identify within your source material? In written texts you will have to carefully scrutinise the grammar, text structure, and vocabulary. In visual texts your attention will turn to the components of the image, how they are arranged, the use of colour, the vantage point of the image, and where the eye is drawn to in the image.
13 Are there inconsistencies in the discursive structures within your source material?
14 What other source materials are relevant in keeping the discourses that you are investigating in existence?

SUGGESTED READING

Fairclough, N. 2003, *Analysing Discourse. Textual Analysis for Social Research*, Routledge, New York and London.

Mills, S. 1997, *Discourse*, Routledge, London and New York.

Phillips L. and Jørgensen M. W. 2002, *Discourse Analysis as Theory and Method*, Sage Publications, London.

Rose, G. 2001, *Visual Methodologies. An Introduction to the Interpretation of Visual Materials*, Sage Publications, London.

Shurmer-Smith, P. 2002, *Doing Cultural Geography*, Sage Publications, London.

Thiesmeyer, L. (ed.) 2003, *Discourse and Silencing. Representation and the Language of Displacement*, John Benjamins Publishing Company, Amsterdam/Philadelphia.

Tonkiss, F. 1998, 'Analysing discourse', in C. Seale (ed.), *Researching Society and Culture*, Sage, London. pp. 245–60.

Wetherell, M., Taylor, S. and Yates, S. J. 2001, *Discourse Theory and Practice. A Reader*, Sage, Thousands Oaks.

12

Knowing Seeing? Undertaking Observational Research

Robin A. Kearns

CHAPTER OVERVIEW

> ... for a discipline often preoccupied with the visual, it seems…[geography] has not studied the practices of seeing rigorously enough (Crang 1997b, p. 371).

'Seeing is believing', as the saying goes. While visual observation is a key to many types of research, there is more to observation than simply seeing: it also involves touching, smelling, and hearing the environment, and making implicit or explicit comparisons with previous experience (Rodaway 1994). Further, seeing implies a vantage point, a place—both social and geographical—at which we position ourselves to observe and be part of the world (Jackson 1993). What we observe from this place is influenced by whether we are regarded by others as an 'insider' (i.e., one who belongs), an 'outsider' (i.e., one who does not belong and is 'out of place'), or someone in between. The goal of this chapter is to reflect on the reasons why observation is fundamental to geographical research, and to consider critically what it means to observe. It explores various positions the researcher can adopt vis-à-vis the observed—from the viewing of secondary materials such as photographs to participating in the life of a community. Two key contentions are:

1   that observation has tended to be an assumed, and consequently undervalued, practice in geographic research; and
2   that ultimately all observation is participant observation.

In the chapter, I argue that observation has been taken for granted as something that occurs 'naturally'. It therefore has not been regarded as requiring the degree of attention granted to more technical aspects of our methodological repertoire as human geographers (e.g. questionnaire design, survey sampling). With critical reflection, however, observation can be transformed into a self-conscious, effective, and ethically sound practice.

PURPOSES OF OBSERVATION

Among the definitions of **observation** in the *Oxford English Dictionary* is 'accurate watching and noting of phenomena as they occur', implying that observation has an unconstrained quality. To regard observation as random or haphazard would be a mistake, however, for we never observe everything there is to be seen. Observation is the outcome of active choice, rather than mere exposure. Our choice—whether conscious or unconscious—of first, *what* to see, and second, *how* to see it, means that we always have an active role in the observation process. Following Mike Crang, I wish to argue for observation as a way of 'taking part in the world, not just representing it' (Crang 1997b, p. 360).

There is a range of purposes for observation in social scientific research and these can be summarised by three words, which conveniently begin with 'c': counting, complementing, and contextualising. The first purpose—counting—refers to an enumerative function for observation. For example, we might accumulate observations of pedestrians passing various points in a shopping mall or airport in order to establish daily rhythms of activity within these places. Research in the time-geographic tradition has used this approach to chart the ebb and flow of spatio-temporal activity (Shapcott and Steadman 1978; Walmsley and Lewis 1984). Under this observational rationale, other elements of the immediate setting are (at least temporarily) ignored while the focal activity occurs. The resulting numerical data is then easily displayed graphically or analysed statistically. This is an approach to observation that may be useful for establishing trends but is ultimately too reductionist to develop any comprehensive understanding of place.

A second purpose of observation is providing complementary evidence. The rationale here is to gather additional descriptive information before, during, or after other more structured forms of data collection. The intent is to gain added value from time 'in the field' and to provide a descriptive complement to more controlled and formalised methods such as interviewing. Complementary observation might involve spending time in a neighbourhood after completing a household survey and taking notes on the appearance of houses, the types of cars, and the upkeep of gardens. I used this approach in research on housing problems in Auckland and Christchurch. Interviewers were instructed to observe the dwellings of those they interviewed. Their notes added to (and often contrasted with) what people said about their own dwellings (Kearns et al. 1991). Such information complements the aggregated data gathered by more structured means and assists in interpreting the experience of place.

The third purpose of observation might be called contextual understanding. Here the goal is to construct an in-depth interpretation of a particular time and place through direct experience. To achieve this understanding the researcher immerses herself/himself in the socio-temporal context of interest and uses first-hand observations as the prime source of data. In this situation, the observer is very much a participant.

It should be noted at the outset that these purposes are not mutually exclusive. As I will later show by way of examples from research, one can approach observation with mixed purposes, seeking, for instance, to both enumerate and understand context during a period in the field (Kearns 1991a).

TYPES OF OBSERVATION

Some social scientists identify two types of observation: *controlled* and *uncontrolled*. **Controlled observation** 'is typified by clear and explicit decisions on what, how, and when to observe' (Frankfort-Nachmaias and Nachmaias 1992, p. 206). This style of observation is associated with natural science and its experimental approach to research, which has been imported into physical geography. Thus, a geographer might set up an electronic stream gauge to gather data at periodic intervals throughout a flood, resulting in a series of so-called 'observations'. However, such data are collected remotely without the aid of human senses. Indeed, the human eye may have only been involved in the secondary sense of observing the gauge, subsequent to the actual data collection. This recognition that controlled observations can be made through mechanical means adds weight to the common perception that such research is rigorous and easily replicated. However, controlled observation is also limiting in terms of the sensory and experiential input that is admissible as 'findings'. Human geographers are unlikely to employ such controlled methods of observation, except perhaps in the earlier example of pedestrian counts.

In two respects, so-called 'controlled observation' is necessarily limiting. First, there is an imposed focus on particular elements of the known world; and second, it is only *directly* observable aspects that are of interest. Thus, imputed characteristics of place and the feelings of residents may be out of range. Most of the observation conducted by contemporary social and cultural geographers could be described as **uncontrolled observation**. Such observation is certainly directed by goals and ethical considerations, but is not controlled in the sense of being restricted to noting prescribed phenomena. Therefore, although observation refers literally to that which is seen, in social science it may involve more than just seeing. Most obviously, observation also includes listening, a critical aspect of several approaches in human geography, including interviewing and participant observation. Effective listening can assist visual observation by both confirming the place of the researcher as a participant (Kearns 1991b) and by attuning oneself to 'soundscapes' and the aural aspects of social settings (Smith 1994).

One might argue that all research involves observation, or at least comprises a series of observations. Thus, in a social setting, we can 'observe' the population by employing questionnaires through which the researcher establishes the frequency of certain variables (for example, occupation, sex). The activity of conducting a questionnaire survey invariably places the researcher in the position of an 'outsider', marked as 'other' by purpose, if not appearance and demeanour (for example, clothing, age, ethnicity, or type of language used). Identifying a sample and evaluating the responses to questions involve concerns related to the goal of generalisability to broader populations. But the cost of these concerns is that only a restricted subset of social phenomena is deemed to be of interest. These phenomena can easily be isolated from their context, unaccompanied by less directly observable values, intentions, and feelings. Qualitative approaches allow the consideration of human experience, potentially suspending traditional concerns about researcher bias and recognising instead the relationship between the researcher and the people and places he or she seeks to study.

A further distinction can be made between primary and secondary observation in research. The former activity would have us adopt the position of participants in, and interpreters of, human activity, whereas as secondary observers we are interpreters of the observations of others. Examples of secondary observation are analyses of picture postcards available to tourists (Crang 1996) and the photography of one 'racialised' group by a representative of another (Jackson 1992). In this chapter, I will not dwell on this use of secondary materials (which are dealt with more fully in chapter 11), but rather note the all-pervasive nature of participant observation. For, in one sense, a solitary researcher observing images of place is also an active participant in the process. This is because the observer is co-creating meaning through bringing their own perspectives and life experiences to their analysis and interpretation.

PARTICIPANT OBSERVATION

Participant observation is most closely associated with social anthropology (Sanjek 1990; Srivinas et al. 1979). Significantly, its profile among the repertoire of approaches used by human geographers was raised by Peter Jackson (1983) who had studied both geography and social anthropology. The approach has been adopted and adapted by geographers seeking to understand more fully the meanings of place and the contexts of everyday life. Examples include a number of now 'classic' studies within the 'humanistic' tradition such as David Ley's (1974) work on 'Monroe', a neighbourhood in inner-city Philadelphia, John Western's (1981) *Outcast Cape Town*, and Graham Rowles' (1978) research on the ways older people experience place. Like many social geographers, these writers talked to 'locals' in the course of their research, but it was the depth of their involvement in a community, their recurrent contact with people, and their relatively unstructured social interactions that stood out in their work. While many of their contemporaries were solely interested in perception or behaviour, these geographers were concerned with experience.

Developing a geography of everyday experience requires us to move beyond reliance on formalised interactions such as those occuring in interviews. As Mel Evans (1988, p. 203) remarks, 'although an interview situation is still a social situation...it is a world apart from everyday life'. Evans is suggesting that no matter how much we are able to put people at ease before and during an interview, its structured format often removes the researcher from the 'flow' of everyday life in both time and space. In other words, an interview ordinarily has an anticipated length and occurs in a mutually agreeable place often set apart from other social interactions. In contrast, the goal of participant observation is developing understanding through being part of the spontaneity of everyday interactions.

There is a consensus that, although definable, participant observation is difficult to describe systematically. Commentators have remarked on its 'elusive nature' (Alder and Alder 1994), its breadth (Bryman 1984), and the fact that it remains 'ill-defined and ...tainted with mysticism' (Evans 1988, p. 197). Part of the 'mysticism' Evans refers to stems from the fact that there are few systematic outlines of the method, and students who have been curious about the approach have commonly been referred to 'classic' studies such as William Whyte's *Street Corner Society* (1957) for models. One explanation for this tendency to refer to examples rather than to offer step-by-step guidelines is that every participant-observation situation is unique. Another reason offered by Evans (1988, p. 197) is that the success of the approach depends less on the strict application of rules and more upon 'introspection on the part of the researcher with respect to his or her relationship to what is to be (and is being) researched'.

While introspection or reflection on what we see and experience is important, it is surely guidance in the act of observing that is needed. Jackson draws on Kluckhohn (1940) for a concise description of participant observation, defining it as 'conscious and systematic sharing, in so far as circumstances permit, in the life activities and, on occasion, in the interests...of a group of persons' (1983, p. 39). It is therefore the systematic and intentional character of observations that contrasts the activities of a participant observer with those of routine participants in daily life (Spradley 1980). To generalise, participant observation for a geographer involves strategically placing oneself in situations in which systematic understandings of place are most likely to arise.

One rationale for participant observation is a recognition that the mere presence of a researcher potentially alters the behaviour or the dispositions of those being observed. This contention is illustrated in a well-known 'Far Side' cartoon by Gary Larson. In the drawing, two men wearing pith helmets are approaching a thatched hut. The 'primitive' occupants, stereotypically adorned with bones through their noses and wearing head-dresses, are exclaiming 'Anthropologists! Anthropologists!' as they rush to hide their television set. The cartoon ironically suggests that scholarly explorers do not expect 'primitives' to have technology (and that primitives might want to live up to this stereotype). In terms of research methods, the cartoon's message is that the undisguised entry of others into a social situation is bound to alter behaviour. This point for us as qualitative researchers is that conscious participation in the social processes being observed increases the potential for more 'natural' interactions and responses to occur.

Use of the term 'observation' in highly controlled scientific research perhaps tempts us to think too easily in terms of a simple dichotomy between participant and non-participant. According to Atkinson and Hammersley, this is an unhelpful distinction 'not least because it seems to imply that the non-participant observer plays no recognised role at all' (1984, p. 248). Indeed, as the Far Side cartoon succinctly illustrates, there is really no such thing as a non-participant in a social situation: even those who believe that they are present but not participating in a research context often unwittingly alter the research setting. To move beyond this false binary construct of participant/non-participant, Gold (1958) suggests that there is a range of four possible research roles:

1   **complete observer** (for example, a psychologist watching a child through a one-way mirror)
2   **observer-as-participant** (for example, a newcomer to a sport being part of the crowd—see Latimer 1998)
3   **participant-as-observer** (for example, seeking to understand social change in one's own locality—see Ponga 1998)
4   **complete participation** (for example, living in a rural settlement to understand meanings of sustainability—see Scott et al. 1997).

While it is difficult to imagine how being a complete observer might be incorporated into geography, an example could be discrete surveillance in a shopping mall, perhaps with access to closed-circuit television (CCTV). As the references above indicate, work by geographers can be easily categorised according to the remaining three roles. Each represents a form of participant observation, and the difference is essentially a matter of the degree of participation involved. This division implies a continuum of involvement for the observing researcher from detachment to engagement. However, whatever one's positioning vis-à-vis 'the observed' it is important to acknowledge that the act of observation is imbued with power dynamics.

POWER, KNOWLEDGE, AND OBSERVATION

Before considering the stages of observation in the field in greater detail, it is important to reflect on aspects of the process itself. As emphasised earlier, observation involves participating, both socially and spatially. We cannot usually observe directly without being present, and our bodily presence brings with it personal characteristics that mark our identity such as 'race', sex, and age. Belonging to a dominant group in society can mean that we carry with us the power dynamics linked to such an affiliation (Dyck and Kearns 1995). Being a white, adult male, for instance, will invariably create challenges to being a participant in a group whose members do not share those characteristics, such as a new mothers' support group. In other words, our difference in terms of key markers of societal power (or lack thereof) contributes to our (in)ability to be 'insiders' and participants in the quest to understand place (matters of 'insider' and 'outsider' status are also discussed in chapters 2 and 3).

More subtle challenges may be generated by our level of education and affiliation to universities. In undertaking university-based research, we can carry institutional dynamics into our acts of observing through subtle forms of social control. Social control can occur through the ways in which one group (the relatively powerful) are able to maintain watch over members of another (the relatively disempowered). Perhaps the most memorable image of this dynamic is Bentham's '**panopticon**', a circular prison designed to maximise the ability of warders to see into every cell and to watch prisoners (Foucault 1977a). Prisoners do not know exactly when they are being observed but learn to act as if they were always being watched. Foucault sees this surveillance as a form of disciplinary power that is enforced through the layout of the built environment rather than through the exertion of force *per se*. The key to the resulting institutional dynamic is the knowledge on the part of prisoners that they could be observed at any time. This knowledge, according to Foucault, results in self-surveillance and self-discipline.

Foucault's ideas have implications for observation as a research approach. The 'surveillance' to which he refers is a very visual and disembodied form of observation. Gillian Rose (1993) has linked this to the traditional geographical activity of fieldwork. To Rose and other feminists, geography has been an excessively observational discipline characterised by an implicit 'masculine gaze'. The key point is that observation can be a power-laden process deployed within institutional practices. As we are based in, and representative of, academic institutions, it is imperative that we be aware of the ways in which others' behaviour may be modified by our presence (Dyck and Kearns 1995).

A challenge posed by feminist geographers and anthropologists is to see fieldwork as a gendered activity (Bell et al. 1993; Nast 1994; Rose 1993). Their argument is that in being participant observers, we unavoidably incorporate our gendered selves into the arena of observation. An extract from the fieldnotes of Louisa Kivell (1995) illustrates how observation in human geography is far from a simple matter of uni-directional watching; rather it involves interactions that are potentially laden with sexual energy. The resulting situations may shed light on the gendered constitution of the field site itself (Box 12.1).

BOX 12.1   **'AND BLACK UNDERWEAR TOO': THE GENDERED CONSTITUTION OF A FIELD SITE**

Me. Walking onto an orchard looking for the manager with whom I had an appointment to discuss employment relations in his operation. Me. Dressed in my 'orchard clothes', a reflection of my expectation that he would have been out working in his 'orchard clothes' too. My orchard clothes include: dark shorts suitable for ladders, dirt and other eventualities; a plain green T-shirt without any brand labels or other logos; a jumper tied around my waist because I know it can get cold down the apple rows; socks and cross-trainers…Anything else? Oh yes, a band tying my hair out of the way, a watch and a medic alert bracelet, mascara, suntan lotion and deodorant, lip balm, a pen and paper in my pocket and maybe a linger of this morning's perfume. Stop.

A white male wearing his 'orchard clothes' approaches me on a tractor and stops. He smiles, then laughs out a question-come-statement: *'You aren't here looking for a picking job are you?'*

For a moment I am incapable.

I reply. *'As it happens, no. I have an appointment to see Mr Sky but I'm interested to hear what makes you think I wouldn't be picker material.'*

'Oh well… nothing really…it's just that um…in two years I've never seen a girl like you on an orchard before.'

What is a girl like me?

White, 21, pretty, on my own.

My education status, my socio-economic background, my place of origin, most of the other 'girl like me' things are not immediately visible.

What pale concept of a girl like me did he dispatch with his laugh?

(Kivell 1995, p. 49).

STAGES OF PARTICIPANT OBSERVATION

Participant observation is far from haphazard. There are some commonly recognised stages through which the process moves, from choice of research site through to presentation of results. I will review each of these, using as a case example my research in the Hokianga district of Northland, New Zealand. In this work, my objective has been to understand the influence that sense of place has in shaping the social meanings of the local health care system. In the course of this research, I have adopted three of the four roles identified by Gold (1958): observer-as-participant, participant-as-observer, and complete participant (see Kearns 1991b, 1997).

Choice of setting

Choosing a setting for participant observation might be dictated by the goals of a larger research project, in which case the setting may be unfamiliar to the researcher (for example, Scott et al. 1997). In such a case, there will be a need for a good deal of background research on the community in question as well as reconnaissance visits before a period of immersion into community life. However, it is likely that student researchers will choose to study settings at least partially familiar to them. But familiarity can bring pitfalls. There is a danger that the researcher is over-familiar with the community, with the result that there is 'too much participation at the expense of observation' (Evans 1988, p. 205). Indeed some argue that it is just as challenging doing fieldwork in one's own society as it is in an 'alien' one (Srinivas 1979).

What, then, might be the ideal? Possibly the best balance to strive for in choosing a research setting is a mid-point between the 'insider' and 'outsider' statuses discussed earlier. The conventionally recommended stance is that of stranger, but this is not necessarily a position in which one simply does not belong. Rather, it is one in which the researcher's status is what Evans (1988) terms 'marginal' in relation to the community. By 'marginal' I take Evans to mean socially, and possibly spatially, on the edge of a community or group. Thus, although cheering on the terraces at Eden Park (a sports ground in Auckland), Bill Latimer (1998) was marginal because he had never been to a high-profile rugby game before. Coming from northern England, the game of his culture and class was soccer. He was thus able to be a critical, only partially involved, observer of the place of rugby in Auckland (see Box 12.2).

BOX 12.2 AT THE GAME: AN OBSERVER-AS-PARTICIPANT

Saturday March 21st, walking alone to Eden Park I was struck by the sea of decorative clothing and painted faces—blue and white for Auckland; red and black for Canterbury. One man had made himself a hat out of DB Export beer coasters. Once inside the ground I steered away from the loud 'yobs' who had positioned themselves behind the goal posts. I didn't choose a good spot. I felt uneasy as I took my seat between two sets of monotonic droning young men (wailing 'AAAAUUUUUAUCKLAAAAAAND!!!' like Tarzans of the terrace).

An eerie silence accompanied the match, interrupted only by the mo(ro)notonic drone of those seated around me. As I was about to discover, this was the calm before the storm. The Blues scored. Before I was able to offer a congratulatory clap of hands Eden Park erupted. Music blasted onto the terraces and was taken as the cue to scream, dance and throw arms, and their contents, into the air. As the music continued to pump out, cheerleaders thrusted and gyrated suggestively to the very deep, sexy, sensuous bass beat. I was soaked with beer and hit about the body with plastic cups and other missiles. I was also very unimpressed. Each time Auckland scored, a young guy in front of me would stand up and say to his friend, 'did you feeeel that?'. He would then embrace his mate in a hand wrestling fashion which meant that their forearm muscles bulged, and both would look each other in the eye, faces inches apart, and grunt 'AAAAUUUUUUCKLAAAAND!!!'

(Latimer 1998, p. 91).

Access

Gaining entry to social settings and places is potentially a fundamental challenge. A crucial issue is identifying key individuals who can act as gatekeepers, facilitating opportunities to interact with others in the chosen research site. There are some settings into which one can simply walk and take on the role of participant. Investigating the way in which a public shopping mall is used is a good example. Being commonly used and perceived as a public place, there are fewer permissions to be sought than in less 'public' settings such as health clinics. And nor is there a problem with 'blending in', given the diversity of users. One can observe through simply participating in the mall's functions: shopping, resting on the seats provided, or using the food court. But gaining access is potentially more challenging when the place is smaller in scale or less public in character.

Gaining access may well be more straightforward if one has a known role. Even being 'the visiting student' in a workplace may give one a role in a way that just being an anonymous visitor or stranger would not. However, there are often no convenient roles in hospitals or factories, so once ethical approval is gained (see the discussion in chapter 2), perhaps there is good reason to resist being typecast into any role except that of outsider (see Kearns 1997). This ambiguous position worked for me in the health clinics of the Hokianga district. I could not legitimately pass as either a health professional or a patient as local residents knew each other too well, so being a visitor reading the newspaper helped me be reasonably inconspicuous for a short period (see Box 12.3).

BOX 12.3 GAINING ACCESS TO A FIELD SITE

My research in, on, and with Hokianga people began with a period of fieldwork during October 1988. My wife Pat had the opportunity of being a medical *locum tenens* in the district and I was also keen to go north. Once in Hokianga, having a spouse with a temporary part in the health-care system gave me some legitimacy in seeking to gain approval to undertake some research at the hospital and community clinics. The medical director as gatekeeper to the health system knew who I was, and as I was already there the formality of letters and telephone conversations could largely be circumvented. I hastily devised a research plan that involved spending time in the waiting areas of each clinic, where I observed social dynamics with the goal of understanding the social function of these places.

Field relations

The role that the researcher adopts within an observed setting (for example, complete participant or participant-as-observer) will define the character of the relations she or he generates. The idea of impression management is critical here, for the impact you make on those encountered will determine, to a large extent, the ease with which they will interact with you and incorporate you into their place. Embedded within the word *incorporate* is 'corpus', the Latin word for body. My purpose in discussing incorporation is to stress the idea of the researcher's embodiment, and to recognise that, as researchers, we take more than our intentions and notebooks into any situation: we take our bodies also. The way we clothe ourselves, for instance, can be a key marker of who we are, or who we wish to be seen as, in the field. By way of example, while researching the inner-city experiences of psychiatric patients, I chose to wear older clothes to drop-in centres in order to minimise being regarded as yet another health professional or social worker intruding on patients' lives (Kearns 1987). Being a student at the time, it was easy for me to find place-appropriate clothes for a drop-in centre! But a troubling question is whether I could have 'blended in' if I had been attempting to study the more elite social relations of place (for example, the dynamics of a lawyers' convention, or a restaurant frequented by politicians). At the most fundamental level, I would not have had the right clothes to wear. It is generally easier to dress 'down' than 'up' and this perhaps explains in small part why participant observation is more often used in studies of people less powerful than researchers themselves.

Our ability to relate to others in the field depends not just on appearance, but also on the level and type of activity undertaken. To extend the above example, passively 'hanging out' in a psychiatric drop-in centre is one thing, but feigning ability in more expert pursuits is another. This need to pass as an *active* participant is reflected in Phil Crang's (1996) research on the workplace geographies within a Mexican theme restaurant in England. Here the researcher sought to understand the dynamics of performance in the restaurant by being employed as a member of the waiting staff and becoming part of the daily routines of the place.

A further point is that although concern for appearance and clothing is appropriate, it potentially reinforces geographers' fixations with the visual (see Rose 1993). Hester Parr (1998) describes how, while researching the geographical experiences of people with mental illness in Nottingham, she became conscious of non-visual aspects of her 'otherness' such as smell: her perfumed deodorant served to set her apart from those she was attempting conversation with and inhibit free interaction. Parr's reflection serves to remind us that senses such as smell add to the character of place (Porteous 1985) and merit consideration for the way they can mark as 'other' the bodiliness of the researcher (see Rodaway 1994).

A related point influencing field relations is that codes of behaviour are attached to different settings. Parr (1998) discusses how she suddenly established a rapport with Bob, an acutely schizophrenic man with whom communication was difficult. The setting for this 'breakthrough' was a city park, neutral ground which neither the researcher nor the informant regarded as home. This site at which social boundaries were blurred contrasted with the drop-in centre where roles were more established and routine. The lesson is that research relations may be enabled or constrained by the (often unspoken) ways in which social space is codified and regulated. Successful participant observation thus involves not only the (temporary) occupation of unfamiliar places, but also the adoption of alternative ways of using time. Box 12.4 continues an account of my Hokianga research by describing my use of time in community clinics.

BOX 12.4 FIELD RELATIONS IN AN OBSERVATIONAL STUDY

At some of the ten hospital and community clinics I blended into the small crowd of clinic attendees, inconspicuously observing events under the guise of reading the newspaper. At others, however, I was clearly a Pakeha ('white') visitor, as all present were both local and Maori and seemed to know each other well. It was immediately evident that going to the doctor involved more than medical interactions. Rather, the occasion frequently provided an opportunity for locals to tell stories and reflect not only on their own well-being, but also on that of their families and friends. From this participant observation in the clinic waiting areas, I noted that the most frequent conversation category was community concerns. Comments on the deleterious impacts of the restructuring of public services were frequently expressed. Residents adopted a relaxed approach to clinic attendance and their use of waiting areas. Patients were observed arriving well before their appointment time (sometimes in the company of others who had no intention of consulting the doctor or nurse) and lingering afterwards 'having a yarn'. These observations led me to interpret the clinics as de facto community centres, analogous to the village market in other countries. The difference, however, was that the place (the clinics) and the time (clinic day) prompted a considerable amount of conversation that explicitly centred on health concerns

(adapted from Kearns 1991b, p. 525).

Talking and listening

We cannot blend in as researchers unless we participate in the social relations we are seeking to understand. Listening ought to precede talking, in order that we become attuned to what matters in a particular time, place, and social setting (Kearns 1991a) (see Box 12.5). Asking questions can be manipulative, and simply conversing about what otherwise might

---

BOX 12.5 TALKING AND LISTENING: THE EMBODIED OBSERVER

My embodiment as researcher was central to the construction of this knowledge. Within the waiting area I had to position myself in such a way as to neither be threatening (and thus inhibit conversation by gazing at others) nor be overly welcoming of conversational engagement (hence my 'hiding' behind a newspaper). Such choreography was bound to break down, and did. On one occasion two locals offered to help with the crossword puzzle I was half-heartedly completing, and on another, a *kuia* (female elder) entered, kissed and welcomed all present to 'her' clinic, including myself. My corporeality within the observed arena of social interaction thus rendered binary constructs of researcher/researched and subject/object thoroughly permeable. In this *kuia*'s clinic, my conceptions of being an 'autonomous self' were dissected and (re)embodied within their rightful web of socio-cultural relations.

(Kearns 1997, p. 5).

seem obvious may result in a less threatening entry into the social relations of place. The how and where of talking and listening are also crucially important. For research with children, for instance, adopting their level—both physically and in terms of style of language—may be the key to successful observation. Sarah Gregory (1998) found that playing with children on the floor was a useful precursor to asking them about their experiences using consumption goods. In other words, observation is least conspicuous when one is interacting most naturally with the research subjects. The lesson is that as researchers we are our own most crucial tool and 'it is the fact of participation, of being part of a collective contract, which creates the data' (Evans 1988, p. 209).

Recording data

A clipboard or audio recorder are the standard means of recording information in other qualitative approaches involving face-to-face communication, such as interviews. However, because these tools would be disruptive to the flow of conversation or interaction, a participant observer can rarely use them. Rather there is a greater reliance on recollection and a necessity to work on detailed note-taking after a period of field encounters. At the end of any day or session of observation, one is likely to feel tired and not inclined to take out a pen, or go to a computer to record reflections. However, developing a discipline for such 'homework' is a key part of field observation: notes are invaluable sources of data, and prompts to further reflection (Scott et al. 1997). Fieldnotes become a personal text for the researcher to refer to and analyse. They represent the process of transforming observed interaction into written communication (see the discussion in chapter 16 on relationships between writing and research). Jean Jackson (1990, p. 7) describes fieldnotes creatively as 'ideas that are marinating'. Preliminary fieldnotes may be taken on any materials at hand, such as the margins of a newspaper (Kearns 1991b). However, back at 'home base', annotations are now almost invariably entered into a computer, and just as a fear of earlier researchers was destruction of paper notes by fire (Sanjek 1990), a contemporary concern is loss of electronic data. Keeping back-up files and/or print-outs of your field data is thus a crucial precaution.

Analysis and presentation

Analysing the results of any period of observation will vary according to the purposes for which it was undertaken. Observations that have involved counting, or carefully recording each instance of some phenomenon, lend themselves to tables that enumerate occurrences and express data as frequencies or percentages. Observation that has complemented a more explicitly structured research design commonly leads to the presentation of quotations or descriptions that assist in our interpretation of findings derived from other sources. In research into the impact of logging trucks on Hokianga roads and people, for instance, we complemented interviews with community members and analyses of secondary data, such as log-harvest projections, with a first-hand narrative of the experience of driving along selected stretches of road (Collins and Kearns 1998). Elsewhere, an assessment of the impact of a 'walking school bus' scheme on children's and parent's commuting patterns involved not only a calculation of car trips saved but also verbatim narratives from children gathered while the lead author walked with them to school (Kearns et al. 2003).

When observation is embedded in an attempt to reach contextual understanding, a considerable volume of text will typically be accumulated, and strategies for the storage, classification, and analysis of information will need to be carefully considered (for a discussion of some of these issues, see chapter 14). A number of useful texts are also available, for example, Bryman and Burgess (1994). This scale of observational engagement also suggests the merits of using computing software such as *NUD*IST* and *NVivo,* now employed by human geographers (see chapter 15).

Ethical obligations

What are our obligations to those whom we have observed? Clearly if observation has been fleeting and devoid of personal contact (for example, watching pedestrian behaviour) any return of research results to those individuals observed would be impractical and perhaps unnecessary. Indeed the 'observed' in this example are only nominally 'participants' in the research. However, the example of 'reading' the presence of graffiti in the built environment (see Lindsey and Kearns 1994) has the potential to be a little more challenging. Observing the 'what' and 'where' of graffiti is unproblematic as 'tagging' is part of the publicly observed landscape. But the act of inscribing graffiti is invariably illegal, so what are our obligations if we witness 'taggers' at work: to report their breach of the law, or to preserve their anonymity? Arguably, our role as citizens takes precedence and the former stance should hold sway.

Where observation 'involves involvement' in a geographical community or social group, it might be argued that there is an ethical imperative to maintain contact after the formal research period. This imperative may be formalised by the requirements of university ethics committees, but the stronger influence should surely come from the researcher, especially if pre-existing relationships have been developed (or reactivated) through the research process. As Maria Ponga noted in her study of the restoration of a *marae* (meeting house) in her home community in New Zealand, 'there is a social responsibility to carry on the ties. I have tried to keep in touch and send letters thanking people for the information they have given me and keep them updated on my progress. As we are all *whanau* (extended family), this has also had an added dimension of maintaining the family ties' (1998, p. 54). (See also chapters 3 and 13.)

Such obligations may be taken for granted when pre-existing ties are involved, but require careful consideration when social situations are entered into, or generated, for the sake of research. It is generally agreed that cross-cultural fieldwork is particularly problematic (see chapter 3 for a full discussion). This is for two reasons that may be linked to the 'field' metaphor: first, the researcher is potentially venturing onto another's turf; and second, because fieldwork involves a researcher working in a field of knowledge, there is the risk of overlooking local understandings and priorities, and of (possibly unintended) one-way traffic of knowledge from the field (periphery) to the academy (centre) (Kearns 1997). Box 12.6 draws on these ideas to complete the series of examples from my Hokianga research. In such situations, the development of **'culturally safe'** research practice (Dyck and Kearns 1995; Kearns and Dyck, 2004) is important. Such practice recognises the ways in which collective histories of power relations may affect individual research encounters. It also stresses the need for appropriate translation of materials into everyday language, and the return of knowledge to the communities that provided or generated it (Kearns 1997). (See also chapters 2, 3, and 13.)

BOX 12.6   COMPLETING THE CIRCLE: CULTURES, THEORY, AND PRACTICE

While on overseas sabbatical leave in 1995, I had the opportunity of recounting the story of place and health in Hokianga, and connecting its plot lines to the coordinates of other struggles for identity and turf. Drawing on Feinsilver's (1993) Cuban experience, for instance, I could identify the community action as a 'narrative of struggle' in which there is a greater symbolism to health politics than just a defence of local services. However, I was left searching for a rationale for the place of the researcher in the narrative of struggle.

To impose theory (upon observation) without reference to the community would be as foolish as the unfettered importation of exotic wildlife or viruses into New Zealand. Clearly, the use of theory must be regulated. My own form of self-regulation has been to return draft papers to people involved with Hokianga's health trust for comment. In one such draft I had interpreted their struggle as a 'postmodern politics of resistance' (Kearns 1997). The returned manuscript was annotated with the comment from a health trust worker that my words sounded like 'undigested theory'. On reflection, this was a fair assessment. I had, perhaps unwittingly, used theory imported from recent visits to conferences in Los Angeles and Chicago. It was time to return, to digest theory, and reconnect with the source of the story. Such returns are made easier through adoptive *whanau* (extended family) relationships in which research is, at times, indistinguishable from the *aroha* (love, affection) and *korero* (purposeful talk) among friends. Hokianga has taught me about being a bicultural geographer, a role that requires respecting the rituals we can never fully enter, while reforming the rituals of our own research (Kearns 1997, p. 6).

REFLECTING ON THE METHOD

As observers, our goal should be to achieve seeing that is, as the saying goes, believing. However, this chapter has argued that believable observation is the outcome of more than simply seeing; it requires cognisance of the full sensory experience of being in place.

Though a well-established approach—especially within anthropology—participant observation can be reinterpreted as a quintessentially postmodern activity. This is because its goal is to acknowledge difference and, through immersion in a situation, to 'become the other', however provisionally. If the questionnaire is the tool for survey researchers, and the audio recorder for key informant interviewers, researchers themselves are the tool for participant observation. The question remaining is: how do we know if the fruits of participant observation are valid? Evans (1988) reminds us of the very important point that any method is, to a degree, valid when the knowledge that it constructs is considered by stakeholders to be an adequate interpretation of the social phenomena that it seeks to understand and explain (see chapter 5).

Are there disadvantages to reliance on observation? One danger, perhaps, is privileging face-to-face interactions over less localised relations that remain beyond the view of the researcher in the field (Gupta and Ferguson 1997). To believe only what we see would be to make the serious mistake of denying the existence of structures such as social class, or communicative processes such as Internet relationships, that occur 'off-stage'.

Whether we seek to count, to gather complementary information, or to understand the context of place more deeply, the key to taking observation seriously is being attentive to detail as well as acknowledging our positions as researchers. Those recognitions imply that we are aware of both our place within the social relations we are attempting to study and the reasons we have the research agendas that we do (White and Jackson 1995).

KEY TERMS

complete observation

complete participation

controlled observation

'culturally safe'

fieldnotes

observation

observer-as-participant

panopticon

participant-as-observer

participant observation

positionality

secondary observation

uncontrolled observation

REVIEW QUESTIONS

1 What are some of the ethical considerations that arise from observation?
2 In what ways might access to a specific social setting (for example, a netball club, an industrial workplace) be achieved for research purposes?
3 In what ways does observation involve more than seeing?
4 Suggest some ways in which our presence might influence interactions in the research setting.
5 Why, and in what circumstances, might one opt for participant observation as a research method?

SUGGESTED READING

A helpful guide for students using participation in dissertation research is provided by Ian Cook's (1997) chapter in *Methods in Human Geography* (by R. Flowerdew and D. Martin (eds), Addison Wesley Longman). Another accessible resource, with concepts interleaved with research examples, is Mel Evans' chapter in Eyles and Smith's (1988) book *Qualitative Methods in Human Geography* (Polity Press, Cambridge).

13

Participatory Action Research

Sara Kindon

CHAPTER OVERVIEW[1]

Participatory action research (PAR) is one of the fastest emerging approaches in human geography. It involves academic researchers in research, education, and socio-political action with members of community groups as co-researchers and decision-makers in their own right (Thomas-Slayter 1995). As such, it is quite different from many other research methods and demands different types of attitudes and behaviours from a researcher. In this chapter I discuss the overall process of PAR and its cycles of action and reflection. I also discuss different types of relationships and various strategies and techniques that can be used to enable the involvement of research participants in all stages of the process. These aim to establish a more democratic research process, which respects and builds co-researchers' capacity and generates more rich, diverse, and appropriate knowledge for community change. If done well, PAR has many benefits for human geographers, particularly for those committed to challenging unequal power relationships and increasing social justice. PAR can also be challenging to carry out: the emphasis on power, relationships, and change is a potent mix. Finally I consider how we can present PAR-generated research information to a range of audiences in effective and ethical ways.

WHAT IS PARTICIPATORY ACTION RESEARCH?

Participatory action research (PAR) has been defined as:

> [A]n experiential methodology for the acquisition of serious and reliable knowledge upon which to construct power, or counterveiling power, for the poor, oppressed and exploited groups and social classes—the grassroots—and for their […] organizations and movements. Its purpose is to enable oppressed groups and classes to acquire sufficient creative and

transforming leverage as expressed in specific projects, acts and struggles to achieve goals of social transformation (Fals-Borda and Rahman 1991, p. 4).

PAR has been evolving since at least the 1970s and is fundamentally different from many other social science methods because its goal is not just to describe or analyse social reality but to help change it (Pratt 2000). This change occurs through the active involvement of research participants in the focus and direction of the research itself. To clarify, as an academic researcher thinking about embarking on PAR, you would not usually determine a research agenda independently. Rather you would work with a social group (usually regarded as marginalised or disenfranchised as Fals-Borda notes above) to define the issues facing them (see chapter 3). Together you would then generate and analyse information, which would hopefully lead to action and ultimately, positive change for those involved (Bowes 1996; Cameron and Gibson 2004; Cooke 2001; Thomas-Slayter 1995). In short, a PAR researcher does not conduct research *on* a group, but works *with them* to achieve change that *they* desire.

PAR involves a number of stages through which academic and social group members work together to define, address, and reconsider the issues facing them (Parkes and Panelli 2001). Such issues commonly include the lack of access to information or resources, the threat of removal of services or subsidies, or the need to respond to and mitigate further unanticipated events. The emphasis on this iterative cycle of **action–reflection** is one of the key distinguishing features of PAR. It can also enable multiple perspectives of different **stakeholders** to be taken into account throughout the research, which can lead to more informed decision-making and more equitable and potentially sustainable outcomes.

PAR involves attention to power relations and as such can be challenging, particularly in the context of an undergraduate research project. It often involves the researcher in a facilitative rather than 'extractive' role, and demands that s/he pay considerable attention to ethics and issues of representation. That said, PAR can be very rewarding and even if it is not possible to involve research participants deeply in every step of a research project, it may be possible to make your research more participatory by adopting some of the ideas discussed in this chapter.

CONDUCTING 'GOOD' PARTICIPATORY ACTION RESEARCH

PAR is an approach that ideally grows out of the needs of a specific context, research question, or problem, and the relationships between researcher and research participants. It is more about the value orientation of the work and its approach (epistemology) than the specific techniques used, although participatory techniques are certainly important (see Kesby et al. 2004 for discussion of deep versus other forms of **participation**). It is also an approach that values the process as much as the product so that the 'success' of a PAR project rests not only on the quality of information generated, but also on the extent to which skills, knowledge, and participants' capacities are also developed (Cornwall and Jewkes 1995; Kesby et al. 2004; Maguire 1987).

According to some practitioners (see Chambers 1994), the most important aspects of participatory work are the attitudes and behaviours of 'outside' researchers (usually

BOX 13.1 THE IMPORTANCE OF ATTITUDES TO RELATIONSHIPS WITHIN PAR

Attitude of Researcher and Example of Attitude Reflected in what Researcher Might Say to Researched Group (RG)	Relationship between Researcher and Researched Group (RG)	Mode of Participation	Relationship between Research and Researched Group (RG)
Elitist 'Trust and leave it to me. I know best.'	Researcher designs and carries out research; RG representatives chosen but largely uninvolved; no real power sharing.	Co-option	ON
Patronising 'Work with me, I know how to help.' (i.e., I know best.)	Researcher decides on agenda and directs the research; Tasks are assigned to RG representatives with incentives; no real power sharing.	Compliance	ON/FOR
Well meaning 'Tell me what you think, then I'll analyse the information and give you recommendations.' (i.e., I know best.)	Researcher seeks RG opinions, but then analyses and decides on best course of action independently; limited power sharing.	Consultation	FOR/WITH
Respectful 'What is important to you in the research? How about we do it together? Here's my suggestion about how we might go about this.'	Researcher and RG determine priorities, but responsibility rests with researcher to direct the process; some power sharing.	Cooperation	WITH
Facilitative 'What does this mean for you? How might we do the research together? How can I support you to change your situation?'	Researcher and RG share knowledge, create new understandings, and work together to form action plans; power sharing.	Co-learning	WITH/BY
Hands-off 'Let me know if and how you need me.'	RG set their own agenda and carry it out with or without researcher; some power sharing.	Collective action	BY

Adapted from: Parkes and Panelli (2001).

academics or practitioners). These affect the relationships formed with research participants and the outcomes achieved. Whether you, as a researcher, respect people's knowledge or perpetuate unequal power relations and extract information largely for your own benefit depends to an extent on your attitudes and behaviours and the nature of the research relationships you establish. To illustrate this further, Box 13.1 shows common connections between the attitudes of the researcher (illustrated here by things a researcher may say to a researched group), the kind of research relationships they form, the resultant mode of participation possible, and the relationship between the researched group and the research itself.

Researchers using PAR generally strive to adopt and practice the attitudes and behaviours that result in people's co-learning and collective action. They also generally follow an iterative process of action–reflection (see Box 13.2), although the specifics of what actually happens, how, and when vary depending on the particular context and circumstances of those involved.

The cycles of action–reflection outlined in Box 13.2 ideally involve us and the people with whom we are working in each stage. However, this may not be possible within the confines of an undergraduate research project. Do not be put off, as this 'ideal' process can and should be adapted collectively to suit the particular needs and constraints of the situation. For example, in a four-month-long PAR project conducted in 1990 with a Costa Rican women's cooperative, cooperative members decided that it would be best if the primary research into their ongoing economic development were undertaken by me and another student rather than by any of them. They felt that we had more time and would be able to involve everyone equally. In this case, we worked with a core advisory group and external development worker to reflect on our actions as we undertook interviews and analysis. We then ran a participatory workshop and produced a report in cartoon format to invite members' reflection upon and analysis of our findings, and to develop action plans for the future.

What is most important in PAR is that the design and process are negotiated with the researched group and carried out in ways appropriate to the context, the time available, and the people involved, including yourself. Adopting even some of the strategies above will enable 'partial' participation to occur. This will bring benefits to your project and some of your participants (see chapter 3), particularly if they are combined with some of the participatory techniques discussed below (also see Kesby et al. 2004).

The strategies and techniques used within a PAR process can involve and adapt some of the other methods discussed in other chapters of this book if they occur in the context of reciprocal relationships. Common methods and techniques are interviewing and visualisation (sometimes also referred to as **participatory diagramming** or **participatory mapping** where participants create diagrams, pictures, and maps to explore issues and relationships; see Box 13.3). These emphasise shared learning (researcher and researched group), shared knowledge, and flexible yet structured collaborative analysis (*pla notes* 2003). They embody the process of **transformative reflexivity** in which both researcher and researched group reflect on their (mis)understandings and negotiate the meanings of information generated together (see Crang 2003, p. 497).

While the above list of techniques may seem exhaustive, it is not prescriptive. Integrating one or several of them, where appropriate, will enhance your research. However, as Howitt and Stevens suggest in chapter 3, a few participatory techniques will not in and of themselves make your project PAR. For this to occur, the open negotiation of the research design and methodology with the people with whom you are working is critical, as is an emphasis on supporting people's capacity to do their own research and analysis.

To give you some more ideas about what this might mean in practice, Box 13.4 summarises some ideas about how to approach doing PAR. These integrate and reinforce ideas about the attitudes, behaviours, relationships, research design, process, and techniques discussed above.

BOX 13.2 KEY STAGES IN A TYPICAL PAR PROCESS

Phase	*Activities*
Getting started	• Assess information sources.
	• Scope problems and issues.
	• Initiate contact with researched group (RG) and other stakeholders.
	• Seek common understanding about perceived problems and issues.
	• Establish a mutually agreeable and realistic time-frame.
	• Establish a **Memorandum of Understanding** (MoU) if appropriate.
Reflection	On problem formulation, power relations, knowledge construction process.
Building partnerships	• Build relationships and negotiate ethics, roles, and representation with RG and other stakeholders.
	• Establish team of co-researchers from members of RG.
	• Gain access to relevant data and information using appropriate techniques (see Box 13.3).
	• Develop shared understanding about problems and issues.
	• Design shared plans for research and action.
Reflection	Reformulation, reassessment of problems, issues, information requirements.
Working together	• Implement specific collaborative research projects.
	• Establish ways of involving others and disseminating information (see Box 13.3).
Reflection	Evaluation, feedback, re-participation, re-planning for future iterations.
Looking ahead	• Options for further cycles of participation, research, and action with or without researcher involvement.

Adapted from: Parkes and Panelli (2001, p. 98)

BOX 13.3 SOME COMMON STRATEGIES AND TECHNIQUES USED WITHIN PAR

Establish a support base and platform for your research

- *Find and critically review secondary data:* **Secondary data** can help to establish the direction of the research and identify where gaps or contradictions in understanding exist.
- *Involve those who are experts about specific issues and processes:* Local experts always exist and can help facilitate the participation of others and inclusion of their knowledges.
- *Negotiate and establish a memorandum of understanding (MoU) for the research team:*[2] MoUs and the process that leads to them clarify research expectations, agreed norms of behaviour, modes of interaction, and 'ownership' of information generated, and are important for sustaining participatory partnerships and realistic expectations.

Get involved with people and their lives

- *Observe directly (see for yourself):* Visiting people and places is essential. Taking a walk through an area with members of the researched group enables us to observe first-hand and question things directly.
- *Do-it-yourself:* By living like the people we are working with, we can learn something—although never all—of their realities, needs, and priorities.
- *Work with groups:* Groups can be casual or encountered 'randomly'; focus groups that are representative or structured for diversity; or community, neighbourhood, or specific social groups. Group interviews are usually a powerful and efficient way of generating and analysing information.

Use interviewing and story-telling approaches

- *Collect case studies and stories:* Focusing on specific events or cases, such as a household profile or history, or how a group coped with a crisis, is a helpful way of teasing out issues. A variety of cases can reveal and illustrate common themes and important differences.
- *Use open-ended questions and key probes:* Asking questions that start with 'What', 'When', 'Where', Who', or 'How' can generate specific information without leading respondents to particular answers. Probing (i.e., 'What happens when…?' and 'Why is that?') can identify key issues, local rationales, and current activities and procedures (see Kevin Dunn's chapter on interviewing in this book).

Use types of participatory mapping and diagramming such as:

- *Map:* Mapping, drawing, and colouring using locally appropriate materials can represent resources, issues, and relationships in ways that enable more democratic participation than verbal discussions alone. Maps might focus on tangible resources such as land, forests, houses, or services. Diagrams can tease out relationships between people, institutions and resources (see below). Do remember—as Howitt and Stevens note in chapter 3—that participatory mapping and diagramming may sometimes be suspect if used in the wrong context.

- *Timelines and trend/change analysis:* Locally defined chronologies of events showing approximate dates; people's accounts of how customs, practices, and things have changed; ethno-biographies or local histories of particular crops, animals, or trees; changes in land use, population, migration, fuel uses, education, health, credit, and so forth may enable analysis of cause and effect factors over time.
- *Seasonal calendars:* Focusing on seasonal variation of particular factors (for example, rain, crop yields, workload, travel) can enable insights into matters such as climatic variation, labour patterns, migration, diet, and local decision-making processes.
- *Daily time use analysis:* Indicating the relative amount of time, degree of drudgery, and level of status associated with various activities may reveal local power relations and identify the best times for research activities.
- *Institutional or venn diagramming:* Drawing out the relationships between individuals and institutions using overlapping circles signifying the importance or closeness of the relationships enhances understanding of power relations, local and surrounding contexts, and the identification of where there are blocks to, or possibilities for, change.
- *Well-being grouping (or wealth ranking):* Grouping or ranking households according to local criteria, including those considered poorest and worst off, can be a helpful lead into discussions about the livelihoods of the poor and how they cope depending upon the particular cultural context.
- *Matrix scoring and ranking:* Drawing matrices of resources, such as different types of trees, soils, or methods of health provision, then using seeds to score or rank how they compare according to different criteria (such as productivity, fertility, or accessibility, for example) can reveal local preferences (what scores highly) and the aspects that inform decision-making strategies.

Engage people in joint analysis, reflection, and future planning

- *Shared presentations and analysis:* Involving people in the presentation and analysis of the maps, diagrams, and information generated throughout the research shares power and enables information to be checked, corrected, and discussed.
- *Contrast comparisons:* Asking group A to analyse the findings of group B and vice versa can be a useful strategy for raising awareness and establishing dialogue, particularly between different groups. This has been used for gender awareness, asking men, for instance, to analyse how women spend their time.

Further information on these and other strategies and techniques, with examples of their use, are in Pretty et al. (1995).

BOX 13.4 SOME WAYS TO PROMOTE PARTICIPATION IN GEOGRAPHIC RESEARCH

- Involve/be involved with the group with whom you are working as equal decision-makers to define the research questions, goals, and methods, and as co-researchers and analysts of information generated.
- Show awareness that you are an outsider to the group you are researching, even if you are working together as co-researchers.
- Be clear about the potential impacts people's involvement may have and what will happen to information generated (ideally through an MoU).
- Take care not to promise too much or inflate people's expectations of what might happen as a result of the research.
- Develop facilitation skills, which can stimulate initiative and sensitively challenge the status quo without imposing your own agenda.
- Work at fostering participatory processes and research techniques, which will release creative ideas and enthusiasm, but not take too much time for those involved (see Box 13.3).
- Seek out the perspectives and participation of the most vulnerable and marginal people.
- Find ways to limit the dominance of interest groups and more powerful people (including yourself, where appropriate).
- Acknowledge that process is as important as product (and sometimes more important) and factor in enough time to involve people appropriately at various stages of the research, including times for reflection.
- Support the group with whom you are working to share the benefits of their involvement with others and to take initiative to address their concerns.
- Involve the group with whom you are working in the writing and dissemination of relevant information; at the very least acknowledge their contributions to any sole-authored work.
- Practice honesty, integrity, compassion, and respect at all times.
- Keep a sense of humour!

Adapted from: Botes and van Rensburg (2000, pp. 53–4); Kesby et al. (2004); and the author's own experiences.

THE VALUE AND REWARDS OF PARTICIPATORY ACTION RESEARCH

Through attention to attitudes and behaviours, as well as the use of appropriate strategies and techniques to support people's participation in collaborative research and action, it is possible to examine and challenge forms of oppression and inequality. PAR is used most frequently by geographers with an activist agenda to work for social change because it offers a tangible way of being able to put the aims and principles of **critical geography** into practice (Kesby 2000). Often this means specifically addressing issues of racism, ableism, sexism, heterosexism, and imperialism (Ruddick 2004, p. 239) and how these are manifested through people's unequal access to, and control over, resources, or in their positions within inequitable social relationships (See Box 13.5).

Because of this activist orientation, PAR can build capacity and alliances within a community. For example, as part of ongoing PAR work with *Te Iwi o Ngaati Hauiti* in the central North Island of Aotearoa/New Zealand, several *iwi* (tribe) members established themselves as a Community Video Research Team to explore the relationships between place, cultural identity, and social cohesion. They undertook training in video production and community research with an academic colleague and me, and then carried out video interviews with other members of the *iwi*. Sometimes I was a co-interviewer and my colleague a co-videographer; at other times they worked independently and later shared their tapes and analysis with us (Kindon 2003; Kindon and Latham 2002).

BOX 13.5 SELECTED GEOGRAPHERS AND PAR

Geographer	PAR work with...
Jenny Cameron & Katherine Gibson	Economically 'depressed' communities, Australia.
Duncan Fuller	Graffiti artists, Newcastle-upon-Tyne, UK.
J. K. Gibson-Graham	Women in mining communities, Australia.
Mike Kesby	People with HIV/AIDS, Zimbabwe.
Robin Kearns	Primary schools and parents, Auckland, Aotearoa/New Zealand.
Sara Kindon	Indigenous women and men in Indonesia and Aotearoa/New Zealand.
Rob Kitchin	People with disabilities, Ireland.
Audrey Kobayashi	Immigrant and ethnic minority groups, Canada.
Jan Monk	Women's and non-governmental organisations, USA and Mexico.
Carolyn Moser & Cathy McIlwaine	Communities coping with violence, Colombia and Guatemala.
Karen Nairn	Young people, Dunedin, Aotearoa/New Zealand.
Rachel Pain	Young people, County Durham, UK.
Ruth Panelli	Rural communities, Australia and Aotearoa/New Zealand.
Linda Peake	Women's handicraft cooperative, Guyana.
Geraldine Pratt	Philippine Migrant Workers Collective, Vancouver, Canada.
Maureen Reed	Women in logging communities, Vancouver Island, Canada.
Diane Rocheleau	Rural and farming communities, Africa and South America.
David Slater	Third World non-governmental organisations, India.
Janet Townsend	Female rainforest settlers, Colombia and Mexico.

Sources: Pain (2003); Ruddick (2004).

PAR enables rich and varied information embedded within specific 'communities' to be shared, analysed, and evaluated collectively (Cooke 2001). This information may be more accurate and relevant for other uses than had a researcher worked alone. In PAR work with rural communities in Bali, Indonesia, in the early 1990s (Kindon 1995; 1998), men associated with one village used information generated through our regular participatory research meetings and focus groups (see chapter 8) to develop an action plan for their community. The plan addressed the need for better roads to open up access to markets. In the four years that followed, these men established a savings/credit fund and liaised with government agencies to raise enough money to seal a remote road and enable more efficient transport of produce to market. Elsewhere in the village, government planners acted on PAR information generated by women's groups about the need for more accessible healthcare facilities, and established a local health post. On my return to the village in 1998, these two key development needs had been met by the collective actions of these men and women and the support received from government agencies.

In summary, people's participation in their own research may challenge prevailing biases and preconceptions about their knowledge by others in positions of power (Sanderson and Kindon 2004), such as government officials and policy-makers. In addition, PAR can bring about desired change more successfully than 'normal' social science research methods (Brockington and Sullivan 2003; Kesby 2000), and often results in improvements in living or working conditions for those involved (Kesby et al. 2004; Pain 2003, 2004; Parkes and Panelli 2001).

CHALLENGES AND STRATEGIES

There are also challenges associated with collaborative endeavours (Monk et al. 2003) especially where participatory techniques are involved (Pain and Francis 2003). While participation is becoming increasingly popular, not all researchers are doing it well (Parnwell 2003).

Most PAR takes place in a group setting, which is both a strength and a weakness. Particular techniques (like those under participatory mapping and diagramming listed in Box 13.3) require group participation, often in public spaces. This spatial aspect of PAR shapes the construction of knowledge (Brockington and Sullivan 2003; Cooke 2001; Mosse 1994) and it usually tends to generate knowledge that reflects dominant power relations in wider society (Kothari 2001). It is therefore important to pay attention not only to *who* participates but *where* they participate and *how*. Keeping a field diary with this information can be helpful when you come to analyse the products of group work. If funds permit, involving a colleague or friend to keep notes on the process or make video-recordings can provide a detailed and more dispassionate record of where and how people participated (yourself included) for later analysis (Kindon 2003).

In terms of the participatory techniques themselves, because they often appear to be quick and easy to use (Leurs 1997), it can be tempting to use them repeatedly in the same ways, rather than to adapt and modify them to the particular contexts involved (Chambers 1994). Certainly, many current participatory processes associated with development projects involve a sequence of participatory techniques such as community mapping, social well-being ranking, agricultural land-use transects, and institutional diagramming, regardless of the particular context or issues being assessed. This formulaic and researcher-led use of participatory techniques can result in what some academics have called the 'tyranny of participation' (Cooke and Kothari 2001), where any inequalities, particularly between the researcher and researched group, are reinforced (Parkes and Panelli 2001; Wadsworth 1998). A way around these difficulties is to consider who defines participation or who initiates what activities at each stage of the PAR process. Being open to sharing facilitation and innovating techniques in response to specific contexts can play a vital role in helping to monitor who is framing participation and how (Williams et al. 2003). Discussing these aspects early on is a particularly useful way of clarifying expectations, establishing greater collaboration, and specifying roles and responsibilities (Kindon and Latham 2002).

Participatory techniques can generate information quickly, but they are not a substitute for more in-depth social research methods (Kesby 2000) like those discussed elsewhere in this book. Understanding the contexts within which information is generated is critical to our ability to rigorously analyse it. For this reason you might wish to consider first undertaking PAR within a community or location already familiar to you. Within an undergraduate dissertation this could provide you with some of the necessary contextual information, freeing you to focus more energy on the process.

Sometimes, our desire to avoid exploitation or extractive research relationships can mean that we become so involved with our co-researchers that we are unable to work effectively for change. Establishing outside support networks (see Bingley 2002) can help to prevent this situation and sustain our endeavours.

A related point is that long-term relationships, even friendships, with participants and co-researchers commonly develop through PAR and while some studies may become a life-time project (see chapter 3), we typically have to leave the group with whom we have been working. Investing time into a sensitive and appropriate leaving strategy at the beginning of the research can help to avoid raising expectations and assist in navigating the changing status of relationships (Kindon and Cupples, 2003). Formal meetings, celebrations, feedback sessions, visits, and the exchange of gifts may all be appropriate mechanisms to assist with closure.

In other cases, it may be academically and professionally important to maintain a sustained engagement long after the official research project is over. This may be in the capacity of support person, community board member, fund writer, publicist, or campaigner. There may be ethical challenges if your status changes from co-researcher to 'friend', and being realistic about what you can commit to in any of these relationships is vital. Overall, a key way to manage this and other challenges associated with PAR is to be realistic with yourself, your co-researchers, and other stakeholders about what is possible within the time and resources available to you.

PRESENTING RESULTS

In their chapter earlier in this volume, Richie Howitt and Stan Stevens observed that representing people with whom we work is no easy undertaking, even if we involve them in the process. In their work with urban communities in Latin America Cathy McIlwaine and Caroline Moser (2003) propose that a balance is needed with respect to the presentation of information. Information should influence policy makers (to affect change) and should be meaningful to those involved in the initial research. In practice, this requires culturally appropriate ways of sharing knowledge and may, for example, require the production of several reports or presentations for different audiences by different members of the research teams using different media (see Cameron and Gibson 2004).

Project or policy reports are powerful advocacy tools to advance action plans developed during the research. Clear, simple presentations work best, providing policy makers with a sense of the process and how it generated reliable, meaningful 'data' upon which practicable policy can be developed. Presenting the results of PAR at public meetings, conferences, or other gatherings with co-researchers can be appropriate and often enjoyable. If their direct participation is not possible, then discussing what they would like you to emphasise in a presentation can go some way to addressing the power imbalance and lend you some authority to speak on their behalf. Taking the findings 'to the streets' in accessible media (for example, newsletters, magazine articles, plays, posters; see chapter 17) should ideally be part of the iterative process of PAR and can have some of the greatest impact at the local level.

As a student, the results of your work also need to meet the requirements of the academy. It can be challenging to present the 'results' of an iterative and participatory research process within the context of a typical thesis or dissertation, but certainly not impossible.[3] Engaging in PAR provides you with the opportunity to negotiate explicitly how you will use information and how you will represent others' experiences and/or views (Kindon and Latham 2002). Although sometimes time consuming, such steps can temper your powerful position as the sole author in what has been, until now, a collaborative process. Sharing your choices and discussing how you intend to construct your argument continues the participatory process and goes some way to ensuring that your final product respects the people and diversity of issues involved. An MoU item about this at the beginning of the research can save misunderstandings when you later want to quote people or include maps or diagrams produced through the research process.

Within the dissertation itself, including direct quotations from a range of people, which tease out common or disparate threads, can illustrate the multiple perspectives in circulation. Citing a disagreement or exchange between people can highlight where there are tensions or differences of perspective. However, take care to contextualise and analyse these adequately or they could be overwhelming to the reader. In addition, discussing aspects of methodology—so important to the participatory process—can honour people's involvement, acknowledge that process is as important as product, and enrich the analysis of the 'results' produced.

It may be appropriate and courteous to include co-researchers as co-authors on any papers that may emerge from PAR (see for example, Peake 2000; Pratt et al. 1999; Townsend et al. 1995). Finally, we do not have to have our names on publications at all—we can work behind the scenes to enable our co-researchers to publish or disseminate their understandings independently of us. Having multiple research products written by different combinations of people can enrich the knowledge produced and be critically important if ongoing action is to be sustained (see chapter 3).

REFLECTING ON PARTICIPATORY ACTION RESEARCH

A key question of PAR is often: 'to whom is the research relevant?' (Pain 2003, p. 651). As researchers, if we accept that we have an opportunity and an obligation to co-construct responsible geographies (McLean et al. 1997; Williams et al. 2003) then PAR offers us an exciting means of undertaking relevant, change-oriented research. While academe does not usually reward such **activism**, the central role of space in many people's oppression (Ruddick 2004) means that human geographers are uniquely positioned, and morally beholden, to adopt ways of researching that build collaborative communities of inquiry (Reason 1998 cited in Hiebert and Swan 1999, p. 239) and challenge oppression.

Fortunately, certain parts of human geography, such as social geography, have a rich tradition of activism. In addition, PAR is becoming more common within geographic research, providing a growing body of work and experience from which to draw. PAR is not without its challenges, particularly within the confines of student research projects, but it is possible to adopt many of the principles discussed in this chapter to enable a rigorous research approach, which also results in tangible benefits for those involved. Perhaps the greatest challenge of all is for academics, including undergraduate researchers, to 'cross boundaries of privilege and confront their personal stake in an issue, and the ways they are positioned differently from members of the [groups] they work with' (Ruddick 2004, p. 239). Hopefully, this chapter has given you some ideas with which to begin this journey within your own work, and some methodological resources to respectfully and ethically facilitate others' participation throughout the process.

KEY TERMS

action-reflection

activism

critical geography

facilitator

Memorandum of Understanding (MoU)

participatory diagramming

participatory mapping

participation

secondary data

stakeholder

transformative reflexivity

REVIEW QUESTIONS

1 Why is participation important in qualitative research?

2 Find an example of a participatory approach to geographic research in a recent book or journal. How is rigour established and maintained?

3 Given the importance of facilitation in PAR, make a note of the skills and attributes needed to be an effective PAR researcher. How might you develop and/or strengthen these skills and attributes in yourself?

4 Devise a list of ways to make your current research project more participatory. What are some of the implications for how you design and carry out each phase of the research? (You might like to

focus on the implications for who is involved and in what capacity; what kinds of methods will be used; how long each phase might take; and how information will be used and presented.)

5   What are some of the major challenges associated with doing PAR in geography? Make a list and then devise strategies to manage these challenges productively.

SUGGESTED READING

Cameron, J. and Gibson, K. 2004 [in press], 'Participatory action research in a postructuralist vein', *Geoforum*, vol. 35.

Kesby, M. 2000, 'Participatory diagramming: deploying qualitative methods through an action research epistemology', *Area*, vol. 32. no. 4, pp. 423–35.

Kesby, M., Kindon, S. and Pain, R. 2004 [in press], '"Participatory" diagramming and approaches', in R. Flowerdew and D. Martin (eds), *Methods in Human Geography*, 2nd edn, Pearson, London.

Kindon, S. and Latham, A. 2002, 'From mitigation to negotiation: Ethics and the geographical imagination in Aotearoa/New Zealand', *New Zealand Geographer*, vol. 58, no. 1, pp. 14–22.

Kitchin, R. 2001, 'Using participatory action research approaches in geographical studies of disability: some reflections', *Disability Studies Quarterly*, vol. 21, no. 4, pp. 61–9.

Pain, R. 2004 [in press], 'Social geography: participatory research', *Progress in Human Geography*.

Young, L. and Barratt, H. 2001, 'Adapting visual methods: action research with Kampala street children', *Area*, vol. 33, no. 2, pp. 141–52.

Notes

1   Readers of this chapter are strongly encouraged to read also chapter 3 which provides a useful, complementary overview of cross-cultural research ethics, methods, and relationships.

2   The research team may consist of researchers only, researched people only, or both researched people and researchers.

3   If you are using PAR in a thesis for example, and because universities typically expect a thesis or dissertation to be the 'original work' of the student alone, you should discuss matters of authorship with your supervisor when preparing your project.

PART 3

'Interpreting and
Communicating' the Results
of Qualitative Research

14

Coding Qualitative Data

Meghan Cope

CHAPTER OVERVIEW

This chapter defines coding, reviews different types of codes and their uses, and discusses several ways to get started with coding in a qualitative project. Specifically, a distinction is drawn between descriptive codes, which are category labels, and analytic codes, which are thematic, theoretical, or in some way emerge from the analysis. Borrowing from the work of grounded theory's Anselm Strauss, a basic four-point plan is reviewed as a strategy to begin coding focused on looking for conditions, interactions, strategies/tactics, and consequences. The building of a 'codebook' is also discussed, stressing the importance of looking critically at the codes themselves, identifying ways in which they relate, minimising overlap between codes, and strengthening the analytical potential of the coding structure. Finally, several related issues are covered, such as coding with others and viewing the world from the perspective of coding.

INTRODUCTION

Geographers are increasingly engaged in not only doing qualitative research, but also thinking and writing critically about methodologies, including the ways that we evaluate, organise, and 'make sense' of our data through the **coding** process (Cope 2003; Jackson 2001). Coding social data (for example, text, images, talk, interactions) is sometimes derided as tedious, but if you think of it as a kind of detective work it can be intriguing, exciting, and very valuable to the research process.

The purposes of coding are partly **data reduction** (to help the researcher get a handle on large amounts of data by distilling along key **themes**), partly organisation (to act as a 'finding aid' for researchers sorting through data), and partly a substantive process of data exploration, analysis, and theory-building. Further, different researchers use coding for different reasons depending on their goals and epistemologies; sometimes coding is used in an exploratory, inductive way such as in '**grounded theory**' where the purpose is to generate theories from empirical data, while other times coding is used to support a theory or hypothesis in a more deductive manner. Several approaches are discussed here with pointers on how to organise and begin the coding aspect of a research project.

TYPES OF CODES AND CODING

One common type of coding is '**content analysis**,' which is essentially a *quantitative* technique and by no means represents the full extent of coding for qualitative research. Content analysis can be done by 'hand' or by computer (see chapter 15 for a discussion), but either way it is a system of identifying terms, phrases, or actions that appear in a document or video and then counting how many times they appear and in what context. For example, a researcher might be interested in how many times the word 'democracy' is used in newspaper articles from a particular country, or how many and what type of places are mentioned in a television program. Frequently, in content analysis, sampling is used in similar ways to quantitative analysis of populations (see chapter 5 for a discussion); perhaps only front-page newspaper stories are included in the analysis, or a television program is sampled for five minutes out of each hour. Similarly, researchers using content analysis typically subject their coded findings to standard statistical analysis to determine frequencies, correlations, variations, and so on. There are many good guidebooks and instructions for conducting content analysis, including some available on the internet (see, for example, Krippendorff 2003; Neuendorf 2001).

While content analysis is a frequently used type of coding, the primary focus of this chapter is on qualitative approaches to coding. However, one of the basic principles of content analysis has broad implications for all coding activity, and is thus worth exploring further. This is the notion that there are both 'manifest' and 'latent' messages contained in the material (for example, text, images, video). **Manifest messages** are those that are blatant and obvious—these then generate manifest *codes*. For example, if I (as a feminist geographer) were performing content analysis on a set of international newspapers and the term 'sex worker' appeared with some level of frequency, I would take that as a code and proceed to scan subsequent materials for it. However, because places with high levels of prostitution tend to be places where women have few economic opportunities or political rights, I might also code instances of the term 'sex worker' for the **latent message** of the 'status of women' as well.

In much of ethnographic work in which researchers use coding qualitatively, the ideas of manifest and latent codes have parallels in 'descriptive' and 'analytic' codes. **Descriptive codes** can be thought of as category labels. They reflect themes or patterns that are obvious on the surface or are stated directly by research subjects; descriptive codes often answer 'who, what, where, when, and how' types of question. As a sub-set, *in vivo* **codes** are descriptive codes that use the actual phrasing of the subject (Strauss and Corbin 1990). For example, if interviews were done with elderly women who mentioned concern with crime in their neighbourhoods, 'crime' would be an *in vivo* descriptive code—the term appears in the body of the text and describes something important to the subjects.

Ethnographers also develop **analytic codes** to code text (or other forms of data) that reflect a theme the researcher is interested in or one that has already become important. Analytic codes typically dig deeper into the processes and context of phrases or actions. For example, it might become apparent that the elderly women mentioned above were specifically afraid of young men and boys they perceive as threatening while walking down the street, and therefore the analytic code 'fear of youth in public space' might be developed and applied.

Often, descriptive codes bring about analytic codes by revealing some important theme or pattern in the data, or by allowing a connection to be made (for example, crime, fear of youth in public), while other times analytic codes are in place from the beginning of the coding process because they are embedded in the research questions. For instance, if we were interested from the start in how elderly women navigate urban spaces, their personal mobility and impediments to mobility would be themes right from the start that would be reflected in the analytic codes for the project.

THE PURPOSES OF CODING

There are three main purposes for coding qualitative material: data reduction, organisation and the creation of searching aids, and analysis. As the prolific French theorist Henri Lefebvre noted, 'Reduction is a scientific procedure designed to deal with the complexity and chaos of brute observations' (Lefebvre 1991, p. 105). Qualitative research usually produces masses of data in forms that are difficult to interpret or digest all at once, whether the data are in the form of interview transcripts, hours of video, or pages of observation notes. Therefore, some form of reduction, or **abstracting**, is desirable to facilitate familiarity, understanding, and analysis. Coding helps reduce data by putting them into smaller 'packages'. These packages could be arranged by topic, such as 'instances in which environmental degradation was mentioned', or by characteristics of the participants such as 'interviews with women working part-time', or by some other feature of the research context or subjects, such as 'observations in public spaces'. By reducing the 'chaos of brute observations', data reduction helps us get a handle on what we have and allows us to start paying special attention to the contents of our data.

The second purpose of coding is to create an organisational structure and finding aid that will help make the most of qualitative data. Similar to data reduction, the organisational process mitigates the overwhelming aspects of minutiae and allows analysis to proceed by arranging the data along lines of similarity or relation. Constructing and maintaining a complete database of sources, dates (of participant observation, interviews, or focus groups, for example), subject contact information, and other relevant information, while not part of the coding process *per se*, is an important step in organising qualitative material for coding and analysis, and also allows the researcher to find specific data more easily. For example, interview transcripts might be coded not only for their content but also by their circumstances—was the interview conducted in the participant's home, were others present, did the subject seem nervous—which can help organise information. With better Computer-Assisted Qualitative Data Analysis Software (CAQDAS) available now (see chapter 15), organising and searching within electronic documents is greatly simplified. Additionally, coding itself is also an important aspect of organising and searching because it is essentially a process of categorising and qualifying data. 'The organizing part will entail some system for categorizing the various chunks [words, phrases, paragraphs], so the researcher can quickly find, pull out, and cluster the segments relating to a particular research question, hypothesis, construct, or theme.' (Miles and Huberman 1994, p. 57). While the development of the **coding structure** is by no means a simple process, it is one that—if done well—enables the data to be organised in such a way that patterns, commonalities, relationships, correspondences, and even disjunctures are identified and brought out for scrutiny.

The final, and principal, purpose of coding is analysis. While strategies for analytical coding will be examined in greater detail below, at this point it is sufficient to note that the *process* of coding is an integral part of analysis. Rather than imagining that analysis of the data is something that begins after the coding is finished, we should recognize that coding *is* analysis (and is probably never truly 'finished'!). Coding is in many ways a *recursive* juggling act of starting with **initial codes** that come from the research questions, background literature, and categories inherent in the project, and progressing through codes that are more interpretive as patterns, relationships, and differences arise. Coding is *reflexive* as well; as new themes emerge, previously coded material will need to be re-coded to include the new concepts.

HOW TO GET STARTED WITH CODING

The discussion of types of codes from above addressed two main approaches to coding, which may be seen as descriptive and analytic codes, though other terms are also used (for example, initial codes and **interpretive codes**). The key distinction is that one type of code is fairly obvious and superficial and is often what the researcher begins with, such as simple category labels. The other type of code is interpretive, analytic, and has more connections to the theoretical framework of the study; these tend to come later in the coding process after some initial patterns are identified. When coding was (and sometimes still is) done manually, researchers developed a '**codebook**'—a long list of codes that were categorised and organised repeatedly. Although current qualitative software packages typically do not use the term 'codebook', it is a useful concept that has relevance whether the codebook is actually a tangible item in manual coding or merely an abstraction in electronic coding.

To start a codebook, it is easiest to begin with the most obvious qualities, conditions, actions, and categories seen in your data and use them as initial codes. These will emerge quite rapidly from background literature, your own proposal or other research-planning documents, and the themes that stick out for you from gathering qualitative data (for example, memorable statements in interviews, notable actions seen while doing participant observation, keywords that jump out in first readings of historical documents). For example,[1] in my work on how urban children conceptualise city spaces in Buffalo, New York, one of my original interests that was heavily present in my grant proposal was how children in the 8–12-year-old age group define 'neighbourhood' and 'community' (see Box 14.1). These terms are obvious starting points for my codebook.

However, codes can also be too general and become cumbersome. Because much of my children's urban geography research is centred around issues of neighbourhood and community, I found that I needed to break each of these into more specific codes, such as codes for the particular neighbourhoods the children refer to, the use of both 'neighbourhood' and 'community' to mean 'local' (such as in reports from the city newspaper), and the way that school curriculum materials define 'community'. This is a frequent characteristic of coding: an initial category becomes overly broad and must be refined and partitioned into multiple codes.

Bear in mind that the opposite also occurs—some codes die a natural death through lack of use. For instance, in my project I had expected the children, who are for the most part in low-income families, to talk about a lack of money or not being able to afford something they wanted. However, after two years in the project, I have found little evidence of children discussing their own poverty (though that absence is itself an interesting research question). While I will probably keep a 'low-income' code for other purposes, its prevalence is much less than I anticipated in the materials generated by the children. As Miles and Huberman said, 'some codes do not work; others decay. No field material fits them, or the way they slice up the phenomenon is not the way the phenomenon appears empirically. This issue calls for doing away with the code or changing its level' (1994, p. 61).

So, the first step is to make a list of what you think are the most important themes up front, with the understanding that some of these will be split into finer specifics while others will remain largely unused. But how do you know what is important? Anselm Strauss, one of the founders of grounded theory, had a helpful system for beginning this awesome task (best represented in Strauss and Corbin 1990). He suggested paying attention to four types of themes:

- conditions
- interactions among actors
- strategies and tactics
- consequences.

'Conditions' might include geographical context (both social and physical), the circumstances of individual participants, or specific life situations that are mentioned or observed (for example, losing a job, becoming a parent, a child changing schools). By thinking along the lines of 'conditions' and coding only for those the coding process is easily started and you may learn a lot about your data in a short time.

The same is true for limiting your scope to 'interactions among actors'—by focusing on relationships, encounters, conflicts, accords, and other types of interactions, a series of powerful codes will emerge that will be helpful throughout the research. For example, in her research on adolescent girls in the southern United States, Mary Thomas (2004) found that young (fourteen year old) African-American girls' interactions with peers were strongly implicated in the type and level of their sexual activity. Thus, Thomas might have coded her interview transcripts regarding peer factors by *whether*, *how*, and *where* girls engaged in sexual activity, as well as *whom* they were influenced by or interacted with.

'Strategies and tactics'[2] is a little more complicated than Strauss' first two types of themes because it requires a deeper understanding of the things (events, actions, statements) you observe and how they relate to broader phenomena, and it suggests a certain level of purposeful intent among the research subjects that may demand additional inquiry on your part. For example, feminist geographers are often interested in women's survival or 'liveli-hood' strategies in different areas of the world (see, for example, the special issue of *Gender, Place and Culture*, 2004, vol. 11, no. 2). Noting that women in certain economic contexts tend to use particular types of financial survival tactics (say, for example, growing food prod-ucts for sale in a local market) can begin to illuminate broader economic, social, and polit-ical processes that shape women's options and actions, which is a valuable insight for geographic research. Other types of strategies or tactics might involve career decisions, polit-ical activism, housing choices, family negotiations, or even subversion.

Coding for strategies and tactics can be straightforward (and descriptive) in instances where respondents say something like 'I moved in with my mother so that she could care for my baby while I finished job training' or 'I got involved with a local group of residents to raise awareness of environmental contamination in our neighbourhood because I was concerned about property values'. Note the words 'so' and 'because' in these statements, which are good tip-offs that a strategy or tactic is embedded in the text.

Other times, coding for strategies and tactics may be more subtle—and more analytical—as when respondents do not explicitly state their reasons for certain actions, but a connection emerges through observation, review of interview text, or other data. For instance, many geog-raphers (for example, Blumen 2002; Cresswell 1999; Flint 2001; Nagar 2000; Secor 2004) have recently paid attention to ways that people engage in *resistance* against diverse forms of oppres-sion, which may be seen as strategies for empowerment, rights, or merely survival. Orna Blumen (2002, p. 133) took 'dissatisfaction articulated in subtle terms' by ultra-orthodox Jewish women as small but significant indicators of the women's resistance to their families' economic circum-stances, and, more broadly, to the status and roles of women in that community. For the women in Blumen's study, then, referring to fatigue, hoping their husbands would soon find paying work, and 'minor, personal, nonconformist remarks suggestive of ambivalence' (p. 140) could all be coded as tactics of resistance in part because Blumen—through careful qualitative work—had sufficiently analysed the broader context of the women's lives and goals.

Similar to the above, 'consequences' is a slightly more complicated code. On the surface, there are descriptive indicators for consequences, including terms such as 'then', 'because', 'as a result of', and 'due to', that may be used in subjects' statements and can be good clues to consequences and as a first-run could certainly be used in this way. Again, however, there are also more analytically sophisticated ways of discovering and coding consequences that are dependent on the unique empirical settings and events of each study. Some consequences will be matters of time passing and actions taking place that result in a particular outcome—the passage of a law, a change in rules or practices, and so on. However, other consequences are more subtle and personal, or they are not the result of changes over time, and therefore may be trickier to identify and code as such. For example, when Anna Secor (2004) hears from young Kurdish women living in Istanbul that they feel uncomfortable in some areas of the city, she might code her focus group transcripts for the consequences of feeling out of place due to the women's identity as an oppressed minority in Turkey. Coding for 'conse-quences' of this kind requires sensitivity to both the subjects and their community context, but is potentially a rich source of analysis and insight if done with care.

As an example of what a sample of coded material looks like with both descriptive and analytic codes, Box 14.1 demonstrates a small selection of field notes from my children's

BOX 14.1	29 NOVEMBER 2003. AFTER-SCHOOL PROGRAM OBSERVATION NOTES, CHILDREN'S URBAN GEOGRAPHIES RESEARCH

Text: field notes from the quilt project	Descriptive & Category Codes	Analytic Codes & Themes	Notes
As I was setting up, Jakob*, Mariana, and Ari came over and then Izzy and Salomé (a new girl I hadn't met before). We set up at a round table in between the bench and the 'café', near the pool table. The noise level was very high and I had a hard time hearing the children at my table. Next to us, three or four younger boys (Stefan et al.) were playing a war board game and making lots of terrible noises (at one point I asked them to be quieter).	Jakob Mariana Ari Izzy Salomé *Relations*: Izzy and Salomé are friends	Relationship between gender and violent play?	*Early release day from school—kids were wild and bored*
			Tape recording would not have worked here!
	Stefan		
	Research setting *conditions*: loud		
After I explained what I wanted (to use the materials to show your house or apartment building and family), I asked the children what a 'neighbourhood' is. There were varying answers immediately, mostly around the idea of 'a bunch of houses next to each other'. Izzy said 'it's when you have one house and then another one and you all get together to play'. Mariana said, 'I don't live in a neighbourhood, I'm part of the West Side	'Neighbourhood' Play		*Gave very loose instructions to allow children freedom within the project's scope*
			Mariana seems proud of her West Side identification

Community'(!) I couldn't hear very well so I got out my notebook and went around the group to write down answers.	'Community'	Difference between 'neighbourhood' and 'community'	
Ari's answer was very long and complicated with something to do with your 'home friend'. I'd like to revisit the question of what is a neighbourhood in video interviews.	*Tactic*: attention	Children's identification with a community or neighbourhood	*Ari (age 5) seems to crave attention*
			Future work— video interviews
Then I got out my digital camera and took pictures of the group (all five gave full permission for this). Nate came up and wanted to 'see' the camera, which I didn't want to let him do because he is so volatile and unpredictable. Reluctantly, I let	Technology		
	Nate		*All the children love technology and the gizmos we bring in get a lot of attention*
him take a picture of me with the children working on the quilt and retrieved the camera from him immediately. [Ironically, the photo Nate took is one of my favourites of this project!]	*Interactions*: Nate's bullying	Our relationships with specific children	
			Review and code photos

* All children's names have been changed

urban geographies project along with codes, themes, and notes. Even this fairly short piece of text reveals several relationships (friends, bullies), tactics (ways of getting attention), and conditions (chaos, volume), that bear further examination in other project data. Additionally, several analytic themes or questions are seen emerging here: the possible relationship between gender and violent play, some children's pride in perceived community membership (despite living in a blighted physical environment), and the importance of play in defining what a neighbourhood is among the children. Subsequent to the quilt project, and using these and other data, I have started generating a theory of how children define and ascribe meaning to the idea of 'neighbourhood', and this, after all, is the goal of most qualitative research!

DEVELOPING THE CODING STRUCTURE

Using the four types of themes reviewed here will take you a long way toward constructing a codebook and you may find other types of themes that are helpful to you, such as 'meanings', 'processes', or 'definitions'. Using the combination of descriptive and analytic codes you may well have over a hundred codes by this point, which is unwieldy at best and counter-productive at worst. Lists of codes that have not been categorised, grouped, and connected will be hard to remember, have too much overlap, and/or leave too many gaps, and will not enable productive analysis. Therefore, the next step is to develop a coding structure, whereby codes themselves are grouped together depending on their similarities, substantive relationships, and conceptual links. This process requires some amount of work but is well worth the effort, both for ease of coding your material and for discerning significant results from your findings.

Developing the coding structure can proceed in various ways, and there are many resources available that demonstrate different approaches (see Denzin and Lincoln 2000; Miles and Huberman 1994), but the main purpose is to organise the codes—and therefore the data and the analysis process. Some codes will automatically cluster; for example, codes relating to the *setting* of interviews (for example, home, office, public space, clinic), *characteristics* of subjects (for example, age, gender), or other *categories* (for example, occupations, leisure activities, life events). Other codes seem to fit together because of their *common issues*; for example, you might have a group of codes related to people's goals or intentions, or a group of codes related to people's experiences of oppression. Finally, codes based on the *substantive content* of text or actions—and most likely related to the analytic themes you are developing—will create another cluster of codes; for example, perceptions, meanings, places, identities, memories, difference, representations, and associations.

Once the codebook is relatively comfortable (I hesitate to say 'complete') and the coding structure is devised, you will want to go through much of your data again to capture connections that may have been missed the first (or second, or third) time around. Remember that coding is an iterative process that feeds back on itself—only you can decide when it is time to move on. As Miles and Huberman (1994) point out, it is sometimes simpler when time or money pressures put a finality on projects that otherwise could always benefit from 'one more case study' or endless additional tweaking of the coding structure!

CODING WITH OTHERS

Depending on the size and resources of the research project, there may be a case for using multiple coders for the data, which complicates the process considerably. There is an inherent tension in using multiple coders on a project: is the goal to make everyone code as consistently as possible or is the goal to allow each coder to interpret data in her/his way within the bounds of the coding structure in order to capture many diverse meanings? The answer will depend on the project and the epistemological leanings of the lead researcher, but in fact both of these goals are important. In the first instance, reliability of the data is undoubtedly enhanced when several coders independently code a piece of data the same way—a common interpretation of data means there is agreement on its meaning. For the sake of time and data reduction having multiple coders can certainly be helpful, but only if they are truly consistent in their coding, which is rare but could be accomplished by achieving conformity on the meanings of codes and providing thorough definitions for each code. On the other hand, text and video—as social data sources—are inherently subject to multiple interpretations and understandings, all of which may be correct or 'true'. While there may be some interpretations that are far-fetched or extreme, in general we as social researchers will be interested in capturing diverse understandings, and having multiple coders can be a great benefit for the project to make deeper and broader connections from the data.

BEING IN THE WORLD, CODING THE WORLD

By way of conclusion, let me point out that coding is not a mysterious process that must be learned from scratch, but rather is one that we are all already actively practising in our everyday lives. The recognition that we are all constantly interpreting and 'coding' the world around us may be a helpful realisation for getting started in a research project, and can also assist us in critiquing our own practices of data reduction, organisation, and analysis. As Silverman (1991 p. 293) points out, there are many ways of 'seeing' and interpreting the world, and—as social beings—we never really shut those lenses off, so why not embrace diverse interpretations and turn our gaze to the process of interpretation?

> How we code or transcribe our data is a crucial matter for qualitative researchers. Often, however, such researchers simply replicate the positivist model routinely used in quantitative research. According to this model, coders of data are usually trained in procedures with the aim of ensuring a uniform approach…However, ethnomethodology reminds us that 'coding' is not the [sole] preserve of research scientists. In some sense, researchers, like all of us, 'code' what they hear and see in the world around them [all the time]…The ethnomethodological response is to make this everyday 'coding' (or 'interpretive practice') the object of inquiry (Silverman 1991, p. 293).

Being in the world requires us to categorise, sort, prioritise, and interpret social data in all of our interactions. Coding qualitative data is merely a formalisation of this process in order to apply it to research and to provide some structure as a way of conveying our interpretations to others.

KEY TERMS

abstracting

analytic code

codebook

coding

coding structure

content analysis

data reduction

descriptive code

grounded theory

initial codes

interpretive codes

in vivo code

latent message

manifest message

theme

REVIEW QUESTIONS

1   What is the difference between descriptive and analytic codes, how do they relate to one another, and what are their respective uses in coding qualitative data?
2   Why does the author state that coding is analysis?
3   What are some potential benefits and potential problems with having multiple people coding in a project?
4   In what ways do we 'code' events, processes, and other phenomena in everyday life? How might thinking about these help us be better qualitative researchers?

SUGGESTED READING

For an excellent step-by-step guide to coding from a grounded theory perspective, see Strauss and Corbin (1990) and the chapter by Kathy Charmaz (2000) in the venerable volume edited by Denzin and Lincoln, *Handbook of Qualitative Research* (which itself is worth a look although it may require a trip to the library due to its high cost). Alternatively, Miles and Huberman (1994) have a thorough discussion of several different approaches to coding, although their own coding examples are somewhat arcane and confusing. Finally, there are several examples of coding and 'making sense' of data by geographers, including collections by Clifford and Valentine (2003); Flowerdew and Martin (1997); Limb and Dwyer (2001); and Moss (2002).

Notes

1   While it is always difficult to convey examples of coding without recounting the entire scope of the research, it is hoped that these examples from a real research project are sufficiently illustrative to demonstrate different coding approaches.
2   Despite the similar pairing of these two words, I am not referring here to Michel de Certeau's (1984) notion of 'strategy' (a technique of spatial organisation employed by 'the powerful') and 'tactic' (an everyday means of 'making do', typically used by those with few options), though there are certainly potential connections. Rather, I am using the terms in their most literal sense as they are employed in Strauss and Corbin (1990) to convey ideas about how people conceptualise what they want and what they do to try to arrive at those goals.

15

Computers, Qualitative Data, and Geographic Research

Robin Peace and Bettina van Hoven

CHAPTER OVERVIEW

This chapter aims to provide a brief introduction to the use of computers in qualitative human geography research. It focuses on a description of some of the basic aspects of **Computer-Assisted Qualitative Data Analysis Software (CAQDAS)** and suggests several reasons for developing CAQDA skills as part of a researcher's tool kit. A summary of advantages, concerns, and future directions for computer use in human geography research concludes the chapter.

INTRODUCTION

Qualitative data, in general, 'tell it like it is' and thus, provide the researcher with the human detail of stories told about the rich contours of lives. As rich, interesting, and exciting as the respondents' stories are, when turned into 'data' they can also become a source of chaos and headache. In this chapter we offer insight into the question whether or not computers can help us deal with these rich but unstructured data. Of course, qualitative data can also be coded, sorted, retrieved, and manipulated by using coloured pencils, cut and paste techniques, or index cards (see Miles and Huberman 1994 for ways of data reduction and display by hand). Using a computer in qualitative data analysis (QDA) is not simply a matter of replacing these techniques with a program, but it opens up new ways of thinking about data analysis to the researcher. This chapter aims to illustrate this. In addition, the opportunities and limitations of computer software in qualitative research are discussed.

FAQs—frequently asked questions

There are a number of questions that researchers who are new to CAQDAS are likely to be curious about: How many kinds of software are there? Which one should I choose? How long does it take to learn how to use the software? Will the computer do my analysis for me and how will I know if it has got it right? Factual queries aside, many questions are personally motivated and determined, and you will not necessarily find all the answers you are looking for in this chapter. At the end of this chapter, you will find a list of additional references and sources that will provide further guidance on where to find answers and help with making decisions, as well as discussion lists for communicating the joys and troubles of CAQDAS with fellow researchers. Before you start, however, we wish to firmly emphasise that computers *do not do analysis*. Even the most sophisticated software is merely one of many tools in a researcher's tool kit.

Who else is using CAQDAS?

Qualitative researchers in disciplines as disparate as sociology, management studies, nursing, and education have developed extensive literatures on qualitative methods that rely on computer assistance. The CAQDAS (http://caqdas.soc.surrey.ac.uk) and the QSR (http://www.qsr.com.au) web sites, for example, each have extensive lists of such literature discussing either the technique and/or the software, or specific case studies. Some case examples are: Scribner (2003), who discusses the use of CAQDA within an educational case study of rural high school teachers; Eliott and Olver's (2002) study of cancer patients (see also Olver et al. 2002); and Eustace's (1998), exploration of a virtual learning community. Geography, on the other hand, is still lagging behind in the uptake of CAQDAS despite having a well-developed reputation for computational work involving statistics and Geographic Information Systems (GIS). Among the few pieces of geography research cited in the literature on the use of and problems with CAQDAS are Baxter (1998); Crang et al. (1997); and Hinchliffe et al. (1997). For a critique of epistemological issues in computer use in geography, you might find it useful to refer to Peace (1998). Examples of the use of a specific program in geography, QSR N4 (NUD*IST) can be found in van Hoven's (2003) study of rural women in Eastern Germany (see also van Hoven-Iganski 2000), and van Hoven and Poelman's (2003) work on sense of place of Brighton, England, as experienced by lesbian, gay, bisexual, and transgendered (LGBT) people. Despite the small amount of published material there is a growing awareness in geography that computer software can have an important role in qualitative work.

TOOL KIT TECHNOLOGY

In general, you are probably familiar with the use of computer software for your studies. You are likely to have used it for making and editing notes, storing them, searching for and retrieving text, and preparing essays and reports. More specific types of geographical activity that can be effectively handled by computers, and that you are likely to have encountered as well, include statistical analysis, modelling, graphics, cartography, **image processing**, visual imagery, remote sensing, and (artificial intelligence) concept handling (Forer and Chalmers 1987). Before the 1990s (but since the late 1960s) computing in geography was largely associated with **geographic information systems** (GIS), with SPSS (*Statistical*

Programs for the Social Sciences), and SAS (*Statistical Analysis System*) software (Earickson and Harlin 1994; Griffith et al. 1990; Shaw and Wheeler 1994). These are software systems with the capacity to deal with the statistical calculations and manipulations of numeric or digitised 'real world' data—migration statistics, demographic data, census information, or satellite readings. In geographical information systems such as ARCVIEW, the software facilitates links between graphic files (digitised pictures of some kind, such as maps) and **attribute databases** (such as information on the location or movement of some factor) in order to identify patterns or changes over time, for example. SPSS and SAS are specialised statistical programs that are used to perform complex calculations, to test research hypotheses, and convert structured data from numeric to graphical display forms.

Relatively recently, human geographers, along with other social scientists, have looked for computer support for analysing unstructured, qualitative data. Such support has been forthcoming in the form of specialised software that has been 'custom built' for social science qualitative research. Since the 1990s, the range of geographical research activities has been extended to include word searching, data coding, **data storage** and retrieval, **memoing**, **graphic mapping**, hierarchical tree building, concept building, and reflexive report writing (see the Glossary at the end of this volume for explanations of some of these terms if they are unfamiliar to you). It is precisely these activities that are part of CAQDAS.

WHAT IS CAQDAS?

CAQDAS (computer-assisted qualitative data analysis software) is a generic title for a range of software that is specifically designed to handle unstructured, qualitative data. They are different from the data handling and statistical systems mentioned above that have been familiar to geographers in the past.

Computer software that is designed to assist researchers involves a three-way relationship between the 'researcher', the 'research process', and the 'hardware and software'. The individual skills, attributes, and desires of the researcher inform the kind of research that is undertaken, govern the researcher's actions, and influence the kind of analysis that is performed. These two elements (i.e., 'researcher' and 'research processes') are in turn influenced by technology. The researcher uses technology to support or enhance the processes in which s/he is engaged. CAQDAS, no less than other software, rely on this three-way relationship. Electronic technology can now facilitate a wide range of qualitative research processes.

Word searching, a relatively simple task that most word processors can perform with fairly rudimentary instruction from the researcher (and therefore a relatively low level of skill) is at one end of the range. The researcher's aim may be, for example, to find out whether or not the respondents to the study refer to a particular term, such as 'family' (see figure 15.1)[1], and the frequency of references to this term (content analysis). In this case, the 'find' or 'search' tool in the word processor can be used to look for key words and to return a complete record of all occurrences. Using this technique, large amounts of text may be searched quickly. In addition, the copy and paste functions can be used to transfer material electronically to another document without re-typing.

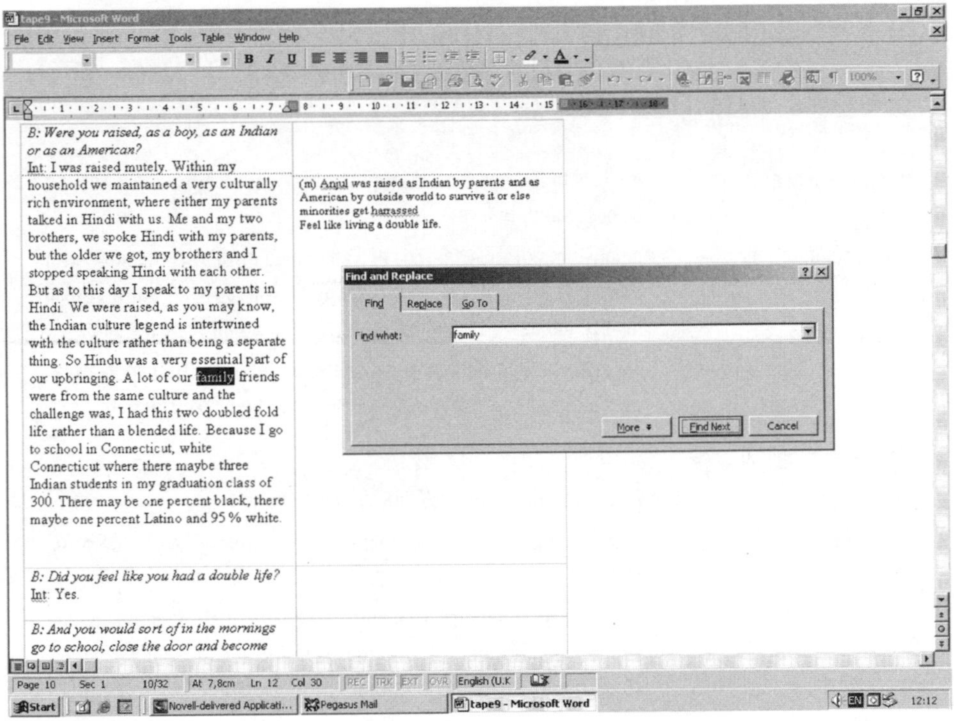

Figure 15.1 Text retrieving in Microsoft Word. Searching for 'family'. Total count in document: nine occurrences of the word in the interviewees' responses.

Concept building, which is a more sophisticated task that requires specialised software and considerable researcher training, exists at the other end of the range. Box 15.1. outlines the specific features of this process.

Different types of software

There is no recipe for choosing the software that will be best for your project. You need to bear in mind the kind of computer you are using, your budget, what access you have to software in your institution, your current skill level and the amount of time you have to learn new skills, and which kind of program is likely to be most useful to you. Rather than give any product specifications or recommendations we summarise some of the key information below. Weitzman and Miles (1995) provide a comprehensive study of twenty-four different software programs (see also Fielding 1994; Fielding and Lee 1998; Grbich 1999; Kelle 1995; Tesch 1990). Some programs have since been updated and upgraded (for example, *NUD*IST* to *NVivo*), while others have been taken out of production (for example, *WinMAX*). Product homepages and mailing lists are usually the best sources for the most up-to-date information (see Key Internet Resources at the end of this chapter). Many sites include screenshots and demonstrations. Some have program reviews and information about training.

BOX 15.1 SOME CHARACTERISTICS OF RESEARCH USING CONCEPT BUILDING BY MEANS OF QUALITATIVE DATA ANALYSIS SOFTWARE

The researcher	Is likely to be experienced in qualitative research, possibly working at postgraduate level.
The research process	Involves qualitative analysis of transcribed in-depth interviews with a large group of respondents (say up to 200 or more) but may also involve intensive specialised analysis of a small (focus) group.
The researcher's question	For example to investigate the 'sense of place' of Brighton as experienced by gay people (see van Hoven and Poelman 2003).
Technology needed	
Hardware:	Computer with Pentium/AMD 133 MHz capacity.
Software:	QDA program (for example, the *Ethnograph, ATLAS/ti, QSR N6, NVivo*).
The researcher's needs	Access to an appropriate computer, software, institutional and user support, ability and time to learn new skills, and an ability to understand the function and limitations of the software.

Ways in which the research process is enhanced through use of the computer:

- Transcribed text can be imported and exported electronically from word-processing program to CAQDA program and back again.
- The 'find' or 'search' tools in the CAQDA program are very sophisticated and can be used to identify a range of relationships and ways in which key words or significant data occur.
- Categories and indexing systems for codes and texts allow for comprehensive retrieval.
- The CAQDA program allows for additional data to be associated with the text, such as memos, notations, diagrams of key relationships, **hierarchical trees**, and graphic relationships.
- Some CAQDA programs allow for interfacing with quantitative databases such as *Excel* or *SPSS*.
- Very large amounts of text may be searched quickly.
- Data can be effectively coded and records of all the codes kept and used for **data retrieval**.
- Concepts can be developed out of the coding processes because the coding can be flexible and fluid through the early stages of the analysis.
- Data can be coded repeatedly so that ideas and concepts can be examined from a number of different angles.
- The ability to retain records of coding patterns and coded material makes it possible for the researcher to rethink and recode—to work recursively.
- Subcoding patterns can be developed from major coding axes so that the detail of concepts can be examined.
- Text can be searched selectively in order to discover links and relations between codes.
- Some CAQDAS allow for graphical data display.
- Theories can be built up, tested, dismantled, rebuilt, and re-examined while the software retains records of the versions, trials, and hunches.

Text retrievers/Textbase managers

These kinds of software are great for doing text analysis where you need to hunt words, strings of words, or characters (such as 'family' in Fig. 15.1.), and retrieve and batch them up into categories and groups. They include software such as *Metamorph*, *Textquest*, and *WordStat*. Some programs' additional capacity facilitates the systematic organisation of words or characters into records based on fields and subsets (i.e., a database). This software includes *askSam*, *Folio VIEWS*, *Maxqda*, and *Readware*.

Code and retrieve

These types of software take the retrieval and management aspects a step further by incorporating capacity for attaching coding. Key words or codes can be applied to data chunks so that relevant sections of texts (rather than individual words or characters) can be retrieved according to a coding formula (see Figure 15.2: note the difference between Figure 15.1 and Figure 15.2, which are both concerned with 'family'). Programs in this range include *HyperQual2*, *Kwalitan*, *Martin*, and *The Ethnograph*.

Code based theory building

Code based theory builders are designed with capacity for retrieval, coding, annotating, memo making, and cross-questioning (see Figure 15.3). They usually have some capacity for graphic representation of coding structures and patterns and increasingly are compatible with quantitative software programs such as *SPSS*, so that you can use multi-method

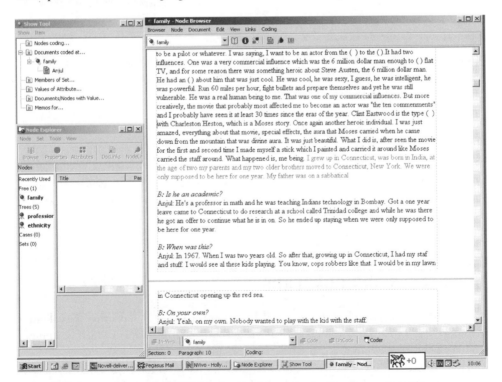

Figure 15.2   Code and retrieve in NUD*IST. Coding 'family' as concept rather than word search.

approaches. Included in this category are programs such as *AQUAD*, *ATLAS/ti*, *HyperRESEARCH*, and *QSR N6/ NVivo*.

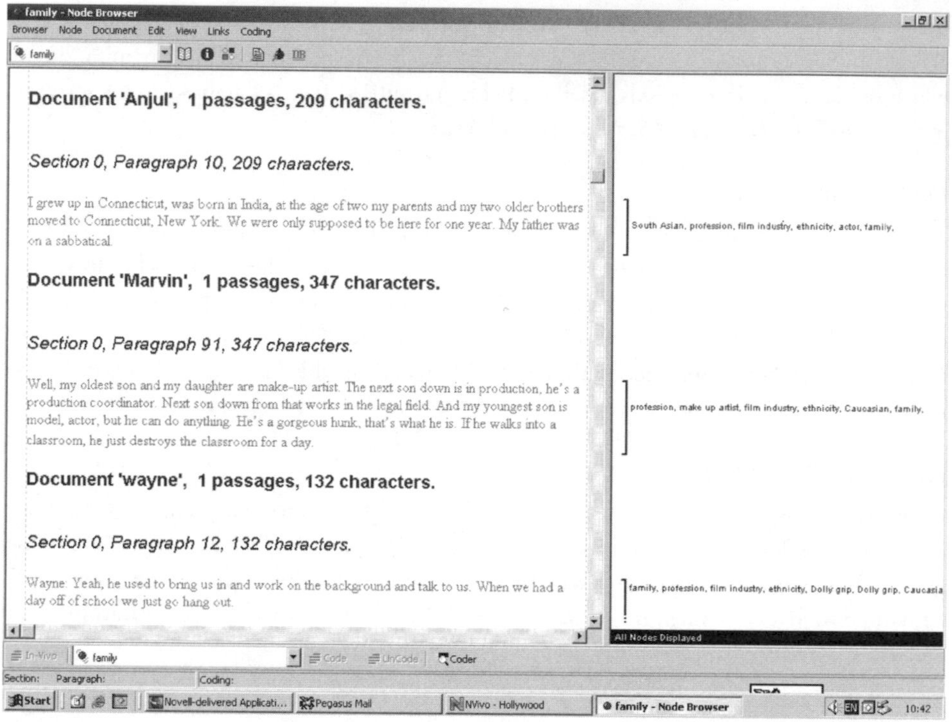

Figure 15.3 Example of a search for 'family': What do male employees in the film industry say about 'family'? The figure also shows the respondents' professions and ethnicity. A differentiation by profession and ethnicity may be possible in a next stage in the analysis.

Graphic display

Graphic display and **conceptual mapping** software programs have been developed to interface with other CAQDA software programs so that coding patterns can be exported from one program and displayed in another. Other graphical display programs include *Decision Explorer*, *MECA*, *Inspiration*, and *IHMC Cmap Tools*.

CONSIDERATIONS FOR CHOOSING CAQDAS: ADVANTAGES AND CONCERNS

In sum, computer technology can be used to support a range of tasks that a qualitative researcher might wish to perform. Box 15.1. already outlined some ways in which a computer program can enhance your research. There are more advantages worth noting: the speed with which examples of text can be retrieved is a significant time saver for the researcher, but so is the ability to manage otherwise unwieldy databases. Some software enables you to keep tabs on data that are off-line; that is, not directly 'machine-readable' and therefore cannot be handled directly by the software. Off-line data might include bibliographies, untranscribed interview data on audio-tape, movie or video clips, static images, or material on compact disk (CD). Being able to make memos and annotations relating to off-line data can successfully extend your database without costly scanning or transcribing processes being involved.

More than 'cut and paste'

Research, at its best, is a recursive process—one in which researchers interact intimately with their data. As Michael Agar (1986, in Crang 1997a, p. 188) suggests, the process of coding and subdividing codes can be 'maddeningly recursive' because the categories that seem stable and appropriate one minute tend to break down as the research progresses, so that new categories must be invented (see chapter 14). This recursivity, this bending back on itself, is one of the great and exciting strengths of qualitative research and, from our experience, using CAQDAS can make the process more efficient and more enjoyable.

In the introduction, we claimed that using a computer in qualitative data analysis is not simply a matter of replacing manual techniques with a program but that it opens up new ways of thinking about data analysis to the researcher. Computer software can make data coding and categorising more flexible. Not only can you experiment freely with various categories, you can also code data more fluidly in different ways. You do not have to make up one coding system for your research project and then allocate data to one set of either/or categories. Programs such as *QSR N6/NVivo* allow you to put the same segments of data under a number of different headings or categories and retrieve them through a range of indexing and searching tools that are activated by the codes the segments of data have been given. You can do multiple coding and then instigate complex inquiries of those coding patterns. This versatility can also enhance 'interactivity' between the researcher and the data.

The vocational argument

Apart from these broad arguments in favour of using computers for qualitative research, there is a vocational argument. If you wish to use a purpose-built program, such as *The Ethnograph*, *ATLAS/ti*, or *QSR N6/NVivo*, there is a specific learning curve associated with each program that can not be circumvented. But being able to do 'fast' research, being able to demonstrate a capacity to analyse more than a dozen in-depth interviews, and having a sense of the versatility and interactive skills involved in qualitative research also makes for a very marketable researcher. Having a wide range of skills as a software user enhances your qualifications. You should consider this seriously when making a decision about whether to invest time in learning to use a particular software program or not.

Some concerns

Broadly, there are two sets of concerns associated with CAQDAS that we wish to raise here. One addresses the use of computers in research in general; the other targets the use of specialised software in particular. Computer technology is not universally accessible. Neither is the ability to link up to the Internet, nor the ability to load up software to facilitate research. Computer technology requires a power supply, a supply of appropriate hardware and software, and a method of gaining access to whatever system support is offered as part of the program. It also requires a decision to commit to a project that entails capital costs, and it requires that all of these elements be in place before the research gets under way. Word processing programs are usually available for use in most research institutions, but not all institutions provide or support more specialised software programs. Trying to finance the purchase of software and software training and support out of your own budget can be very costly. Trying to learn to use new software on your own can be very demoralising.

There are several other concerns that have been raised by researchers discussing and using CAQDAS (not all critiques are by users) and they, too, should be taken into consideration. Richards (1997), for example, cautions against opting for large-scale projects under the illusion that good research involves collecting vast amounts of data. She suggests that although computers have the capacity for prodigious memory work, they should not be used lightly. CAQDAS are as effective working with small databases as they are with larger ones. Box 15.2 outlines further concerns alongside some advantages mentioned above. A relatively serious concern is the overemphasis of programs on grounded theory (discussed further in chapter 14). The research process induced by *QSR N6/NVivo*, for example, pretty much follows the analytical steps of grounded theory (coding, categorising, memoing, constant comparison). However, Barry (1998, p. 2.6) helpfully suggests that:

> researchers will be more likely to take what they can from the software and use supplementary non-computerised methods, than to confine themselves to the limitations of computer methods. Perhaps first time qualitative researchers might be tempted to start with 'grounded theory' as a method and with computerized data analysis as a tool...However once qualitative researchers find their feet they will soon be happy to reject methods and tools that will not serve their type of data and their type of problem.

BOX 15.2 CAQDAS: ADVANTAGES AND CONCERNS

Advantages	*Concerns*
Managing large quantities of data	Obsession with volume
Convenient coding and retrieving	Mechanistic data analysis/taken-for-granted mode of data handling
Comprehensive and accurate text searches	Exclusion of non-text data
Quick identification of deviant cases	Over-emphasis on 'grounded theory'
More time to explore 'thick data' as clerical tasks become easier	Loss of overview
Playful relationship with data—enhanced creativity	The machine takes over—alienation from data
	Makes qualitative research look more 'scientific'
	Limitations for connecting with geographical data such as GIS-type systems (van Hoven 2003)

Our message, therefore, is that undergraduates and graduates, as well as established researchers, need to remember that there are complex configurations of practical/technical and theoretical/political issues to bear in mind when assessing the role of computing in their own explorations of qualitative research. Computer software does offer exciting new developments and capacities, and it also offers computer users the chance to acquire marketable skills and a sense of conceptual confidence and flexibility that may be harder to achieve with other methods. Qualitative research using computer software demands, above all else, a high degree of researcher reflexivity. Any full-scale move to using computers to help make sense of qualitative research will entail on-going reflection and critique.

CONCLUSION—FUTURE DIRECTIONS

We hope that more geographers who experiment with CAQDA software will publish accounts of their experiences and methods and the field will be opened up for widespread discussion and debate. An exciting new development might see the production of purpose-built software for interfacing between GIS programs and CAQDA software in much the same way that *QSR N6/NVivo* and *SPSS* programs are now compatible. Increasingly there will be a trend towards working across qualitative/quantitative boundaries to produce multi-method work that draws research insights from the widest possible background. Such work will depend on the capacities of computers to manage databases—to store, organise, retrieve, and display symbolic information—in ways that make it possible to deal with data more efficiently and with greater versatility, to reduce drudgery, and increase flexibility and to provide researchers with interactive, portable, and valued skills.

KEY TERMS

attribute database
code and retrieve software
computer-assisted qualitative data analysis
    software (CAQDAS)
concept building
conceptual mapping
data retrieval
data storage

geographic information system (GIS)
graphic mapping
hierarchical trees
memoing
text retriever software
theory building software
word searching

REVIEW QUESTIONS

1   Qualitative data have been described on the one hand as 'rich' and as 'chaotic' on the other. Discuss the ways in which these attributes are appropriate descriptors for qualitative data.

2   Discuss the ways in which qualitative and quantitative data are different and require different styles and technologies for their management.

3   Computers are frequently described as 'tools'. Discuss some of the specific characteristics of computers that are indicative of this.

4   The initials 'CA' in the acronym 'CAQDA' refer to the particular relationship that computers have to the analytic processes involved in research. The idea that computers 'assist' the analyst is a far cry from the notion that computers 'do research'. Discuss the relationships between data analysis and computer technologies in qualitative research.

5   Qualitative research is often described as a 'recursive' process. What is meant by recursivity? How do recursive approaches assist qualitative analysis? What might be an example of a recursive process in qualitative research?

6   Choose any one of the four generic types of CAQDA software (described in this chapter) and use the Internet to explore the capacities of the software in that category. Compare your findings with someone who chose a different category. Discuss which kinds of software would be appropriate for any research project you know about.

SUGGESTED READING

Barry, C. 1998, 'Choosing Qualitative Data Analysis Software: Atlas/ti and Nudist Compared', *Sociological Research Online,* vol. 3, no. 3, Available: <http://www.socresonline.org.uk/3/3/4.html> (Accessed: 2 November 2004).

Coffey, A. and Atkinson, P. 1996, *Making Sense of Qualitative Data, Complementary Research Strategies,* Sage, Thousand Oaks.

Denzin, N. and Lincoln, Y. (eds), 1994, *Handbook of Qualitative Analysis,* Sage, Thousand Oaks.

Dey, I. 1993, *Qualitative Data Analysis: A User-Friendly Guide for Social Scientists,* Routledge, London.

Fielding, N. and Lee, R. 1998, *Computer Analysis and Qualitative Research,* Sage, London and Thousand Oaks.

Gahan, C. and Hannibal, H. 1998, *Doing Qualitative Research Using QSR NUD*IST,* Sage, London and Thousand Oaks.

Gibbs, G. R., 2002, *Qualitative Data Analysis: Explorations with NVivo,* Open University Press, Buckingham.

Kelle, U. (ed.) 1995, *Computer-Aided Qualitative Data Analysis: Theory, Methods and Practice,* Sage, London and Thousand Oaks.

Miles, M. B. and Huberman, A. M. 1994, *Qualitative Data Analysis: A Sourcebook of New Methods,* Sage, Thousand Oaks.

Weitzman, E. and Miles, M. 1995, *Computer Programs for Qualitative Data Analysis: Software Sourcebook,* Sage, Thousand Oaks.

KEY INTERNET RESOURCES

This internet resource list is subdivided into seven categories:
* Finding out more about CAQDA
* Finding out more about qualitative research
* Finding out more about computers
* Product pages for specific software packages

- Electronic journals
- Email discussion lists
- Internet sites for geographers

Finding out more about CAQDA

CAQDAS (Computer Assisted Qualitative Data Analysis Software) Networking Project, <http://www.caqdas.soc.surrey.ac.uk> (Accessed: 11 March 2004).

Sociological Research Online, <http://www.socresonline.org.uk/> (Accessed: 11 March 2004).

Using Computers in Sociological Research: Discussion Forum, Sociological Research Online, <http://www.socresonline.org.uk/socresonline/threads/computers/computers.html> (Accessed: 11 March 2004).

Finding out more about qualitative research

Association for Qualitative Research, <http://www.latrobe.edu.au/www/aqr/about/aboutaqr.htm> (Accessed: 11 March 2004).

Qualitative Analysis: what's that?, <http://info.ippt.gov.pl/~zkulpa/quaphys/QAnalys.html> (Accessed: 11 March 2004).

Qualitative Comparative Analysis, <http://www.nwu.edu/IPR/publications/qca.html> (Accessed: 11 March 2004).

QualPage! resources for qualitative researchers, <http://www.qualitativeresearch.uga.edu/QualPage/> (Accessed: 11 March 2004).

Text analysis software sources, <http://www.intext.de/TEXTANAE.HTM> (Accessed: 11 March 2004).

Finding out more about computers

Exploring the Internet, Nicky Ferguson, *Social Research Update*, <http://www.soc.surrey.ac.uk/sru/SRU4.html> (Accessed: 11 March 2004).

Glossary of Internet Terms, Enzer Matisse 1994–8, <http://www.matisse.net/files/glossary.html> (Accessed: 11 March 2004).

PCWebopaedia, <http://www.pcwebopedia.com/index.html> (Accessed: 11 March 2004).

Product pages for specific software packages

Atlas/ti, <http://www.atlasti.de/index.html > (Accessed: 11 March 2004).

AQUAD, <http://www.aquad.de/eng/e-index.htm> (Accessed: 11 March 2004).

AskSam, <http://www.asksam.com/> (Accessed: 11 March 2004).

Decision Explorer, <http://www.banxia.com/demain.html> (Accessed: 11 March 2004).

The Ethnograph v5.0, <http://www.QualisResearch.com/> (Accessed: 11 March 2004).

FolioViews, <http://www.folio.com/folio/Factsv41.cfm> (Accessed: 11 March 2004).

HyperQual, <http://home.satx.rr.com/hyperqual/> (Accessed: 11 March 2004).

HyperRESEARCH 1.65 Software for Qualitative Data Analysis, <http://www.researchware.com/hr/index.html> (Accessed: 11 March 2004).

IHMC Cmap Tools, <http://www.ihmc.us/> (Accessed: 11 March 2004).

Inspiration Software, Inc., <http://www.inspiration.com/> (Accessed: 11 March 2004).

KWALITAN, <http://www.kwalitan.net/ebgels/index.html> (Accessed: 11 March 2004).

Martin, <http://www.son.wisc.edu/resources/simonds/martin/martin.htm> (Accessed: 11 March 2004).

Maxqda, <http://www.maxqda.com> (Accessed: 11 March 2004).

MECA, <http://www.hss.cmu.edu/departments/sds/faculty/carley.html> (Accessed: 11 March 2004).

METAMORPH™ Intelligent Text Retrieval, <http://www.thunderstone.com/jump/Metamorph.html> (Accessed: 11 March 2004).

QSR N6/NVivo, <http://www.qsr.com.au/> (Accessed: 11 March 2004).

Readware, <http://www.readware.com/> (Accessed: 11 March 2004).

SAS Institute, <http://www.sas.com/> (Accessed: 11 March 2004).

SPSS Statistical Product and Service Solutions, < http://www.spss.com/> (Accessed: 11 March 2004).

TextQuest, <http://www.textquest.de/> (Accessed: 11 March 2004).

WordStat, <http://www.simstat.com/wordstat.htm> (Accessed: 11 March 2004).

Electronic journals

The following journals provide online access to articles dealing with issues of computer use in qualitative research.

Forum Qualitative Social Research, <http://www.qualitative-research.net/fqs/fqs-eng.htm> (Accessed: 11 March 2004).

International Journal of Qualitative Methods, <http://www.ualberta.ca/~ijqm/english/engframeset.html> (Accessed: 11 March 2004).

The Qualitative Report: an online journal dedicated to qualitative research and critical inquiry, <http://www.nova.edu/ssss/QR/index.html> (Accessed: 11 March 2004).

Social Research Update, <http://www.soc.surrey.ac.uk/sru/Sru.html> (Accessed: 11 March 2004).

Sociological Research Online, <http://www.socresonline.org.uk/socresonline/> (Accessed: 11 March 2004).

Email discussion lists

Qual Research, <http://www.jiscmail.ac.uk/lists/QUAL-RESEARCH.html> (Accessed: 11 March 2004).

Qualitative Research, <http://www.jiscmail.ac.uk/lists/QUALITATIVE-RESEARCH.html> (Accessed: 11 March 2004)

Qual-software, <http://www.jiscmail.ac.uk/lists/qual-software.html> (Accessed: 11 March 2004).

QSR Forum, <http://www.qsr.com.au/resources/qsrForum/qsr_forum.htm> (Accessed: 11 March 2004).

Internet sites for geographers

Internet Resources for Geographers (journals, maps, organisations, datasets, educational resources, software), <http://www.colorado.edu/geography/virtdept/resources/contents.htm> (Accessed: 11 March 2004).

The Virtual Geography Department, <http://www.colorado.edu/geography/virtdept/contents.htm> (Accessed: 11 March 2004).

Note

1   The examples in Figures 15.1 to 15.3 draw on a study undertaken in 2000 by Bettina van Hoven on gendered experiences in the film industry. This material was also used in a student assignment on CAQDAS and for a student dissertation (see, for example, van Duinen and van Hoven 2003).

16 Writing Qualitative Geographies, Constructing Geographical Knowledges

Juliana Mansvelt and Lawrence D. Berg

CHAPTER OVERVIEW

In this chapter we examine the process of 'writing-up the results' of qualitative research in human geography. Our aim, however, is to contest the simplistic understanding of the relationship between research, writing, and the production of knowledge that arises from describing the process in this manner. Indeed, the very phrase 'writing-up' implies that we are somehow able to unproblematically reproduce the simple truth(s) of our research in our writing. In this framework for understanding research, writing becomes a mirror that serves to innocently reflect the reality of research 'findings'. In contrast, we draw upon post-structuralist approaches to argue that writing is not merely a mechanical process that reflects the 'reality' of qualitative research findings, but, instead, writing constitutes in part how and what we know about our research. Writing is thus not so much a process of writing-UP, as one of **writing-IN**, a perspective which has significant implications for how research is conceptualised.[1]

STYLES OF PRESENTATION

Part of our argument in this chapter revolves around the idea that a number of powerful **dichotomies**—such as subject/object, researcher/researched, data/conclusions, and research/writing—currently exist and that these dichotomies structure our understanding of research. These dichotomies have developed historically as part of a positivist framework that, we suggest, limits our understanding of the writing process. We thus feel it is important to present readers with a very brief history of the development of positivist thought in human geography before moving on to discuss an alternative approach to writing human geography.

Positivist and neo-positivist approaches: universal objectivity

The philosophical approach to scientific knowledge known as **positivism** was founded by Auguste Comte (1798–1857), a French philosopher and sociologist (see Gregory 1978; Kolakowski 1972). Comte argued that scientific knowledge of the world arises from observation only. The notion of a singular truth was associated with this and positivists of Comte's tradition had significant difficulties with issues and questions arising from the relationship between truth and phenomena such as religion, ethics, morals, and metaphysics.

The logical positivists, whose work developed as a critique of strict positivism during the 1920s, differed from the Comtean positivists in their conception of scientific knowledge. They accepted the validity of more than just empirically verifiable statements. In this sense, Comte allowed only statements arising from empirically verifiable knowledge (that is, information available to the senses) as the basis of factual knowledge (or truth). The logical positivists, on the other hand, acknowledged the existence of two kinds of factual statements: analytical statements, the truth of which is contained in their internal logic (for example, if A=B and B=C, then A=C); and synthetic statements, whose truth is proven through recourse to empirical observation (for example, if we observe high levels of homelessness in areas with low provision of state housing, our empirical observations could lead us to conclude that the incidence of homelessness is a consequence of particular state housing policies). As you may appreciate from the previous example, numerical correlation is not the same as causation. Assessing the validity of analytical statements derived from empirical observations is thus problematic, and particularly so in social science.

Karl Popper (1959) recognized this and developed an alternative form of neo-positivist thought he termed 'critical rationalism'. Unlike the logical positivists, who focused upon verification as the basis of knowledge, Popper argued that falsification should be the basis for making decisions about the validity of factual statements. His argument was based on the notion that we can never know for sure whether a particular hypothesis was true or not (such as whether a lack of state housing does result in more homelessness), but we do have the ability to ascertain if such statements are false (for example, by finding examples of where incidence of homeless is low in areas of minimal state housing provision). Under critical rationalism, then, we never prove something but instead we can either disprove something (or prove it to be false through the process of falsification), or accept it to be contingently 'true' (until it has been proved false). According to Popper, scientific knowledge was much more contingent than conceptualised by the logical positivists, since present 'truths' were always open to future falsification.

Although few geographers have ever fully taken up the ideas of any single school of positivist thought, positivism of one sort or another has played a foundational role in the way that many geographers have come to understand the world. This became most explicit during the so-called 'quantitative revolution' of the 1960s (Gregory 1978; Guelke 1978), which saw geography develop as a broadly positivist 'science'. Geographers maintained a strict distinction between facts and values (Gregory 1978); giving emphasis to observational statements over theoretical ones (Berg 1994a) and often universalising their findings across all contexts (Barnes 1989). They also made a strict distinction between objective and subjective knowledge.

Objective knowledge is seen as 'scientific', rigorous, and detached, and consequently valid. It is constituted in opposition to subjective knowledge, which is personal, value-based, non-scientific, and non-academic (and therefore unacceptable as a basis for establishing 'the' truth). Objective knowledge is founded on interrelated and highly gendered notions of rationality, disembodied reason, and universality (Berg 1994a; 1997; Bondi 1997). Trevor Barnes and Derek Gregory (1997, p. 15) suggest 'scientific geographers' thus imagined themselves:

> as a person—significantly, almost always a man—who had been elevated above the rest of the population, and who occupied a position from which he could survey the world with a detachment and clarity that was denied to those closer to the ground (whose vision was supposed to be necessarily limited by their involvement in the mundane tasks of ordinary life).

Knowledge from the disembodied vantage point of the objective researcher, looks the same from any perspective—it is monolithic, universal, and totalising. This concept of un-located and disembodied rational knowledge draws on powerful metaphors of mobility (the researcher can move to any and all perspectives) and transcendence (the researcher is not part of the social relations she or he is examining, but instead can rise above them to see everything) for its rhetorical power to convince readers of its claims to the truth (see Barnes and Gregory 1997; Haraway 1991).

In adopting a broadly positivist model for their work, geographers also developed a specific approach to writing their research. They developed commonly used approaches or forms of writing (or what we call '**tropes**') in their academic studies that attempted to erase the authorial self from their written work. Similarly, they tried to create, through their writing, distance between themselves as researcher/author and their research objects. These tropes are most evident in the practice of writing in the third person—a practice that is still prevalent in much academic writing today. Many geography undergraduate students, for example, are still required to use the formal third-person narrative form in their essay assignments. The notion of universal knowledge underpins writing in the third person and it is also intended to erase the imprint of the author on the text and to ensure distancing of the author from the research. In other words, third-person narratives are needed to maintain impartiality and objectivity, two cornerstones of the positivist model. The third-person narrative constructs an '**objective modality**' (Fairclough 1992). This effectively removes the author from his/her writing while at the same time implying the author's full agreement with the statements being made. In so doing, it does the work of transforming interpretative statements into factual statements (see Box 16.1).

Writing in the objective mode is often accompanied by **nominalisation**, a process that further removes the writer from the text (see Box 16.1). Nominalisation involves the transformation of adjectives and verbs into nouns. It occurs, for example, when in the process of researching, researchers and research subjects are rhetorically transformed into things such as 'the research'; or when actions and processes are given particular kinds of argumentative power as nouns, such as can be found in statements such as 'the analysis suggests' (Fowler 1991). Nominalisation deletes a great deal of helpful and important information from sentences. For example, it deletes information about the participants—normally the agent or the person 'doing' something and the affected participant, or the person having something 'done to' them. It also changes the **modality**—that is, the writer's degree of agreement with the statement—and it tends to hide details about the circumstances relating to a set of actions. Nominalisation creates *mystification* because it permits concealment, hiding the participants, indicators of time or place, and stance. It also results in *reification*, whereby complex, uncertain, and often contradictory processes, such as are involved in human geographic research, assume the much more certain status of 'things'. Thus, the complex processes of research are smoothed over into a one-dimensional and simple thing: 'the research' (see, for example, Fowler 1991, p. 80). Ironically, while positivist epistemology is founded on the idea that any statement can be contested through recourse to empirical evidence and logic, the language used to communicate research findings within this framework implies an unquestionable accuracy that is a very poor approximation of the messiness of social life.

Interestingly writers drawing on positivist approaches have shown ambivalence with regard to their own writing practices. On the one hand, they have explicitly acted as if language has no impact on meaning; yet ironically they have implicitly acknowledged—through their insistence on writing in the third person—the significant role that language plays in constructing knowledge and meaning.

BOX 16.1 REMOVING THE WRITER—THIRD PERSON AND NOMINALISATION

Writing in third person and a process called nominalisation help create a more formal written text. This has the effect of distancing the author from the narrative being constructed and creating a sense of neutrality and objectivity.

As you read these sentences consider how the use of third person, by removing terms that describe oneself (such as 'I') and substituting descriptors of others (for example, the investigator) creates a sense of distance, from the research and the research subjects, and makes the statement appear more factual.

'The investigator examined five types of place-based knowledge.'
'The researcher demonstrated that understandings of home are complex.'
'One tries not to influence the responses gained from interview questions.'

Nominalisation is the process of turning verbs into nouns. It involves taking actions and events and changing them into objects, concepts or things—making sentences seem more formal and abstract. Like writing in third person, nominalisation contributes to a sense of detachment from the text (and the research), removing both personal reflections and the context of the subject being discussed.

For example, the verb 'developed' is nominalised to the noun 'development':
'I *developed* a framework for analysing interviews' (first person narrative) might become 'The *development* of a framework for analysing interviews'.

Below are two more examples of text. In the informal text, few verbs have been nominalised. In the second paragraph is an example of more formal research writing where verbs and verb phrases have been nominalised. As you read these two examples, think how the agency of the researcher appears to be removed in the second portion of text, concealing the researcher's emotions and experiences. Note for example, how the first sentence in the formal text suggests there is much to be learnt from the research (now assumed the status of a thing), rather than the researcher-led processes which constituted it as implied by the more informal excerpt.

Informal Text:
Designing and conducting the research was a learning process for me. Potential participants often refused to be involved in the study and I found this very frustrating. It was also troubling to know other research subjects felt as if they were being coerced into participating. Analysing the research findings produced limited insights into the research question. I concluded that my research project was ill-conceived!

Formal Text:
Much was learnt from the design and conduct of the research. Potential participants' refusal to be involved in the study caused frustration. It was a matter of concern that some individuals felt their participation was subject to researcher coercion. Research analysis provided limited insights into the research question. The research was ill-conceived.

The formality achieved through the use of third person and processes of nominalisation may have the effect of producing an author as an all-seeing and all-knowing (seemingly objective) surveyor of the research, rather than an active participant, complicit in the production of both text and research. Such distancing is an illusion, negating the ways in which power and subjectivity are constituted through the research process.

Post-positivist approaches: situated knowledges

Although the positivist-oriented science model dominated during the quantitative theoretical period of the 1960s and 1970s, its **hegemony** (or conceptual dominance) is now contested in geography by post-positivist approaches such as humanism, Marxism, and political economy, poststructuralism (for example, Barnes 1993; Berg 1994b; 2001; Dixon and Jones 1996). In particular, feminist **poststructuralist** writers (Anzaldúa 1987; Frankenberg and Mani 1993; Massey 1993; Mohanty 1991) have been keen to confront the universalism, mastery, and disembodiment inherent in positivist notions of objectivity, criticising masculinist and Eurocentric concepts of universal knowledge (see also Berg 2004; Berg and Kearns 1998; Bondi 1997; England 1994). Such ideas, they suggest, play a significant role in marginalising those who do not fit into dominant conceptions of social life.

Donna Haraway's (1991) evocative metaphor of *situated knowledges* provides perhaps the most useful approach to contest universalist forms of knowledge. She argues that within dominant ideologies of scientific knowledge, objectivity must be seen as a 'God Trick' of seeing everything from nowhere. She proposes a different concept of 'objectivity', one that attempts to situate knowledge by making the knower accountable to their *position*. All knowledge is the product of specific embodied knowers, located in particular places and spaces: 'there is no independent position from which one can freely and fully observe the world in all its complex particulars' (Barnes and Gregory 1997, p. 20). Research that draws upon situated knowledges is thus based on a much different notion of objectivity from that posed by positivists, and this conception of objectivity also requires a different form of writing practice.

Work by Isabel Dyck (1997) provides an excellent example of the importance of 'position' and the kind of 'truths' situated knowledge might produce (also see England 1994). Dyck reflects on the importance of her own position as a white middle-class Canadian academic and the impact this had on two different research projects she undertook to examine the time–space strategies adopted by Indo-Canadian immigrant women in Vancouver. She found that immigrant women were more willing to speak with her about certain aspects of their lives than others because she was not seen as a threat to their own social networks and relationships within the Indo-Canadian community in Vancouver. At the same time, as an outsider, she was occasionally excluded from aspects of Indo-Canadian women's lives that were defined as culturally sensitive. Her research thus points to the specificity of position and the importance of recognising the politics of position in research processes.

Poststructuralists and feminists also contest those approaches to inquiry that conceptualise writing and language as simple reflections of 'reality'. They argue that 'language lies at the heart of all knowledge' (Dear 1988, p. 266). It should be made clear, however, that such arguments do not assume that language and ideas are the same as 'real' phenomena, objects, and material things. Instead, arguments about the centrality of language express the fact that all processes, objects, and things are understood by humans through the medium of language. Thus, while we might experience the very material process of hitting our 'funny bone' on a table in ways that do not necessarily entail language (for example, as pain), we come to understand the process and the objects involved through language (with categories such as table, funny bone, pain, etc.). Accordingly, language must be seen as not merely reflective, but instead as *constitutive* of social life (for example, Barnes and Duncan 1992; Bondi 1997; Dear 1988).

The poststructuralist critiques of both the **mimetic** concept of language and of disembodied concepts of universal objectivity have significant implications for writing practices. If language were constitutive of knowledge and meaning, then it would seem to matter *how* we write our knowledges of the world. Likewise, if we are to *locate* our knowledge, then we must locate ourselves as researchers and writers within our own writing. Accordingly, poststructuralist writers reject the ostensibly 'objective' modality of writing their work in the third person. Instead, they opt for locating their knowledge-defining objectivity as something to be found not through distance, impartiality, and universality, but through contextuality, partiality, and **positionality**. However, as Gillian Rose (1997) has argued, given the difficulty in completely understanding the 'self', it may be virtually impossible for authors to fully locate themselves in their research. Notwithstanding such difficulties, it is possible for authors to go some way towards locating themselves within their work. Certainly the first step is to reject the third-person narrative, replacing it with a first-person narration of our essays.[2] At the same time, it is not enough to merely adopt the first-person narrative form. Instead, it is important to both reflect upon and analyse how one's position in relation to the processes, people, and phenomena we are researching actually affects both those phenomena and our understanding of them. Again, Isabel Dyck's (1997) study of 'two research projects' discussed above provides an excellent example of how we might undertake such analyses. Thus rather than writing ourselves *out* of our research, we write ourselves back *in*. This is, perhaps, one of the most important distinctions to be made between what we will refer to as the 'writing-UP' (distanced, universal, and impartial) and the 'writing-IN' (located, partial, and situated knowledge) models. Another significant difference arises from the ways that post-positivists conceptualise the relationship between observation and theory.

BALANCING DESCRIPTION AND INTERPRETATION— OBSERVATION AND THEORY

The role of 'theory' and the constitution of 'truth'

We argue in this section that there currently exist a number of powerful dichotomies— observation/theory, subject/object, researcher/researched, data/conclusions, and research/ writing—that structure our understanding of research. It is important to remember that these dichotomies are not recent developments in Western thought. Instead, they arose within the long history of dualistic thinking in Western philosophy (Berg 1994a; Bordo 1986; Derrida 1981; Foucault 1977b; Jay 1981; Le Doeff 1987; Lloyd 1984; Nietzsche 1969). These dichotomies became racialised and gendered through a long historical process of developing a singular Eurocentric and masculine concept of rational thought. For example through a process that Susan Bordo (1986) terms the 'Cartesian masculinisation of thought', Descartes' mind–body distinction came to define appropriate forms of knowledge. The mind was conceptualised as rational and it came to be a property of European men. The body was seen as irrational (have you ever heard the phrase 'mind over matter'?) and was associated with everything that was not European or masculine: women, racial minorities, and sexual dissidents for example. In other words, the mind was unmarked but the body was a mark of difference. Further, Descartes' dualistic philosophy of knowledge formed the basis for the dominant present-day conception of objectivity as impartial, distanced, and disembodied knowledge. Accordingly, Cartesian dualistic thinking forms the foundation of positivist thought (Karl Popper, of whom we spoke earlier, for example, was a well-known adherent of mind–body dualism).

As we have already discussed, positivist-inspired geographers make a rigid distinction between objective and subjective knowledge and between theory and observation. As with the observation/theory binary, the so-called 'objective' is valued at the expense of the subjective. Such hierarchically valued dichotomies form parts of a whole series of other binary concepts—including (but not limited to) mind/body, masculine/feminine, rationality/irrationality, and research/writing—that are interlinked through complex processes of signification (Derrida 1981; Jay 1981; Le Doeff 1987; Lloyd 1984). In this way, for example, observation is equated with objectivity, mind, masculinity, rationality, and research. Theory is constituted as lacking, and it is associated with all those other negatively valued concepts: the subjective, the body, the feminine, and the irrational.

Conceptualising one side of the binary as a *lack* of the other leads to a devaluation of the subordinate term. Thus, in the case of those positivists who conceive of theory as a lack of empirical observation, the ways in which theory constitutes our understanding of empirical 'reality' (in addition to explaining it) are underestimated. Indeed, positivist constructions of factual knowledge as phenomena that are available to the senses (empirically observable) tend to efface the very theoretical nature of positivist thinking itself. As we have already suggested, positivism has both a history and a geography associated with Europe. It is an epistemology—a theory of knowledge—that has developed relatively recently and has come to dominate contemporary intellectual life in the West. Nonetheless, it is not the only theory of knowledge; rather, it is one of many competing theories of knowledge. However, because it is dominant, or hegemonic, it rarely has to account for its own epistemological frameworks. With this in mind, we argue for 'recognition that we cannot insert ourselves into the world free of theory, and neither can such theory ever be unaffected by our experiences in the world' (Berg 1994a, p. 256). Observations are thus *always already* theoretical, just as theory is always touched by our empirical experience. Recognition of this relationship has important consequences for the way we write-IN our work (and WORK-in our writing).

Writing and researching as mutually constitutive practices

Metaphors that allude to research as 'exploration' or 'discovery' are hard to avoid, so taken for granted are their meanings (how often have you heard lecturers speak of their research in terms of 'exploring', 'examining', 'discovering', and 'uncovering'?). This is particularly the case with the so-called 'writing-up' of the research. The term writing-up powerfully articulates the written aspect of the research process in a way that engenders it somehow less significant and/or less problematic than other aspects of the research process. Writing-up is usually seen as a phase that occurs at the end of a research program; indeed, many textbooks about conducting research (this one included) include the section on 'writing-up' at the end of the book (for example, Flowerdew and Martin 1997; Kidder et al. 1986; Kitchin and Tate 2000). Writing is also often seen as a neutral activity though, ironically, scientific and positivist modes of writing and thinking are subject to rhetoric, creativity, and intuition (Bailey et al. 1999a).

The 'writing-up phase' may be discussed in such a way that it appears to be merely a matter of presenting the results and conclusions in an appropriate format. We argue here that in writing research the researcher is not so much presenting her or his findings as re-presenting the research through a particular medium. Re-presentation speaks of the mediated character of the process of writing research.

Rather than reflecting the outcome of a particular research endeavour, we believe the act of writing is a means by which the research is constituted—or given form—and that this process occurs throughout the research process. For example, keeping in mind the constitutive character of language, we can see that any attempt to write research involves a process of selecting categories and language to describe complex phenomena and relationships. But we are getting at much more than that here. Research and writing are iterative processes, and writing helps shape the research as much as it reflects it. At the larger scale of disciplinary practices and epistemological conventions, as we have suggested above, the way we conceptualise the author (as distant and impartial or as involved and partial, for example) has significant implications for the ways that the very processes of research itself can be understood. For us, then, writing is not so much a matter of writing-UP as of writing-IN, a perspective that has considerable implications for how qualitative research is conceptualised and undertaken.

It is unhelpful to assume that the 'writing of research' is a phase that occurs entirely at the end of a research program. Writing is not devoid of the political, personal, and moral issues that are a feature of undertaking research. Further, the separation between 'fieldwork' and writing is artificial (Denzin 1994). Whatever the qualitative research technique utilised, some means of recording the researcher's interpretations, impressions, and analysis must be used, and though such accounts may be recorded on tape, memory stick, or video, the words with which they are constructed are an integral part of the research, not simply a result, recollection, or recording of it. The research cannot be separated from the labels, terms, or categories used to describe it and interpret it, because it is through these that the research is made meaningful.

For example, after I (Juliana) had conducted several qualitative interviews with local authority Economic Development Officers for my PhD research, I realised that using the word 'traditional' as a label for a certain form of local economic initiative was problematic. This was because definitions of 'traditional economic initiatives' were contested by officers and because the term appeared to position local authorities who undertook this type of initiative as 'old-fashioned' or 'not progressive'. I learnt a valuable lesson about the power embodied in words I had simply utilised from the literature on local economic development and about the kind of assumptions embedded in my own research agenda. This understanding enabled me to construct my questions (and consequently my entire research project) in a different way.

I (Lawrence) have had similar experiences of re-orienting research agendas in a project I undertook with two colleagues (McClean et al. 1997). This research helped define some of the historical geographies of Maori tribal land losses in the Porirua region of New Zealand—but it also involved a research 'partnership' with Ngati-Toa Rangatira, a Maori tribal organisation whose lands formed the focus of the research. In this instance, because of our commitment to a research partnership with Ngati-Toa Rangatira, the 'writing-up' of the research was only the initial phase of an iterative process of negotiating the production of knowledge between the three researchers and the *iwi* (tribe). I am not suggesting here, however, that negotiated knowledge is intrinsically better than other forms of knowledge. Instead, what I want to point out is that the process of making explicit the act of negotiation helps to make the research accountable in ways that are appropriate given the specificity of positions and power relations. All research is caught up with power relations, and to deny this is to deny an important aspect of knowledge production (see chapters 2 and 3). Taking this process seriously has enabled me to rethink the role of writing in my intellectual endeavours (see McClean 1997).

Thoughts, observations, emotions, and interpretations that occur during the research thus become important components of any research endeavour, not because they record events or ideas but because they are signifiers of them (in this sense, they act to 'define' complex constellations of ideas and thoughts about the research in more simplified categories of knowledge). Whether interpretations are noted by way of a personal diary, log, video, or audio recording they can provide insight into the researcher's own speaking position and how this is articulated, challenged, and modified through the research journey.

Writing-IN is not a matter of 'telling'—it is about knowing the world in a certain way. The process of writing constructs what we know about our research but it also speaks powerfully about who we are and where we speak from. As we have suggested in a previous section, the detached third-person writing style so common in academic journals and reports implies that the researcher is omnipotent—that they have a perspective that is all-seeing and all-knowing. However, what may appear to be the truth spoken from 'everywhere' is actually a partial perspective spoken from some*where* and by some*one*. Knowledge does not, according to a poststructuralist perspective, exist independently of the people who created it—knowledges are partial and geographically and temporally located. As the researcher writes and inscribes meaning in the qualitative text they are actually constructing a particular and partial story. Richardson (1994) suggests that writing creates a particular view of not only what we are talking about, but also of ourselves. Power is connected with speaking position through text, so a qualitative researcher should consider not only the standpoint spoken from in constructing a research account, but also the implications of their interpretations for those who may have been involved in the research and on the structuring and power relations in everyday life.

Because the practice of writing is not neutral, the voices of qualitative researchers do not need to hide behind the detached 'scientific' modes of writing. Such modes of writing position the researcher as a disembodied observer of the truth, rather than a (re)presenter and creator of a particular and partial truth. The researcher is an instrument of the research and accordingly we suggest they should acknowledge their position in ways that demonstrate the connection between the processes of research and writing. **Reflexivity** is the term often used for writing self into the text. Kim England (1994, p. 82) defines this as 'self-critical sympathetic introspection and the self conscious analytical scrutiny of self as researcher'. A reflexive approach can make researchers more aware of asymmetrical (i.e., where a researcher has more social power and influence than their participants) or exploitative relationships, but it cannot remove them (England 1994, p. 86; also see Rose 1997 and chapters 2 and 3 of this volume). One way in which reflexivity can be encouraged in the writing-IN of qualitative research is by the use of personal pronouns (for example, I, we, my, our).

However, it is important that the use of personal pronouns does not become merely an emotive tool. Alison Jones (1992) suggests that in academic spheres the use of 'I' may result in the insertion of 'emotion' as a replacement for 'reason' thereby creating a work of 'fiction' hiding power relations as much as it might make them explicit. Employing reflexivity through use of first person should instead make explicit the politics associated with the personal voice and draw attention to assumptions embedded in research texts. Reflexivity is also concerned with constructing research texts in a way that gives consideration to the voices of those who may have participated in the research. Reflexivity is about writing critically, in a way that reflects the researcher's understanding of their position in time and place, their particular standpoint, and the consequent partiality of their perspective. Writing situated accounts may involve acknowledging the role of emotions in research (Widdowfield 2000) and thinking about how one's positionality is 'mutually constituted through the relational context of the research process' (Valentine 2003, p. 377). This understanding of the dialogic nature of research and writing (in the sense of a 'dialogue' between various aspects of the research process) enables qualitative researchers to acknowledge in a meaningful way how their assumptions, values, and identities constitute the geographies they create. It also provides an opportunity to play and experiment with writing as a way of knowing and representing.

Richardson (1994) believes that to write 'mechanically' shuts down the creativity and sensibilities of the researcher. She encourages researchers to explore text and genre in the (re)presentation of qualitative research through a variety of media, including oral and visual. Richardson suggests researchers experiment with diverse forms of the written word (prose, poetry, play, autobiography) and write research pieces that are not conventionally linear in format and structure. We support Richardson's (1994) metaphorical construction of writing as '**staging** a text' and wish to encourage geographical researchers to consider how they are (re)presenting the research 'actors', creating the plot, action, and dialogue of a research 'tale'; how they are constructing the stage, the setting of the 'research' play; and to whom (i.e., the audience) the 'production' is aimed.

Of course, most undergraduate geography students will be required to write their research within a given format, the essay or report (for some advice on the conventions associated with these forms of writing, see Hay (2002), Hay, et al. (2000) or Kitchin and Tate (2000) and chapter 17 of this book). Nevertheless, it may be possible to convince your lecturer to allow you to produce another form of geographic representation: a play, a video, a poem, a short story, a poster-board, to name a few options. Despite writing constraints and 'staging' conventions imposed by self and audience (such as for an 'academic' publication or

BOX 16.2   WRITING IN—ALTERNATIVE REPRESENTATIONS

The unconventionality of Marcus Doel and David Clarke's (1999) staging of an 'academic' article is conveyed by its unusual title 'Dark Panopticon. Or, Attack of the Killer Tomatoes'. In this paper, which appeared in *Environment and Planning D: Society and Space,* the authors write as if in a dream world. Their piece is simultaneously fragmentary and powerful. The form of writing here is cleverly indicative of poststructuralist perspectives through which various arguments and thoughts are constructed. In it, narratives of dream, text from other academics, and authorial thoughts are presented as a complex reflexive tapestry. The narratives contained within the article are disjointed and struggled over, and the readers invited on hallucinatory journeys through real and imagined spaces. These are spaces that reflect the ways in which depersonalisation, de-individuation, and fatigue characterise both ways of thinking about the world and commodity relations. As you read the following excerpt consider how theoretical stance and textual staging are integrated through this 'alternative' approach:

> Flash-darks touch the flesh of the world, giving rise to all manner of ontic unease. To be touched by the Dark Panopticon is exemplified for us in the display of greengrocery that greets countless millions as they flow into the world's markets, supermarkets, and hypermarkets. And what we feel here—is it only us?—is an unprecedented and almost unbearable brutality against the flesh of the world: not simply the flesh of humans or animals, but above all else the flesh of vegetables and soft fruit. In particular we are horrified by violence against tomatoes. Yet as we shall tease out in due course, tomatoes, like all objects in the consumer society and data in the surveillance society, take their revenge. The tomatoes strike back...

(Doel and Clarke 1999, p. 429)

a thesis) we want to argue that there is no single correct way to 'stage' a text (see Box 16.2). By exploring the varied ways in which the text can be staged, and how in such staging different stories may be emphasised and other voices may come to the fore, the researcher has the potential to create dynamic and interesting research pieces that engage and challenge both writer and reader.

Issues of validity and authenticity

The interpretative nature of qualitative research has given rise to a considerable amount of debate concerning how the **validity** and authenticity of qualitative research accounts might be assessed (see Bailey et al. 1999a; Baxter and Eyles 1997). The reflexive writing-IN of research experiences and assumptions is not a licence for sloppy research or monographs based solely on personal opinion. Rigour, integrity, and honesty in writing-IN are no less important in qualitative research than they are in quantitative research. Works by writers such as Mike Davis (1990), Gillian Rose (1993), and Cole Harris (1997) provide telling examples of critical qualitative research and rigorous analysis of socio-spatial relations.

The truth and validity of knowledge arising from geographical and social science research has been the subject of discussion for a considerable period of time. More than two decades ago, for example, Harrison and Livingston (1980) suggested that the conduct of research is necessarily linked to what it is possible to know and how we can know it. Poststructuralist thinking has also challenged the assumption of a singular truth and the privileging of certain claims to knowledge. Associated with this is what has been termed the 'crisis of representation' (Marcus and Fisher 1986). That is, doubts have arisen over researchers' authority to speak for others in the conduct and communication of research (Alvermann et al. 1996). In recent years, an increased sensitivity to power and control on the part of some qualitative researchers has encouraged a rethinking of research design and implementation (Glesne and Peshkin 1992, p. 10), and it has also meant a growing concern over the textual appropriation (how researchers appropriate participants' voices) of data in the writing of research accounts (Opie 1992). More recently, Baxter and Eyles (1997) have argued that geographers need to be more explicit about how rigour has been achieved throughout the research process. The process of writing-IN qualitative research requires, therefore, that writers explicitly state the criteria with which a reader may assess the 'trustworthiness' of a given piece of research (see chapter 5 for a discussion). Addressing this issue is difficult because it involves qualitative writers grappling with the tensions between the complexity and richness of information that emerges from qualitative research and the need to produce some sort of 'standardised' evaluation criteria (Baxter and Eyles 1997).

The poststructuralist challenge to a singular notion of truth and a growing awareness of issues of representation do present difficulties for assessing the validity of qualitative research. Much of the debate surrounding the validity of qualitative writing rests upon how terms such as 'rigour', 'validity', 'reliability', and 'truthfulness' are defined. A related issue is whether these definitions, which have often been used as 'objective' measures of the quality of quantitative research, are applicable to qualitative endeavours (see chapter 5). Poststructuralist thinking casts doubt on foundational arguments that seek to anchor a text's authority in terms such as reliability, validity, and generalisability (Denzin 1994).

A debate by two geographers in 1991 and 1992 issues of *The Professional Geographer* highlights some of the issues surrounding reading and evaluating texts and the validity of qualitative approaches. The exchange between Erica Schoenberger (1991; 1992), and Linda McDowell (1992) is significant because it was written at a time when in-depth interviewing was not used extensively in industrial and economic geography. This debate is interesting not only because it centred upon contested definitions of validity but also because it raised issues of meaning and interpretation, audience, and representation through the language that constituted these articles. It demonstrates powerfully the multiple reading of texts and the care needed in constructing qualitative interpretation. Schoenberger sought to argue for the legitimacy of qualitative forms of interviewing, but in doing so suggested how quantitative definitions of reliability (defined by Schoenberger as the stability of methods and findings) and validity (accuracy and truthfulness of findings) might be applied to qualitative research. McDowell disagreed with Schoenberger's concept of validity as interpretation that is verifiable and that corresponds to some external truth. She suggested that Schoenberger's definition was based on a continued adherence to a positivist-inspired quantitative research model, as demonstrated by the language through which her arguments were constructed. Schoenberger (1992) addressed McDowell's criticisms by referring to issues of intended audience (positivist geographers), power and interpretation, suggesting McDowell had misinterpreted her claims.

If concepts such as validity are contested, how then is it possible to construct rigorous research texts? Clifford Geertz (1973) has argued that good qualitative research comprises 'thick' description. Such descriptions take the reader to the centre of an experience, event, or action, providing an in-depth study of the context and the reasons, intentions, understandings, and motivations that surround that experience or occurrence. Though an understanding of 'the heart of the matter' is not independent of researcher interpretation and it will differ according to researcher and 'researched' (Denzin 1994), we believe it is possible to produce 'thick' descriptions of the world in which we live. While it may not be possible to assess the authenticity of such partial descriptions, the validity of the interpretations upon which they are constructed can be examined. Mike Davis (1990, pp. 253–57), for example, provides a particularly compelling description of the makeshift prisons and holding centres for the urban underclass who make up the more than 25,000 prisoners in 'the carceral city' found in a three-mile radius of Los Angeles city hall (see Box 16.3). His descriptions, meticulously researched and referenced, are as much novel-like evocations of city life as they are academic descriptors.

Communicating qualitative research is thus about choices; for example, over what to present, to whom, and how (Strauss and Corbin 1990, p. 247). Though such choices are not always conscious and not necessarily made in circumstances of our own choosing, researchers can attempt to approach transparency in research (that is, accountability to their perspective and position) through reflexively acknowledging and making explicit those choices that have influenced the creation, conduct, interpretation, and writing-IN of the research. Such choices are likely to be guided by principles of ethics, truthfulness, and rigour (see chapters 2 and 3). Transparency may make researchers, and the audiences for whom they write, more aware of the constraints on interpretation, of the limitations imposed by the 'textual staging', and of the implications of the former for research participants. For

BOX 16.3 WRITING FORTRESS L.A.

The demand for law enforcement lebensraum in the central city, however, will inevitably bring the police agencies into conflict with more than mere community groups. Already the plan to add two highrise towers, with 200-400 new beds, to County Jail on Bauchet Street downtown has raised the ire of planners and developers hoping to make nearby Union Station the center of a giant complex of skyscraper hotels and offices. If the jail expansion goes ahead, tourists and developers could end up ogling one another from opposed highrises. One solution to the conflict between carceral and commercial redevelopment is to use architectural camouflage to finesse jail space into the skyscape. If buildings and homes are becoming more prison- or fortress-like in exterior appearance, then prisons ironically are becoming architecturally naturalized as aesthetic objects. Moreover, with the post-liberal shift of government expenditure from welfare to repression, carceral structures have become the new frontier of public architecture. As an office glut in most parts of the country reduces commissions for corporate highrises, celebrity architects are rushing to design jails, prisons, and police stations.

An extraordinary example, the flagship of an emerging genre, is Welton Becket Associates' new Metropolitan Detention Centre in Downtown Los Angeles, on the edge of the Civic Centre and the Hollywood Freeway. Although this ten-story Federal Bureau of Prison's facility is one of the most visible new structures in the city, few of the hundreds of thousands of commuters who pass it by every day have any inkling of its function as a holding and transfer center for what has been officially described as the 'managerial elite of narco-terrorism'. Here, 70% of federal incarcerations are related to the War on Drugs. This postmodern Bastille—the largest prison built in a major US urban center in generations—looks instead like a futuristic hotel or office block, with artistic charms (like the high-tech trellises on its bridge-balconies) comparable to any of Downtown's recent architecture. But its upscale ambience is more than mere façade. The interior of the prison is designed to implement a sophisticated program of psychological manipulation and control: barless windows, a pastel color plan, prison staff in preppy blazers, well-tended patio shrubbery, a hotel-type reception area, nine recreation areas with nautilus workout equipment, and so on. In contrast to the human inferno of the desperately overcrowded County Jail a few blocks away, the Becket structure superficially appears less a detention than a convention center for federal felons—a 'distinguished' addition to Downtown's continuum of security and design. But the psychic cost of so much attention to prison aesthetics is insidious. As one inmate whispered to me in the course of a tour, 'Can you imagine the mindfuck of being locked up in a Holiday Inn?' (Mike Davis 1990, pp. 256–7).

example, the choices surrounding the use of research participants' quotes in a written text comprise far more than a simple matter of how, where, how many, and in what form participants' voices are to be included. The inclusion of quotations raises issues of representation, authority, appropriation, and power (see Opie 1992 for a discussion on how textual appropriation may be reduced). Kay Anderson (1999, pp. 83–4), for example, provides a particularly compelling description of the juxtaposition of identities and spaces in Redfern, an inner-city suburb of Sydney closely identified with spaces of 'Aboriginality' (see Box

16.4). Anderson weaves together quotes from research participants, evidence gathered from archival research, and rich theoretical writing to argue for understanding Redfern as a hybrid space of porous and fluid identities and spaces. Her work manages quite subtly to acknowledge issues of power in research and representation, while simultaneously providing us with a vivid description of life on the Block.

BOX 16.4 RETHINKING REDFERN—WRITING QUALITATIVE RESEARCH

On the Block [a small area of Redfern, an inner-city suburb of Sydney] itself, in 1994 the dominant language group was Banjalang, but a wide range of other place-based dialect groups were present, including Eora (Sydney region), Wiradjuri (Nowra), Kamlaroi (Dubbo and Moree), and many other groups from throughout New South Wales and Queensland. In addition, approximately two-thirds of the total number of rent-payers on the block were women, a significant minority of whom (among those interviewed) were married or partnered to Tongans, Fijians, Torres Strait Islanders, and members of other ethnicities. In most cases the men did not live with the women, who supported their children and funded the periodic visits of husbands or partners, friends and relatives. Sociability has always been both fractious and friendly. Some tenants saw the Block as 'home'; others perceived their place of birth as home; most considered they had multiple homes, including Redfern. In the words of a tenant known on the Block as a community elder and who has since refused to leave it: 'Redfern is an Aboriginal meeting place. People come from all over the country to get news of friends and family'. Now a member of the housing coalition which has been formed to fight the AHC [Aboriginal Housing Company], the same woman recently stated that Redfern has long been a place where children taken from their relatives encountered relatives or information that would lead to those relatives (*Melbourne Age*, 1 February 1997). Another woman had this to say in an interview for a recent documentary: 'People who come from interstate or wherever make to Sydney. Their first aim is the Block because they gotta know who's who and where's where and where to go from here' (ABC TV 1997).

The 'traffic of relating' on the Block opens up fresh ways of thinking about home and community in a context of more widely invoked images of 'flight', 'flow', 'crossings', 'travel' and transnational exchange in contemporary cultural geography. Models of mixing that work with the idea that cultures are porous and fluid are particularly apt in relation to this case study. There is, as I have suggested, no 'pure' culture at Redfern, no crisp boundaries of inside and outside, even for so stigmatised an area. This is not only a methodological issue. It is also an epistemological problem in that the boundaries of researchable communities are not secure and areas never exist as discrete entities (Anderson 1999, pp. 83–4).

Jamie Baxter and John Eyles (1997) suggest the criteria of credibility, transferability, dependability, and confirmability are useful general principles for guiding an evaluation of the rigour (trustworthiness) of a piece of qualitative research. They see these categories as broadly equivalent to the concepts of validity, generalisability, reliability, and objectivity that have been used to evaluate the quality of quantitative research endeavours. We believe it is important to keep in mind the constructed-ness of these concepts, to avoid using them as universal assessment criteria and to avoid engaging in comparative analysis of qualitative studies. Notwithstanding this, Baxter and Eyles' principles have much to commend them in that they may assist in evaluating the internal consistency and rigour of a piece of research. The application of these principles should encourage researchers to explore and make explicit their own research agendas and assumptions and to elaborate on how they believe their research text constitutes the 'truth' about a particular subject (see Box 16.5). While transparency is not in itself ultimately achievable, if conscious reflexive writing produces qualitative texts that are open to scrutiny by research participants and audience, and if they present challenges to taken-for-granted ways of seeing and knowing, and provoke and promote questions about 'place' in the world, then perhaps this goes some way towards establishing the 'validity' of a qualitative research text. Communicating qualitative research is as much about how we know, as it is about what we know.

BOX 16.5   DISTANCING VERSUS REFLEXIVE WRITING

Leisure researcher Sherry Dupuis (1999) rejected models of writing that refused to acknowledge her positionality, individuality, and creativity in research. She believes writing about emotions, experiences, and contradictions and inconsistencies in research findings can actually assist in understanding the experiences of research participants. In the following excerpt she argues for a recognition of the ways in which qualitative researchers construct rather than simply reflect the stories of others.

> What continues to worry me more, however, is how this sense that we <u>could</u> distance ourselves from our work leads to the false perception that we are telling <u>other's stories</u>. Somehow we believe that when we write our texts devoid of any sense of our selves and using the words of our participants, the stories we are telling are solely our participants' stories. Related to this, Daly (1995, 1997) talked about how the traditional emphasis in qualitative research has been the idea that our findings and our theories 'emerge from the data' (Glaser & Strauss, 1967) much like mist rises from a meadow. The assumption is that knowledge is something that researchers 'find' or 'discover' (Eisner, 1985; Golden-Biddle & Locke, 1997; Richards & Richards, 1991; Webb, 1992). Daly (1995, 1997) challenged this assumption arguing that theory does <u>not</u> emerge from the data—it emerges from the researchers: that is, it is drawn out of the data by those who collect it. Knowledge is cultivated and constructed, not found.

(Dupuis 1999, p. 48)

CONCLUSION

We have discussed the importance of language in the social construction of knowledge, how power is articulated through dichotomies, and how meaning is inscribed in language. We believe models of writing that construct the writer as a disembodied narrator are inappropriate for communicating qualitative research. Our focus has been on written rather than visual texts, as writing remains the predominant means of communicating qualitative research. The breaking down of dichotomies, through an interpretative understanding of writing and researching as mutually constitutive processes, and an understanding of which principles might guide valid qualitative research are critical to writing 'good' qualitative research. It is also crucial to understand how power and meaning are inscribed in the words that constitute the research process, to recognise researchers' subjectivities, standpoint, and locatedness (shifting and partial though they might be), and to acknowledge the voices of those with whom we undertake research. We believe that doing this enables a qualitative researcher to have confidence in the 'validity' of their interpretations. Consequently this chapter has not been a 'how to' guide, but a means of raising important issues that are inherent in the writing-IN process.

KEY TERMS

dichotomy

hegemony

mimetic

modality

neo-positivism

nominalisation

objective

objective modality

positionality

positivism

poststructuralism

reflexivity

situated knowledge

staging

subjective

trope

validity

writing-IN

REVIEW QUESTIONS

1   What implications do poststructuralist perspectives have for writing qualitative research?
2   In what ways is the term 'writing-up' misleading?
3   Why should writing be seen as an integral part of the entire research process?
4   How can a researcher endeavour to produce 'trustworthy' research?

SUGGESTED READING

Baxter, J. and Eyles, J. 1997, 'Evaluating qualitative research in social geography: establishing "rigour" in interview analysis', *Transactions of the Institute of British Geographers*, vol. 22, no. 4, pp. 505–25.

Bondi, L. 1997, 'In whose words? On gender identities, knowledge and writing practices', *Transactions of the Institute of British Geographers*, vol. 22, pp. 245–58.

Dupuis, S. L. 1999, 'Naked truths: towards a reflexive methodology in leisure research', *Leisure Sciences*, vol. 21, no. 1, pp. 43–64.

Jones, A. 1992, 'Writing Feminist Educational Research: Am "I" in the Text?', in S. Middleton and A. Jones (eds), *Women and Education in Aotearoa,* Bridget Williams Books, Wellington.

McNeill, D. 1998, 'Writing the new Barcelona', in T. Hall and P. Hubbard (eds), *The Entrepreneurial City: Geographies of Politics, Regime and Representation,* John Wiley, London.

Richardson, L. 1994, 'Writing. A Method of Inquiry', in N. K. Denzin and Y. S. Lincoln (eds), *Handbook of Qualitative Research,* 2nd edn, Sage, Thousand Oaks, CA.

Rose, G. 1997, 'Situating knowledges: Positionality, reflexivities and other tactics', *Progress in Human Geography,* vol. 21, pp. 305–20.

Notes

1   Readers seeking specific 'how to' advice on stylistic conventions associated with the presentation of research are advised to consult chapter 17 of this volume; Hay (2002); Hay et al. (2002); Kneale (1999); or Stanton (1996) in conjunction with the conceptual material of this chapter.

2   It is appropriate to note however that it can be difficult institutionally to present some forms of research this way. For instance, social or environmental impact statements prepared by government departments or consulting firms will frequently not list authors, where indeed the 'we' would be poorly defined. Moreover, neither group would want individuals to be sued for their opinions.

From Personal to Public: Communicating Qualitative Research for Public Consumption

Dydia DeLyser and Eric Pawson

CHAPTER OVERVIEW

Qualitative researchers can communicate their research to general audiences, and this chapter suggests several strategies. Because writing is a formative part of the research process, and a means of presenting findings, we offer techniques to focus creativity, and convince an audience. We explore written work, public talks, and web pages, and describe effective ways to share our research with informants, the media, and the broader community.

INTRODUCTION

How do qualitative researchers set about communicating their findings? In our case, it's a cold, wet Monday morning. Sitting in a quiet room with a large whiteboard, we talk about relevant books and articles we have read in the weeks before. But what exactly is our focus, and what will our argument be?

We use the whiteboard for brainstorming and sorting out our ideas, as we strive to identify the focusing questions and themes (these now appear in the 'chapter overview' guide above) that will structure our argument. We talk about the things we would really like to say and where, if anywhere, they will 'fit'. We revisit what we have read, and talk through how that can be used to substantiate, elaborate, or illustrate the points on the whiteboard. Our arguments become clearer as we modify them, revise them, and flesh them out.

What is the purpose of these opening paragraphs? They tell a story, or **anecdote**, which is designed to get your attention and address the chapter's major themes. Since you are still reading, perhaps the ploy is working. And if this strategy worked for us, then it will probably work for you when you are communicating the results of your own research. Telling a story, one that encapsulates the main points you wish to make, is a good way to start. It need not be personal; in fact, many successful anecdotes come directly from the writer's own qualitative data.

Our opening story (from data on our experience with writing) describes a writing and communication *process* that has parallels in the process you use when you write for your instructors/supervisors, your web readers, or the public to whom you give your talk. Our story emphasises interaction, suggesting that writing is a *social process*, intimately linked with thinking, reading, and discussing. It implies that we cannot know what we want to say or how we will say it until we have written and talked through a plan, elaborating it with notes and reading. This is not a new idea: 'How can I know what I think till I see what I say?' asked Graham Wallas back in 1926 (in Boyle 1997, p. 238). Writing to communicate is not the end-point of research, rather it is central to the thinking process that *is* research (Richardson 2000).

If you can communicate your ideas to others, and learn more about them as you talk them through, you'll be more successful in communicating in formal situations. You will be well prepared and more confident about what you are saying and why you are taking the risk of saying it. In other words, you will have something you want to communicate.

WHY COMMUNICATE?

Why should we communicate the results of our research? Obviously, unless we do, we will not pass the paper, we will fail our course, or we will not get our degree. We will let down our respondents and ourselves. But those motivations are negative. We can also see positive reasons for communicating the results of our research, the fruits of our learning; like, for example, the fact that when we share with others the new understandings we have gained from our research we convey, and possibly help to create, new and different worlds. We may have important messages about a diverse range of topics, and, by sharing our findings we may inspire others to take up action as well. Indeed, many feel deeply committed to helping people and environments, and sharing the results of our research can honour that commitment. Plus, frankly, it can also just be fun (Hay 2002). But once we decide it is important to communicate our research, we must decide who to communicate it to.

The initial answer may be surprising: we first communicate our research with ourselves. We write first for ourselves, and to ourselves, because the very act of writing reveals what it is that we think and know, and what we do not (Richardson 2000). In other words, writing is an *iterative process* (Kitchin and Tate 2000), whereby we read, write, and research in interlinked phases, with each activity clarifying the direction we need to take with the others. Reading makes clearer what we might write, and vice versa. Writing helps to elucidate what we think, and being clearer on what we think enables us to communicate those thoughts to better effect.

Indeed, the writing process itself is *formative*; writing is an essential part of clarifying thinking (Becker 1986). 'Writing *is* thinking' says Harry Wolcott (1990b, p. 21). A good grade, or a good public reception for a talk, is dependent on how clearly we can communicate our thoughts, which means that our thoughts themselves have to be clear. In order for them to become clear it helps to practice writing to oneself, writing in drafts 'for your eyes only' before submitting them to broader scrutiny. You will see that, as you write, ideas you had will become clearer, and that ideas you did not know you had will form. It also helps to write (whether a rough plan, a first draft, or something more complete), and then put that writing aside for a little while. You will be a different person when you return to it, an hour, or a day later. Your brain will have reflected on the ideas; you will have a fresher perspective.

Though you are your own **audience** and critic, we each need an external audience as well. Who is the audience for your research? As researchers, we have a public audience. We are accountable within the academy (to meet course or degree requirements, or to our peers) and we have obligations beyond it (for example, to those who worked with us as respondents or gave us access to networks). It is often best not to go directly to these audiences without a trial, or pilot. A pilot study 'in the field' is widely accepted as good research method (see chapter 10, for example); piloting one's writing or talk is less frequently talked about, but equally helpful.

Further, even though we often save 'writing-up' (see Chapter 16 for a discussion of this phase) for the last minute, if we understand writing as part of the thinking and research process, then there will already be *something* written on paper, or outlined in one's head, that can be piloted with an external audience. Try the grandmother test. Can your grandmother understand your thoughts, your draft paper, your thesis outline? She may be a Nobel laureate; she might be a lifelong homemaker, but she will likely be a sympathetic audience with whom you should be able to communicate your ideas. If she is not clear on what you are saying and why, restate things so she will be. This is also the role of your supervisor, dissertation adviser, or instructor; but explaining your work to somebody outside your field is a sure way to clarify what it is you wish to say.

Because the academic life is one that takes place within *social networks* and has *social responsibilities*, each of us must be able to explain our ideas to ourselves—as the foundation for explaining them to wider audiences. Grandmothers and supervisors can help us to sharpen our thinking, writing, and communicating, yet they are not the final arbiters of our work. Sharing our research, with examiners, with those who helped us, and with wider networks of people who have stakes in our areas of investigation, is an essential part of the role of researcher (see the discussion in chapters 3, 5, and 13 for example). In order to fully participate in the academic world we have to contribute to the academic life that has provided us with our opportunity; we do that most often by writing (Becker 1986).

Depending on which part of the audience we are communicating with, the ground rules vary. Your university or department will most probably have publicised its expectations for your term paper, dissertation, or thesis. Follow that guidance. If in doubt, ask your academic advisers. More challenging are obligations to other audiences. How do we share our research, how do we 'share the field' as Julie Cupples and Sara Kindon (2003) put it? Their view is unequivocal: 'sharing the field is essential both in terms of the training of future researchers and as a means of giving back something to those who have helped us' (2003, p. 224; see also DeLyser 2001; and Routledge 2001). In other words, we have obligations to those who follow us, as well as to those who have helped us get to where we are. Different strategies may be necessary for each group. Although placing a copy of your paper or thesis in the library, for example, is usually sufficient for the former, the latter group may appreciate something quite different.

COMMUNICATING WITH A GENERAL AUDIENCE

We communicate with our audience in four main ways: the written word, the spoken word, through our body language, and with visual representations. Though discipline-specific written presentations of one's research are used commonly to fulfill course or degree requirements, they may not be the best way to give something back to the participants in one's research network. There may be more accessible ways of passing on our insights. Vehicles such as short articles for local newsletters, or reports abstracted from a dissertation or thesis for, say, local officials (in government agencies for example) enable the language, length, and tone of the feedback to be tailored to the audience concerned. Informants themselves are often interested, and sharing your findings with them is one way of showing your appreciation of their contribution to your work (see chapters 3 and 13 for related discussions). You can, of course, share more than your findings: Julie Cupples, for example, found that the women who had worked with her in Nicaragua particularly appreciated receiving copies of interview transcripts (Cupples and Kindon 2003). Since it may take some time before your report or thesis is finished, providing transcripts first can be a way to give something back to informants in a more timely manner.

Releasing written material through the media can be effective too. Before undergraduate field trips in New Zealand, local newspapers are usually alerted about the group's research projects and impending arrival in the locality. This is a polite way of informing people that student researchers are in the vicinity and may also serve as an appeal for tolerance and cooperation. Often the newspaper will then summarise the outcomes of such projects—an effective form of feedback.

A word of caution, however: reporters may have a different interest in, and reading of, the research that you have done, and may represent your work in ways having unforeseen consequences. When Iain Hay led a second-year class in work on fear of crime in Unley, a local government area in Adelaide, South Australia, the results were consistent with the results of other studies, revealing low levels of fear. But the local press, receiving copies of the class report, saw things differently, with one paper headlining 'Grim nights in a suburb of fear', and another 'Fear of crime shackles Unley', thus undoing a lot of good work with public agencies that had helped with the research. Although over time such agencies began to pay more attention to how fear of crime constrained people's behaviours, when it happened a 'student project intended to demonstrate [this] became an instrument of oppression', by raising fear levels due to the sensational reporting (Hay 1995, p. 269).

The media can perhaps best be treated with caution. But the results of student research can also reach an interested audience through clearly worded letters to the editor of the local newspaper (Hay and Bass 2002). If your topic is potentially sensitive, or if it could be misconstrued by different parties, then it may be better to give targeted feedback, using talks. Talks are an excellent means of involving your audience, and giving them the opportunity to participate with you by listening and asking questions. In fact, presentations like slide shows given in community gathering places can be a creative and fun way to reach and engage your respondents. You may also wish to make a poster or a map describing your project and display that at a place accessible to the community you worked with; when you first put it up you can invite respondents to see it, and you can give a short presentation about it (Lydia Pulsipher, personal communication). Still, whether given off campus, or on, these talks do need careful preparation (see Hay 2002), even if only to overcome the natural fear that many of us hold about public speaking. Practice helps, as does the grandmother test. Both underline the things that can draw in an audience, as well as those that will put them to sleep (see Box 17.1).

BOX 17.1   SOME KEY 'DO'S' AND 'DON'TS' FOR PUBLIC PRESENTATIONS

Do:

- Prepare: if you know your stuff, you will be less nervous about presenting it, and give your audience more confidence in what you are saying. Practise your presentation, perhaps delivering it to your resolute grandmother.
- Make sure you have high-quality content: your audience has come first to hear what you have to say, only second to hear how you will say it.
- Use visuals that *add to* what you have to say. Use them when and where you need them, as illustrations of your point(s).
- Interact: engage actively with an audience by including them in the picture. Perhaps start with an anecdote, and relate what you are saying to the people and place you are talking in. Leave time for questions.

Don't:

- Use extensive, bulleted **PowerPoint** outlines: they remove your audience's need to listen to what you have to say, which likely cannot be reduced to a simple list of bullet points in the first place (see Tufte 2003, who found that such presentations, by oversimplifying complex engineering analysis and therefore causing problems to go unresolved, actually contributed to the loss of the Space Shuttle *Columbia*).
- Mumble: ask your audience if they can hear you. They won't thank you if they can't. Speak as clearly as you can. A clearly spoken presentation conveys the speaker's confidence in her work (see Strunk and White 1959, p. xi, who even advise, 'If you don't know how to pronounce a word, say it loud!'—it is better to clearly mispronounce a word than to leave what you said, and therefore what you meant, unintelligible. Pace yourself, and look at your audience as much as you can to engage them, and make sure they are following you.

Another means of communicating research results is via a web site, an effective tool in a range of circumstances, and with varying audiences. Setting up web pages while doing the research is another aspect of the formative process of writing. Plus, an attractive web site may draw an early audience, and can give you contacts working in similar fields, or potential respondents. A web site is also a way to give something back to your department: it may attract others to think about coming to study there in the future.

Web sites require design as careful as any other means of communication (see Krug 2000; Thatcher et al. 2002). Follow a template if your university or department has one, and use your entry page as an overview of your work. It is the 'front room' rather than the whole 'house'; you can construct more detailed pages further into your site. Balance words with images, tables, and maps, but be aware of the politics and legalities of visual representation: we can use only images for which we have permission; and must be cautious not to misrepresent our research subjects by picturing them insensitively—that is, picturing them in ways devoid of context, or placing them in inappropriate juxtapositions (Cupples and Kindon 2003, p. 224).

STRUCTURE AND CREATIVITY

Today few people write in longhand, directly on paper. The personal computer has revolutionised our abilities to write and to make revisions to our writing. But the notion of 'word processing' can be a dangerous misnomer, implying that the computer does all the work, taking agency away from the writer, and stifling creativity. However you choose to write, remember that *you* control the process.

One way to facilitate that control is to keep the structural basics for any piece of communication firmly in mind. Box 17.2 illustrates these for written work, but the importance of structure is just as central for a successful poster or talk.

BOX 17.2   STRUCTURAL BASICS

- Begin with clear research questions: they narrow the world of possibilities, and allow us as writers to focus our attention, thus sharpening our creative abilities.
- Develop an outline, using it to communicate with yourself, remind you of points you want to make, and quotes you wish to engage. Allow it to change as your paper changes, and as you progress in your writing project.
- Use sub-headings. When your ideas need to shift, call attention to such important transitions with descriptive sub-headings. Use them in first drafts, or later, when you see a shift in your argument or the need to call more attention to a specific point.
- Develop clear paragraphs, advancing usually just one idea in each. Locate the thesis statement (the 'point' of the paragraph) at the paragraph's beginning or end, and use the middle to build that idea. 'Clinch' the paragraph with a summary statement or a question that leads clearly to the next part of the paper.

Writers facing projects like term papers or theses may feel initially that any externally imposed form or structure hinders creativity, forcing our work into 'boring' moulds and 'stifling' formats. Pausing to consider highly restrictive forms like the *haiku* or the sonnet, however, reveals rather that such structures can be stimulants to creativity. More productive, then, is a view that *structure harnesses creativity.* Indeed, writers use structure to *focus* their creative energies.

As an example, consider film. Because most Hollywood films (and many others besides) must run between 90 and 110 minutes in length, and because, in standard screenplay format, one page becomes 1 minute in the final film, nearly every script must be between 90 and 110 pages long—the novice screen writer who writes drastically more or less will likely not be taken seriously. Further, because many film audiences grant a new movie just 10 minutes of their time before switching off, screen writers face a 10 minute (and therefore ten page) limit in which they *must* hook their audiences, demonstrating to them what and who the film is about, showing them why they will want to stay to the end. Finally, screen writers must accomplish everything primarily with dialogue and visuals—descriptive or explanatory narration is seldom successful. Since nearly every film you have ever watched likely fits these rigid restrictions, you can begin to understand the creativity that such limitations can render.

Successful academic writers and speakers also use structure in carefully considered ways. Box 17.3 highlights some of the key techniques that enable us to highlight personal style and voice, to showcase the richness of qualitative data, and, indeed, to express originality within clear structures. Using them helps us communicate more clearly, giving us the best chance of convincing our audience of the pertinence of what we wish to say.

BOX 17.3 USING STRUCTURE IMAGINATIVELY

- Show, don't tell'. Use your data to make your story unfold. Whenever you make an assertion based on your data, *show* your readers how you know this is so by backing it up with data. For example, in a paper based on interviews, show readers how you know what you know by including compelling quotes from those interviews to support your own statements.
- Write with carefully chosen verbs and nouns; avoid modifiers. Modifiers (like adjectives and adverbs) weaken prose while verbs and nouns strengthen it. Forms of the verb 'to be' (is, was, were) can be stifling because they lack action, and deny agency. Choose active verbs and precise nouns for the action or situation you have in mind.
- Use anecdotes that are directly on the point to draw your reader in, and present your argument powerfully.

CONVINCING THE AUDIENCE

How do we convince an audience and ourselves of the value of the research that we have done? Everything said about communication in this chapter so far will help: clear thinking, good preparation, transparent structure. Most audiences today are well past the stage where they need to be convinced of the worth of qualitative research *per se*; but it is still necessary to describe and justify the methods we have used, demonstrating why these methods were the most appropriate for the questions we have set out to answer (Boyle 1997).

Qualitative research, unlike some quantitatively based reports (often designed to be interpreted through their tables and summaries), cannot be 'skimmed', because it is in the very details, richness, and diversity that the author's points become clear (Richardson 2000).

But how much data is 'enough', and to what extent should respondents be quoted: briefly or at length? In general, audiences will follow longer quotes best when the words relate directly to the point the writer seeks to make. Limit the length of quotes by omitting unneeded passages, and consider paraphrasing certain sections, quoting only the relevant words. You may find it useful to look in journals that commonly report the results of qualitative research, like *Cultural Geographies* or *Social and Cultural Geography*, to see examples of how best to make a point with emphatic, colourful, and telling quotations.

On the other hand, be aware that whenever you make a point, you must have data to back it up. If your point is nuanced, or central to your argument, show that with data reflecting these issues: use several short quotes from interviews, for example, to show a variety of respondents' views. Again, you need not show them all—careful selection of a few will indicate that breadth to your reader or listener. You will convey your points best when you stay close to your own data, avoiding making claims the data will not support.

This counts in public presentations as well. When delivering your talk or answering questions, be honest, basing your comments on your own research and knowledge, without bluffing your way through material or answers you do not know. And, in all arenas, avoid **plagiarism**. When we use the works of others without proper acknowledgement, be these from books, articles, newspapers, or web sites, it undermines our credibility and is generally very easy for an experienced audience to detect.

CONCLUSION

It is now two weeks since we started to write this chapter although, in reality, the writing began months ago with reading and exchanges of emails about developing ideas. On that wet Monday, when we began, we tried to focus the task, then allowed ourselves time for more reading; we accepted the messiness of our first drafts, and enabled our thoughts to gel over days spent doing other things. Finally, we scheduled enough time for revisions. So where do we now stand?

In general, as qualitative researchers, we will all stand well positioned to produce strong and polished work if we use a transparent structure (one that is clear to the audience) to harness our creativity, and if we stay close to our data as we build our arguments. Still, when we read the published works of others, we may lose sight of all the iterations their efforts involved. Instead, we see the finished product of someone else's work as a streamlined whole, missing the complex and not-always-forward-moving steps in the process. In fact, this is a common mistake found far beyond the bounds of qualitative research.

When people today quote American astronaut Neil Armstrong's famous 1969 words upon setting first foot on the moon, 'One small step for [a] man; one giant leap for mankind', they, in some ways, are celebrating *his* accomplishment, *his* moment of glory. But his Apollo 11 mission came only after years of effort, of research, training, and analysis (by women as well as men), as well as many other missions—none without risk—each leading in different increments to that first footfall. Like Armstrong's step, our research and communication proceed incrementally—in an iterative process of reading, writing, thinking, and talking—in small steps adding up to greater accomplishments.

KEY TERMS

anecdote
audience

plagiarism
PowerPoint

REVIEW QUESTIONS

1   What are four ways to communicate our research, and which audience might each best serve?
2   How is writing a social process?
3   How can structure serve to harness creativity?
4   How can we attempt to make sure our work is geared properly for our audience?
5   How are the processes of writing, reading, and doing research all related?

SUGGESTED READING

Becker, H. S. 1986, *Writing for Social Scientists. How to Start and Finish Your Thesis, Book, or Article*, University of Chicago Press, Chicago.

Cupples, J. and Kindon, S. 2003, 'Returning to university and writing the field', in R. Scheyvens and D. Storey (eds), *Development Fieldwork. A Practical Guide*, Sage Publications, London.

DeLyser, D. forthcoming. 'Writing it Up', in J. P. Jones III and B. Gomez, (eds), *Research Methods in Geography*, Blackwell, London.

Hay, I., (ed.) 2002, *Communicating in Geography and the Environmental Sciences*, 2nd edn, Oxford University Press, Melbourne.

Manalo, E. and Trafford, J. 2004, *Thinking to Thesis. A Guide to Graduate Success at All Levels*, Pearson Education, Auckland.

Tufte, E. 2003, *The Cognitive Style of PowerPoint*, Graphics Press LLC, Cheshire.

Wolcott, H. 1990, *Writing Up Qualitative Research*, Sage, Newbury Park.

Glossary

abstracting

Reducing the complexity of the 'real world' by generating summary statements on the basis of common processes, experiences, or characteristics in the data. (See also *data reduction*.)

accidental sampling

See *convenience sampling*.

action–reflection

Periods of action followed by times when participants reflect on what they have done and what can be learned. The learning informs the next phase of action creating an iterative cycle of action and reflection. This process enables change to occur throughout the research process. (See also *reflexivity*.)

activism

Political and practical action usually intended to bring about social, economic, or other change. (See also *applied people's geography* and *critical geography*.)

aide-mémoire

A list of topics to be discussed in an interview. May contain some clearly worded questions or key concepts intended to guide the interviewer. Alternative term for *interview guide*.

analytic code

A code that is developed through analysis and is theoretically informed, a code based on themes that emerge from relevant literature and/or the data. (See also *interpretive code*; compare with *descriptive code*.)

analytical log

Critical reflection on substantive issues arising in an interview. Links are made between emergent themes and the established literature or theory. (See also *personal log*.)

anecdote

A story often personalised to the author or presenter, and directly related to the point of the paper or presentation, that captures the attention of an audience, and persuades them of the importance, relevance, and/or interest of what they are reading or hearing.

applied people's geography

This term was coined by David Harvey to refer to geographical research that is consciously 'part of that complex of conflictual social processes which give birth to new geographical landscapes' (Harvey 1984, p. 7). (See also *activism* and *critical geography*.)

archival research

Research based on documentary sources (for example, public archives, photographs, newspapers).

archives

Narrowly defined as the non-current records of government agencies but also including company and private papers. Typically managed by a specialist in a government agency dedicated to the records' long-term use and preservation. A distinction can be made between archives as surviving records and archives as the institution dedicated to their preservation.

archivist

Professional curator of non-current records who has expertise in the accession, arrangement, and preservation of such records (in contrast to the current files of a central or local government agency that are controlled by records managers).

asymmetrical power relation

A research situation in which informants are in positions of influence relative to the researcher. (See also *potentially exploitative power relation* and *reciprocal power relation*.)

attribute database

A set of information compiled from measurable characteristics, such as the census.

audience

Those people with whom you wish to communicate the results of your research. Identifying who constitutes the audience is fundamental to the success of communicating with them.

bias

Systematic error or distortion in a data set that might emerge as a result of researcher prejudices or methodological characteristics (for example, case selection, non-response, question wording, interviewer attitude).

bulletin board

An electronic medium devoted to sending and receiving messages for a particular interest group (for example, the about.com Geography Bulletin Board at <http://geography.about.com/mpboards.htm?once=true&> (Accessed: 16 September 2004).

canon

A body of work, such as texts, held by some critics to be the most important of their kind and therefore worthy of serious study by all interested in the field.

case

Example of a more general process or structure that can be theorised. (See also *case study*.)

case study

Intensive study of an individual, group, or place over a period of time. Research is typically done in situ.

CAQDAS

Acronym for computer-assisted qualitative data analysis software.

CATI

See *Computer-Assisted Telephone Interviewing*.

chain sampling

See *snowball sampling*.

closed questions

Questions in which respondents are offered a limited series of alternative answers from which to select. Respondents may be asked to select, for example, one or more categories, rank items in order of importance or select a point on a scale measuring the intensity of an opinion. (Compare with *open questions* and *combination questions*.)

codebook

An organisational tool for keeping track of the codes in a project, including their meanings and applications, as well as notes regarding the coding process.

code and retrieve software

Specialist software packages that allow text to be segmented or grouped for coding and display. They facilitate electronic marking up, cutting, sorting, reorganising, and collecting traditionally done with scissors, paper, and sticky tape. Examples include Kwalitan and The Ethnograph.

coding

The processes of assigning qualitative or quantitative 'values' to chunks of data or categorising data into groups based on commonality or along thematic lines for the purposes of describing, analysing, and organising data.

coding structure

The organisation of codes into meaningful clusters, hierarchies, or categories.

collaborative research

Research designed, conducted, interpreted, and disseminated by a team of local and non-local members, with local members directing the process or sharing equally in decision-making.

colonial research

Imposed, often exploitative research in both imperial and non-imperial contexts that maintains distance from, and domination of, the marginalized 'others' that it seeks to study and which denies the validity of their knowledge, ways of knowing, experience, and concerns. (Compare with *decolonising research, inclusionary research,* and *postcolonial research*.)

combination questions

Questions made up of both *closed* and *open* components. Their closed component offers respondents a series of alternative answers to choose between while their open component allows respondents to suggest an additional answer, not listed in the closed component, or to elaborate on the reason why a particular option was selected in the closed component.

common questions

Asked in oral history interviews of each participant. They build up varying views and information about certain themes. (Compare with *orientation questions, specific questions,* and *follow-up questions*.)

complete observation

A situation in which observation is overwhelmingly one-way and the researcher's presence is masked such that s/he is shielded from participation.

complete participation

A situation in which the researcher's immersion in a social context is such that s/he is first and foremost a participant. As a result of this level of immersion, the researcher may need to adopt critical distance to achieve an observational stance. That critical distance might be gained by reflection out-of-hours in the field, or through short-term exits from the field.

computer-assisted cartography

Any hardware or software that is used to facilitate map making. *Geographic Information Systems* (GIS) belong under this heading.

Computer-Assisted Qualitative Data Analysis Software (CAQDAS)

Both a general acronym and the specific acronym for the CAQDAS network based in Surrey, United Kingdom.

computer-assisted telephone interviewing (CATI)

Questionnaire/interview conducted by telephone with questions being read directly from a computer file and responses being recorded directly onto a computer file.

concept building

Refers to the process of entering and *coding* data in a systematic way that relates to the research question being asked. The ability of a software package to support the systematic organisation of concepts leads to that software being categorised as theory building software. (See also *concept mapping*.)

conceptual framework

Intellectual structure underlying a research project that emerges from an integration of previous literature, theories, and other relevant information. The conceptual framework provides the basis for framing, situating, and operationalising research questions.

conceptual mapping

As for *concept building*, but refers to the specific ability to visually represent data in some form. For example, QSR NUD*IST software uses *hierarchical tree* structures and ATLAS/ti uses network diagrams. Inspiration and Decision Explorer are purpose-built conceptual mapping programs for qualitative research.

conditions of use form

Sometimes known as an *informed consent form*, a form outlining what will happen to the material research participants share with you—what their rights are, who will own copyright, where recordings will be stored, and for how long, what they will be used for…(See also *Memorandum of Understanding*.)

constructionist approach

An approach for challenging assumptions of coherence and truth within positivist knowledge (sometimes referred to as either rationalist, objectivist, or Cartesian knowledge (see *positivism*)). Draws attention to social practices in the production of all knowledge, including scientific knowledge.

confederate

Someone thought by other research study participants to be another participant but who is, in fact, part of the research team.

confirmability

Extent to which results are shaped by respondents and not by researcher's biases.

content analysis

See *latent content analysis* and *manifest content analysis*.

controlled observation

Purposeful watching of worldly phenomena that is strictly limited by prior decisions in terms of scope, style, and timing. (Compare with *uncontrolled observation*.)

convenience sampling

Involves selecting cases or participants on the basis of expedience. While the approach may appear to save time, money, and effort, it is unlikely to yield useful information. Not recommended as a *purposive sampling* strategy.

credibility

The plausibility of an interpretation or account of experience.

critical geography

Various ideas and practices that are committed to challenging unequal power relationships, developing and applying critical theories to geographical problems, and working for political change and social justice. (See also *activism* and *applied people's geography*.)

critical inner dialogue

Constant attention to what an informant is saying, including *in situ* analysis of the themes being raised, and a continual assessment of whether the researcher fully understands what is being said.

critical reflexivity

See *reflexivity*.

criterion sampling

Choosing all cases that satisfy some predetermined standard.

cultural protocols

Local, community, or group defined codes of appropriate behaviour, interaction, and communication to which outsider researchers are expected to adhere.

'culturally safe'

Having knowledge of the history, beliefs, and practices of minority groups and maintaining awareness of these factors.

data cleaning

Identifying and correcting errors of *coding* in a data set.

data management software

A generic term for any software that facilitates the entry, organisation, retrieval, and/or coding and mapping of input data.

data reduction

Using categorisation and qualification to lump data together into larger packages, thereby reducing the complexity and number of data points but increasing the level of understanding of trends, processes, or other insights. (See also *abstracting*.)

data retrieval

Refers to the process of getting access to data that has already been entered into a computer system.

data storage

Refers to the process of introducing data into a computer system so that it may be archived in some way (for example, as a document, spreadsheet, or graphics image).

debriefing

Procedure by which information about a research project (some of which may have been withheld or misrepresented) is made known to participants once the research is complete.

decode

To analyse in order to understand the hidden meanings in a text.

decolonising research

Research whose goals, methodology, and use of research findings contest imperialism and other oppression of peoples, groups, and classes by challenging the cross-cultural discourses, *asymmetrical power relationships*, and institutions on which they are based. (See also *applied people's geography*, *inclusionary research*, and *postcolonial research*.)

deconstruction

A method for challenging assumptions of coherence and truth within a *text* by revealing inconsistencies, contradictions, and inadequacies (for example, where matters that are problematical have been naturalised).

deduction

Reasoning from principles to facts. (Compare with *induction*).

dependability

Minimisation of variability in interpretations of information gathered through research. Focuses attention on the researcher-as-instrument and the extent to which interpretations are made consistently.

dependent variable

A study item whose characteristics are considered to be influenced by an *independent variable*. For example, flooding is heavily dependent on rainfall.

descriptive code

A *code* describing some aspect of the social data, typically aspects that are fairly obvious. (See also *manifest message* and *initial code*. Compare with *analytic code*.)

deviant case sampling

Selection of extraordinary cases (for example, outstanding successes, notable failures) to illuminate an issue or process of interest.

dichotomy

A division or binary classification in which one part of the dichotomy exists in opposition to the other (for example, light/dark, rich/poor). In most dichotomous thinking, one part of the binary is also more positively valued than the other.

disclosure

When a researcher reveals information about her/himself or the research project, or when research participants reveal information about themselves.

disconfirming case

Example that contradicts or calls into question researchers' interpretations and portrayals of an issue or process.

discourse

There is no fixed meaning for discourse. This term has accrued a number of meanings that are in circulation in both academic and popular cultures. Even amongst cultural theorists, whose ideas human geographers draw upon, discourse is used in differing ways (for example, Mikhail Bakhtin's double-voiced discourse). In this book, discourse is understood in the contexts used by Michel Foucault. To make matters more complex he employed the term in at least three different ways: (i) as written/visual texts or statements that have meaning and effect, (ii) an individual system or group of texts or statements that have meaning, and (iii) a regulated practice of rules and structures that govern particular texts or statements. Particular attention in this book is given to his third definition because it is this rule-governed quality of discourse that is of primary importance to geographers. This definition of discourse evokes how it shapes social practices, impacting upon our actions, attitudes, and perceptions. (See also *discourse analysis*.)

discourse analysis

Method of investigating rules and structures that govern and maintain the production of particular written, oral, or visual *texts*. (See also *discourse*.)

document

In archival research, an individual archived item such as a memorandum or letter that may be handwritten or typed that constitutes a single item or part of a larger file.

discursive structures or formations

A key concept of Foucauldian *discourse analysis*. The rules and structures governing the production of *discourse* that effect the way individuals think, act, and express themselves; for example, through travel, comportment, clothes, make-up.

eclecticism

An approach characterised by extensive borrowing of ideas from different *discourses* and their incorporation into a single argument.

episteme

In the writings of Michel Foucault, episteme refers to the whole sets of discursive structures/formations within which a culture thinks. An episteme refers to the social processes by which certain statements about the world are considered as knowledge and others are dismissed. Episteme therefore requires critically addressing the range of methodologies that a culture employs at a particular time as 'commonsense' to allow certain statements to become knowledge about particular people, events, and places. (See also *discursive structures/formations*.)

epistemology

Ways of knowing the world and justifying belief. (See also *ontology*.)

essentialism

The idea that words (language) have some clear, apparent, and fundamental meaning, rather than being given a meaning by users (readers, writers).

ethics

Refers to the moral conduct of researchers and their responsibilities and obligations to those involved in the research.

ethnography

A research method dependent on direct field observation in which the researcher is involved closely with a social group or neighbourhood. Also an account of events that occur within the life of a group, paying special attention to social structures, behaviour, and the meaning(s) of these for the group.

extreme case sampling

See *deviant case sampling*.

facilitator

The person who encourages or moderates the discussion in a *focus group*. In participatory action research, a person who helps others to learn by guiding an appropriate process, rather than imposing their own agenda, using techniques that enable people's self-reflection and analysis.

faction

A blend of 'fact' and 'fiction'. Usually refers to the tendency to weave interesting imaginary elements (for example, dialogue) into an otherwise factual account.

factoid

A 'fact' that is considered to be of dubious origins or accuracy.

FAQ

Acronym for 'frequently asked question'.

fieldnotes

An accumulated written record of the fieldwork experience. May comprise observations and personal reflections. (Compare with *research diary*.)

fieldwork diary

See *fieldnotes*.

files

A set of archived papers—typically held together by a paperclip—created by an official agency and relating to a common topic or theme. Usually organised in reverse chronological order with the newer material overlaying older documents.

finding aids

Archives equivalent to a library catalogue, typically taking the form of a list of accession of *files* by name as originally organised by creating agencies. Some archives now have computer-based systems that allow material to be located by use of key words.

focus group

A research method involving a small group of between six and ten people discussing a topic or issue defined by a researcher, with the researcher facilitating the discussion.

focused interview

Technique in which an interviewer poses a few predetermined questions but has flexibility in asking follow-up questions.

follow-up questions

Sometimes known as *prompts*, these are questions that permit the interviewer to ask the participant to elaborate on certain elements of an earlier response.

funnelling

Interview question ordering such that the topics covered move from general issues to specific or personal matters. (Compare with *pyramid structure*.)

genealogy

Refers to the ideas of Michel Foucault that question histories of human societies, especially how certain knowledge excludes certain individuals from civil society through, for example, particular portrayals of sexuality, insanity, and illness. To conduct this critique Foucault (1980, p. 50) refers to the term genealogy as an interpretation which can account for the knowledges, discourses, and objects of human societies without reference to the notion of the Cartesian subject; an individual, unified self with agency and control over itself through thought and reason. Instead, of a unified self, Foucault's writing focuses on the processes that he thought were crucial in the constitution of a person's subjectivity.

generalisability

The degree to which research results can be extrapolated to a wider population group than that studied.

geographic information system (GIS)

A generic title for a number of integrated computer tools for the processing and analysing of geographical data, including specialized software for input (digitising) and output (printing or plotting) of mappable data. GIS is not the name of a specific software package.

GIS

See *geographic information system*.

graphic mapping

In *CAQDA*, the graphical representation of concepts, often using nodes and links; conceptual network builders have graphic mapping capacity.

graphics software

Any computer program for the display and manipulation of pictures.

grounded theory

A systematic inductive (data-led) approach to building theory from empirical work in a recursive and reflexive fashion. That is, using a method of identifying themes or trends from the data, then checking through the data (or collecting more), then refining the themes using repeated checks with the data to build theory that is thoroughly 'grounded' in the real world. Initiated by Glaser and Strauss (1967) and reinterpreted and refined greatly since then by these and other authors.

haptical quality

The immediate impact on the senses of a *text*, such as a film.

hegemony

A social condition in which people from all sorts of social backgrounds and classes come to interpret their own interests and consciousness in terms of the *discourse* of the dominant or ruling group. The hegemony of the dominant class is thus based, in part at least, on the (unwitting) consent of the subordinate classes. Such consent is created and reconstituted through the web of social relations, institutions, and public ideas in a society.

hermeneutics

The study of the interpretation of meaning in *texts*: whether there is assumed to be a single dominant meaning, or a multiplicity of meanings.

hierarchical tree building

The system for graphically representing coded and categorised data in a software program such as NUD*IST™.

iconography

The identification and description of symbols and images.

iconology

A search for deep symbolical images that provide a representation of the values of an individual or a group.

image processing

Refers to the digital manipulations to which images are subjected in electronic systems.

inclusionary research

Decolonising research projects that empower marginalised and oppressed peoples, groups, and classes with training and tools that they can use to transform their situations and conditions. (See also *postcolonial research*.)

independent variable

A study item whose characteristics are considered to cause change in a dependent variable. For example, the independent variable rainfall may promote flooding (the *dependent variable*).

induction

Process of generalisation involving the application of specific information to a general situation or to future events. (Compare with *deduction*.)

informant

Person interviewed by a researcher. Some refer to those who are interviewed as 'subjects' or 'respondents'. Others argue that someone who is interviewed, as opposed to simply observed or surveyed, is more appropriately referred to as an informant. That is because an interview informant is likely to have a more active and informed role in the research encounter.

informed consent

Informant/subject agreement to participate in a study having been fully apprised of the conditions associated with that study (for example, time involved, methods of investigation, likely inconveniences, and possible consequences).

informed consent form

See *conditions of use form.*

initial codes

Codes that are pre-determined in some way, usually because they are a prominent theme in the research questions or are inherent in the topic of the research. (See also *descriptive codes.*)

insider

A research position in which the researcher is socially accepted as being 'inside', or a part of, the social groups or places involved in the study. (Compare with *outsider.*)

interpretive codes

Codes that emerge from analysis and interpretation of the data along themes and toward theory generation. (See also *analytic codes.*)

interpretive community

Involves established disciplines with relatively defined and stable areas of interest, theory, and research methods and techniques. Influences researchers' choice of topics and approaches to, and conduct of, study.

intersubjectivity

Meanings and interpretations of the world created, confirmed, or disconfirmed as a result of interactions (language and action) with other people within specific contexts. (See also *subjectivity* and *objectivity.*)

intertextuality

The necessary interdependence of a *text* with those that have preceded it. Any text is built upon and made meaningful by its associations with others.

interview

A means of data collection involving an oral exchange of information between the researcher and one or more other people.

interview guide

A list of topics to be covered in an interview. May contain some clearly worded questions or key concepts intended to guide the interviewer. (Compare with *interview schedule.*)

interview schedule

Ordered list of questions that the researcher intends to ask informants. Questions are worded similarly and are asked in the same order for each informant. In its most rigid form, an interview schedule is a questionnaire delivered in face-to-face format. (Compare with *interview guide.*)

in vivo code

A term from *grounded theory* for a descriptive code that uses the actual phrasing of the subjects for the code's name.

landscape

Landscape is used broadly to mean a built, cultural, or physical environment (and even the human body), which can be 'read' and interpreted.

latent content analysis

Assessment of implicit themes within a text. Latent content may include ideologies, beliefs, or stereotypes. (Compare with *manifest content analysis*.)

latent message

The underlying or implied meanings of data; compare to *manifest message*.

life history

An interview in which data on the experiences and events of a person's life are collected. The aim is to gain insights into how a person's life may have been affected by institutions, social structures, relations, rites of passage, or other significant events. (Compare with *oral history*.)

literature review

Comprehensive critical summary and interpretation of resources (for example, publications, reports) and their relationship to a specific area of research.

manifest content analysis

Assessment of the surface or visible content of text. Visible content may include specific words, phrases, or the physical space dedicated to a theme (for example, column centimetres in a newspaper or time in a video). (Compare with *latent content analysis*.)

manifest message

The plainly visible content of the data; compare to *latent message*.

margin-coding

A simple system of categorising material in transcripts. Typically involves marking the transcript margin with a colour, number, letter, or symbol code to represent key themes or categories.

maximum variation sampling

Form of *sampling* based on high diversity aiming to uncover systematic variations and common patterns within those variations.

memoing

In qualitative software systems: a process whereby the researcher may write memos or reflections on the research process as s/he works and then incorporate these memos as electronic data for further investigation.

Memorandum of Understanding (MoU)

A document specifying the aims, process, roles, responsibilities, and rights of parties involved in a research project. (See also *conditions of use form*.)

metaphor

An expression applied to something to which it is not literally applicable in order to highlight an essential characteristic.

mimetic

Miming or imitating.

mixed methods

A combination of techniques for tackling a research problem; the term is often used specifically to mean a combination of quantitative and qualitative methods.

modality

See *objective modality* and *subjective modality*.

moderator

See *facilitator*.

multiple voices

A reference to the need to listen to alternative literatures, texts, expressions, or opinions, and therefore avoid the assumption that there is only one view of merit.

nominalisation

The transformation of verbs and adjectives into nouns. Nominalisation reduces information available to readers and it mystifies social processes by hiding actions and the identity of actors.

NUD*IST

A software system for qualitative data analysis developed by Richards and Richards at Qualitative Research Solutions in Australia. The acronym stands for Nonnumerical, Unstructured Data: Indexing, Searching, Theorising.

NVivo

A software package to help organise and analyse qualitative data. Allows importing and coding of textual data, text editing, coded data retrieval and review, word and coding pattern searches, and data import/export to quantitative analysis software.

objective/objectivity

Unaffected by feelings, opinions or personal characteristics. Often contrasted with *subjectivity*. (See also *intersubjectivity*.)

objective modality

A form of writing that implicitly hides the writer's presence in the text (for example, third-person narrative form) but which clearly signals agreement with the statement being made. (Compare with *subjective modality*.)

observation

Most literally, purposefully watching worldly phenomena. Increasingly broadened beyond seeing to include apprehending the environment through all our senses (for example, sound, smell) for research purposes.

observer-as-participant

A research situation in which the researcher is primarily able to observe but in so doing is also participating in a social situation. (Compare with *participant-as-observer*.)

ontology

Beliefs about the world. Understanding about the kinds of things that exist in the universe and the relations between them. (See also *epistemology*.)

open questions

Questions in which respondents are able to formulate their own answers, unrestricted by choosing between pre-determined categories. (Compare with *closed questions* and *combination questions*).

opportunistic sampling

Impromptu decision to involve cases or participants in a study on the basis of leads uncovered during fieldwork.

oral history

A prepared *interview* of a particular kind conducted in question-and-answer format with a person who has first-hand knowledge of a subject of interest. (Compare with *life history*.)

oral methods

Verbal techniques, such as *interviews* or *focus groups*, as opposed to written methods for seeking information.

Orientalism

As used by Edward Said (1978), a key postcolonial term (see *postcolonialism*) referring to Western (mis)representations and construction of an imagined Orient in discourses that serve to produce and legitimise imperialism.

orientation questions

Used in *oral history* interviews to establish the participant's background. (Compare with *common questions*, *specific questions,* and *follow-up questions*).

Other

The non-Self, groups and peoples perceived as fundamentally different from one's self and against which a person might compare themselves and establish their own social position, meaning, and identity. Also taken to mean that which is oppositional to the mainstream—marginal or outside the dominant ideology. Initially developed by Simone de Beauvoir in her 1949 book *The Second Sex* to characterise patriarchal representations and subjugation of women, the term was extended by Franz Fanon (1967) and Edward Said (1978) to the cross-cultural representations and relationships that underlie *colonialism*.

outsider

A research position in which the researcher is rendered 'outside' a social circle, or feels 'out of place' on account of differences such as visible appearance, unfamiliarity, or inability to speak the language or vernacular used. (Compare with *insider*.)

panopticon

A circular prison with cells surrounding a central warders' station. In the panopticon, inmates may be observed at any time but they are not aware of the observation.

paradigm

Set of values, beliefs, and practices shared by a community (e.g., members of an academic discipline) that provides a way of understanding the world.

participant

Person taking part in a research project. Usually the *informant*, rather than a member of the research team.

participant checking

Informant's review of the transcript of their contribution to an *interview* or *focus group* for accuracy and meaning. May also involve the informant reviewing the overall research output (for example, thesis, report). Also serves as a means of continuing the involvement of informants in the research process.

participant-as-observer

A research situation in which the researcher is primarily a participant in a social situation or gathering place, but in so doing can maintain sufficient critical distance to observe social dynamics and interactions. (Compare with *observer-as-participant*.)

participant observation

A fieldwork method in which the researcher studies a social group while being a part of that group.

participation

A process in which people play active roles in decision-making and other activities affecting their lives.

participatory diagramming

A technique whereby a group of people, with support from a *facilitator*, collectively produce a visual representation (for example, drawing, diagram, chart, mind-map, sketch) for subsequent analysis using locally appropriate materials (for example, stones, leaves, chalk, ground, pens, paper, whiteboards), criteria, and symbols. Diagrams usually convey relationships between key stakeholders, institutions or resources, sometimes over different time periods. (See also *participatory mapping*.)

participatory mapping

A technique whereby a group of people, with support from a *facilitator*, collectively produce a 'map' for subsequent analysis using locally appropriate materials, criteria, and symbols. Maps usually focus on material aspects of life such as a watershed, a village, a body, or the distribution of particular resources within a particular area. (See also *participatory diagramming*.)

pastiche

A *text* that is a medley drawn from various sources.

'pencil only' rule

A typical archival convention to ensure the protection of file materials, it requires that researchers make notes in pencil only. This is rendered somewhat redundant by the increasing use of personal computers.

personal log

Recorded reflections on the practice of an *interview*. Includes discussions of the appropriateness of the order and phrasing of questions, and of the *informant* selection. Also contains assessments of matters such as research design and ethical issues. (See also *analytical log*.)

pilot study

Abbreviated version of a research project in which the researcher practices or tests procedures to be used in a subsequent full-scale project.

plagiarism

Failure to acknowledge the source of ideas, illustrations, or text. In the worst cases, sections of text are lifted verbatim and reproduced, without quotation marks, as if the author's own. In many universities, plagiarised work—which is often easy to spot—automatically fails.

population

The larger group from which a *sample* has been selected for inclusion in a study. In quantitative research, based on *probability* (random) *sampling*, it is assumed that the sample has been selected such that the mathematical probability of sample characteristics being reproduced in this broader population can be calculated. In qualitative research, where *purposive sampling* is used, no such assumption is made

postcolonial research

Research that rejects imperialism and the goals, attitudes, representations, and methods of imposed, 'colonial' research and instead seeks to conduct research that is welcomed and that fosters egalitarian relationships and openness, values local knowledge and ways of knowing, and contributes to self-determination and locally defined welfare. (See also *decolonising research* and *inclusionary research*. Contrast with *colonial research*.)

postcolonialism

An approach to knowledge that seeks to represent voices of the *'other'*, especially colonised peoples and women, and to recognise knowledge that has been ignored through processes of colonisation and patriarchy.

positionality

A researcher's social, locational, and ideological placement relative to the research project or to other participants in it. May be influenced by biographical characteristics such as class, race, and gender, as well as various formative experiences.

positivism

An approach to scientific knowledge based around foundational statements about what constitutes truth and legitimate ways of knowing. There are a number of variants of positivist thought but central to all is the construction of a singular universal and value-free knowledge based on empirical observation and the scientific method.

postmodernism

A movement in the humanities and social sciences that includes *postcolonialism* and which embraces the pluralism of multiple perspectives, knowledges, and voices rather than the grand theories of modernism. Individual interpretation is considered partial because it is to some degree socially contingent and constituted.

poststructuralism

A school of thought that endeavours to link language, subjectivity, social organisation, and power.

potentially exploitative power relation

A research situation in which the researcher is in a position of power relative to the research participant. (See also *asymmetrical power relation* and *reciprocal power relation*.)

power

In Foucauldian discourse analysis, power is central to thinking about *discourse* as something that has an impact. It is through power that the elements of discourse have effects on what people do, think, and how they express themselves. Yet, power is not conceptualised in terms of acting upon people in an oppressive way. Rather, the individual is seen as an effect of power. That is, power makes things possible as well as restricting possible actions and attitudes. These possibilities are instances of power/knowledge relationships. (See also *power/knowledge*.)

power/knowledge

A key concept of Foucauldian discourse analysis. Foucault argues that the relationship between power and knowledge is essential to thinking about the effects of *discourse*. He argues that statements that are accepted as knowledge are themselves the outcome of power struggles. For example, what has constituted geographical knowledge in universities has been a constant struggle over different versions of what constituted space/place.

PowerPoint

Proprietary presentation graphics software, originally designed for business presentations, that has been widely adopted in classrooms and the academy. Be aware that its use risks promoting style over substance, and that audiences can generally spot this very easily.

preliminary meeting

In *oral history*, a first meeting between interviewer and *respondent* designed to establish rapport, clarify ethical responsibilities and rights, explore the parameters of the pending interview/s, and work through other matters of mutual interest or concern; an important step for both parties after which additional preparations may be made for interview.

pre-testing

See *pilot study*.

primary observation

Research in which the investigator is a participant in, and interpreter of, human activity involving her/his own experience. (Compare with *secondary observation*.)

primary question

Interview question used to initiate discussion of a new topic or theme. (Compare with *probe question*.)

probability sampling

Sampling technique intended to ensure a random and statistically representative *sample* that will allow confident generalisation to the larger *population* from which the sample was drawn. (Compare with *purposive sampling*).

probe question

A gesture or follow-up question used in an interview to explore further a theme or topic already being discussed. (See also *prompt*. Compare with *primary question*.)

prompt

A follow-up question in an *interview* designed to deepen a response (for example, 'why do you say that?'; 'what do you mean?'.) (See also *probe question*. Compare with *primary question*.)

provenance

Organisational principle for *archives* that stresses the importance of the original internal arrangement of a collection of *files* and the order of information in files as devised by their creating agencies as a means of understanding past events.

purposive sampling

Sampling procedure intended to obtain a particular group for study on the basis of specific characteristics they possess. (Compare with *probability sampling*.) Aims to uncover information-rich phenomena/participants that can shed light on issues of central importance to the study.

purposeful sampling

See *purposive sampling*.

pyramid structure

Order of interview questions in which easy-to-answer questions are posed at the beginning of the interview while deeper or more philosophical questions/issues are raised at the end. (Compare with *funnelling*.)

quantitative methods

Statistical and mathematical modelling approaches used to understand social and physical relationships.

quota sampling

Selecting sampling elements on the basis of categories known or assumed to exist in the universal population.

random sampling

See *probability sampling*.

rapport

A productive interpersonal climate between informant and researcher. A relationship that allows the informant to feel comfortable or confident enough to offer comprehensive answers to questions.

reactive effects

The influence a research method or researcher has on the individuals or phenomena under observation.

reciprocal power relation

A research situation in which researcher and *informant* are in comparable social positions and experience relatively equal costs and benefits of participating in the research. (See also *asymmetrical power relation* and *potentially exploitative power relation*.)

records

A generic term for files, maps, plans, and other documents held in an *archive*.

recruitment

The process of finding people willing to participate in a research project. Recruitment strategies can range from asking people 'on the street' (perhaps to fill in a questionnaire) to inviting key individuals to participate (in a focus group, for example).

reflexivity

Self-critical introspection and a self-conscious scrutiny of oneself as a researcher. (See also *action–reflection*.)

regime of truth

A key concept of Foucauldian discourse analysis. Foucault argues that within a particular time and society there is a predisposition to particular statements that become accepted as truths or commonsense. Foucault stressed that these statements must be examined with these social circumstances. It is this social-cultural context that both gives texts their sense and makes them compelling. (See also *discourse* and *discourse analysis*.)

relativism

An approach to knowledge in which it is held that there is no means for significantly differentiating between the merits of arguments. Suggests that there are no absolute, unequivocal standards of true/false or right/wrong.

reliability

Extent to which a method of data collection yields consistent and reproducible results when used in similar circumstances by different researchers or at different times. (See also *validity*.)

replicability

Able to be repeated or tested to see how general the particular findings of a study are in the wider *population*.

representation

The way in which something (the world, human behaviour, a city, the landscape) is depicted, recognising that this cannot be an exact depiction. An important insight from poststructuralist thinkers is that representations not only describe the social world but also help to shape or constitute it.

research diary

A place for recording observations in the process of being reflexive. Contains thoughts and ideas about the research process, its social context, and the researcher's role in it. The contents of a research diary are different to those of the fieldnotes, which more typically contain qualitative data, such as records of observations, conversations, and sketch maps.

respondent

See *informant*.

rigour

Accuracy, exactitude, and trustworthiness.

sample

Phenomena or participants selected from a larger set of phenomena or a larger *population* for inclusion in a study.

sampling

Means of selecting phenomena or participants for inclusion in a study. A key difference between qualitative and quantitative inquiry is in the logic underpinning their use of *purposive* and *probability* (random) *sampling* respectively.

sampling frame

A list or register (for example, electoral roll, phone directory) from which respondents for a questionnaire are drawn.

saturation

The point in the data gathering process when no new information or insights are being generated. This is one method used by researchers to determine when to stop gathering data.

secondary data

Information collected by people/agencies and stored for purposes other than for the research project for which they are being used (for example, census data being used in an analysis of socio-economic status and water consumption).

secondary observation

Research in which the data are the observations of others (for example, photographs).

secondary question

Interview prompts that encourage the informant to follow up or expand on an issue already discussed. See also *follow-up questions*.

semiology

See *semiotics*.

semiotics

The system or language of signs (sometimes referred to as semiology). (See also *signifier* and *signified*.)

semi-structured interview

Interview with some predetermined order, but which nonetheless has flexibility with regard to the position/timing of questions. Some questions, particularly sensitive or complex ones, may have a standard wording for each *informant*. (Compare with *structured interview* and *unstructured interview*.)

sign

Written or other image/mark that represents something else. Comprises *signifier* and *signified*.

signified

The meaning derived from a *signifier* (or from a set of signifiers, such as a text).

signifier

Images such as written marks, or features of the landscape with which meaning is associated.

situated knowledge

A metaphor that evokes recognition of the positionality (or contextual nature) of knowledges. The inscription and creation of knowledge is always partial and 'located' somewhere.

snowball sampling

A sampling technique that involves finding participants for a research project by asking existing informants to recommend others who might be interested. From one or two participants the number of people involved in the project 'snowballs'. Also known as chain sampling.

social structure

See *structure*.

sound document

The outcome and output from an *oral history* interview.

specific questions

These relate to interviewees' individual experiences and are developed through follow-up work. (Compare with *orientation questions, common questions,* and *follow-up questions*).

staging

A theatrical metaphor for writing-in research that encourages geographical researchers to consider how the construction of a research text is actually a form of cultural production. The author of the text is a creator, director, and performer in the particular narrative he or she is constructing.

stakeholder

Any individual or group that has an interest in a project because of how it may benefit, harm, or exclude them.

standardised questions

A uniform set of questions that are repeated for all *interviews* or *focus groups* in a research project, contrasting with spontaneous questions that develop out of the conversational flow of an interview or focus group.

structure

A structure is a functioning system (for example, social, economic, or political) within which individuals are located, within which all events are enacted, and which are reproduced and transformed by those events.

structured interview

Interview that follows a strict order of topics. Usually the order is set out in an *interview schedule*. The wording of questions for each interview may also be predetermined. (Compare with *unstructured interview* and *semi-structured interview*.)

subaltern

Oppressed, exploited, marginalised minority peoples and groups. The term derives from the work of Antonio Gramsci and from the 'subaltern studies' project undertaken by Indian historians since the early 1980s that endeavoured to write history from 'below', but is often used in a wider sense.

subject

See *informant*.

subjective/subjectivity

Refers to the insertion of the personal resources, opinions, and characteristics of a person into a research project. Often contrasted with objectivity. (See also *intersubjectivity*.)

subjective modality

A form of writing that explicitly acknowledges the writer's presence in the text (e.g., first-person narrative form) and clearly signals their agreement or disagreement with the statement being made. (Compare with *objective modality*.)

text

Traditionally synonymous with the written page, but now used more broadly to refer to a range of source forms including oral texts (including semi-structured interviews and oral histories), images (including painting, photographs, and maps) as well as written and print texts (including newspapers, letters, and brochures).

text based managers

Software with capacity for managing and organising data, creating subsets of data for further analysis, and searching and retrieving combinations of words, phrases, coded segments, memos or other material. Examples include askSam, FolioVIEWS and MAXqda.

text retriever software

Computer program for recovering data by category on the basis of keywords that appear in the data; for finding words, phrases, or other character strings; and for finding things that are misspelt, sound alike, mean the same thing, or have certain patterns. Examples include Metamorph, The Text Collector, WordCruncher, ZyINDEX, and Sonar Professional.

textual analysis

Reading and constant reinterpretation of texts as a set of *signs* or signifying practices.

textual community

Group of individuals who share certain understandings of the meaning of texts.

theme

In *coding*, an important process, commonality, characteristic, or theory that emerges from the data and can be used to analyse and abstract the data.

theory building software

Computer programs that deal with relationships between data categories to develop higher-order classifications and categories, and to formulate and test propositions or assertions. Examples include AQUAD, ATLAS/ti, HyperRESEARCH, and N6.

transcript

Written record of speech (for example, interview, focus group proceedings, film dialogue). May also include textual description of informant gestures and tone.

transferability

Extent to which the results of a study might apply to contexts other than that of the research study.

transformative reflexivity

A process through which a researcher and researched group reflect on their (mis)understandings and negotiate the meanings of the information generated together. The shared process has the potential to transform each person's own understandings.

triangulation

Use of multiple or mixed methods, researchers, and information sources to confirm or corroborate results.

trope

Figure of speech that allows writers or producers of other forms of *text* to say one thing but mean something else. May involve use of metaphor or metonymy.

typical case sampling

Selection of samples that illustrate or highlight that which is considered typical or normal.

uncontrolled observation

Purposeful watching of worldly phenomena that is relatively unconstrained by restrictions of scope, style, and time. (Compare with *controlled observation*.)

unstructured interview

Interview in which there is no predetermined order to the issues addressed. The researcher phrases and raises questions in a manner appropriate to the informants' previous comment. The direction and vernacular of the interview is informant driven. (Compare with *structured interview* and *semi-structured interview*.)

validity

The truthfulness or accuracy of data compared with acceptable criteria. (See also *reliability*.)

vernacular

Occurring in the location where it originated. Vernacular language is the language of a place.

warm-up

A set of pre-interview techniques intended to enhance rapport between interviewer and *informant*. May include small talk, sharing food, or relaxed discussion of the research.

word processing

A generic concept which includes the use of computer capacity to create, edit, and print documents.

word searching

The process of looking for individual words in an electronic text.

writing-IN

The active and situated process of writing in which the author engages with the ways in which meanings are constructed through the creation of his/her text.

References

Abraham, F. 1982, *Modern Sociological Theory: An Introduction,* Oxford University Press, New Delhi.

Adelman, C. (ed.) 1981, *Uttering, Muttering: Collecting, Using and Reporting Talk for Social and Educational Research,* Grant McIntyre, London.

Agar, M. 1986, *Speaking of Ethnography,* Sage, Beverly Hills.

Agar, M. and MacDonald, J. 1995, 'Focus groups and ethnography', *Human Organization,* vol. 54, no. 1, pp. 78–86.

Agius, P., Davies, J., Howitt, R., Jarvis, S. and Williams, R. 2004, 'Comprehensive Native Title Negotiations in South Australia', in M. Langton, M. Teehan, L. Palmer and K. Shain (eds), *Honour Among Nations? Treaties and Agreements with Indigenous People,* Melbourne University Press, Melbourne.

Agius, P., Howitt, R. and Jarvis, S. 2003, *Different visions, different ways: lessons and challenges from the native title negotiations in South Australia,* Paper presented to the Native Title Conference, Alice Springs, June 2003.

Aitken, S. C. and Zonn, L. E. 1993, 'Weir(d) sex: representation of gender–environment relations in Peter Weir's *Picnic at Hanging Rock* and *Gallipoli*', *Environment and Planning D: Society and Space,* vol. 11, no. 2, pp. 191–212.

Alder, P. A. and Alder, P. 1994, 'Observational techniques', in N. K. Denzin and Y. S. Lincoln (eds), *Handbook of Qualitative Research,* Sage, Thousand Oaks.

Alvermann, D. E., O'Brien, D. G. and Dillon, D. R. 1996, 'On writing qualitative research', *Reading Research Quarterly,* vol. 31, pp. 114–20.

American Historical Association 2003, *Statement on Standards of Professional Conduct* (online), Available: <http://www.historians.org/PUBS/Free/ProfessionalStandards.htm> (Accessed: 10 September 2004).

Anderson, K. J. 1999, 'Reflections on Redfern', in E. Stratford (ed.), *Australian Cultural Geographies,* Oxford University Press, Melbourne.

—— 1995, 'Culture and nature at the Adelaide Zoo: at the frontiers of "human" geography', *Transactions of the Institute of British Geographers,* vol. 20, no. 3, pp. 275–94.

—— 1993, 'Place narratives and the origins of inner Sydney's Aboriginal settlement, 1972–73', *Journal of Historical Geography,* vol. 19, no. 3, pp. 314–35.

Anderson, K. J. and Gale, F. (eds) 1992, *Inventing Places: Studies in Cultural Geography,* Longman Cheshire, Melbourne.

Anfara, V. A., Brown, K. M. and Mangione, T. L. 2002, 'Qualitative analysis on stage: making the research process more public', *Educational Researcher,* vol. 31, no. 7 (October), pp. 28–38.

Anzaldúa, G. 1987, *Borderlands/La Frontera: The New Mestiza,* Spinsters/Aunt Lute Press, San Francisco.

Askew, L and McGuirk, P. M. 2004. 'Watering the suburbs: distinction, conformity and the suburban garden', *Australian Geographer*, vol. 35, pp 17–37.

Atkinson, P. and Hammersley, M. 1984, 'Ethnography and participant observation', in N. K. Denzin and Y. S. Lincoln (eds), *Handbook of Qualitative Research*, Sage, Thousand Oaks.

Ayres, L. 1997, Defining and Managing Family Caregiving in Chronic Illness: Expectations, Explanations and Strategies, PhD thesis, University of Illinois at Chicago.

Babbie, E. 2001, *The Practice of Social Research,* 9th edn, Wadsworth, Belmont, CA.

—— 1998, *The Practice of Social Research,* 8th edn, Wadsworth, Belmont, CA.

—— 1992, *The Practice of Social Research,* 6th edn, Wadsworth, Belmont, CA.

Bailey, C. 2001, 'Geographers doing household research: intrusive research and moral accountability', *Area*, vol. 33, no. 1, pp. 107–10.

Bailey, C., White, C. and Pain, R. 1999a, 'Evaluating qualitative research: dealing with the tension between "science" and "creativity"', *Area*, vol. 31, no. 2, pp. 169–83.

—— 1999b, 'Response', *Area*, vol. 31, no. 2, pp. 183–4.

Baker, A. R. H. 2003, *Geography and History, Bridging the Divide,* Cambridge University Press, Cambridge.

—— 1997, 'The dead don't answer questionnaires: researching and writing historical geography', *Journal of Geography in Higher Education*, vol. 21, no. 2, pp. 231–43.

Banks, M. 2001, *Visual Methods in Social Research*, Sage Publications, London.

Barnes, T. J. 1993, 'Whatever happened to the philosophy of science?', *Environment and Planning A*, vol. 25, pp. 301–4.

—— 1989, 'Place, space and theories of economic value: Contextualism and essentialism', *Transactions of the Institute of British Geographers*, NS 14, pp. 299–316.

Barnes, T. J. and Duncan, J. 1992, 'Introduction: writing worlds', in T. J. Barnes and J. Duncan (eds) *Writing worlds: discourse, text and metaphor in the representation of landscape,* Routledge, London.

Barnes, T. J. and Gregory, D. 1997, 'Worlding geography: geography as situated knowledge', in T. J. Barnes and D. Gregory (eds), *Reading Human Geography: the poetics and politics of inquiry*, Arnold, London.

Barret, M. 1991, *The Politics of Truth: From Marx to Foucault*, Polity Press, Cambridge.

Barry, C. 1998, 'Choosing Qualitative Data Analysis Software: Atlas/ti and Nudist Compared', *Sociological Research Online*, vol. 3, no. 3, Available: <http://www.socresonline.org.uk/3/3/4.html> (Accessed: 2 November 2004).

Barthes, R. 1973, *Mythologies*, translated by A. Lavers, Paladin, London.

Baxter, J. 1998, Exploring the Meaning of Risk and Uncertainty in an Environmentally Sensitized Community, PhD thesis, Department of Geography, McMaster University, Ontario.

Baxter, J. and Eyles, J. 1999a, 'The utility of in-depth interviews for studying the meaning of environmental risk', *Professional Geographer*, vol. 51, no. 2, pp. 307–20.

—— 1999b, 'Prescription for research practice? Grounded theory in qualitative evaluation', *Area*, vol. 31, no. 2, pp. 179–81.

—— 1997, 'Evaluating qualitative research in social geography: establishing "rigour" in interview analysis', *Transactions of the Institute of British Geographers*, vol. 22, no. 4, pp. 505–25.

Bazely, P. 1997, 'NUD*IST 4: —— Survey research: How do I set up data input for a survey to link structured responses (e.g. in SPSS) with qualitative data in NUD.IST 4?', *User Support Notes*, Available: <http://kerlins.net/bobbi/research/nudist/resources/bazeley1.html> (Accessed: 4 February 2005).

Becker, H. S. 1986, *Writing for Social Scientists. How to Start and Finish Your Thesis, Book, or Article*, University of Chicago Press, Chicago.

Bedford, T. and Burgess, J. 2002, 'The focus-group experience', in M. Limb and C. Dwyer (eds), *Qualitative Methodologies for Geographers: Issues and Debates*, Edward Arnold, London.

Bell, D. 1991, 'Art and land in New Zealand', *New Zealand Journal of Geography*, vol. 92, pp. 15–17.

Bell, D. and Binnie, J. 2000, *The Sexual Citizen: Queer Politics and Beyond*, Polity Press, Cambridge.

Bell, D., Binnie, J., Cream, J. and Valentine, G. 1994, 'All hyped up and no place to go', *Gender Place and Culture*, vol. 1, no. 1, pp. 31–48.

Bell, D., Caplan, P. and Karim, W. J. 1993, *Gendered Fields: Women, Men and Ethnography*, Routledge, London.

Bennett, K. 2002, 'Interviews and focus groups', in P. Shurmer-Smith (ed.), *Doing Cultural Geography*, Sage, London.

Berg, B. L. 1989, *Qualitative Research Methods for the Social Sciences*, Allyn & Bacon, Boston.

Berg, L. D. 2004, 'Scaling knowledge: towards a critical geography of critical geography', *GeoForum*, vol. 35, no. 5, pp. 553–8.

—— 2001, 'Masculinism, emplacement and positionality in peer review', *The Professional Geographer*, vol. 53, no. 4, pp. 511–21.

—— 1997, *Banal geographies*, Paper presented to the Inaugural International Conference of Critical Geographers, Vancouver, Canada, 10–13 August 1997.

—— 1994a, 'Masculinity, place, and a binary discourse of theory and empirical investigation in the human geography of Aotearoa/New Zealand', *Gender, Place and Culture,* vol. 1, no. 2, pp. 245–60.

—— 1994b, 'Masculinism, power and discourses of exclusion in Brian Berry's "Scientific" Geography", *Urban Geography*, vol. 15, pp. 279–87.

—— 1993, 'Between modernism and postmodernism', *Progress in Human Geography*, vol. 17, pp. 490–507.

Berg, L. D. and Kearns, R. A. 1998, 'America Unlimited', *Environment and Planning D: Society and Space*, vol. 16, pp. 128–32.

Berg, L. and Mansvelt, J. 2000, 'Writing in, speaking out: communicating qualitative research findings', in I. Hay (ed.), *Qualitative Research Methods in Human Geography*, Oxford University Press, Melbourne.

Berger, T. R. 1991, *A Long and Terrible Shadow: White Values, Native Rights in the Americas*, Douglas & McIntyre and University of Washington Press, Vancouver and Seattle.

Bernard, H. R. 1988, *Research Methods in Cultural Anthropology*, Sage, Newbury Park.

Berreman, G.D. 1972, *Hindus of the Himalayas: Ethnography and Change*, 2nd edn, University of California Press, Berkeley.

Bertrand, J. T., Brown, J. E. and Ward, V. M. 1992, 'Techniques for analyzing focus group data', *Evaluation Review*, vol. 16, no. 2, pp. 198–209.

Billinge, M., Gregory, D. and Martin, R. 1984, 'Reconstructions', in M. Billinge, D. Gregory and R. L. Martin (eds), *Recollections of a Revolution: Geography as Spatial Science*, Macmillan, London.

Bingley, A. 2002, 'Research ethics in practice', in L. Bondi et al. (eds), *Subjectivities, Knowledges and Feminist Geographies: The Subjects and Ethics of Research*, Rowman & Littlefield, London.

Binnie, J. and Valentine, G. 1999, 'Geographies of sexuality—a review of progress', *Progress in Human Geography*, vol. 23, pp. 176–87.

Bishop, P. 2002, 'Gathering the land: the Alice Springs to Darwin rail corridor', *Environment and Planning D: Society and Space*, vol. 20, pp. 295–317.

Blaikie, P. and Brookfield, H. 1987, *Land Degradation and Society*, Methuen, London.

Blake, K. 2001, 'In search of Navajo sacred geography', *The Geographical Review*, vol. 91, no. 4, pp. 715–24.

Blumen, O. 2002, 'Criss-crossing boundaries: ultraorthodox Jewish women go to work', *Gender, Place and Culture*, vol. 9, no. 2, pp. 133–51.

Blunt, A. 2003, 'Home and identity', in A. Blunt, P. Gruffudd, J. May, M. Ogborn and D. Pinder (eds), *Cultural Geography in Practice*, Arnold, Euston.

Bogdan, R. 1974, *Being Different: The Autobiography of Jane Frey*, Wiley, London.

Bogdan, R. C. and Biklen, S. K. 1992, *Qualitative Research for Education: An Introduction to Theory and Methods*, 2nd edn, Allyn & Bacon, Boston.

Bondi, L. 1997, 'In whose words? On gender identities, knowledge and writing practices', *Transactions of the Institute of British Geographers*, vol. 22, pp. 245–58.

Bonnet, A. 1996, 'Constructions of "race", place and discipline: geographies of "racial" identity and racism', *Ethnic and Racial Studies*, vol. 19, no. 4, pp. 864–83.

Bordo, S. 1986, 'The Cartesian masculinization of thought', *Signs*, vol. 11, pp. 439–56.

Botes, L. and van Rensburg, D. 2000, 'Community participation in development: nine plagues and twelve commandments', *Community Development Journal*, vol. 35. no. 1, pp. 53–4.

Bouma, G. D. 1996, *The Research Process*, 3rd edn, Oxford University Press, New York.

—— 1993, *The Research Process*, rev. edn, Oxford University Press, New York.

Bowes, A. 1996, 'Evaluating and empowering research strategy: reflections on action-research with South Asian women', *Sociological Research Online*, vol. 1, no. 1, Available: <http://www.socresonline.org.uk/1/1/1.html#top>, (Accessed: 23 September 2004).

Boyle, M. and Rogerson, R. 2001, 'Power, discourse and city trajectories', in R. Paddison (ed.), *Handbook of Urban Studies*, Sage, London.

Boyle, P. 1997, 'Writing up—some suggestions', in R. Flowerdew and D. Martin (eds), *Methods in Human Geography. A Guide to Students Doing a Research Project*, Addison Wesley Longman, Harlow.

Brannen, J. (ed.) 1992a, *Mixing Methods: Qualitative and Quantitative Research*, Avebury, Aldershot, USA.

—— 1992b, 'Combining qualitative and quantitative approaches: an overview', in J. Brannen (ed.), *Mixing Methods: Qualitative and Quantitative Research*, Avebury, Aldershot, USA.

Bridge, G. and Dowling, R. 2001, 'Microgeographies of retailing and gentrification', *Australian Geographer*, vol. 32, no. 1, pp. 93–107.

Brockington, D. and Sullivan S. 2003, 'Qualitative research', in R. Scheyvens and D. Storey (eds), *Development Fieldwork: A Practical Guide*, Sage, London.

Bryant, R. and Bailey, S. 1997, *Third World Political Ecology*, Routledge, New York.

Bryman, A. 1984, 'The debate about quantitative and qualitative research: a question of method or epistemology?', *The British Journal of Sociology*, vol. 35, pp. 75–92.

Bryman, A. and Burgess, R. G. (eds) 1994, *Analyzing Qualitative Data*, Routledge, London.

Burawoy, M., Burton, A., Ferguson, A., Fox, K., Gamson, J., Gartrell, N., Hurst, L., Kurzman, C., Salzinger, L., Schiffman, J. and Ui, S. 1991, *Ethnography unbound: power and resistance in the modern metropolis*, University of California Press, Berkeley.

Burgess, J. 1996, 'Focusing on fear: The use of focus groups in a project for the Community Forest Unit, Countryside Commission', *Area*, vol. 28. no. 2, pp. 130–5.

—— 1988, 'Exploring environmental values through the medium of small groups: 2. Illustrations of a group at work', *Environment and Planning A*, vol. 20, no. 4, pp. 457–76.

Burgess, J., Limb, C. and Harrison, C. M. 1988, 'Exploring environmental values through the medium of small groups: 1. Theory and practice', *Environment and Planning A*, vol. 20, no. 3, pp. 309–26.

Burgess, J. and Wood, P. 1988, 'Decoding docklands: place advertising and the decision-making strategies of the small firm', in J. Eyles and D. M. Smith (eds), *Qualitative Methods in Human Geography*, Polity Press, Cambridge.

Burgess, R. G. 1996, (ed.) *Studies in Qualitative Methodology: Computing and Qualitative Research*, vol. 5, JAI Press, London.

—— 1982a, 'Elements of sampling in field research', in R. G. Burgess (ed.), *Field Research: A Sourcebook and Field Manual*, George Allen & Unwin, London.

—— 1982b, 'Multiple strategies in field research', in R. G. Burgess (ed.), *Field Research: A Sourcebook and Field Manual*, George Allen & Unwin, London.

—— 1982c, 'The unstructured interview as a conversation', in R. G. Burgess (ed.), *Field Research: A Sourcebook and Field Manual*, George Allen & Unwin, London.

Burman, E. and Parker, I. 1993, 'Against discursive imperialism, empiricism and constructionism: thirty-two problems with discourse analysis', in E. Burman and I. Parker (eds), *Discourse Analytic Research: Repertoires and Readings of Texts in Action*, Routledge, London.

Burton, R. F. 1886, *The Arabian Nights*, Benares Edition, London.

Buston, K. 1997, 'NUD*IST in Action: Its Use and its Usefulness in a Study of Chronic Illness in Young People', *Sociological Research Online*, vol. 2, no. 3, Available: <http://www.socreson-line.org.uk/welcome.html>, (Accessed: 23 September 2004).

Butler, R. 1997, 'Stories and experiments in social inquiry', *Organisation Studies*, vol. 18, no. 6, pp. 927–48.

Cameron, J. 1992, Modern-Day Tales of Illegitimacy: Class, Gender and Ex-Nuptial Fertility, MA Minor Thesis, Department of Geography, University of Sydney.

Cameron, J. and Gibson, K. 2004 [in press], 'Participatory action research in a poststructuralist vein', *Geoforum*, vol. 35.

Cameron, L. 2001, 'Oral history and the Freud archives: incidents, ethics and relations', *Historical Geography*, vol. 29, pp. 38–44.

Carey, M. A. 1994, 'The group effect in focus groups: Planning, implementing and interpreting focus group research', in J. M. Morse (ed.), *Critical Issues in Qualitative Research Methods*, Sage, Thousand Oaks.

Carroll, J. and Connell, J. 2000, '"You gotta love this city": The Whitlams and inner Sydney', *Australian Geographer*, vol. 31, no. 2, pp. 141–54.

Casey, M. J., Wyatt, G., Rager, A., Arnevik, C., Pfarr, D., Anderson, J., Everett, L. and Busman, L. 1996, *Addressing Nonpoint Source Agricultural Pollution in the Minnesota River Basin: Findings from Focus Groups Conducted with Farmers, Agency Staff, Crop Consultants and Researchers, December 1995*, Study Conducted for the Minnesota Department of Agriculture (online), Available: <http://www.soils.umn.edu/research/mn-river/doc/fgrptweb.html>, (Accessed: 4 January 2005).

Cavendish, A. P. 1964, 'Early Greek philosophy', in D. J. O'Connor (ed.), *A Critical History of Western Philosophy*, The Free Press, New York.

Ceglowski, D. 1997, 'That's a good story, but is it really research?', *Qualitative Inquiry*, vol. 3, no. 2, pp. 188–99.

Chakrabarti, R. 2004, Constrained spaces of prenatal care: South Asian women in New York City, Unpublished research proposal, Department of Geography, University of Illinois at Urbana-Champaign.

Chambers, R. 1994, 'The origins and practice of participatory rural appraisal', *World Development*, vol. 22, no. 7, pp. 953–69.

Charmaz, K. 2000, 'Grounded theory: objectivist and constructivist methods', in N. K. Denzin, and Y. S. Lincoln, *Handbook of Qualitative Research*, 2nd edn, Sage Publications, Thousand Oaks, CA.

Clarke, G. 2001, 'From ethnocide to ethnodevelopment? Ethnic minorities and indigenous peoples in Southeast Asia', *Third World Quarterly*, vol. 22, no. 3, pp. 413–36.

Clifford, N. and Valentine, G. (eds) 2003, *Key Methods in Geography*, Sage, London.

Cloke, P., Cook, I., Crang, P., Goodwin, M., Painter, J. and Philo, C. (eds) 2004, 'Talking to people', in *Practising Human Geography*, Sage, London.

Cloke, P., Cooke, P., Cursons, J., Milbourne, P. and Widdowfield, R. 2000, 'Ethics, reflexivity and research: encounters with homeless people', *Ethics, Place and Environment*, vol. 3, no. 2, pp. 133–54.

Coffey, A. and Atkinson, P. 1996, *Making Sense of Qualitative Data, Complementary Research Strategies*, Sage, Thousand Oaks.

Collins, D. and Kearns, R. 1998, *Avoiding the Log-jam: Exotic Forestry, Transport and Health in Hokianga*, Working Paper No. 8, Department of Geography, The University of Auckland.

Connell, R. W. 1991, 'Live fast and die young: the construction of masculinity among young working-class men on the margin of the labour market', *Australia and New Zealand Journal of Sociology*, vol. 27, no. 2, pp. 141–71.

Cook, I. 2000, '"Nothing can ever be the case of 'us' and 'them' again": exploring the politics of difference through border pedagogy and student journal writing', *Journal of Geography in Higher Education*, vol. 24, no. 1, pp. 13–27.

—— 1997, 'Participant observation', in R. Flowerdew and D. Martin (eds), *Methods in Human Geography*, Addison Wesley Longman, Harlow.

Cooke, B. 2001, 'The social psychological limits of participation?', in B. Cooke and U. Kothari (eds), *Participation: The New Tyranny?*, Zed Books, London.

Cooke, B. and Kothari, U. 2001, 'The case for participation as tyranny', in B. Cooke and U. Kothari (eds), *Participation: The New Tyranny?*, Zed Books, London.

Coombs, H. C. 1978, *Kulinma: Listening to Aboriginal Australians*, Australian National University Press, Canberra.

Coombs, H. C., McCann, H., Ross, H. and Williams, N. M. 1989, *Land of Promises: Aborigines and development in the East Kimberley*, Centre for Environmental Studies, ANU and Aboriginal Studies Press, Canberra.

Cooper, A. 1995, 'Adolescent dilemmas of landscape, place and religious experience in a Suffolk parish', *Environment and Planning D: Society and Space*, vol. 13, pp. 349–63.

—— 1994, 'Negotiating dilemmas of landscape, place and Christian commitment in a Suffolk parish', *Transactions of the Institute of British Geographers*, vol. 19, pp. 202–12.

Cooper, D. and Herman, D. 1995 'Getting the family right', in D. Herman and C. Stychin (eds), *Legal Inversions: Lesbians, Gay Men, and the Politics of Law*, Temple University Press, Philadelphia, pp. 142–62.

Cope, M. 2003, 'Coding qualitative data', in Clifford, N. and G. Valentine (eds), *Key Methods in Geography*, Sage Publications, Thousand Oaks, CA.

Cornwall, A. and Jewkes, R. 1995, 'What is participatory research?', *Social Science and Medicine*, vol. 41, pp. 1667–76.

Costello, L. and Hodge, S. 1998, 'Queer/Clear/Here: Destabilising Sexualities and Spaces', in Stratford, E. (ed.), *Australian Cultural Geographies*, Oxford University Press, Melbourne, pp. 131–52.

Cousins, M. and Houssain, A. 1984, *Michel Foucault*, Macmillan, Basingstoke.

Cox, K. R. 1981, 'Bourgeoise thought and the behavioural geography debate', in R. K. Cox and R. G. Golledge (eds), *Behavioural Problems in Geography Revisited*, Methuen, New York.

Crang, M. 2003, 'Qualitative methods: touchy, feely, look-see?', *Progress in Human Geography*, vol. 27, no. 4, pp. 494–504.

—— 1997a, 'Analyzing qualitative materials', in R. Flowerdew and D. Martin (eds), *Methods in Human Geography: A Guide for Students Doing Research*, Addison Wesley Longman, Harlow, pp. 183–96.

—— 1997b, 'Picturing practices: research through the tourist gaze', *Progress in Human Geography*, vol. 21, pp. 359–73.

Crang, M., Hudson, A., Reimer, S. and Hinchliffe, S. 1997, 'Software for qualitative research: 1. Prospectus and overview', *Environment and Planning A*, vol. 29, no. 5, pp. 771–87.

Crang, P. 1996, 'It's showtime: on the workplace geographies of display in a restaurant in southeast England', *Environment and Planning D: Society and Space*, vol. 12, pp. 675–704.

Cresswell T. 1999, 'Embodiment, power and the politics of mobility: the case of female tramps and hobos', *Transactions of the Institute of British Geographers*, vol. 24, no. 2, pp. 175–92.

Crush, J. 1993, 'Post-colonialism, de-colonization, and geography', in A. Godlewska and N. Smith (eds), *Geography and Empire*, Blackwell, Oxford.

Cupples, J. and Harrison, J. 2001, 'Disruptive Voices and the Boundaries of Respectability in Christchurch, New Zealand', *Gender, Place and Culture*, vol. 8, no. 2, pp. 189–204.

Cupples, J. and Kindon, S. 2003, 'Returning to university and writing the field', in R. Scheyvens and D. Storey (eds), *Development Fieldwork. A Practical Guide*, Sage Publications, London.

Daniels, S. and Cosgrove, D. 1988, 'Introduction: iconography and landscape', in D. Cosgrove and S. Daniels (eds), *The Iconography of Landscape: Essays on the Symbols, Representation, Design and Use of Past Environments*, Cambridge University Press, Cambridge.

Davis, C. M. 1954, 'Field techniques', in P. E. James and C. F. Jones (eds), *American Geography: Inventory and Prospect*, Syracuse University Press for the AAG, Syracuse.

Davis, Mark 1997, *Gangland: Cultural Elites and the New Generationalism*, Allen & Unwin, Sydney.

Davis, Mike 1990, *City of Quartz: Excavating the future in Los Angeles*, Verso, London.

Dear, M. 1988, 'The postmodern challenge. Reconstructing human geography', *Transactions of the Institute of British Geographers*, NS 13, pp. 262–74.

deCerteau, M. 1984, *The practice of everyday life*, University of California Press, Berkeley, CA.

Deloria, V. Jr. 1988, [1969], *Custer Died for Your Sins: an Indian Manifesto*, Norman, University of Oklahoma Press, Oklahoma.

DeLyser, D. forthcoming. 'Writing it Up', in J. P. Jones III and B. Gomez, (eds), *Research Methods in Geography*, Blackwell, London.

—— 2001, '"Do you really live here?' Thoughts on insider research', *Geographical Review*, vol. 91, nos. 1 & 2, pp. 441–53.

DeLyser, D. and Starrs, P. F. 2001, 'Doing fieldwork: editors' introduction', *The Geographical Review*, vol. 91, no. 1–2, p. iv.

Dennis, R. 2001, 'Reconciling geographies, representing modernities', in I. Black, and R. Butlin (eds), *Place, Culture an Identity, Essays in Honour of Alan R. H. Baker*, Les Presses de l'Université Laval, Quebec.

Denzin, N. K. 1994, 'The art and politics of interpretation', in N. K. Denzin and Y. S. Lincoln (eds), *Handbook of Qualitative Research*, Sage, Thousand Oaks, CA.

—— 1978, *The Research Act*, 2nd edn, McGraw Hill, New York.

Denzin, N. K. and Lincoln, Y. S. 2000, *Handbook of Qualitative Research*, 2nd edn, Sage, Thousand Oaks, CA.

—— 1994, 'Introduction: entering the field of qualitative research', in N. K. Denzin and Y. S. Lincoln (eds), *Handbook of Qualitative Research*, Sage, Thousand Oaks, CA.

Derrida, J. 1981, *Dissemination*, translated by B. Johnson, University of Chicago Press, Chicago.

—— 1978, *Writing and Difference*, translated with an introduction and additional notes by A. Bass, University of Chicago Press, Chicago.

—— 1976, *Of Grammatology*, translated by G. Spivak, The Johns Hopkins University Press, Baltimore and London.

de Vaus, D. A. 1995, *Surveys in Social Research*, UCL Press, London.

Dey, I. 1993, *Qualitative Data Analysis: A User-Friendly Guide for Social Scientists*, Routledge, London.

Dillman, D.A. 1978, *Mail and Telephone Surveys: The Total Design Method for Surveys*, John Wiley, New York.

Dissertation Proposal Writing Tutorial Undated (online), Available: <http://www.people.ku.edu/~ebben/tutorial_731.htm> (Accessed: 29 September 2004).

Dixon, D. P. and Jones III, J. P. 1996, 'For a supercalifragilisticexpialidocious scientific geography', *Annals of the Association of American Geographers*, vol. 86, pp. 767–79.

Doel, M. A. and Clarke, D. B. 1999, 'Dark panopticon. Or, attack of the killer tomatoes', *Environment and Planning D: Society and Space*, vol. 17, no. 4, pp. 427–50.

Donovan, J. 1988, 'When you're ill, you've gotta carry it', in J. Eyles and D. M. Smith (eds), *Qualitative Methods in Human Geography*, Polity Press, Cambridge.

Douglas, J. D. 1985, *Creative Interviewing*, Sage, Beverly Hills.

Douglas, L., Roberts, A. and Thompson, R. 1988, *Oral History: A Handbook*, Allen & Unwin, Sydney.

Driver, F. 1988, 'Historicity and human geography', *Progress in Human Geography*, vol. 12, no. 4, pp. 479–83.

Duberman, M., Vicinus, M. and Chauncey, G. 1990, *Hidden From History. Reclaiming The Gay and Lesbian Past*, Meridian Press, New York.

Duinen, I. van and Hoven, B. van 2003, '"We have to be extra special…" Gender gedifferentieerde ervaringen in de werkplaats van de Hollywood filmindustrie', *Agora,* vol. 9, no. 3, pp. 33–5.

Duncan, J. S. 1999, 'Complicity and resistance in the colonial archive: some issues in the method and theory of historical geography', *Historical Geography*, vol. 27, pp. 119–28.

—— 1992, 'Elite landscapes as cultural (re) production: the case of Shaughnessy Heights', in K. Anderson and F. Gale (eds), *Inventing Places: Studies in Cultural Geography*, Longman Cheshire, Melbourne.

—— 1987, 'Review of urban imagery: urban semiotics', *Urban Geography*, vol. 8, no. 5, pp. 473–83.

Duncan, J. and Duncan, N. 1988, 'Re-reading the landscape', *Environment and Planning D: Society and Space*, vol. 6, no. 2, pp. 117–26.

Dunn, K. M. 2003, 'New cultural geographies in Australia: the social and spatial constructions of culture and citizenship', in B. J. Garner (ed.), *Geography's New Frontiers,* Conference papers No. 17, Geographical Society of New South Wales, Gladesville, pp. 189–200.

—— 2001, 'Representations of Islam in the politics of mosque development in Sydney', *Tijdschrift voor Economische en Social Geografie* vol. 92, no. 2, pp, 291–308.

—— 1997, 'Cultural geography and cultural policy', *Australian Geographical Studies*, vol. 35, no. 1, pp. 1–11.

—— 1995, 'The landscape as text metaphor', in G. Dixon and D. Aitken (eds), *IAG Conference Proceedings 1993*, Monash Publications in Geography, Melbourne.

—— 1993, 'The Vietnamese concentration in Cabramatta: Site of avoidance and deprivation, or island of adjustment and participation?', *Australian Geographical Studies*, vol. 31, no. 2, pp. 228–45.

Dunn, K. M. and Mahtani, M. 2001, 'Media representations of ethnic minorities', *Progress in Planning*, vol. 55, no. 3, pp. 163–72.

Dunn, K. M. and Roberts, S. 2003, 'The social construction of an Indo-Chinese-Australian neighbourhood in Sydney: The case of Cabramatta', in L. Wei (ed.), *Enclaves to Ethoburbs*, John Hopkins Press, Baltimore.

Dunn, K. M., McGuirk, P. M. and Winchester, H. P. M. 1995, 'Place making: the social construction of Newcastle', *Australian Geographical Studies*, vol. 33, no. 2, pp. 149–66.

Dupuis, S. L. 1999, 'Naked Truths: Towards a Reflexive Methodology in Leisure Research', *Leisure Sciences*, vol. 21, no. 1, pp. 43–64.

Durack, M. 1986 [1959], *Kings in Grass Castles*, Corgi Books, London.

Durham, M. 2001, 'The Conservative Party, New Labour and the Politics of the Family', *Parliamentary Affairs*, vol. 54, pp. 689–91.

Dyck, I. 1999, 'Using qualitative methods in medical geography: deconstructive moments in a subdiscipline?', *Professional Geographer*, vol. 51, no. 2, pp. 243–53.

—— 1997, 'Dialogue with difference: A tale of two studies', in J. P. Jones III, H. L. Nast and S. M. Roberts (eds), *Thresholds in Feminist Geography: difference, methodology, representation*, Rowman & Littlefield, Lanham.

Dyck, I. and Kearns, R. 1995, 'Transforming the relations of research: towards culturally safe geographies of health and healing', *Health and Place*, vol. 1, no. 3, pp. 137–47.

Earickson, R. and Harlin, J. 1994, *Geographic Measurement and Quantitative Analysis*, Prentice Hall, Upper Saddle River.

Edmonds, M. 1995, 'Why don't we tell them what they want to hear? Native title, politics and the intransigence of ethnography', J. Finlayson and D. E. Smith (eds), *Native Title: Emerging Issues for Research, Policy and Practice*, Research Monograph No. 10, Centre for Aboriginal Economic Policy Research, The Australian National University, Canberra, pp. 1–8.

Edwards, E. 2003, 'Negotiating spaces', in J. M. Schartz and J. R. Ryan (eds), *Picturing Place Photography and the Geographical Imagination,* I. B. Tauris, London and New York.

Edwards, J. A. and Lampert, M. D. (eds) 1993, *Talking Data: Transcription and Coding in Discourse Research,* Lawrence Erlbaum Associates, Hillsdale, New Jersey.

Eichler, M. 1988, *Nonsexist Research Methods: A Practical Guide*, Allen & Unwin, Boston.

Eliott, J. A. and Olver, I. N. 2002, 'The discursive properties of 'hope': a qualitative analysis of cancer patients' speech', *Qualitative Health Research*, vol. 12, no. 20, pp. 173–93.

England, K. V. L. 1994, 'Getting personal: reflexivity, positionality, and feminist research', *Professional Geographer*, vol. 46, pp. 80–9.

—— 1993, 'Suburban pink collar ghettos: the spatial entrapment of women', *Annals of the Association of American Geographers,* vol. 83, no. 2, pp. 225–42.

Eustace, K. 1998, 'Ethnographic study of a virtual learning community', *Internet Research: Electronic Networking Applications and Policy,* vol. 8, no. 1, pp. 83–4.

Evans, M. 1988, 'Participant observation: the researcher as research tool', in J. Eyles and D. M. Smith (eds), *Qualitative Methods in Human Geography*, Polity Press, Cambridge.

Evans, V. and Sternberg, J. 1999, 'Young people, politics and television current affairs in Australia', *Journal of Australian Studies*, December, pp. 103–9.

Eyles, J. 1988, 'Interpreting the geographical world: qualitative approaches in geographical research', in J. Eyles and D. M. Smith (eds), *Qualitative Methods in Human Geography*, Polity Press, Cambridge.

Eyles, J. and Smith, D. M. (eds) 1988, *Qualitative Methods in Human Geography*, Polity Press, Cambridge.

Fairclough, N. 2003, *Analysing Discourse. Textual Analysis for Social Research*, Routledge, New York and London.

—— 1992, *Discourse and Social Change*, Polity Press, Cambridge.

Fals-Borda, O. and Anisur Rahman, M. 1991, *Action and Knowledge: Breaking the Monopoly with Participatory Action Research*, Intermediate Technology Publications Ltd, London.

Fanon, F. 1967 [1963], *The Wretched of the Earth*, translated by C. Farrington, Harmondsworth and London.

Feinsilver, J. M. 1993, *Healing the Masses: Cuban health politics at home and abroad*, University of Columbia Press, Berkeley.

Feitelson, E. 1991, 'The potential of mail surveys in Geography: some empirical evidence', *Professional Geographer*, vol. 43, pp. 190–205.

Fielding, N. 1999, 'The norm and the text: Denzin and Lincoln's handbooks of qualitative method', *British Journal of Sociology*, vol. 50, no. 3, pp. 525–34.

—— 1995, 'Choosing the right software program', *ESRC Data Archive Bulletin*, no. 58, Available: <http://kennedy.soc.surrey.ac.uk/caqdas/choose.htm>, (Accessed: 8 February 1999).

—— 1994, 'Getting into computer-aided qualitative data analysis', *ESRC Data Archive Bulletin,* September, no. 57, Available: <http://kennedy.soc.surrey.ac.uk/caqdas/getting.htm>, (Accessed: 8 February 1999).

Fielding, N. and Lee, R. 1998, *Computer Analysis and Qualitative Research*, Sage, London.

Fincher, R. and Panelli, R. 2001, 'Making space: women's urban and rural activism and the Australian state', *Gender, Place and Culture*, vol. 8, no. 2, pp. 129–48.

Findlay, A. M. and Li, F. L. N. 1997, 'An auto-biographical approach to understanding migration: the case of Hong Kong emigrants', *Area*, vol. 29, no. 1, pp. 34–44.

Fink, A. and Kosecoff, J. 1988, *How to Conduct Surveys: A Step-by-Step Guide*, 2nd edn, Sage Publications, Beverly Hills.

Fish, S. 1980, *Is There a Text in this Class? The Authority of Interpretive Communities*, Harvard University Press, London.

Fisher, J. F. 1990, *Sherpas: Reflections on Change in Himalayan Nepal*, University of California Press, Berkeley.

Flick, U. 1992, 'Triangulation revisited: strategy of validation or alternative?', *Journal for the Theory of Social Behaviour,* vol. 2, no. 2, pp. 175–97.

Flint, C. 2001, 'Right-wing resistance to the process of American hegemony: the changing political geography of nativism in Pennsylvania, 1920–1998', *Political Geography*, vol. 20, no. 6, pp. 763–86.

Flowerdew, R. and Martin, D. (eds) 1997, *Methods in Human Geography*, Addison Wesley Longman, Harlow.

Flyvbjerg, B. 1998, *Rationality and Power: Democracy in Practice*, translated by S. Sampson, University of Chicago Press, Chicago.

Foddy, W. 1993, *Constructing Questions for Interviews and Questionnaires*, Cambridge University Press, Cambridge.

Forbes, D. K. 1999, 'Globalisation, postcolonialism and new representations of the Pacific Asian metropolis', in P. Dicken, P. Kelly, L. Kong, K. Olds and H. Yeung (eds), *The Logic(s) of Globalisation*, Routledge, London.

—— 1993, 'Multiculturalism, the Asian connection and Canberra's urban imagery', in G. Clark, D. Forbes and R. Francis (eds), *Multiculturalism, Difference and Postmodernism,* Longman Cheshire, Melbourne.

Forer, P. and Chalmers, L. 1987, 'Geography and information technology: issues and impacts', in P. G. Holland and W. B. Johnston (eds), *Southern Approaches: Geography in New Zealand*, New Zealand Geographical Society (Inc.), Christchurch.

Foucault, M. 1982, 'The subject and power', in H. Dreyfus and P. Rabinow (eds), *Beyond Structuralism and Hermeneutics*, Harvester, Brighton.

—— 1981, 'The order of discourse', in R. Young (ed.), *Untying the Text: A Poststructuralist Reader*, RKP, London pp 48–78.

—— 1980, *Power/Knowledge*, Harvester, Brighton.

—— 1978, *The History of Sexuality: An Introduction*, vol. I, Penguin, Harmondsworth.

—— 1977a, *Discipline and Punish: the birth of the prison*, Pantheon, New York.

—— 1977b, *Language, counter-memory, practice: Selected essays and interviews*, Cornell University Press, Ithaca.

—— 1972, *The Archaeology of Knowledge*, translated by A. Sheridan Smith, Pantheon, New York.

Fowler, F. 2002, *Social Survey Methods*, Sage, Thousand Oaks, CA.

Fowler, R. 1991, *Language in the News: Discourse and Ideology in the Press*, Routledge, London.

Frankenberg, R. and Mani, L. 1993, 'Crosscurrents, crosstalk: Race, 'postcoloniality' and the politics of location', *Cultural Studies*, vol. 7, pp. 292–310.

Frankfort-Nachmias, C. and Nachmaias, D. 1992, *Research Methods in the Social Sciences*, 4th edn, Edward Arnold, London.

Freire, P. 1976, *Education: the Practice of Freedom*, Writers and Readers Publishing Cooperative, London.

—— 1972a, *Cultural Action for Freedom,* Penguin, Harmondsworth.

—— 1972b, *Pedagogy of the Oppressed,* Penguin, Harmondsworth.

Furer-Haimendorf, C. von 1984, *The Sherpas Transformed: Social Change in a Buddhist Society of Nepal*, Sterling Publishers, New Delhi.

—— 1975, *Himalayan Traders: Life in Highland Nepal*, J. Murray, London.

—— 1964, *The Sherpas of Nepal: Buddhist Highlanders*, J. Murray, London.

Gade, D.W. 2001, 'The languages of foreign fieldwork', *The Geographical Review*, vol. 91, no. 1–2, pp. 370–9.

Gahan, C. and Hannibal, M. 1998, *Doing Qualitative Research Using QSR NUD*IST*, Sage, London.

Gale, G. F. 1964, *A Study of Assimilation,* Libraries Board of South Australia, Adelaide.

Gale, S. J. 1996, *75 years: The Anniversary of University Geography in Australia,* Department of Geography, University of Sydney, Sydney.

Gardner, R., Neville, H. and Snell, J. 1983, 'Vietnamese Settlement in Springvale', *Environmental Report No. 14,* Monash University Graduate School of Environmental Science, Melbourne.

Garlick, S. 2002, 'Revealing the unseen: tourism, art and photography', *Cultural Studies,* vol 16, no. 2, pp. 289–305.

Geertz, C., 1984, 'Anti-anti-relativism', *American Anthropologist,* vol. 86, pp. 263–77.

—— 1980, 'Blurred genres', *American Scholar,* vol. 49, pp. 165–79.

—— 1973, *The Interpretation of Culture: selected essays,* Basic Books, New York.

Geographical Review 2001, Special Issue on 'Doing Fieldwork', *The Geographical Review,* vol. 91, no. 1–2.

George, K. 1999a, *A Place of Their Own: The Men and Women of War Service Land Settlement at Loxton after the Second World War,* Wakefield Press, Adelaide.

—— 1999b, *City Memory, A Guide and Index to the City of Adelaide Oral History Collection,* Corporation of the City of Adelaide.

Gibson, C. 2003, 'Digital divides in New South Wales: a research note on social–spatial inequality using 2001 Census data on computer and Internet technology', *Australian Geographer,* vol. 34, pp. 239–57.

Gibson, K., Cameron, J. and Veno, A. 1999, *Negotiating Restructuring and Sustainability: A Study of Communities Experiencing Rapid Social Change,* Australian Housing and Urban Research Institute Working Paper, AHURI, Melbourne. Also available: <http://www.ahuri.edu.au/global/docs/wkpap_11.pdf> (Accessed: 23 September 2004).

Gibson-Graham, J. K. 1994, '"Stuffed if I know!": Reflections on post-modern feminist social research', *Gender, Place and Culture,* vol. 1, no. 2, pp. 205–24.

Gilbert, M. 1994, 'The politics of location: doing feminist research at "home"', *Professional Geographer,* vol. 46, pp. 90–6.

Gill, R. 1996, 'Discourse analysis: practical implementations', in J. T. E. Richardson (ed.), *Handbook of Qualitative Methods for Psychology and the Social Sciences,* British Psychological Society, Leicester. pp. 141–56.

Gillham, B. 2000, *Developing a Questionnaire,* Continuum, London.

Glaser, B. G. and Strauss, A. L. 1967, *The Discovery of Grounded Theory: strategies for qualitative research,* Aldine, Chicago.

Glesne, C and Peshkin, A. 1992, *Becoming Qualitative Researchers: an introduction,* Longman, New York.

Gold, J. R. 1980, *An Introduction to Behavioural Geography,* Oxford University Press, Oxford.

Gold, R. L. 1958, 'Roles in sociological field observation', *Social Forces,* vol. 36, pp. 219–25.

Golledge, R. 1997, 'On reassembling one's life: overcoming disability in the academic environment', *Environment and Planning D: Society and Space,* vol. 15, no. 4, pp. 391–409.

Goss, J. 1988, 'The built environment and social theory: towards an architectural geography' *Professional Geographer,* vol. 40, no. 4, pp. 392–403.

Goss, J. D. 1993, 'Placing the market and marketing place: tourist advertising of the Hawaiian Islands, 1972–1992', *Environment and Planning D; Society and Space,* vol. 11, pp. 663–88.

Goss, J. D. and Leinbach, T. R. 1996, 'Focus groups as alternative research practice: Experience with transmigrants in Indonesia', *Area,* vol. 28, no. 2, pp. 115–23.

Gough, K. 1968, 'Anthropology and omperialism', *Monthly Review,* vol. 19, no. 11, pp.12–27.

Gould, P. 1988, 'Expose yourself to geographic research', in J. Eyles (ed.), *Research in Human Geography*, Blackwell, Oxford.

Grbich, C. 1999, *Qualitative Research in Health. An Introduction*, Sage, London.

Green, J., Frauquiz, M. and Dixon, C. 1997, 'The myth of the objective transcription: Transcribing as a situated act', *TESOL Quarterly*, vol. 31, no.1, pp. 172–6.

Gregory, D. 1994, 'Paradigm', in R. J. Johnston, D. Gregory and D. M. Smith (eds), *The Dictionary of Human Geography*, Blackwell, Oxford.

—— 1978, *Ideology, Science and Human Geography*, Hutchinson, London.

Gregory, S. 1998, Consuming the Cool: Children's Popular Consumption Culture, MA thesis, Department of Geography, The University of Auckland.

Griffith, D., Desloges, J. and Amrhein, C. 1990, *Statistical Analysis for Geographers*, Prentice Hall Engineering, Science and Mathematics, New Jersey.

Guelke, L. 1978, 'Geography and logical positivism', in D. Herbert and R. J. Johnston (eds), *Geography and the Urban Environment*, vol. 1, Wiley, New York.

Gupta, A. and Ferguson, J. 1997, *Anthropological Locations: Boundaries and Grounds of a Field Science*, University of California Press, Berkeley.

Hall, C. 1982, 'Private archives as sources for historical geography', in A. R. H. Baker and M. Billinge (eds), *Period and Place: Research Methods in Historical Geography*, Cambridge University Press, Cambridge, pp. 274–8.

Hall, S. 1980, 'Encoding/decoding', in *Culture, Media, Language: working papers in cultural studies*, Centre for Contemporary Cultural Studies, Hutchinson, London, pp. 123–38.

—— (ed.), 1997, *Representation: Cultural Representations and Signifying Practices*, Sage, London.

Hammersley, M. 1992, 'Deconstructing the qualitative–quantitative divide', in J. Brannen (ed.), *Mixing Qualitative and Quantitative Research*, Avebury, Aldershot, USA.

Hammersley, M. and Atkinson, P. 1983, *Ethnography: Principles in Practice*, Tavistock, London.

Hanlon, J. 2001, 'Spaces of interpretation; archival research and the cultural landscape', *Historical Geography*, vol. 29, pp. 14–25.

Haraway, D. 1991, 'Situated knowledges. The science question in feminism and the privilege of partial perspective', in D. Haraway (ed.), *Simians, Cyborgs and Women: The reinvention of nature*, Routledge, London.

Harley, J. B. 1992, 'Deconstructing the map', in T. Barnes and J. Duncan (eds), *Writing Worlds: Discourse, Text and Metaphor in the Representation of Landscape*, Routledge, London.

Harris, C. 2002, *Making Native Space, Colonialism, Resistance, and Reserves in British Columbia*, UBC Press, Vancouver.

—— 2001, 'Archival Fieldwork', *Geographical Review*, vol. 91, nos. 1 & 2, pp. 328–34.

—— 1997, *The Resettlement of British Columbia: Essays on colonialism and geographical change*, University of British Columbia Press, Vancouver.

—— 1978, 'The Historical Mind and the Practice of Geography', in D. Ley and M. Samuel (eds), *Humanistic Geography*, Croom Helm, Chicago, pp. 123–37.

Harrison, C. M. and Burgess, J. 1994, 'Social constructions of nature: a case study of conflicts over the development of Rainham marshes', *Transactions of the Institute of British Geographers*, vol. 19, no. 3, pp. 291–310.

Harrison, R.T. and Livingstone, D.N. 1980, 'Philosphy and problems in human geography: a presuppositional approach', *Area*, vol. 12, pp. 25–30.

Hartig, K. V. and Dunn, K. M. 1998, 'Roadside memorials: interpreting new deathscapes in Newcastle, New South Wales', *Australian Geographical Studies*, vol. 36, no. 1, pp. 5–20.

Harvey, D. 1984, 'On the history and present condition of geography: an historical materialist manifesto', *Professional Geographer,* vol. 36, pp. 1–11.

Hay, I. 2003a, 'Ethical practice in geographical research', in G. Valentine and N. Clifford (eds), *Key Methods in Geography*, Sage, London.

—— 2003b, 'From "Millennium" to "Profiles": Geography's Oral Histories across the Tasman', *Proceedings of the 22nd Conference of the New Zealand Geographical Society*, 6–11 July, University of Auckland, New Zealand, pp. 5–6.

—— 2002, *Communicating in Geography and the Environmental Sciences*, 2nd edn, Oxford University Press, Melbourne.

—— 1998, 'Making moral imaginations: research ethics, pedagogy, and professional human geography', *Ethics, Place and Environment*, vol. 1, no. 1, pp. 55–75.

—— 1996, *Communicating in Geography and the Environmental Sciences*, Oxford University Press, Melbourne.

—— 1995, 'The strange case of Dr Jekyll in Hyde Park: fear, media and the conduct of an emancipatory geography', *Australian Geographical Studies*, vol. 33, no. 2, pp. 257–71.

Hay, I., and Bass, D. 2002, 'Making news in geography and environmental management', *Journal of Geography in Higher Education*, vol. 26, no. 1, pp. 129–42.

Hay, I., and Israel, M. 2001, '"Newsmaking geography": communicating geography through the media', *Applied Geography*, vol 21, no. 2, pp. 107–25.

Hay, I., Bochner, D. and Dungey, C. 2002, *Making the Grade. A guide to successful communication and study*, 2nd edn, Oxford University Press, Melbourne.

Hay, I., Hughes, A. and Tutton, M. 2004, 'Monuments, memory and marginalisation in Adelaide's Prince Henry Gardens', *Geografiska Annaler B.,* vol. 86, no. 3, pp. 200–15.

Head, L. 2000, *Second Nature. The History and Implications of Australia as Aboriginal Landscape*, Syracuse University Press, New York.

Heath, A.W. 1997, 'The proposal in qualitative research', *The Qualitative Report* (online), vol. 3, no. 1, Available: <http://www.nova.edu/ssss/QR/QR3-1/heath.html> (Accessed: 9 September 2004).

Heathcote, R. L. 1975, *Australia*, Longman, London.

Heidegger, M. 1996 [1927], *Being and Time*, translated by J. Stambaugh, State University of New York Press, Albany.

Herlihy, P. H. 2003, 'Participatory research mapping of indigenous lands in Darien, Panama', *Human Organization*, vol. 62, no. 4, pp. 315–31.

Herlihy, P. H. and Knapp, G. 2003, 'Maps of, by, and for the peoples of Latin America', *Human Organization*, vol. 62, no. 4, pp. 303–14.

Herman, R. D. K. 1999, 'The Aloha State: place names and the anti-conquest of Hawai'i', *Annals of the Association of American Geographers*, vol. 89, no. 1, pp. 76–102.

Herman, T. and Mattingly, D. 1999, 'Community, justice, and the ethics of research: negotiating reciprocal research relations', in J. D. Proctor and D. M. Smith (eds), *Geography and Ethics: Journeys in a Moral Terrain*, Routledge, London.

Herod A. 1999, 'Reflections on interviewing foreign elites: praxis, positionality, validity and the cult of the insider', *Geoforum*, vol. 30, pp. 313–27.

—— 1993, 'Gender issues in the use of interviewing as a research method', *Professional Geographer*, vol. 45, no. 3, pp. 305–17

Hessey, R. 1997, 'I, Caesar', *Sydney Morning Herald*, Metro Section, 14–20 February.

Hiebert, W. and Swan D. 1999, 'Positively Fit: a case study in community development and the role of participatory research', *Community Development Journal*, vol. 34, pp. 356–64.

Hinchliffe, S., Crang, M., Reimer, S. and Hudson, A. 1997, 'Software for qualitative research: 2. Some thoughts on "aiding" analysis', *Environment and Planning A*, vol. 29, no. 5, pp. 1109–24.

Hirst, P. A. 1979, *On Law and Ideology*, Macmillan, London.

Hoad, N. 2000, 'Arrested development or the queerness of savages: resisting evolutionary narrative of difference', *Postcolonial Studies*, vol. 3, no. 2, pp. 133–58.

Hodge, R. and Kress, G. 1980, *Social Semiotics,* Polity Press, Cambridge.

Hoggart, K., Lees, L. and Davies, A. 2002, *Researching Human Geography*, Arnold, London.

Holbrook, B. and Jackson, P. 1996, 'Shopping around: focus group research in North London', *Area*, vol. 28, no. 2, pp. 136–42.

Holland, P. 1991, 'Poetry and landscape in New Zealand', *New Zealand Journal of Geography*, vol. 92, pp. 8–9.

Holland, P. G. and Hargreaves, R. P. 1991, 'The trivial round, the common task: work and leisure on a Canterbury Hill Country run in the 1860s and 1870s', *New Zealand Geographer*, vol. 47, no. 1, pp. 19–25.

Holland, P., Pawson, E. and Shatford, T. 1991, 'Qualitative resources in geography' [Special Issue], *New Zealand Journal of Geography*, vol. 92.

Holt-Jensen, A. 1988, 'Multiple meanings: shopping and the cultural politics of identity', *Environment and Planning A*, vol. 27, pp. 1913–30.

Hooks, B. 1990, *Yearning: Race, Gender, and Cultural Politics*, South End Press, Boston.

Hoppe, M. J., Wells, E. A., Morrison, D. M. and Wilsdon, A. 1995, 'Using focus groups to discuss sensitive topics with children', *Evaluation Review*, vol. 19, no. 1, pp. 102–14.

Horowitz, I. L. 1967, 'The Rise and Fall of Project Camelot', in I. Horowitz, *The Rise and Fall of Project Camelot: studies in the relationship between science and practical politics*, MIT Press, Cambridge.

Horvath, R. J. 1971, 'The Detroit Geographical Expedition and Institute Experience', *Antipode*, vol. 3, no. 1, pp. 73–85.

Hoven, B. van 2003, 'Analysing qualitative data using CAQDAS', in N. Clifford and G. Valentine (eds), *Key Methods in Geography*, Sage, London.

Hoven, B. van and Poelman, A. 2003, 'Using Computers for Qualitative Data Analysis: An Example Using NUD*IST', *Journal of Geography in Higher Education*, vol. 27, no. 1, pp. 113–20.

Hoven-Iganski, B. van 2000, *Made in the GDR. The Changing Geographies of Women in the Post-Socialist Rural Society in Mecklenburg-Westpomerania,* KNAG/NGS, Utrecht.

Howitt, R. 2003, 'Scale', in J. Agnew, K. Mitchell and G. Toal (eds), *A Companion to Political Geography*, Blackwell, Oxford.

—— 2002a, 'Worlds turned upside down: inclusionary research in Australia', *Proceedings of the Association of American Geographers Conference,* Los Angeles, March 2002. Available: <http://www.es.mq.edu.au/~rhowitt/AAG2002.panel.htm>, (Accessed: 23 September 2004).

—— 2002b, 'Decolonizing Research: ethical and methodological issues', *Proceedings of the Institute of Australian Geographers Conference*, ANU, Canberra.

—— 2002c, 'Scale and the other: Levinas and geography', *Geoforum,* vol. 33, pp. 299–313.

—— 2001, *Rethinking Resource Management: justice, sustainability and indigenous peoples,* Routledge, London.

—— 1997, 'Getting the scale right: the geopolitics of regional agreements.' *Northern Analyst,* vol. 2, pp. 15–17.

—— 1992, 'The political relevance of locality studies: a remote Antipodean viewpoint', *Area,* vol. 24, no. 1, pp. 73–81.

Howitt, R., Crough, G. and Pritchard, B. 1990, 'Participation, power and social research in Central Australia', *Australian Aboriginal Studies,* vol. 1, pp. 2-10.

Howitt, R. and Jackson, S. 1998, 'Some things do change: indigenous rights, geographers and geography in Australia', *Australian Geographer,* vol. 29, no. 2, pp. 155–73.

Howitt, R. and Suchet-Pearson, S. 2003, 'Ontological pluralism in contested cultural landscapes', in K. Anderson, M. Domosh, S. Pile and N. Thrift (eds), *Handbook of Cultural Geography,* Sage, London.

Huggan, G. 1995, 'Decolonizing the map', in B. Ashcroft, G. Griffiths and H. Tiffin (eds), *The Post-Colonial Studies Reader,* Routledge, London.

Hughes, A. 1999, 'Constructing economic geographies from corporate interviews: insights from a crosscountry comparison of retailer–supplier relationships', vol. 30, *Geoforum,* 363–74.

Hutchins, M. 1993, *Talking History, A Short Guide to Oral History,* Bridget Williams Books and Historical Branch of Internal Affairs, Wellington.

Institute of International Studies, University of California, Berkeley 2001, *Dissertation Proposal Workshop* (online), Available: <http://globetrotter.berkeley.edu/DissPropWorkshop/> (Accessed: 9 September 2004).

Ivanitz, M., 1999, 'Culture, ethics and participatory methodology in cross-cultural research', *Australian Aboriginal Studies,* vol. 2, pp. 46–58.

Jackson, J. 1990, '"I am a field note": Fieldnotes as a symbol of professional identity', in R. Sanjek (ed.), *Fieldnotes: The Makings of Anthropology,* Cornell University Press, Ithica.

Jackson, P. 2001, 'Making sense of qualitative data', in M. Limb and C. Dwyer (eds), *Qualitative Methodologies for Geographers,* Oxford University Press, London.

—— 1999, 'Constructions of culture, representations of race: Edward Curtis' "way of seeing"', in K. Anderson and F. Gale (eds), *Cultural Geographies,* Longman, Melbourne.

—— 1992, 'Constructions of culture, representations of race: Edward Curtis's "way of seeing"', in K. Anderson and F. Gale (eds), *Inventing Places: Studies in Cultural Geography,* Longman Cheshire, Melbourne.

—— 1983, 'Principles and problems of participant observation', *Geografiska Annaler,* vol. 65B, pp. 39–46.

Jackson, P. and Holbrook, B. 1995, 'Multiple meanings: shopping and the cultural politics of identity', *Environment and Planning A,* vol. 27, pp. 1913–30.

Jackson, P. and Penrose, J. (eds), 1993, *Constructions of Race, Place and Nation,* University College London Press, London.

Jackson, P. A. 1993, 'Changing ourselves: a geography of position', in R. J. Johnston (ed.), *The Challenge for Geography,* Basil Blackwell, Oxford.

Jackson-Lears, T. 1985, 'The concept of cultural hegemony: problems and possibilities', *American Historical Review,* vol. 90, pp. 567–93.

Jacobs, J. M. 1999, 'The labour of cultural geography', in E. Stratford (ed.), *Australian Cultural Geographies*, Oxford University Press, Melbourne.

—— 1996, *Edge of Empire: Postcolonialism and the City*, Routledge, London.

—— 1993, '"Shake 'im this country": the mapping of the Aboriginal sacred in Australia—the case of Coronation Hill', in P. Jackson and J. Penrose (eds), *Constructions of Race, Place and Nation*, University College Press, London.

—— 1992, 'Culture of the past and urban transformation: The Spitalfield Market redevelopment in East London', in K. J. Anderson and F. Gale (eds), *Inventing Places: Studies in Cultural Geography*, Longman Cheshire, Melbourne.

Jarrett, R. L. 1994, 'Living poor: Family life among single parent African American women', *Social Problems*, vol. 41, no. 1, pp. 30–49.

Jay, N. 1981, 'Gender and dichotomy', *Feminist Studies*, vol. 7, pp. 38–56.

Jick, T. D. 1979, 'Mixing qualitative and quantitative methods: triangulation in action', *Administrative Science Quarterly*, vol. 24, December, pp. 602–11.

Johnson, A. 1996, '"It's good to talk": The focus group and the sociological imagination', *The Sociological Review*, vol. 44, no. 3, pp. 517–38.

Johnson, R. B. 1997, 'Examining the validity structure of qualitative research', *Education*, vol. 118, no. 2, pp. 282–90.

Johnston, R. J. 1983, *Philosophy and Human Geography: An Introduction to Contemporary Approaches*, Edward Arnold, London.

—— 1979, *Geography and Geographers: Anglo-American Human Geography Since 1945*, Edward Arnold, London.

—— 1978, *Multivariate Statistical Analysis in Geography: A Primer on the General Linear Model*, Longman, New York.

Jones, A. 1992, 'Writing Feminist Educational Research: Am 'I' in the Text?', in S. Middleton and A. Jones (eds), *Women and Education in Aotearoa*, Bridget Williams Books, Wellington.

Jones, J. P. III, Nast, H. J. and Roberts, S. M. (eds) 1997, *Thresholds in Feminist Geography: Difference, Methodology, Representation*, Rowman & Littlefield, Lanham, MD.

Johnston, R. J., Gregory, D., Pratt, G. and Watts, M.(eds) 2000, *The Dictionary of Human Geography*, Blackwell, Oxford.

Jorgensen, J. 1971, 'On Ethics and Anthropology', *Current Anthropology*, vol. 12, no. 3, pp. 321–56.

Judd, C. M., Smith, E. R. and Kidder, L. H. 1991, *Research Methods in Social Relations*, 6th edn, Holt, Rinehart and Winston, Sydney.

Katz, C. 1994, 'Playing the field: questions of fieldwork in geography', *Professional Geographer*, vol. 46, no. 1, pp. 67–72.

Kearns, R. 1997, 'Constructing (Bi)cultural geographies: research on, and with, people of the Hokianga District', *New Zealand Geographer*, vol. 52, pp. 3–8.

—— 1991a, 'Talking and listening: avenues to geographical understanding', *New Zealand Journal of Geography*, vol. 92, pp. 2–3.

—— 1991b, 'The place of health in the health of place: the case of the Hokianga special medical area', *Social Science and Medicine*, vol. 33, pp. 519–30.

—— 1987, 'In the Shadow of Illness: A Social Geography of the Chronically Mentally Disabled in Hamilton, Ontario', PhD dissertation, Department of Geography, McMaster University.

Kearns, R and Dyck, I. 2004 (in press) 'Culturally safe research', in D. Wepa (ed.), *Cultural Safety in Aotearoa New Zealand*, Pearson Education, Auckland.

Kearns, R. A., Collins, D. C. A. and Neuwelt, P. M. 2003, 'The walking school bus: extending childrens' geographies', *Area,* vol. 35, pp. 285–92.

Kearns, R. A., Smith, C. J. and Abbott, M. W. 1991, 'Another day in paradise? Life on the margins in urban New Zealand', *Social Science and Medicine*, vol. 33, pp. 369–79.

Keen, J. and Packwood, T. 1995, 'Case study evaluation', *British Medical Journal*, vol. 311, no. 7002, pp. 444–8.

Kelle, U. 1997a, 'Capabilities for theory building and hypothesis testing in software for computer aided qualitative data analysis', *The Data Archive Bulletin*, vol. 65, no. 10, Available <http://www.data-archive.ac.uk/> (Accessed: 4 February 2005).

—— 1997b, 'Theory building in qualitative research and computer programs for the management of textual data', *Sociological Research Online*, vol. 2, no. 2, Available <http://www.socresonline.org.uk/welcome.html>, (Accessed: 23 September 2004).

—— 1995, 'An overview of computer-aided methods in qualitative research', in U. Kelle (ed.), *Computer-Aided Qualitative Data Analysis: Theory, Methods and Practice*, Sage, London.

Kellehear, A. 1993, *The Unobtrusive Researcher: A Guide to Methods*, Allen & Unwin, Sydney.

Kesby, M. 2000, 'Participatory diagramming: deploying qualitative methods through an action research epistemology', *Area*, vol. 32, no. 4, pp. 423–535.

Kesby, M., Kindon, S. and Pain, R. 2004, '"Participatory" diagramming and approaches', in R. Flowerdew and D. Martin (eds), *Methods in Human Geography*, 2nd edn, Pearson, London.

Kidder, L. H., Judd, C. M. and Smith, E. R. 1986, *Research Methods in Social Relations*, CBS Publishing, New York.

Kindon, S. 2003, 'Participatory video in geographic research: a feminist practice of looking?' *Area*, vol. 35, no. 2, pp. 142–53.

—— 1998, 'Of mothers and men: challenging gender and community myths in Bali, Indonesia', in I. Guijt and M. Kaul Shah (eds), *The Myth of Community: Gender Issues in Participatory Development*, Intermediate Technology Publications Ltd., London.

—— 1995, 'Exploring empowerment methodologies with women and men in Bali', *New Zealand Geographer*, vol. 51, no. 1, pp. 10–12.

Kindon, S. and Cupples, J. 2003, 'Anything to declare: the politics and practicalities of leaving the field', in R. Scheyvens and D. Storey (eds), *Development Fieldwork: A Practical Guide*, Sage, London.

Kindon S. and Latham, A. 2002, 'From mitigation to negotiation: Ethics and the geographical imagination in Aotearoa/New Zealand', *New Zealand Geographer*, vol. 58, no. 1, pp. 14–22.

Kirby, S. and Hay, I. 1997, '(Hetero)sexing space: gay men and 'straight' space in Adelaide, South Australia', *Professional Geographer*, vol. 49, no. 3, pp. 295–305.

Kirk, J. and Miller, M. 1986, *Reliability and Credibility in Qualitative Research*, Sage, Beverly Hills.

Kitchin, R. 2001, 'Using participatory action research approaches in geographical studies of disability: some reflections', *Disability Studies Quarterly*, vol. 21, no. 4, pp. 61–9.

Kitchin, R. and Tate, N. 2000, *Conducting Research in Human Geography: Theory, Methodology and Practice*, Longman, London.

Kitson Clark, G. 1969, *Guide for Research Students Working on Historical Subjects,* 2nd edn, Cambridge University Press, Cambridge.

Kitzinger, J. 1994, 'The methodology of focus groups: The importance of interaction between research participants', *Sociology of Health and Illness*, vol. 16, no. 1, pp. 103–21.

Kivell, L. 1995, 'Sex-gender and race: constructing a harvest workforce', MA thesis, Department of Geography, The University of Auckland.

Kluckhohn, F. R. 1940, 'The participant observer technique in small communities', *American Journal of Sociology*, vol. 46, pp. 331–43.

Kneale, P. 1999, *Study Skills for Geography Students*, Arnold, London.

Kobayashi, A. 1994, 'Coloring the field: gender, "race", and the politics of fieldwork', *Professional Geographer,* vol. 46, no. 1, pp. 73–80.

Kolakowski, L. 1972, *Positivist Philosophy: From Hume to the Vienna Circle*, Penguin, London.

Kong, L. 1999, 'Cemeteries and columbaria, memorials and mausoleums: narrative and interpretation in the study of deathscapes in geography', *Australian Geographical Studies*, vol. 37, no. 1, pp. 1–10.

—— 1998, 'Refocussing on qualitative methods: problems and prospects for research in a specific Asian context', *Area*, vol. 30, no. 1, pp. 79–82.

Kothari, U. 2001, 'Power, knowledge and social control in participatory development', in B. Cooke and U. Kothari (eds), *Participation: The New Tyranny?*, Zed Books, London.

Krippendorff, K. 2003, *Content Analysis: An Introduction to its Methodology*, Sage, Thousand Oaks, CA.

Krueger, R. 1998, *Analyzing and Reporting Focus Group Results*, Focus Group Kit 6, Sage, Thousand Oaks, CA.

—— 1994, *Focus Groups: A Practical Guide for Applied Research*, 2nd edn, Sage, Thousand Oaks, CA.

Krug, S. 2000, *Don't make me think! A common sense approach to web usability,* Que, Indianapolis.

Kunstler, H. 1994, *The Geography of Nowhere*, Touchstone, USA.

Kurtz, M. 2001, 'Situating practices: the archives and the file cabinet', *Historical Geography*, vol. 29, pp. 26–37.

Labovitz, S. and Hagedorn, R. 1981, *Introduction to Social Research*, 3rd edn, McGraw-Hill, Sydney.

Lane, R. 1997, 'Oral histories and scientific knowledge in understanding environmental change: a case study in the Tumut region, NSW', *Australian Geographical Studies,* vol. 35, no. 2, pp. 195–205.

Lane, R. and Waitt, G. 2001, 'Authenticity in tourism and Native Title: place, time and spatial politics in the East Kimberley', *Social and Cultural Geography*, vol 2. no. 4, pp. 381–404.

Latimer, B. 1998, 'Masculinity, Place and Sport: Rugby Union and the Articulation of the 'New Man' in Aotearoa/New Zealand', MA thesis, Department of Geography, The University of Auckland.

Law, L. 2000, *Sex Work in Southeast Asia. The Place of Desire in a Time of AIDS*, Routledge, London and New York.

Lawson, V. 1995, 'The politics of difference: examining the quantitative/qualitative dualism in post-structuralist feminist research', *Professional Geographer*, vol. 47, no. 4, pp. 449–57.

Le Doeff, M. 1987, 'Women and philosophy', in T. Moi (ed.), *French Feminist Thought: A Reader*, Basil Blackwell, Oxford.

Lefebvre, H. 1991, *The Production of Space*, Blackwell, Oxford.

Le Heron, R., Penny, G., Paine, M., Sheath, G., Pedersen, J. and Botha, N. 2001, 'Global supply chains and networking: a critical perspective on learning challenges in the New Zealand dairy and sheepmeat commodity chains', *Journal of Economic Geography*, vol. 1, no. 4, pp. 439–56.

Lee, R. 2000, *Unobtrusive Methods in Social Research*, Open University Press, Buckingham.

—— 1992, 'Teaching qualitative geography: a JGHE written symposium', *Journal of Geography in Higher Education*, vol. 16, no. 2, pp. 123–6.

Lees, L 2004, 'Urban geography: discourse analysis and urban research', *Progress in Human Geography*, vol. 28, no. 1, pp. 101–7.

Leurs, R. 1997, 'Critical reflections on rapid and participatory rural appraisal', *Development in Practice*, vol. 7, no. 3, pp. 290–3.

Levinas, E. 1969, *Totality and Infinity: an essay on exteriority*, Duquesne, translated by A. Lingis, University Press, Pittsburgh.

Levitas, R. 1997, *The Inclusive Society?: Social Exclusion and New Labour*, Macmillan, Basingstoke.

Ley, D. 1974, *The Black Inner City as Frontier Outpost*, Monograph No. 7, Association of American Geographers, Washington, D.C.

Limb, M. and Dwyer, C. (eds) 2001, *Qualitative Methodologies for Geographers: Issues and Debate*, Arnold, London.

Lincoln, Y. S. and Guba, E. G. 2000, 'Paradigmatic controversies, contradictions, and emerging confluences', in Denzin, N. K. and Lincoln, Y. S. (eds), *Handbook of Qualitative* Research, 2nd edn, Sage, Thousand Oaks, CA.

—— 1985, *Naturalistic Inquiry*, Sage, Beverly Hills, CA.

—— 1981, *Effective Evaluation*, Jossey-Bass, San Francisco.

Lindsay, J. M. 1997, *Techniques in Human Geography*, Routledge, London.

Lindsey, D. and Kearns, R. A.1994, 'The writing's on the wall: Graffiti, territory and urban space', *New Zealand Geographer*, vol. 50, pp. 7–13.

Linstead, S. and Grafton-Small, R. 1990, 'Organisational bricolage', in B. Turner (ed.), *Organisational Symbolism*, Walter de Gruyter, Berlin.

Lloyd, G. 1984, *The Man of Reason: 'male' and 'female' in Western philosophy*, Methuen, London.

Longhurst, R. 2000, '"Corporeographies" of pregnancy: "bikini babes"', *Environment and Planning D: Society and Space*, vol. 18, pp. 453–72.

—— 1996, 'Refocusing groups: Pregnant women's geographical experiences of Hamilton, New Zealand/Aotearoa', *Area*, vol. 28, no. 2, pp. 143–9.

—— 1995, 'The geography closest in—the body…the politics of pregnability', *Australian Geographical Studies*, vol. 33, pp. 214–23.

Lowenthal, D. and Prince, H. 1965, 'English landscape tastes', *Geographical Review*, vol. 47, no. 4, pp. 449–57.

Lunt, P. and Livingstone, S. 1996, 'Rethinking the focus group in media and communications research', *Journal of Communication*, vol. 46, no. 2, pp. 79–98.

Lutz, C. A. and Collins J. L. 1993, *Reading National Geographic*, University of Chicago Press, Chicago.

Maccoby, E. and Maccoby, N. 1954, 'The interview: a tool of social science', in G. Lindzey (ed.), *Handbook of Social Psychology*, Addison-Wesley, Cambridge, Massachusetts.

Mackenzie, S. 1989, *Visible Histories: Women and Environments In a Post-War British City*, McGill-Queen's University Press, Montreal.

Maguire, P. 1987, *Doing participatory research: a feminist approach*, Centre for International Education, University of Massachusetts, Amherst.

Manning, K. 1997, 'Authenticity in constructivist inquiry: methodological considerations without prescription', *Qualitative Inquiry*, vol. 3, no. 1, pp. 93–104.

Manalo, E. and Trafford, J. 2004, *Thinking to Thesis. A Guide to Graduate Success at All Levels*, Pearson Education, Auckland.

Marcus, G. E. and Fisher, M. M. J. 1986, *Anthropology as Cultural Critique: An Experimental Moment In the Human Sciences*, University of Chicago Press, Chicago.

Markwell, K. 2002, 'Mardi Gras tourism and the construction of Sydney as an international gay and lesbian city', *GLQ*, vol. 8, nos. 1–2, pp. 81–100.

Markwell, K. 1997, 'Dimensions of a nature-based tour', *Annals of Tourism Research*, vol. 24, no. 1, pp. 131–55.

Massey, D. B. 1993, 'Power-geometry and a progressive sense of place', in J. Bird, B. Curtis, G. Robertson and L. Tickner (eds), *Mapping the futures*, Routledge, London.

Massey, D. and Meegan, R. (eds) 1985, *Politics and Method—Contrasting Studies in Industrial Geography*, Methuen, London.

May, T. 2001, *Social Research: Issues, Methods and Process*, 3rd edn, Open University Press, Buckingham.

—— 1997, *Social Research: Issues, Methods and Process*, 2nd edn, Open University Press, Buckingham.

—— 1993, *Social Research: Issues, Methods and Process*, Open University Press, Buckingham.

Maya People of Southern Belize, Toledo Maya Cultural Council, and Toledo Alcades Association 1997, *Maya Atlas: the Struggle to Preserve Maya Land in Southern Belize,* North Atlantic Books, Berkeley.

Mayhew, R. 2003, 'Researching Historical Geography', in A. Rogers and H. Viles (eds), *The Student's Companion to Geography*, 2nd edn, Blackwell, Oxford.

Mays, N. and Pope, C. 1997, 'Rigour and qualitative research', *British Medical Journal*, vol. 310, no. 6997, pp. 109–13.

McBride, B. 1999, 'The (post)colonial landscape of Cathedral Square: urban redevelopment and representation in the "Cathedral City"', *New Zealand Geographer,* vol. 55, no. 1, pp. 3–11.

McClean, R., Berg, L. D. and Roche, M. M. 1997, 'Responsible geographies: co-creating knowledges in Aotearoa', *New Zealand Geographer*, vol. 53, no. 2, pp. 9–15.

McCracken, J. 1991, 'Looking at photographs', *New Zealand Journal of Geography*, vol. 92, pp. 12–14.

McDowell, L. 1998, 'Illusions of power: interviewing local elites', *Environment and Planning A,* vol. 30, pp. 2121–32.

—— 1992, 'Valid games? A response to Erica Schoenberger', *Professional Geographer*, vol. 44, no. 2, pp. 212–15.

McDowell, L. and Court, G. 1994, 'Performing work: bodily representations in merchant banks', *Environment and Planning D: Society and Space*, vol. 12, pp. 727–50.

McFarlane, T. and Hay, I. 2003, 'The battle for Seattle: protest and popular geopolitics in *The Australian* newspaper', *Political Geography*, vol. 22, pp. 211–32.

McGregor, G. 1994, *EcCentric Visions: Re-Constructing Australia*, Wilfred Laurier University Press, New York.

McGuirk, P. M. 2002, 'Producing the capacity to govern in global Sydney: a multiscaled account', *Journal of Urban Affairs*, vol. 25, pp. 201–23.

McGuirk, P. M. and Rowe, D. 2001, '"Defining moments" and refining myths in the making of place identity: the Newcastle Knights and the Australian Rugby League grand final', *Australian Geographical Studies*, vol. 39, no. 1, pp. 52–66.

McIlwaine, C. and Moser, C. 2003, 'Poverty, violence and livelihood security in urban Colombia and Guatemala', *Progress in Development Studies*, vol. 3, no. 2, pp. 113–30.

McIntyre, J. 2001, *Guide to Writing a Research Proposal* (online), Available: <http://www.education. uts.edu.au/research/degrees/guide.html> (Accessed: 9 September 2004).

McKay, D. 2002, 'Negotiating positionings: exchanging life stories in research interviews', in Moss, P. (ed.) *Feminist Geography in Practice*, Blackwell, Oxford.

McKendrick, J. H. 1996, *Multi-method Research in Population Geography: A Primer to Debate*, The University of Manchester, Population Geography Research Group, Manchester.

McLafferty, S. 2003, 'Conducting questionnaire surveys' in N. Clifford and G. Valentine (eds), *Key Methods in Geography*, Sage, London, pp. 87–100.

McLean, R., Berg, L. and Roche, M. 1997, 'Responsible geographies: co-creating knowledge in Aotearoa, New Zealand', *New Zealand Geographer*, vol. 53, no. 2, pp. 9–15.

McManus, P. A. 2000, 'Beyond Kyoto? Media representations of an environmental issue', *Australian Geographical Studies*, vol. 38, no. 3, pp. 306–19.

McNay, L. 1994, *Foucault: A Critical Introduction*, Polity Press, Cambridge.

McNeill, D. 1998, 'Writing the new Barcelona', in T. Hall and P. Hubbard (eds), *The Entrepreneurial City: Geographies of Politics, Regime and Representation*, John Wiley, London.

Mee, K. J. 1994, 'Dressing up the suburbs: representations of Western Sydney', in K. Gibson and S. Watson (eds), *Metropolis Now: Planning and the Urban in Contemporary Australia*, Pluto Press, Sydney.

Mee, K. and Dowling R. 2003, 'Reading *Idiot Box*: film reviews intertwining the social and cultural', *Social and Cultural Geography*, vol. 4, no. 2, pp. 185–215.

Meinig, D. W. 1986, *The Shaping of America: a geographical perspective on 500 years of history*, Yale University Press, New Haven.

Merlan, F. 1996, 'Formulations of claim and title: a comparative discussion', in J. Finlayson and A. Jackson-Nakano (eds), *Heritage and Native Title: Anthropological and Legal Perspectives*, Australian Institute of Aboriginal and Torres Strait Islander Studies, Canberra, pp. 165–77.

Merton, R. K. 1987, 'The focussed interview and focus groups: Continuities and discontinuities', *Public Opinion Quarterly*, vol. 51, no. 4, pp. 550–66.

Miles, M. B. and Huberman, A. M. 1994, *Qualitative Data Analysis: An expanded sourcebook*, 2nd edn, Sage Publications, Thousand Oaks, CA.

——— 1984, *Qualitative Data Analysis: a Sourcebook of New Methods*, Sage, Beverly Hills.

Mills, S. 1997, *Discourse*, Routledge, London and New York.

Minichiello, V., Aroni, R., Timewell, E. and Alexander, L. 1995, *In-Depth Interviewing: Principles, Techniques, Analysis*, 2nd edn, Longman Cheshire, Melbourne.

——— 1990, *In-Depth Interviewing: Researching People*, Longman Cheshire, Melbourne.

Mishler, E. 1986, *Research Interviewing: Context and Narrative*, Harvard University Press, Cambridge, Massachusetts.

Mohammad, R. 1999, 'Marginalisation, Islamism and the production of the "Other's" "Other"', *Gender, Place and Culture*, vol. 6, no. 3, pp. 221–40.

Mohanty, C. T. 1991, 'Cartographies of struggle: Third world women and the politics of feminism', in C. Mohanty, A. Russo and L. Torres (eds), *Third World Women and the Politics of Feminism*, University of Indiana Press, Bloomington.

Monk, J. and Hanson, S. 1982, 'On not excluding half of the human in human geography', *Professional Geographer*, vol. 34, pp. 11–23.

Monk, J., Manning, P. and Denman, C. 2003, 'Working together: feminist perspectives on collaborative research and action', *ACME: An International E-Journal for Critical Human Geographies*, vol. 2, no. 1, pp. 91–106.

Morgan, D. L. 1997, *Focus Groups as Qualitative Research*, 2nd edn, Sage, Thousand Oaks.

—— 1996, 'Focus groups', *Annual Review of Sociology*, vol. 22, pp. 129–52.

—— (ed.) 1993, *Successful Focus Groups: Advancing the State of the Art*, Sage, Newbury Park.

Morgan, D. L. and Krueger, R. A. 1993, 'When to use focus groups and why', in D. L. Morgan (ed.), *Successful Focus Groups: Advancing the State of the Art*, Sage, Newbury Park.

Moser, C. A. and Kalton, G. 1983, *Survey Methods in Social Investigation*, Heinemann, London.

Moss, P. 2002, *Feminist Geography in Practice*, Blackwell, Oxford.

—— 2001, *Placing Autobiography in Geography*, Syracuse University Press, Syracuse.

—— 1995, 'Reflections on the 'gap' as part of the politics of research design', *Antipode*, vol. 27, no. 1, pp. 82–90.

Mosse, D. 1994, 'Authority, gender and knowledge: theoretical reflections on the practice of participatory rural appraisal', *Development and Change*, vol. 25, pp. 497–526.

Mostyn, B. 1985, 'The content analysis of qualitative research data: a dynamic approach', in M. Brown, J. Brown and D. Canter (eds), *The Research Interview: Uses and Approaches*, Academic Press, London.

Muller, S. 1999, Myths, media and politics. Implications for koala management decisions in Kangaroo Island, South Australia, paper presented to Institute of Australian Geographers' conference, 27 September to 1 October, Sydney.

Mullings, B. 1999, 'Insider or outsider, both or neither: some dilemmas of interviewing in a cross-cultural setting', *Geoforum*, vol. 30, pp. 337–50.

Munt, S. R. 1998, 'Sisters in exile: the lesbian nation', in A. Rosa (ed.), *New Frontiers of Spaces, Bodies and Gender*, Routledge, London and New York, pp. 3–19.

Myers, G. 1998, 'Displaying opinions: Topics and disagreement in focus groups', *Language in Society*, vol. 27, pp. 85–111.

Myers, G. and MacNaghten, P. 1998, 'Rhetorics of environmental sustainability: commonplaces and places', *Environment and Planning A*, vol. 30, pp. 333–53.

Myers, G., Klak, T. and Koehl, T. 1996, 'The inscription of difference: news coverage of the conflicts in Rwanda and Bosnia', *Political Geography*, vol. 15, no. 1, pp. 21–46.

Nader, L. 1974, 'Up the anthropologist—perspective gained from studying up', in D. Hymes, *Reinventing Anthropology*, Vintage Books, New York, pp. 284–311.

Nagar, R. 2000, '*Mujhe Jawab Do!* (Answer Me!): women's grass-roots activism and social spaces in Chitrakoot (India)', *Gender, Place and Culture*, vol. 7, no.4, pp. 341–62.

Nast, H. 1994, 'Opening remarks: Women in the field', *Professional Geographer*, vol. 46, pp. 54–66.

National Council on Public History 2003, *NCPH Ethics Guidelines* (online), Available: <http://ncph.org/ethics.html>, (Accessed: 18 August 2004).

National Research Foundation (South Africa) undated, *Proposal Writing Resources* (online), Available: <http://www.nrf.ac.za/methods/proposals.htm> (Accessed: 9 September 2004).

Nelson, C., Treichler, P. and Grossberg, L. 1992, 'Cultural studies: an introduction', in L. Grossberg, C. Nelson and P. Treichler (eds), *Cultural Studies*, Routledge, New York.

Nelson, S. 2003, 'It's I mean like uh disrespectful', *Times Higher Educational Supplement*, 28 March, p. 16.

Nettlefold, P. A. and Stratford, E. 1999, 'The production of climbing landscapes-as-texts', *Australian Geographical Studies*, vol. 37, no. 2, pp. 130–41.

Neuendorf, K. 2001, *The Content Analysis Guidebook*, Sage Publications, Thousand Oaks, CA. (See online accompaniment at: <http://academic.csuohio.edu/kneuendorf/content/>.)

NHMRC (National Health and Medical Research Council) 2003, *Values and Ethics—Guidelines for Ethical Conduct in Aboriginal and Torres Strait Islander Health Research*, NHMRC, Canberra.

Nicholson, B. 2000, 'Something there is...', in K. Reed-Gilbert (ed.), *The Strength of Us as Women: Black Women Speak*, Ginninderra Press, Canberra, pp. 27–30.

Nicholson, H. 2002, 'Telling travelers' tales: the world through home movies', in T. Creswell, and D. Dixon (eds), *Engaging film, geographies of mobility and identity*, Rowman & Littlefield, Lanham, MD.

Nietzsche, F. W. 1969, *On the Genealogy of Morals*, translated by W. Kaufmann and R. J. Hollingdale, Vintage, New York.

Nietschmann, B. Q. 2001, 'The Nietschmann syllabus: a vision of the field', *Geographical Review*, vol. 91, nos 1–2, pp. 175–84.

—— 1997, 'Protecting indigenous coral reefs and sea territories, Miskito Coast, RAAN, Nicaragua', in S. Stevens, (ed.), *Conservation Through Cultural Survival: Indigenous Peoples and Protected Areas*, Island Press, Washington, D.C., pp. 193–224.

—— 1995, 'Defending the Miskito reefs with maps and GPS: mapping with sail, scuba, and satellite', *Cultural Survival Quarterly*, vol. 18, no. 4, pp. 34–7.

—— 1987, 'The third world war', *Cultural Survival Quarterly*, vol. 11, no. 3, pp. 1–16.

—— 1979, *Carribean Edge: the Coming of Modern Times to Isolated People and Wildlife*, Bobbs-Merrill, Indianapolis, IN.

—— 1973, *Between Land and Water: the Subsistence Ecology of the Miskito Indians, Eastern Nicaragua*, Seminar Press, New York.

Nolan, N. 2003, 'The ins and outs of skateboarding and transgression in public space in Newcastle, Australia', *Australian Geographer*, vol. 34, no. 3, pp. 311–27.

Oakley, A. 1981, *From Here to Maternity: Becoming a Mother*, Penguin, Harmondsworth.

O'Brien, K. 1993, 'Improving survey questionnaires through focus groups', in D. L. Morgan (ed.), *Successful Focus Groups: Advancing the State of the Art*, Sage, Newbury Park.

O'Connell-Davidson, J. and Layder, D. 1994, *Methods, Sex and Madness*, Routledge, London.

Ogborn, M. 2003, 'Knowledge is power: Using archival research to interpret state formation', in A. Blunt, P. Grufford, J. P. May, M. Ogborn and D. Pinder (eds), *Cultural Geography in Practice*, Arnold, London, pp. 9–20.

Oliver, W. H. 2002, *Looking for the Phoenix*, Bridget Williams Books, Wellington.

Olver, I. N., Eliott, J. A. and Blake-Mortimer, J. 2002, 'Cancer patients' perceptions of Do Not Resuscitate orders', *PsychoOncology*, vol. 11, no. 3, pp. 181–7.

O'Neill, P. M. 2001, 'Financial narratives of the modern corporation', *Journal of Economic Geography*, vol. 1, pp. 181–99.

Opie, A. 1992, 'Qualitative research, appropriation of the other and empowerment', *Feminist Review*, vol. 40, pp. 52–69.

Oppenheim, N. 1992, *Questionnaire Design, Interviewing and Attitude Measurement*, Pinter, London.

Oritz, S. M. 1994, 'Shopping for sociability in the mall', *Research in Community Sociology*, vol. 4 (supplement), pp. 183–99.

Ortner, S. B. 1999, *Life and Death on Mt. Everest: Sherpas and Himalayan Mountaineering*, Princeton University Press, Princeton.

—— 1989, *High Religion: A Cultural and Political History of Sherpa Buddhism*, Princeton University Press, Princeton.

——— 1978, *Sherpas Through Their Rituals*, Cambridge University Press, Cambridge.

Padfield, M. and Procter, I. 1996, 'The effect of the interviewer's gender on the interviewing process: a comparative enquiry', *Sociology*, vol. 30, pp. 355–66.

Pain, R. 2004 [in press] 'Social geography: participatory research', *Progress in Human Geography*.

——— 2003, 'Social geography: on action-oriented research', *Progress in Human Geography*, vol. 27, no. 5, pp. 677–85.

Pain, R. and Francis, P. 2003, 'Reflections on participatory research', *Area*, vol. 35, no. 1, pp. 46–54.

Panofsky, E. 1957, *Meaning in the Visual Arts,* Doublebay Anchor, New York.

Parfitt, J. 1997, 'Questionnaire design and sampling', in R. Flowerdew and D. Martin (eds), *Methods in Human Geography. A Guide for Students Doing a Research Project*, Longman, Harlow.

Park, P. 1993, 'What is participatory research? A theoretical and methodological perspective', in P. Park, M. Brydon-Miller, B. Hall and T. Jackson (eds), *Voices of Change: Participatory Research in the United States and Canada*, Bergin & Garvey, Westport, CT.

Parkes, M. and Panelli, R. 2001, 'Integrating catchment ecosystems and community health: the value of participatory action research', *Ecosystem Health*, vol. 7, no. 2, pp. 85–106.

Parnwell, M. 2003, 'Consulting the poor in Thailand: enlightenment or delusion?', *Progress in Development Studies*, vol. 3, no. 2, pp. 99–112.

Parr, H. 1998, 'Mental health, ethnography and the body', *Area*, vol. 30, pp. 28–37.

Pavlovskaya, M. 2004, 'Other transitions: multiple economies of Moscow households in the 1990s', *Annals of the Association of American Geographers*, vol. 94, no. 2, pp. 329–51.

Patton, M. Q. 2002, *Qualitative Evaluation and Research Methods*, 3rd edn, Sage, Beverly Hills.

——— 1990, *Qualitative Evaluation and Research Methods*, 2nd edn, Sage, Beverly Hills.

Pawson, E. 1991, 'Monuments, memorials and cemeteries: icons in the landscape', *New Zealand Journal of Geography*, vol. 92, pp. 26–7.

Pawson, E. and Teather, E. 2002, 'Geographical Expeditions: assessing the benefits of a student-driven fieldwork method', *Journal of Geography in Higher Education,* vol. 26, no. 3, pp. 275–89.

Peace, R. 1998, 'CAQDAS/NUD*IST: computer assisted qualitative data analysis software/non-numerical, unstructured data. Indexing, searching and theorising—a geographical perspective', in E. Bliss (ed.), *Proceedings of the Second Joint Conference, Institute of Australian Geographers and New Zealand Geographical Society*, January 1997, New Zealand Geographical Society, Hamilton, pp. 382–5.

Peake, L. (on behalf of Red Thread Women's Development Programme) 2000, *Women Researching Women: Methodology Report and Research Projects on the Study of Domestic Violence and Women's Reproductive Health in Guyana*, Interamerican Bank, Georgetown, Guyana.

Pearson, L. J. 1996, Place Re-identification: the 'Leisure Coast' as a Partial Representation of Wollongong, BSc Honours thesis, School of Geography, University of New South Wales.

Pearson, L. J. and Dunn, K. M. 1999, 'Reidentifying Wollongong: dispossession of the local citizenry', *Proceedings of the Australian University Tourism and Hospitality Education 1999 National Research Conference*, Adelaide.

Perry, P. 1969, 'Twenty-five years of New Zealand historical geography', *New Zealand Geographer*, vol. 25, no. 2, pp. 93–105.

Philip, L. J. 1998, 'Combining quantitative and qualitative approaches to social research in human geography—an impossible mixture?', *Environment and Planning A*, vol. 30, pp. 261–76.

Phillips, L. and Jørgensen, M. W. 2002, *Discourse Analysis as Theory and Method,* Sage Publications, London.

Phillips, N. and Hardy, C. 2002, *Discourse Analysis Investigating Processes of Social Construction,* Sage Publications, Thousand Oaks, CA.

Pickles, J. 1992, 'Texts, hermeneutics and propaganda maps', in T. J. Barnes and J. S. Duncan (eds), *Writing Worlds*, Routledge, London.

Pickles, K. 2002, 'Kiwi icons and the Re-Settlement of New Zealand as Colonial Space', *New Zealand Geographer*, vol. 58, no. 2, pp. 5–16.

Pile, S. 1992, 'Oral history and teaching qualitative methods', *Journal of Geography in Higher Education*, vol. 16, no. 2, pp. 135–43.

pla notes, December 2003, IIED, London.

Platt, J. 1988, 'What can case studies do?', *Studies in Qualitative Methodology*, vol. 1, pp. 1–23.

Poland, B. D. 1995, 'Transcription quality as an aspect of rigor in qualitative research', *Qualitative Inquiry*, vol. 1, no. 3, pp. 290–310.

Ponga, M. 1998, 'I Nga ra o Mua: (Re)Constructions of symbolic layers in Te Poho-o-Hinemihi Marae', MA thesis, Department of Geography, The University of Auckland.

Popper, K. 1959, *The Logic of Scientific Discovery*, Hutchinson, London.

Porteous, D. J. 1985, 'Smellscape', *Progress in Human Geography*, vol. 9, pp. 356–78.

Potter, J. 1996, 'Discourse analysis and constructionist approaches: theoretical background', in J. T. E. Richardson (ed.), *Handbook of Qualitative Methods for Psychology and the Social Sciences*, British Psychological Society, Leicester.

Powell, J. M. 1988, *An Historical Geography of Modern Australia: The Restive Fringe*, Cambridge University Press, Cambridge.

—— 1973, *Yeomen and bureaucrats: the Victorian Crown Lands Commission, 1878–79*, Oxford University Press, Melbourne.

Pratt, G. 2002, 'Studying immigrants in focus groups', in P. Moss (ed.), *Feminist Geography in Practice: Research and Methods*, Blackwell, Oxford.

Pratt, G. 2000, 'Participatory action research', in R. Johnston, D. Gregory, G. Pratt and M. Watts (eds), *Dictionary of Human Geography*, 4th edn, Blackwell, Oxford.

Pratt, G. in collaboration with the Philippine Women's Centre 1999, 'Is this Canada? Domestic Workers' Experiences in Vancouver, B.C.', in J. Momson (ed.), *Gender, Migration and Domestic Service*, Routledge, London.

Pretty, J., Guijt, I., Thompson, J. and I. Scoones (eds) 1995, *Participatory Learning and Action: A Trainer's Guide*, IIED, London.

Professional Geographer 1994, Special Issue on 'Women in the Field', *Professional Geographer,* vol. 46, no. 1.

Przeworski, A. and Salmon, F. 1995, *The Art of Writing Proposals: Some Candid Suggestions for Applicants to Social Science Research Council Competitions* (online), Available: <http://www.ssrc.org/publications/for-fellows/art_of_writing_proposals.page> (Accessed: 9 September 2004).

Pulvirenti, M. 1997, 'Unwrapping the parcel: an examination of culture through Italian home ownership', *Australian Geographical Studies*, vol. 35, no. 1, pp. 32–9.

Punch, K. F. 2000, *Developing Effective Research Proposals*, Sage, London.

Raitz, K. B. 2001, 'Field observations, archives, and exploration', *Geographical Review*, vol. 91, nos. 1 & 2, pp. 121–31.

Reason, P. and Rowan, J. (eds) 1981, *Human Inquiry: A sourcebook of new paradigm research*, John Wiley & Sons, Chichester.

Reed, M. and Harvey, D. 1992, 'The new science and the old: complexity and realism in the social sciences', *Journal for the Theory of Social Behaviour*, vol. 22, no. 4, pp. 353–80.

Reinharz, S. 1992, *Feminist Methods in Social Research*, Oxford University Press, New York.

Reynolds, H., 1998, *This Whispering In Our Hearts*, Allen & Unwin, Sydney.

Richards, L. 1997, 'Computers and Qualitative Analysis', *The International Encyclopedia of Education*, Elsevier Science, Oxford.

—— 1990, *Nobody's Home: Dreams and Realities in a New Suburb*, Oxford University Press, Melbourne.

Richards, L. and Richards, T. 1995, 'Using hierarchical categories in qualitative data analysis', in U. Kelle (ed.), *Computer-Aided Qualitative Data Analysis: Theory, Methods and Practice*, Sage, London. Also available: <http://www.qsr.com.au/otherinfo/papers/hierarchies.html> (Accessed: 8 February 1999).

Richardson, L. 2000, 'Writing: A Method of Inquiry', in N. K. Denzin and Y. S. Lincoln, (eds), *Handbook of Qualitative Research*, 2nd edn, Sage, London.

—— 1994, 'Writing. A Method of Inquiry', in N. K. Denzin and Y. S. Lincoln (eds), *Handbook of Qualitative Research*, Sage, Thousand Oaks, CA.

Rimmer, P. J. and Davenport, S. 1998, 'The geographer as itinerant: Peter Scott in flight, 1952–1996', *Australian Geographical Studies*, vol. 36, no. 2, pp. 123–42.

Rivera, M. 1997, *Various definitions of geography* (online), Available: <http://www2.westga.edu/~geograph/define.html>, (Accessed: 22 August 2004).

Roberts, J. and Sainty, G. 1996, *Listening to the Lachlan*, Sainty and Associates, Potts Point.

Robertson, B. M. 2000, *Oral History Handbook*, 4th edn, Oral History Association of Australia SA Branch Inc, Adelaide.

—— 1994, *Oral History Handbook*, Oral History Association of Australia, Adelaide.

Robinson, G. 1998, *Methods and Techniques in Human Geography*, John Wiley & Sons, Chichester.

Rodaway, P. 1994, *Sensuous Geographies: Body, Sense, Place*, Routledge, London.

Rose, C. 1988, 'The concept of reach and the Anglophone minority in Quebec', in J. Eyles and D. Smith (eds), *Qualitative Methods in Human Geography*, Polity Press, Cambridge.

Rose, D. B. 1999 'Indigenous ecologies and an ethic of connection', in N. Low (ed.), *Global Ethics and Environment*, Routledge, London.

—— 1997 'Situating Knowledges: Positionality, Reflexivity, and Other Tactics', *Progress in Human Geography*, vol. 21, no. 3, pp. 305–20.

—— 1996a, 'Histories and rituals: land claims in the Territory', in B. Attwood (ed.), *In the Age of Mabo: History, Aborigines and Australia*, Allen & Unwin, Sydney, pp. 35–52.

—— 1996b, *Nourishing Terrains: Australian Aboriginal views of landscape and wilderness*, Australian Heritage Commission, Canberra.

Rose, G. 2003, 'Family Photographs and domestic spacings: a case study', *Transactions of the Institute of British Geographers,* vol. 28, pp. 5–18.

—— 2001, *Visual Methodologies. An Introduction to the Interpretation of Visual Materials*, Sage Publications, London.

—— 1997, 'Situating knowledges: Positionality, reflexivities and other tactics', *Progress in Human Geography*, vol. 21, pp. 305–20.

—— 1996, 'Teaching visualised geographies: towards a methodology for the interpretation of visual materials', *Journal of Geography in Higher Education,* vol. 20, no. 3, pp 281–94.

—— 1993, *Feminism and Geography,* University of Minnesota Press, Minneapolis.

Routledge, P. 2002, 'Travelling East as Walter Kurtz: identity, performance and collaboration in Goa, India', *Environment and Planning D: Society and Space,* vol. 20, no. 4, pp. 477–96.

—— 2001, 'Within the river. Collaboration and methodology', *Geographical Review,* vol. 91, nos. 1 & 2, pp. 113–20.

Rowles, G. D. 1978, *Prisoners of Space: Exploring the Geographical Experience of Older People,* Westview Press, Boulder.

Rowley, C. D. 1971a, *Outcasts in White Australia: Aboriginal Policy and Practice Volume II,* Australian National University Press, Canberra.

—— 1971b, *The Remote Aborigines: Aboriginal Policy and Practice Volume III,* Australian National University Press, Canberra.

—— 1970, The *Destruction of Aboriginal Society: Aboriginal Policy and Practice Volume I.* Canberra, Australian National University Press.

Rowse, T., 2000, *Obliged To Be Difficult: Nugget Coombs' Legacy in Indigenous Affairs,* Cambridge University Press, Cambridge.

Ruby J. 1995, *Secure the Shadow; Death and Photography in America,* MIT Press, Cambridge, MA.

Ruddick, S. 2004, 'Activist geographies: building possible worlds', in P. Cloke, P. Crang and M. Goodwin (eds), *Envisioning Human Geographies,* Arnold, London.

Ruming, R., Mee, K. and McGuirk, P. M. 2004, 'Questioning the rhetoric of social mix: courteous community or hidden hostility', *Australian Geographical Studies,* vol. 42, no. 2, pp. 234–48.

Said, E. 1993, *Culture and Imperialism,* Vintage Books, New York.

—— 1978, *Orientalism,* Vintage Books, New York.

Sanderson, E. and Kindon, S. 2004, 'Progress in participatory development: opening up the possibility of knowledge through progressive participation', *Progress in Development Studies,* vol. 4, no. 2, pp. 114–26.

Sanjek, R. (ed.) 1990, *Fieldnotes: the Makings of Anthropology,* Cornell University Press, Ithaca.

Sarantakos, S. 2005, *Social Research,* 3rd edn, Palgrave, Melbourne.

—— 1993, *Social Research,* MacMillan, South Melbourne.

Sauer, C. 1941, 'Foreword to historical geography', *Annals of the Association of American Geographers,* vol. 31, no. 1, pp.1–24.

Sausseur, F. de, 1983, *Course in General Linguistics,* Duckworth, London.

Sayer, A. 1992, *Method in Social Science: A Realist Approach,* 2nd edn, Routledge, London.

Sayer, A. and Morgan, K. 1985, 'A modern industry in a declining region: links between method, theory and policy', in D. Massey and R. Meegan (eds), *Politics and Method: Contrasting Studies in Industrial Geography,* Methuen, London.

Schaffer, K. 1988, *Women and the Bush: Forces of Desire in the Australian Cultural Tradition,* Cambridge University Press, Cambridge.

Schein, R. H. 1997, 'The place of landscape: a conceptual framework for interpreting an American scene', *Annals of the Association of American Geographers,* vol. 87, no. 4, pp. 660–80.

Schoenberger, E. 1992, 'Self-criticism and self-awareness in research: a reply to Linda McDowell', *Professional Geographer,* vol. 44, pp. 215–18.

—— 1991, 'The corporate interview as a research method in economic geography', *Professional Geographer*, vol. 43, no. 2, pp. 180–9.

Schollmann, A., Perkins, H. C. and Moore, K. 2000, 'Intersecting global and local influences in urban place promotion: the case of Christchurch, New Zealand, *Environment and Planning D: Society and Space*, vol. 32, pp. 55–76.

School of Global Studies, 1998, *Essay Format and Essay Writing for Geography Students*, School of Global Studies, Massey University, Palmerston North.

Scott, K., Park, J., Cocklin, C. and Blunden, G. 1997, *A Sense of Community: An Ethnography of Rural Sustainability in the Mangakahia Valley, Northland,* Occasional Publication 33, Department of Geography, The University of Auckland.

Scribner, J. P. 2003, 'Teacher learning in context: the special case of a rural high school', *Education Policy Analysis Archives,* vol. 11, no. 12.

Secor, A. 2004, '"There is an Istanbul that belongs to me": citizenship, space, and identity in the city', *Annals of the Association of American Geographers*, vol. 94, no. 2, pp. 352–68.

—— 2003, 'Citizenship in the city: identity, community and rights among women migrants to Istanbul', *Urban Geography*, vol. 24, no. 2, pp. 147–68.

Seebohm, K. 1994, 'The nature and meaning of the Sydney Mardi Gras in a landscape of inscribed social relations', in R. Aldrich (ed.), *Gay Perspectives II: More Essays in Australian Gay Culture,* Department of Economic History with the Australian Centre for Gay and Lesbian Research, University of Sydney, Sydney.

Sekaran, U. 1992, *Research Methods for Business: A Skill Building Approach*, 2nd edn, John Wiley & Sons Inc., New York.

Shapcott, M. and Steadman, P. 1978, 'Rhythms of urban activity', in T. Carlstein, D. Parkes and N. Thrift (eds), *Human Activity and Time Geography*, John Wiley & Sons, New York.

Shaw, G. and Wheeler, D. 1994, *Statistical Techniques in Geographical Analysis*, Halsted Press, New York.

Shaw, W. S. 2000, 'Ways of Whiteness: Harlemising Sydney's Aboriginal Redfern', *Australian Geographical Studies*, vol. 38, no. 3, pp. 291–305.

Sheridan, G. 2001, 'Dennis Norman Jeans: historical geographer and landscape interpreter extraordinaire', *Australian Geographical Studies*, vol. 39, no. 1, pp. 96–106.

Sherraden, M. n.d., *How to do Focus Groups* (online), Available: <http://www.ln.edu.hk/mkt/courses/howtodofocusgroups.doc> (Accessed: 29 September 2004).

Shopes, L. 2000, 'International Review Boards Have a Chilling Effect on Oral History', *Perpectives OnLine* (online), Available: <http://www.theaha.org/perspectives/issues/2000/009/009vie.cfm9>, (Accessed: 14 January 2004).

Shurmer-Smith, P. 2002, *Doing Cultural Geography*, Sage Publications, London.

Sides, C.H. 1992, *How to Write and Present Technical Information*, 2nd edn, Cambridge University Press, Oakleigh, Victoria.

Silverman, D. 1993, *Interpreting Qualitative Data: Methods for Analysing Talk, Text and Interaction,* 2nd edn, Sage, London.

—— 1991, *Interpreting Qualitative Data: Methods of Analysing Talk, Text and Interaction*, 1st edn, Sage Publications, Thousand Oaks, CA.

Singer, A. and L. Woodhead (1988), *Disappearing World: Television and Anthropology*, London, Boxtree & Granada Television.

Skelton, T. 2001, 'Girls in the club: researching working girls' lives', *Ethics, Place and Environment*, vol. 4, no. 2, pp. 167–73.

Smith, A. 1994, *New Right Discourses on Race and Sexuality*, Cambridge University Press, Cambridge, Mass.

Smith, D. A. 2003, 'Participatory mapping of community lands and hunting yields among the Buglé of Western Panama', *Human Organization*, vol. 62, no. 4, pp. 332–41.

Smith, K. 2003, 'Pushing the boundaries: the exclusion of disability rights groups from political influence in Victoria', *Australian Geographer*, vol. 34, no. 3, pp. 345–54.

Smith, L. T. 1999, *Decolonizing Methodologies: Research and Indigenous Peoples*, University of Otago Press & Zed Books, Dunedin and London.

Smith, S. J. 1994, 'Soundscape', *Area*, vol. 26, pp. 232–40.

—— 1988, 'Constructing local knowledge: The analysis of self in everyday life', in J. Eyles and D. M. Smith (eds), *Qualitative Methods in Human Geography*, Polity Press, Cambridge.

—— 1981, 'Humanistic method in contemporary social geography', *Area*, vol. 15, pp. 355–8.

Sparke, M. 1998, 'A map that roared and an original atlas: Canada, cartography and the narration of a nation', *Annals of the Association of American Geographers*, vol. 88, no. 3, pp. 463–95.

Spate, O. H. K. and Learmonth, A. 1967, *India and Pakistan: A General and Regional Geography*, Methuen, London.

Spradley, J. P. 1980, *Participant Observation*, Holt, Rinehart & Wilson, New York.

Srivinas, M. N., Shah, A. M. and Ramaswamy, E. A. 1979, *The Fieldworker and the Field: Problems and Challenges in Sociological Investigation*, Oxford University Press, Delhi.

Stacey, J. 1988, 'Can there be a feminist ethnography', *Women's Studies International Forum*, vol. 11, pp. 21–7.

Stake, R. 1995, *The Art of Case Study Research*, Sage, Thousand Oaks.

Stanley, L. and Wise S. 1993, *Breaking Out Again: Feminist Ontology and Epistemology*, 2nd edn, Routledge, London.

Stanton, N. 1996, *Mastering Communication*, 3rd edn, MacMillan, London.

Starkey, A. (video recording) and George, K. (interviews) 2003, *Balfour's City Site, 1910–2003*, Corporation of the City of Adelaide.

Stevens, S. (forthcoming), 'Struggles Over Forests: Contestation and Conservation in the Chomolungma/Mt. Everest Region of Nepal', in M. Steinberg (ed.), *Forests, Fields, and Fallows: Contested Resources in Politicized Indigenous Landscapes*, University of Texas Press, Austin.

—— 2004, 'Imperialism, Sharwas (Sherpas), and Protected Areas in the Chomolungma (Sagarmatha/Mt. Everest) Region of Nepal', Paper presented to the Association of American Geographers Centennial Meeting, Philadelphia, PA, March 2004.

—— 2003, 'Tourism and deforestation in the Mt. Everest region of Nepal', *Geographical Journal*, vol. 169, no. 3, pp. 255–77.

—— 2001, 'Fieldwork as Commitment', *Geographical Review*, vol. 91, no. 1–2, pp. 66–73.

—— 1997, 'Consultation, Co-management, and Conflict in Sagarmatha (Mt. Everest) National Park, Nepal', in S. Stevens (ed), *Conservation Through Cultural Survival: Indigenous Peoples and Protected Areas*, Island Press, Washington, D. C., pp. 63–97.

—— 1993, *Claiming the High Ground: Sherpas, Subsistence, and Environmental Change in the Highest Himalaya*, University of California Press, Berkeley.

Stevens, S. and Sherpa, M. N. 1993, 'Indigenous Peoples and Protected Areas: New Approaches to Conservation in Highland Nepal', in L. S. Hamilton, D. P. Bauer and H. F. Takeuchi (eds), *Parks, Peaks, and People*, East-West Center, Program on Environment, Honolulu, HI.

Stewart, D. W. and Shamdasani, P. N. 1990, *Focus Groups: Theory and Practice*, Sage, Newbury Park.

Stratford, E. 2002, 'On the edge: a tale of skaters and urban governance', *Social and Cultural Geography*, vol. 3, no. 2, pp. 193–206.

—— 2001, 'The Millennium Project on Australian Geography and Geographers: An Introduction', *Australian Geographical Studies*, vol. 39, no. 1, pp. 91–5.

—— (ed.) 1999, *Australian Cultural Geographies*, Oxford University Press, Melbourne.

—— 1998, 'Public spaces, urban youth and local government: the skateboard culture in Hobart's Franklin Square', in R. Freestone (ed.), *20th Century Urban Planning Experience, Proceedings of the 8th International Planning History Conference*, University of New South Wales, Sydney.

—— 1997, 'Memory work in geography and environmental studies: some suggestions for teaching and research', *Australian Geographical Studies*, vol. 35, no. 2, pp. 208–21.

Stratford, E. and Harwood, A. 2001, 'The regulation of skating in Australia: an overview and commentary on the Tasmanian case', *Urban Policy and Research*, vol. 19, no. 2, pp. 61–76.

Strauss, A. and Corbin, J. 1990, *Basics of Qualitative Research. Grounded Theory, Procedures and Techniques*, Sage, Newbury Park.

Strunk, William, Jr., and White, E. B. 1959, *The Elements of Style*, Macmillan, New York.

Stychin, C. F. 2003, *Governing Sexuality. The Changing Politics of Citizenship and Law Reform*, Hart Publishing, Oxford and Portland, Oregon.

Suchet, S. 2002, '"Totally wild"? Colonising discourses, indigenous knowledges and managing wildlife', *Australian Geographer*, vol. 33, no. 3, pp. 141–57.

Sudman, S. and Bradburn, N. M. 1982, *Asking Questions: A Practical Guide to Questionnaire Design*, Jossey-Bass, San Francisco.

Sweet, C. 2001, 'Designing and conducting virtual focus groups', *Qualitative Market Research: An International Journal*, vol. 4, no. 3, pp. 130–5.

Swenson, J. D., Griswold, W. F. and Kleiber, P. B. 1992, 'Focus groups: Method of inquiry/intervention', *Small Group Research*, vol. 23, no. 4, pp. 459–74.

Symonds, J. A. 1896, *A Problem of Modern Ethics*, privately printed, London.

Symposium on Computing and Qualitative Geography, 1995, University of Durham, 11–12 July, Available: <http://www.helsinki.fi/neu/lists/qual-software/0034.html>, (Accessed: 8 February 1999).

Tashakkori, A. and Teddlie, C. 1998, *Mixed Methodology: Combining Qualitative and Quantitative Approaches*, Sage, Thousand Oaks, CA.

Taylor, C. 1984, 'Foucault on freedom and truth', *Political Theory*, vol. 12, no. 2, pp. 152–83.

Tesch, R. 1990, *Qualitative Research. Analysis Types and Software Tools*, Falmer Press, Basingstoke.

—— (ed.) 1989, 'Computer Software and Qualitative Analysis: A Reassessment', in G. Blank, E. Brent and J. L. McCartney (eds), *New Technology in Sociology: Practical Applications in Research and Work*, Transaction Books, New Brunswick.

Thatcher, J., Waddell, C. and Burks, M. 2002, *Constructing Accessible Websites*, Glasshaus, Birmingham, UK.

Thiesmeyer, L. (ed.) 2003, *Discourse and Silencing. Representation and the Language of Displacement*, John Benjamins Publishing Company, Amsterdam/Philadelphia.

Thomas, M. 2004, 'Pleasure and propriety: teen girls and the practice of straight space', *Environment and Planning D: Society and Space*, vol. 22, no. 5, pp. 773–89.

Thomas-Slayter, B. 1995, 'A brief history of participatory methodologies', in R. Slocum, L. Wichart, D. Rocheleau and B. Thomas-Slayter (eds), *Power, Process and Participation: Tools for Change*, Intermediate Technology Publications Ltd, London.

Thompson, P. 2000, *The Voice of the Past: Oral History*, 3rd edn, Oxford University Press, New York.

Thompson, S. 1994, 'Suburbs of opportunity: the power of home for migrant women', in K. Gibson and S. Watson (eds), *Metropolis Now: Planning and the Urban in Contemporary Australia*, Pluto, Sydney.

Thrift, N. J. 1996, *Spatial Formations,* Sage, Thousand Oaks.

Tonkiss, F. 1998, 'Analysing discourse', in C. Seale (ed.), *Researching Society and Culture*, Sage, London. pp. 245–60.

Townsend, J. with Arrevillaga, U., Bain, J., Cancino, S., Frenk, S., Pacheco, S. and Perez, E. 1995, *Women's Voices from the Rainforest*, Routledge, London.

Tremblay, M. A. 1982, 'The key informant technique: a non-ethnographic application', in R. G. Burgess (ed.), *Field Research: A Sourcebook and Field Manual,* Allen & Unwin, London.

Tuan, Y. F. 1991, 'Language and the making of place: a narrative–descriptive approach', *Annals of the Association of American Geographers*, vol. 81, no. 4, pp. 684–96.

Tufte, E. 2003, *The Cognitive Style of PowerPoint*, Graphics Press LLC, Cheshire.

Tully, J. 1995, *Strange Multiplicity: Constitutionalism in an age of diversity*, Cambridge University Press, Cambridge.

Turner, F. J. 1920, *The Frontier in American History*, Henry Hold, New York.

Valentine, G. 2003, 'Geography and ethics: in pursuit of social justice—ethics and emotions in geographies of health and disability research', *Progress in Human Geography*, vol. 27, no. 3, pp. 375–80.

—— 2002, 'People like us: negotiating sameness and difference in the research process', in. Moss, P. (ed.), *Feminist Geography in Practice: Research and Methods*, Blackwell, Oxford.

—— 1997, 'Tell me about…: using interviews as a research methodology', in R. Flowerdew and D. Martin (eds), *Methods in Human Geography: A Guide for Students Doing a Research Project*, Longman, Harlow.

—— 1993, '(Hetero)sexing space: lesbian perceptions and experiences of everyday spaces', *Environment and Planning D: Society and Space*, vol. 11, no. 4, pp. 395–413.

—— 1989, 'The geography of women's fear', *Area*, vol. 21, no. 4, pp. 385–90.

Valentine, G., Skelton, T. and Butler, R. 2003, 'Coming out and outcomes: negotiating lesbian and gay identities with, and in, the family', *Environment and Planning D: Society and Space*, vol. 21, pp. 479–99.

Wadsworth, Y. 1998, '*What is Participatory Action Research?*', Action Research International Paper 2. Available: <http://www.scu.edu.au/schools/gecm/ar/ari/p-ywadsworth98.html>. (Accessed: 4 February 2005).

Waitt, G. 1999, 'Naturalizing the primitive: a critique of marketing Australia's indigenous peoples as hunter gatherers', *Tourism Geographies*, vol. 1, no. 2, pp. 142–63.

—— 1997, 'Selling paradise and adventure: representations of landscape in the tourist advertising of Australia', *Australian Geographical Studies*, vol. 35, no. 1, pp. 47–60.

Waitt, G. and Head, L. 2002, 'Postcards and frontier mythologies: sustaining views of the Kimberley as timeless', *Environment and Planning D: Society and Space*, vol. 20, pp. 319–44.

Waitt, G. and McGuirk, P. M. 1996, 'Marking time: tourism and heritage representation at Millers Point, Sydney', *Australian Geographer*, vol. 27, no. 1, pp. 11–29.

Waitt, G., McGuirk, P., Dunn K., Hartig, K. and Burnley I. 2000, *Introducing Human Geography: Globalisation, Difference and Inequality*, Pearson Education Australia, Sydney.

Walmsley, D. S. and Lewis G. I. 1984, *Human Geography: Behavioural Approaches*, Longman, New York.

Walsh, B. and Lavalli, T. 1996, 'Comparative Review of NUD*IST, Atlas/ti, Folio Views', *Microtimes*, no. 162, Available: <http://www.microtimes.com/162/research.html> (Accessed: 8 February 1999).

Ward, B. 1972, *What's Wrong with Economics?*, MacMillan, London.

Ward, R. 1958, *The Australian Legend*, Oxford University Press, Melbourne.

Ward, V. M., Bertrand J. T. and Brown, L. F. 1991, 'The comparability of focus group and survey results: Three case studies', *Evaluation Review*, vol. 15, no. 2, pp. 266–83.

Warde, A. 1989, 'Recipes for a pudding: a comment on locality', *Antipode*, vol. 21, no. 3, pp. 274–81.

Wearing, B. 1984, *The Ideology of Motherhood: A Study of Sydney Suburban Mothers,* George Allen & Unwin, Sydney.

Webb, B. 1982, 'The art of note-taking', in R. G. Burgess (ed.), *Field Research: A Sourcebook and Field Manual*, Allen & Unwin, London.

Webb, E. J., Campbell, D. T., Schwartz, R. D. and Sechrest, L. 1966, *Unobtrusive Measures: Non-reactive Research in the Social Sciences*, Rand McNally, Chicago.

Weinstein, D. and Weinstein, M. 1991, 'Georg Simmel: sociological flaneur bricoleur', *Theory, Culture and Society*, vol. 8, pp. 151–68.

Weitzman, E. and Miles, M. 1995, *Computer Programs for Qualitative Data Analysis: Software Sourcebook*, Sage, Thousand Oaks.

Welsh, I. 1996, *Trainspotting*, W. W. Norton, London.

Western, J. C. 1981, *Outcast Cape Town*, University of Minnesota Press, Minneapolis.

White, P. and Jackson, P. A. 1995, '(Re)theorising population geography', *International Journal of Population Geography*, vol. 1, pp. 111–23.

Whyte, W. F. 1982, 'Interviewing in field research', in R. G. Burgess (ed.), *Field Research: A Sourcebook and Field Manual*, Allen & Unwin, London.

Whyte, W. H. 1957, *Street Corner Society*, University of Chicago Press, Chicago.

Widdowfield, R. 2000, 'The place of emotions in academic research', *Area*, vol. 32, no. 2, pp. 199–208.

Wiles, J. 2003, 'Daily geographies of caregivers: mobility, routine, scale', *Social Science and Medicine*, vol. 57, pp. 1307–25.

Wilkinson, A. 1999, 'New Labour and Christian Socialism', in G. R. Taylor (ed.), *The Impact of New Labour*, Macmillan, Basingstoke, pp. 37–50.

Williams, G., Srivastava, M., Corbridge, S. and Veron, R. 2003, 'Enhancing pro-poor governance in Eastern India: participation, politics and action', *Progress in Development Studies*, vol. 3, no. 2, pp. 159–78.

Williams, M. 1992, 'Archives in geographical research', in A. Rogers, H. Viles and A. Goudie (eds), *The Students Companion to Geography*, Blackwell, Oxford.

Williamson J. E. 1978, *Decoding Advertisements: Ideology and Meaning in Advertising*, Marion Boyars, London.

Wilson, A. G. 1972, 'Theoretical geography: some considerations', *Transactions of the Institute of British Geographers,* vol. 7, pp. 31–44.

Winchester, H. P. M. 2000, 'Qualitative research and its place in geography', in I. Hay (ed.), *Qualitative Research Methods in Human Geography*, Oxford University Press, Melbourne.

—— 1999, 'Interviews and questionnaires as mixed methods in population geography: The case of lone fathers in Newcastle, Australia', *Professional Geographer*, vol. 51, no. 1, pp. 60–7.

—— 1996, 'Ethical issues in interviewing as a research method in human geography', *Australian Geographer*, vol. 27, no. 1, pp. 117–31.

—— 1992, 'The construction and deconstruction of women's role in the urban landscape', in F. Gale and K. Anderson (eds), *Inventing Places: Studies in Cultural Geography*, Longman Cheshire, Melbourne.

Winchester, H. P. M. and Costello, L. N. 1995, 'Living on the street: social organisation and gender relations of Australian street kids', *Environment and Planning D: Society and Space*, vol. 13, pp. 329–48.

Winchester, H. P. M. and Dunn, K. M. 1999, 'Cultural geographies of film: tales of urban reality', in K. J. Anderson and F. Gale (eds), *Inventing Places: Studies in Cultural Geography*, Addison Wesley Longman, Melbourne.

Winchester, H. P. M., McGuirk, P. M. and Dunn, K. M. 1997, 'Uncovering Carrington', in J. Moore, J. Ostwald and A. Chawner (eds), *Hidden Newcastle: The Invisible City and the City of Memory*, Gadfly Media, pp. 174–81.

Winchester, H. P. M., McGuirk, P. M. and Everett, K. 1999, 'Celebration and control: Schoolies Week on the Gold Coast Queensland', in E. Teather (ed.), *Embodied Geographies: Spaces, Bodies and Rites of Passage*, Routledge, London.

Wolcott, H. 1990a, 'On seeking—and rejecting—validity in qualitative research', in E. Eisner and A. Peshkin (eds), *Qualitative Inquiry In Education: the continuing debate*, Teachers College Press, New York.

—— 1990b, *Writing Up Qualitative Research*, Sage, Newbury Park.

Wolf, D. (ed.) 1996, *Feminist Dilemmas in Fieldwork*, Westview, Boulder, CO.

Wolf, E. (1982), *Europe and The People Without History*, University of California Press, Berkeley.

Wood, L. A. and Kroger, R. O. 2000, *Doing Discourse Analysis: Methods for Studying Action in Talk and Text*, Sage, Thousand Oaks, CA.

Wood, L. and Williamson, S. 1996, *Consultants' Report on Franklin Square: Users, Activities and Conflicts*, UNITAS Consulting, Hobart.

Wooldridge, S. W. 1955, 'The status of geography and the role of fieldwork', *Geography*, vol. 40, pp. 73–83.

Wrigley, E. A. 1970, 'Changes in the philosophy of geography', in R. J. Chorley and P. Haggett (eds), *Frontiers in Geographical Teaching*, Methuen, London.

Young, L. and Barratt, H. 2001, 'Adapting visual methods: action research with Kampala street children', *Area*, vol. 33, no. 2, pp. 141–52.

Zeigler, D. J., Brunn, S. D. and Johnson, J. H. 1996, 'Focusing on Hurricane Andrew through the eyes of the victims', *Area*, vol. 28, no. 2, pp. 124–9.

Zelinsky, W. 2001, 'The Geographer as Voyeur', *The Geographical Review*, vol. 91, no. 1–2, pp. 1–8.

Zimmerer, K. S. and Bassett, T. J. (eds) 2003, *Political Ecology: an Integrative Approach to Geography and Environment–Development Studies*, Guilford Press, New York.

Index